From Settler to Citizen

From Settler to Citizen

*New Mexican Economic Development and
the Creation of Vecino Society, 1750–1820*

Ross Frank

UNIVERSITY OF CALIFORNIA PRESS
Berkeley   Los Angeles   London

University of California Press
Berkeley and Los Angeles, California

University of California Press, Ltd.
London, England

© 2000 by
The Regents of the University of California

Library of Congress Cataloging-in-Publication Data

Frank, Ross, 1957–
    From settler to citizen : New Mexican economic development and the creation of Vecino
society, 1750–1820 / Ross Frank.
        p.   cm.
    Includes bibliographical references and index.
    ISBN 0-520-22206-7 (cloth : alk. paper)
    1. New Mexico—Economic conditions.   2. New Mexico—History.
HC107.N6 F73   2000
338.9789'009'033—dc21

                                                                                00-034381

Manufactured in the United States of America

09 08 07 06 05 04 03 02 01 00
10 9 8 7 6 5 4 3 2 1

The paper used in this publication meets the minimum requirements of ANSI/NISO Z39.48-
1992 (R 1997) (*Permanence of Paper*). ∞

To my parents,
and to the people of Arroyo Hondo, New Mexico

CONTENTS

LIST OF ILLUSTRATIONS AND TABLES / *ix*

PREFACE / *xiii*

ACKNOWLEDGMENTS / *xvii*

A NOTE ABOUT TRANSLATIONS / *xxi*

ABBREVIATIONS / *xxiii*

Introduction / *1*

Chapter 1. "Like a Ball in the Hands of Fortune":
New Mexican Economy through the 1770s / *13*

Chapter 2. "If We Should Lose New Mexico a Second Time":
Bourbon Reform, Indian Policy, and the Alliances of the 1780s / *65*

Chapter 3. "This Type of Commerce Cannot Remedy Itself":
Obstacles to Economic Growth in New Mexico and
the Bourbon Response / *76*

Chapter 4. New Mexican Economic Development, 1780–1820 / *119*

Chapter 5. Creating Vecinos: Cultural Transformation / *176*

Conclusion / *223*

NOTES / *235*

GLOSSARY OF COLONIAL SPANISH TERMS / *285*

BIBLIOGRAPHY / *295*

INDEX / *315*

ILLUSTRATIONS AND TABLES

FIGURES

1. Deaths in New Mexico caused by hostile Indians and recorded in provincial burial records, 1700–1819 / *36*

2. New Mexico population summary, 1740–1785 / *48*

3. Tithe rentals for New Mexico, 1750–1780 / *53*

4a. Santa Clara baptisms and burials, 1776–1790 / *58*

4b. Population change in Santa Clara, 1776–1790 / *59*

5. Expenditures for presidios internos from the treasuries of Mexico and Durango, 1770–1811 / *84*

6. Total estimated outlay for presidios internos and associated expenses, 1770–1810 / *91*

7. Plan of the cuartel, Presidio of Santa Fe, 1791 / *113*

8. New Mexico tithe rentals, 1732–1819 / *129*

9. Growth in value of tithe rental relative to vecino population, New Mexico, 1760–1820 / *130*

10. "Peace Expenditures," Extraordinary Fund, Province of New Mexico, 1786–1793 / *135*

11. Distribution of goods and services purchased within New Mexico, using the "Peace Expenditures," Extraordinary Fund, 1786–1791 / *136*

12. Vecino-Indio marriages as a percentage of those represented in
diligencias matrimoniales, New Mexico, 1700–1839 / *179*

PLATES

1. Pueblo manta, early style / *16*

2. Río Grande blanket with banded and serrate designs / *18*

3. Chronology of Pueblo pottery types / *160*

4. Puname Polychrome jar / *161*

5. San Pablo Polychrome jar / *162*

6. Trios Polychrome jar, Zia Pueblo / *163*

7. Puebla chocolate jar, blue-on-white talavera ware / *164*

8. Ako Polychrome jar / *165*

9. Acomita Polychrome jar / *166*

10. Laguna Mission Church interior, 1940 / *168*

11. Ogapoge Polychrome jar / *170*

12. Powhoge Polychrome storage jar / *171*

13. Kiua Polychrome storage jar, Cochití Pueblo / *172*

14. Nambé Polychrome storage jar / *173*

15. Board chest, late eighteenth or early nineteenth century / *191*

16. Framed chest, late eighteenth or early nineteenth century / *192*

17. Harinero, late eighteenth or early nineteenth century / *193*

18. Two bultos of Santo Jo' / *229*

19. Two retablos of the Man of Sorrows / *231*

MAPS

1. The Province of New Mexico, circa 1790 / *4*

2. The Provincias Internas, circa 1785 / *11*

3. The northward spread of the horse in the western United States / *39*

4. Portions of the Province of New Mexico, Miera y Pacheco map, 1779 / *40*

5. Ojo Caliente detail, Miera y Pacheco map, 1779 / *44*

6. A detail of Miera y Pacheco's map of the Albuquerque region, 1779 / *45*

7. A portion of the Laguna region and north, Miera y Pacheco map, 1779 / *46*

8. Northern interregional explorations, 1770–1800 / *102*

9. The Pueblo pottery-making area, by linguistic group / *157*

TABLES

1. Comparison of household occupations, Nueva Vizcaya and
New Mexico, 1790 / *138*

2. Summary of the transaction described by Fray Juan Augustín de Morfí in
paragraph 14 of "Account of Disorders, 1778" / *144*

3. Summary of the transaction described by Fray Juan Augustín de Morfí in
paragraph 15 of "Account of Disorders, 1778" / *145*

4. Summary of the transaction described by Fray Juan Augustín de Morfí in
paragraph 16 of "Account of Disorders, 1778" / *146*

5. Comparison of peso de la tierra values, New Mexico, 1776 and 1791 / *149*

PREFACE

Those who write about history at the beginning of the third millennium should not have to discover to their surprise that their work has political implications. Mine does. I grew up in Arroyo Hondo, a small village in northern New Mexico about 12 miles north of Taos. I arrived a few months after my fourth birthday in 1960, part of a plan by my parents to relocate from Los Angeles, prompted by anti-urban feelings and a fire that burned down our home there. My childhood in Arroyo Hondo was marked by ethnic, social, and economic difference: I was an Anglo and lived in a middle-class household run by parents with college educations. None of this kept me from thinking about what had created the world of my neighbors—*Vecinos* of Arroyo Hondo.

I attended the public school system in Taos. One spring afternoon in Taos High School, the principal called the student body into the gym for a special assembly. There an elected official from the area addressed a few hundred of us on a matter that seemed to him of some urgency. He began by telling us that some Latinos had taken to calling themselves Chicanos in the name of fostering solidarity and group identity. The term "Chicano," he informed us solemnly, had its roots in the slang of the uneducated, and it meant something vulgar and dirty, like trash. We should never consider ourselves or our culture Chicano. Instead, the people from northern New Mexico should think of themselves as Spanish Americans. We could trace our heritage back to the Spanish conquistadores who settled this land and could be proud of our lineage. Do not, he warned us, use the word *Chicano* as a label for ourselves or for others.

At the time I found this lecture somewhat confusing, but nonetheless arresting enough to file away with other assorted incidents of my career in high school. Today I find the story interesting in a number of ways. In the first place, it was not as if the Taos High School of 1974 were a hotbed of Chicano consciousness or activism. Those who did roam the halls exchanging Chicano handclasps as often as not showed a self-chiding skepticism about the whole matter. "Chicano powder!" they would exclaim. I suspect that most of my contemporaries discovered Chicano activism in college. This politician, however, clearly had some grave concerns about the effect that Chicano ideology might be having on Taoseños of high school age, and the school officials apparently had enough concern to convene an assembly to inoculate us against Chicanismo. At a more fundamental level, I believe that this view of a distinct ethnic identity held by New Mexicans of Spanish descent, those whom the speaker called "Spanish American," points to a vision of history which connects directly to the political issues of race, ethnicity, and history that continue to seethe beneath the often deceptively calm surface of New Mexican communities.

I am aware that by arguing that vecino cultural distinctiveness took shape at the end of the colonial period, I challenge those who have grown accustomed to thinking of Spanish New Mexicans as conveniently separate from Mexicans by virtue of centuries of traditions inherited directly from Spain. At the same time, I argue that by 1800 the Hispanic racial and ethnic mixtures that arose in New Mexico—*Castas* and *Genízaros*—all became *Españoles* in increasing contrast to Pueblo Indians. For Chicanos who today conceive of their ethnic identity as a subaltern blend of Spanish and Indian, having emerged from colonial New Mexico, this argument may represent an unwanted complication.

For Native Americans, especially, the implications of my work will also demand scrutiny of the methodologies I used in my research. It is difficult enough to interpret what Spanish colonial documents say about the actions of New Mexican vecinos, individually or as a society. A non-Indian scholar using the materials in historical archives written by Spanish officials to help understand the actions and motivations of Pueblo, Comanche, Apache, or other Indian people in the eighteenth century treads on fragile ground indeed. Spanish documents do contain representations of Native American voices. The difficulty lies in recovering a convincing sense of Indian agency from materials intended to convey very different information. Here the items made by the Pueblos for their own use, for trade, and for export—such as Pueblo pottery or blankets—can suggest economic and cultural changes over time or in relation to Spanish society. Pueblo interpreters of cultural history today and in the past serve as crucial guides in the process of evaluating written materials and in understanding the religious and cultural context of historical objects. With a variety of sources and techniques, the obstacles of time and cultural perspective can be surmounted to some degree, but the issue of my own racial, cultural, social, and institutional affiliations will remain as potent as ever.[1]

This state of affairs is as it should be. I view this book as a project in the recovery of almost invisible yet important pieces of the late colonial world of vecinos, Pueblo Indians, and the non-Pueblo Native American groups in New Mexico. That such a project is necessary suggests the costs that some groups of people and individuals had to bear in the past: Their histories were erased to enable others to create a more compelling history for themselves. I will be satisfied if this work helps us understand the nature and significance of those erasures. Perhaps it will also add to the resources available to descendants of the people who appear in this book as they present their own histories.

ACKNOWLEDGMENTS

The time and resources required to complete this book came in large part from the Mellon Foundation Postdoctoral Research Fellowship in Comparative Race and Ethnicity that I held at Stanford University during the 1995–1996 academic year. The Department of Ethnic Studies at the University of California, San Diego, my academic home, provided its blessing for my year off from teaching, and I accomplished a good deal of revision during the sabbatical provided by UCSD during the fall quarter of 1996. In addition, a grant from the UCSD Academic Senate allowed me to employ Ruby C. Tapia, who, along with Paula Marie Seniors, provided invaluable research assistance during the final stretch.

In addition to the large number of intellectual debts I have accumulated while writing this work, debts I have endeavored to account for along the way in the usual academic manner, several groups have sustained me in this project in ways that require special acknowledgment and thanks:

To my colleagues in the Department of Ethnic Studies at UCSD—Ramón A. Gutiérrez, Yen Le Espiritu, George Lipsitz, Charles Briggs, Jane Rhodes, Leland Saito, Paule Cruz Takash, and Jonathan Holloway—I cannot express adequate thanks for the intellectual stimulus, discussion, friendly support, counsel, and inspiration they have provided me. The manner in which a group of professors from many disciplines has created such a hospitable environment for innovative work never ceases to amaze me.

The research and writing of the dissertation that formed the foundation of this work required more than intellectual sustenance. Access to collections of Spanish colonial documents in the United States and Mexico made it possible to pursue the research project I had envisioned: At the New Mexico State Records Center and Archives in Santa Fe, Myra Ellen Jenkins, Stanley M. Hordes, and J. Richard Salazar have been a constant source of succor over the years. I am indebted to Vivian Fisher and Walter Brem, among a solicitous and professional staff at the Bancroft Library at the University of California, Berkeley. Victoria San Vicente of the Coordinación de Archivos Históricos, Roberto Beristáin, and Roberto Pedraza (reprographics) at the Archivo General de la Nación in Mexico City provided a great deal of help and advice in various aspects of my search for particular archival materials.

My perusal of the Archivo Histórico and the Archivo del Cabildo of the Cathedral of Durango occurred as a result of kind interest and aid on the part of a number of individuals. My thanks to the archbishop of Santa Fe, Monsignor Robert F. Sanchez, Maria Ochoa, archivist for the Archdiocese of Santa Fe, and Professor Glafira Magaña Perales (head of the Departamento de Archivos Eclesiásticos, AGN) for arranging my introduction to the archivist of the Cathedral of Durango. Monseñor Juan Antonio Díaz Acosta, on behalf of Archbishop Antonio López Avina, kindly allowed me free access to both sections of the Cathedral Archive during my two week-long visits to Durango. While there, Licenciado Marco Aurelio Mendoza Gomes (president), Licenciado Rene Chacón González (secretary general), and Licenciado María de Lourdes López Aranda granted me permission to use the material in the Archivo del Supremo Tribunal de Justicia, which also houses the papers of Juan José Zambrano (the building was once Zambrano's mansion).

Chihuahua proved an archival treasure, largely due to the efforts of Raymundo Palacios Carlos, archivist of the Archivo Histórico Municipal located in the Presidencia Municipal. Señor Palacios and his assistants passed freshly catalogued boxes of documents directly into my waiting arms. I offer my thanks to Ana Belinda Ames Russek of the Museo Regional de la Universidad Autónoma de Chihuahua and Elisa Ma. Ames Russek, the cultural adviser, who made sure I profited even as I unsuccessfully searched for Río Grande Pueblo pottery in regional collections.

Roberto Moreno de los Arcos, then director of the Instituto de Investigaciones Históricas, Universidad Nacional Autónoma de México, kindly offered the hospitality of the institute during my year in Mexico and effected my affiliation. While I was in the Federal District, Virginia Guedea orchestrated my welcome at the Instituto de Investigaciones Históricas. I profited handsomely by the invitation of Ignacio "Nacho" del Río to join his Seminario del Norte. Nacho, and his colleagues and students, provided a constant source of knowledge and information within easy reach, which added a great deal to my research. In addition to the discussions with Nacho and others at the institute, I thank my fellow researchers at the AGN for frequent conversations, sometimes about things historical, and for the occasional item of interest to me that they turned up in their own research. Martín González de la Vara, Brian Conal Belanger, Michael Ducey, Ana Laura Romero López, and Rodrigo Martínez come immediately to mind.

The concepts that form the substance of this work received important doses of useful criticism at early stages from Richard E. Ahlborn, James N. Gregory, Francis H. Harlow, Ramón A. Gutiérrez, Angela Moyano Pahissa, Marc Simmons, Lonn Taylor, and Eric Van Young. A number of people have been especially generous with their own research and have made manuscripts, data, and publications available to me that I could not have obtained otherwise. I thank them here, with assurances that they are in no way responsible for the use I have made of their work: Richard E. Ahlborn, John O. Baxter, Charles R. Cutter, Larry Frank (my father), Ramón A. Gutiérrez, Francis H. Harlow, Curtis Schaafsma, Marc Simmons, Lonn Taylor, William B. Taylor, and Mark Winter. Ramón Gutiérrez, Robert Katt, Steve Elster, and three anonymous readers gave me numerous suggestions that have improved the organization and substance of this work. At the University of California Press, Monica McCormick, Suzanne Knott, and copyeditor Sarah MacLennan Kerr worked beyond the call of duty to bring this project to its published form.

I especially am grateful for permission to reproduce the images of objects included in this work. These were obtained from the curatorial and permissions staffs of the School of American Research, the Museum of New Mexico (Laboratory of Anthropology, Museum of Indian Art and Culture, Palace of the Governors, and Museum of International Folk Art), the Taylor Museum of the Colorado Springs Fine Arts Center, the Museum of the University of Colorado (Boulder), the Harwood Foundation of the University of New Mexico, and the Millicent Rogers Museum. Al Luckett and Joshua Baer also agreed to allow important examples to be included in this book. My thanks go as well to the artist and sometime photographer William Acheff and to my father, for providing the clay and wooden subjects. Nancy Hunter Warren took exquisite photographs of *santos* for a different project and magnanimously allowed me to use some of them here.

Friends and families extended other kinds of sustenance that enabled me to complete this book. My parents, Alyce and Larry Frank, transplanted me to northern New Mexico at the age of four, and although it took eighteen more years for me to even begin to realize it, they also instilled in me most, if not all, of the elements that made me interested in the culture and history of late colonial New Mexico. For their indoctrination I offer this work to them as some measure of repayment, but even that cannot convey my appreciation for their love, encouragement, and constant support. I also express my gratitude to the Gomez Mont family(ies), who provided my real education while I was in Mexico. Finally, to Carina Chiang I owe a good deal of the happiness and inner strength that allow me to indulge myself in nosing around in the affairs of people who lived during the eighteenth and early nineteenth centuries.

A NOTE ABOUT TRANSLATIONS

Unless otherwise noted, I translated the Spanish documents that I discuss in this work from archival or printed sources. A few notes concerning these translations seem appropriate. Accents normally do not appear in eighteenth-century documents. Quotations of Spanish material retain the original orthography except where inconsistencies might confuse the reader (e.g., *becino* instead of *vecino*). In general, I followed the same formula in translations from the Spanish: I did not add accents and left proper names in their original spelling. Only when a conventional spelling exists because of the position of the subject (e.g., Revillagigedo instead of Revilla Gigedo), or when multiple or alternative spellings appear (e.g., Cisneros and Sisneros, José and Joseph), did I alter the spelling of proper names according to modern orthography, with the exception of a few cases in which the original spelling seemed more authentic (e.g., Zuñi instead of Zuni Pueblo).

Few documents written in New Mexico had the benefit of an educated public notary to compose materials according to proper legal and bureaucratic standards. Consequently, the syntax can appear convoluted and somewhat arbitrary, and punctuation often simply does not exist. In such cases, I first tried to translate the material literally and in the phraseology of the original. I then rearranged the syntax as necessary when unwieldy sentences threatened to obscure, rather than convey, the original meaning of the author. In some cases I also replaced words that seemed awkward or out of context in English with words or phrases that relaxed to some extent the literal translation of the original. Brackets enclose additions to the translation in cases in which previously mentioned, [implied], or understood words, or a translator's explanatory note, proved necessary to understanding the excerpt. In translations made by other people, the translator's additions or comments appear in brackets, as in the printed original, and I enclosed mine in {curly brackets}. Finally, when a translated word seemed to have special significance, I included the original Spanish in (parentheses). Ultimately, I guided the decisions I made in translating material for this work by the principle that the author deserved an English hearing in his or, occasionally, her own voice.

ABBREVIATIONS

Each of the following abbreviations represents an archival source referred to in the text. The abbreviation for the archive is followed by volume number, expediente or section, and page, folio, or microfilm frame number. Reference numbers from standard published guides appear whenever possible, such as the Twitchell numbers for the Spanish Archives of New Mexico; Chávez for the Archives of the Archdiocese of Santa Fe; Chapman for the Archivo General de las Indias; and the Ignacio del Río designations for the Archivo Franciscano at the Biblioteca San Augustín in Mexico City. The Archivo del Catedral de Durango, in Durango, Mexico, has been microfilmed by the University Library at New Mexico State University, Las Cruces, since I completed my research for this study. The citations here do not include the document's location in the microfilm series, but the order of the physical documents should correspond to that of the microfilm.

ARCHIVES OF THE ARCHDIOCESE OF SANTA FE, NEW MEXICO

AASF:BA	Book of Baptisms
AASF:BU	Book of Burials
AASF:DM	Diligencias Matrimoniales
AASF:MI	Loose Documents, Mission

ARCHIVO DEL CATEDRAL DE DURANGO, MEXICO

ACD:CB	Archivo del Cabildo
ACD:CO	Archivo Histórico, Ramo de Correspondencia
ACD:DZ	Archivo Histórico, Ramo de Diezmos
ACD:PA	Archivo Histórico, Ramo de Padrones

ACD:VA   Archivo Histórico, Ramo de Varios
AFBN   Archivo Franciscano, Biblioteca San Augustín (old Biblioteca Na-
            cional), Mexico City
AGI:GUAD   Ramo de Guadalajara

ARCHIVO GENERAL DE LA NACIÓN, MEXICO CITY

AGN:AC   Ramo de Alcabalas
AGN:CA   Ramo de Californias
AGN:HI   Ramo de Historias
AGN:MAP   Mapoteca
AGN:PI   Ramo de Provincias Internas
AGN:RC   Ramo de Reales Cédulas

CHI:RG   Registro de Propiedades, Archivos Históricos, Chihuahua, Mexico

ARCHIVO HISTÓRICO, PALACIO MUNICIPAL, CHIHUAHUA, MEXICO

CPM:CI   Sección Civil
CPM:GO   Sección Gobierno
CPM:HA   Sección Hacienda
CPM:JU   Sección Justicia
CPM:NO   Sección Notaria

PALACIO GOBIERNO, DURANGO, MEXICO

DUR:PG   Archivo Histórico
HTOZ   Hemenway Collection, Tozzer Library, Harvard University, Cam-
            bridge, Massachusetts
NMSRCA   New Mexico State Records Center and Archives, Santa Fe, New
            Mexico
PBAN   Pinart Collection, Bancroft Library, University of California, Berke-
            ley, California
RHUN   Ritch Collection, Huntington Library, San Marino, California
SANM I   Spanish Archives of New Mexico, series I, land grant records
SANM II   Spanish Archives of New Mexico, series II, provincial records

Introduction

This book tells two interwoven stories. The first traces the economy of
the Spanish colonial province of New Mexico from the 1750s until just before Mexico won its independence from Spain in 1821. It documents a brief
but critical period of intensive economic growth beginning in the 1780s that
lasted for about three decades and identifies the major forces and events that
brought about this development. The story of economic development places
New Mexico squarely within the broader history of the northern provinces of
New Spain.

Economic change helped to define the dominant society and culture that
emerged from the eighteenth century, the subject of the second story. The
struggle for subsistence and cooperative defense against raids by Apache and
Comanche bands had brought Pueblo Indians, Spanish settlers, and *Castas**
closer together before the 1780s. A decade later, the booming overland trade
created the conditions for *Vecinos*† to begin to usurp Pueblo Indian lands,
markets, and craft production. Out of this era of economic prosperity, vecinos created the roots of the Hispanic culture that still enriches the region.

The book is organized into an introduction, five chapters, and a conclusion. The introduction outlines the ethnic geography of New Mexico as it developed from the period of Spanish invasion and first settlement at the end

---

*Definitions of Spanish terms and other words that appear in italics can be found in the
glossary.
†As used here, the Spanish word *Vecino* refers to the non-Indian settlers of New Mexico. The
term, literally "neighbor," took on a meaning that included a sense of belonging to the province in late colonial New Mexican documents. Settlers were commonly referred to by Franciscans or provincial officials as "vecinos" as distinct from "Indios," the inhabitants of the pueblos,
who represented another kind of neighbor.

of the sixteenth century to the 1750s. The first three chapters focus on the economic history of New Mexico from 1750 to about 1810 and on the province's place within the larger region of northern New Spain. The cultural and social implications of economic change figure lightly in the early chapters and become increasingly important in chapters 4 and 5.

Chapter 1 begins by laying out the economy of New Mexico in about 1750, with careful attention to the relationships between Pueblo Indian communities on the Río Grande and Spanish settlers and officials. This portion of the chapter explores several questions: How did the Pueblos participate in the Spanish economy of the province? To what extent did the Spanish population use force to take advantage of Indian goods and labor? What effect did the relationship of the Pueblos to the Spanish economy have on Indian livelihoods and Pueblo autonomy? The second part of chapter 1 recounts the tremendous adversity experienced from the 1760s into the 1780s by Pueblo Indian and Spanish settlers alike, first from attacks launched by Apache, Comanche, and Navajo raiding parties and then from a virulent outbreak of smallpox. Underlying this narrative of tragedy, the analysis gauges the effect that warfare and disease had on the population of the province and how each blow affected the growth and structure of the New Mexican economy.

The larger economic, political, and administrative concerns of policymakers who governed New Spain during the late colonial period forms the subject of chapter 2. Reform of economic policy, implemented by a more powerful and efficient bureaucracy, became the hallmark of the Spanish Bourbon kings. Carlos III (1759–1788) and his ministers extended reform to the Spanish possessions in America. Chapter 2 follows the Bourbon Reforms to northern New Spain and locates the central role that New Mexicans played in a new military strategy directed at the Apache and Comanche bands in the region. The resulting Spanish alliance with the Comanche in 1786 protected mining and commercial centers in the north from attack and freed New Mexico from one important obstacle to economic development.

Chapter 3 investigates a series of other obstacles to economic growth and development in New Mexico, identified by Bourbon administrators and New Mexican governors, and their attempts to solve these problems. In each case, the Bourbon response demonstrated an understanding of the serious issues that faced the northern provinces and the willingness and ability to project tremendous power into farthest reaches of New Spain. However, Spanish officials could not always control the effects of their policies or ensure that they provided the intended solution.

Bourbon economic initiatives did encourage economic growth in late colonial New Mexico. Chapter 4 presents the evidence for a boom beginning during the 1780s, led by a surge in trade with other northern provinces—just the kind of economic activity envisioned by Bourbon policymakers and administrators. Increased exports from New Mexico and expanded food and

craft production began to integrate New Mexico more closely into a northern interregional economy. The chapter then analyzes how trade and increased productivity altered the internal economy of the province. Vecinos
responded to new opportunities for gain by adopting coercive economic relationships to extract goods from Pueblo Indians, and in the process they
dramatically changed craft production in both populations.

Chapter 5 explores the social and cultural transformation of Hispanic
New Mexicans and connects them directly to the economic changes of the
1780s and 1790s. The incentives created by the economic boom helped to
form a vecino society that identified itself in contradistinction to the Pueblo
Indians. Encroachment on Indian lands in order to increase agricultural and
livestock production paralleled the end of close cooperation in warfare and
increasing intermarriages between vecinos and Pueblo Indians. A prosperous vecino population expressed its emerging identity through religious patronage and the creation of New Mexican variants of Spanish and Mexican
cultural forms, discernible in *santos* and in furniture. By the end of the eighteenth century, the strength of vecino society had drawn the Franciscan missionaries away from protecting the interests of the Pueblo Indians and provoked new forms of political and cultural resistance in the Río Grande
pueblos.

A brief concluding section suggests ways in which this view of late colonial
New Mexico alters the general understanding of economic change after
1821, when Mexican independence from Spain opened the border with the
United States to overland trade from Missouri.

THE ETHNIC GEOGRAPHY OF NEW MEXICO TO 1750

When Francisco Vásquez de Coronado led the first Spanish conquistadores
to New Mexico in 1540, the 60,000 to 80,000 Pueblo Indians (*Indios de
pueblo*) lived in as many as 150 distinct villages. Pueblo people had cultivated
many of the richest agricultural lands in the Río Grande Valley continually
since the fourteenth century.[1] Each group of Pueblos spoke one of three
distinct language groups: Tanoan, Keres, or Zuñi. Members of the Tanoan
pueblos spoke one of at least six distinct and mutually unintelligible dialects
that had developed much earlier from a common ancestral tongue. The geographical distribution of these language groups indicates the complexity of
the Pueblo world that faced Spanish colonizers (see Map 1). Tanoan speakers lived on a north-south axis roughly centered on the Río Grande Valley.
The northernmost Pueblos of Taos and Picurís spoke Tiwa. Farther south, a
group of pueblo-dwellers along the Río Grande and its Río Chama tributary
spoke Tewa. Next came the Tano-speaking pueblo-dwellers in the Santa Fe
area, including Galisteo Pueblo. Towa speakers flanked this region on both
sides: Jémez to the west, and Pecos to the east. Proceeding to the south, the

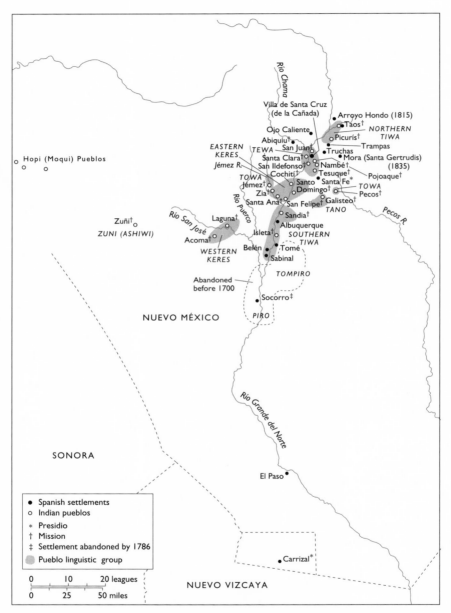

Map 1. The Province of New Mexico, circa 1790. *Source:* Adapted from Peter Gerhard, *The North Frontier of New Spain* (Princeton, N.J.: Princeton University Press, 1982), 315.

large province of Tiguex stretched from just north of present-day Albuquerque to Socorro in the south; its inhabitants spoke a southern version of Tiwa. The pueblos of Sandía and Isleta form the modern representatives of Tiguex. Farther south and east lived groups of Piro and Tompiro villagers, distantly related to the other Tanoan-speaking groups.

In addition to the complex movement of peoples that the distribution of the Tanoan villages suggests, the Keres group of Pueblos settled on an east-west axis that met the Tanoan progression at the Río Grande between present-day Santa Fe and Albuquerque. These people descended from the earlier groups that had built and occupied the sophisticated settlements of Chaco Canyon. Acoma formed the center of the western Keres villages (which later included Laguna Pueblo), and the eastern Keres pueblos included San Felipe, Santa Ana, Zia, Santo Domingo, and Cochití. To the west of Acoma, the Zuñi villagers (the original "Cities of Cíbola") spoke a language unrelated to any other in the region; they represent another story of migration and resettlement. Still farther west, Shoshone-speaking Hopi people settled in a group of villages in northeastern Arizona.

PUEBLO SOCIAL STRUCTURE, RELIGION, AND WORLDVIEW

The complicated religious and social bonds that knit settlements into vibrant communities mirrored the geographical and linguistic relationships among the Pueblos. Together these socioreligious structures tied the Native American peoples of the Río Grande region loosely together within a "Pueblo worldview." The internal organization of each pueblo not only reflected a method of ordering social and political relations but also expressed a complex religious system that maintained the harmonious function and balance of natural forces on which the Pueblos relied for their survival.[2] Today, through the many changes over six centuries, nineteen Río Grande pueblos in New Mexico and the group of Hopi pueblos in northeastern Arizona continue a way of life based on these ancient traditions.

The group of western pueblos, encompassing Acoma, Laguna, Zuñi, and the Hopi villages, had a similar social structure based on matrilineal clans. In western Pueblo households, only persons who came from different clans could marry, and the life of the new family centered primarily around the wife's relatives. Each clan took its name from an important actor in the religious mythology of the Pueblo. For example, Zuñi Pueblo has Eagle, Badger, Corn, and Crane clans, among others. Moreover, each clan might have its own subgroupings. Some pueblos remained small enough that the members of a clan consisted of a web of families all related to a common female ancestor. Larger pueblos had clans that contained a number of different family lineages. This arrangement emphasized the ways in which the clan system organized Pueblo social relations. In these pueblos, the clan system incorporated households into a framework of reciprocal relations and also served as a communal repository for ceremonial information.[3]

Just as the clan performed the central task of social organization among the western pueblos, the eastern pueblos divided into halves, or moieties, that served to pattern social and ceremonial relations. For the Tewa pueblos (San Juan, Santa Clara, San Ildefonso, Nambé, Tesuque, and Pojoaque) and the Tiwa pueblos (Taos and Picurís in the north, and Sandía and Isleta in the south), the moieties represented Summer People and Winter People. Within these divisions, households participated in the social-religious life of the pueblo through *kiva* societies, associations dedicated to performing the ceremonial functions centered around special structures, called kivas, in which religious instruction and observance took place. In the Tiwa and Tewa pueblos, families traced their lineage through the relatives of both the mother and the father.

Each of the Tanoan-speaking and northeastern Keres pueblos borrowed some traits from its neighbors over centuries of coexistence. The Tewa and Tiwa pueblos have social structures that some anthropologists have labeled clans, but these do not serve to regulate marriage or organize households into groups connected by kinship. The Tanoan clanlike groupings probably grew out of the influence of their Keresan neighbors. Similarly, the eastern Keres pueblos have borrowed moieties from the Tewa. Turquoise and Squash (or Pumpkin) People correspond to the Winter and Summer divisions within the Tanoan pueblos. The eastern Keres have matrilineal clans and have also incorporated other religious associations, such as Medicine societies. The relationship between close proximity and cultural borrowing becomes equally clear in the development of the Towa-speaking Jémez people, who organize kinship within exogamous, matrilineal clans clearly borrowed from the Keres.

Overlaying the social organization of each of the pueblos, the kachina cult provided the religious focus for the Pueblo world. Kachinas (or katsinas) are supernatural beings who can bless the Pueblos and humankind with rain, fertile crops, good hunting, and general well-being. Religious ceremonies and public dances provide the Pueblo people with opportunities to call on the kachinas to continue the natural cycle of life. A number of Pueblo myths identify kachinas with the Anasazi people, the Pueblo ancestors who occupied the great cities built into cliffs, like Mesa Verde in southwestern Colorado, one of the most famous surviving examples. In essence, the Pueblos made gods out of ancestral spirits. From the evidence of mural paintings on the interior kiva walls of pueblos occupied before the Spanish conquest, the kachina cult reached the Río Grande in the early to mid–fourteenth century. The early Spanish chroniclers described kivas as well as the masked dancers (also called kachinas) in colorful costumes who impersonated the kachinas in dance ceremonies. Specialists disagree about the exact path the kachina ceremonial complex took before spreading across the Pueblo area, but the masked gods and rites of impersonation clearly link the southwestern kachina cult to religious practices in central and western Mexico.[4] Perhaps the arrival of the new religious cult during a period of migration into the Pueblo region facilitated the connection between the Anasazi and the kachina.

Depending on the historical development of a particular pueblo, either the clans or the kiva societies organized by moiety held the esoteric ceremonial information required for participation in the inner workings of the kachina cult and other religious associations. In the case of the western pueblos (Zuñi, Acoma, and Laguna), and to a lesser extent the eastern Keres pueblos and Jémez, clans connected (and still connect) religious ceremony to kinship networks, and in this manner they served to organize the social and cultural fabric of whole villages. In the other pueblos of Tanoan descent, the dual division of the pueblos provided by the moiety system alongside the kiva societies expressed a network of relationships animated by the kachina religion. The kachina cult not only connected and ordered complex webs of kinship, family, and other social groupings within pueblos but also engaged all of the peoples in the region in a conscious religious observance in common that kept the world in balance and in a productive relationship with humankind.[5]

For the Río Grande Pueblos, the seventeenth century brought the Spanish and disaster. Epidemic diseases contributed to a dramatic population decline, from 60,000–80,000 to about 17,000 just before the Pueblo Revolt of 1680. Smallpox killed up to one-third of the Pueblo population in 1636, and another epidemic struck four years later. By the 1630s other factors made the Pueblo people even more susceptible to disease. Attacks of the Apache on the Zuñi, Piro, and Tompiro Pueblos limited the land that the Indians could cultivate. By the 1670s the Tompiro had abandoned their pueblos south and east of present-day Albuquerque because of population loss from disease, prolonged drought, and the inability to prevent Apache raids.[6]

During the eighteenth century, Franciscan missionaries attacked Pueblo institutions in order to convert the Indians to Christianity and force them to conform to Spanish patterns of social behavior. Spanish officials and colonists also demanded labor and tribute from the pueblos through the ownership of *encomiendas*. All told, Spanish coercion represented the deciding factor in the decline of the Pueblo population by 70 to 80 percent during the first century of Spanish occupation and settlement.

PUEBLO INDIANS AND FRANCISCANS
IN THE EIGHTEENTH CENTURY

Spanish secular and religious institutions changed dramatically in New Mexico after the Pueblo Revolt of 1680 and the permanent reconquest of New

Mexico in 1692 by Diego de Vargas. The encomienda system of tribute ended with the rebellion of 1680, and the *repartimiento,* which had extracted Pueblo labor for Spanish farms and haciendas, continued after the reconquest as a much looser form of rotational labor draft, limited to the benefit of Spanish governors and *alcaldes mayores.*[7] As a result, the Pueblos retained much of their communal agricultural land, despite encroachments by vecinos and provincial officials during the eighteenth century.

The Franciscan missionaries continued to reside in their missions inside the pueblos, acting as the spiritual leaders of a nominally converted, Christian Indian congregation. As a result of the revolt, the Franciscans lost the means to effect any further fundamental change in the underlying religion of the Pueblos or to advocate social behavior that might lead to the adoption of Spanish cultural values.[8]

The religious reports concerning the spiritual condition of the Pueblo Indians demonstrate the weak position of the missionary in New Mexico. In 1760 Bishop Pedro Tamarón y Romerál made serious charges about the level of spiritual care given the Pueblo Indians in the report he wrote after his official visitation of the New Mexican missions: "I soon observed that those Indians were not indoctrinated. They do recite the catechism in Spanish, following their *fiscal,* but since they do not know this language, they do not understand what they are saying. The missionaries do not know the languages of the Indians, and as a result the latter do not confess except at the point of death, and then with the aid of an interpreter."[9] After repeated admonitions about the necessity of learning the native languages in order to impart the faith, the *custos* responded in no uncertain terms that the friars held no interest in study, "nor . . . would they do anything about it even if further precepts were applied."[10] Tamarón's appraisal of the state of Pueblo Indian Catholicism seems mild compared with that of the next visitor. Fray Francisco Atanasio Domínguez, who visited the province in 1776 on behalf of the Franciscan provincial, found a general lack of commitment to the Catholic faith and placed most of the blame on the Indians themselves, rather than on lack of effort by the missionaries: "Their repugnance and resistance to most Christian acts is evident, for they perform the duties pertaining to the Church under compulsion, and there are usually many omissions."[11]

The two visitors grasped to some degree both the relationship between the continued observance of traditional Native ceremonies and the perfunctory nature of the Pueblo Indian conversion to Christianity, as well as the helplessness of the missionaries in the face of Native opposition to change. Tamarón expressed his concern that the Indians had retained idolatrous practices, especially in relation to the kiva. In these underground chambers, religious meetings, dances, and ceremonies continued in secrecy, uninterrupted by Spanish interference. After an inspection in which he could not "find proof of anything evil," Tamarón ordered the missionaries to watch carefully in the future. The friars in turn "argued the difficulty of depriving them [the Indians] of that dark and strange receptacle, which is also a temptation to evil."[12]

Domínguez described the Pueblos' "scalp dance," held to celebrate victory in battle over their Plains Indian enemies, and objected to the attention paid to the gory trophies and to the glorification of the warrior who took the scalp—practices that he said "are tainted by the idea of vengeance." He credited the friars with trying to stop the scalp dance but added that "they have only received rebuffs, and so the fathers are unable to abolish this custom and many others." In response to this type of resistance, the New Mexican missionaries rationalized that the Pueblo Indians remained neophytes and deserved special tolerance. Domínguez noted, "Under such pretexts they will always be neophytes and minors with the result that our Holy Faith will not take root and their malice will increase."[13]

The Franciscans in New Mexico faced a sophisticated system of cultural resistance among the Pueblos that allowed them to absorb foreign elements and yet not integrate them into the Indian worldview. According to anthropologists, Pueblo societies "compartmentalized" non-Pueblo elements, such as the body of Catholic teachings, and in this manner prevented the teachings from influencing traditional Indian patterns of belief.[14]

The Pueblo adaptation to Spanish political control also illustrates the process of compartmentalization. A royal decree of 1620 called for the establishment of Spanish secular officials in each Indian community, chosen within the pueblo without any outside supervision. The secular administration comprised a governor, alcaldes to assist him in governing within the pueblo, fiscales responsible for the affairs of the community lands and irrigation ditches, and *sacristanes* who staffed and maintained the mission church.[15] The Spanish Crown assumed that secular government would further the process of civilizing and Christianizing the Indians.

In New Mexico, before the revolt the Pueblos elected these officials under the close supervision of the resident friar, but afterward the Franciscans had no power to affect Native elections. Religious officials inside the pueblos appointed and controlled secular officials and used them in an executive capacity to deal with people or problems outside the Pueblo social and cultural system. In the Tewa pueblos, each of the two internal ceremonial organizations (moieties) had a full complement of secular officials, from governor to deputy fiscales, appointed by some combination of *cacique,* war captain, and other religious clan or kiva leaders. The cacique generally appointed officers to the secular positions in the Keresan pueblos.[16]

At Taos Pueblo, the traditional war leader handled part of the outside business. A council of leaders, made up of previous holders of the important Native religious and secular offices, advised the cacique, rather than the person holding the position of governor, which the Spanish had imposed on the pueblo. The secular officials made no fundamental policy decision on any issue, as the council resolved and directed matters of importance from behind the scenes. Nor did the cacique take active control of the council; he simply represented the stable repository of power.[17] In practice, the secular government imposed by the Spanish ensured that no person directly involved in the important social and religious affairs of Pueblo life became accountable to any outside authority.

NONSEDENTARY INDIAN GROUPS

A complicated series of historical factors acted upon the ethnic geography of New Mexico by the mid–eighteenth century.[18] The various groups that made up the Apache peoples surrounded the province (see Map 2). The Spanish reconquest of the Pueblo Indians had left New Mexico largely at peace with its nomadic Indian neighbors. Attacks from the south, coupled with drought during the 1660s, forced the abandonment in the 1670s of the Tompiro pueblos, located between Socorro and the later Spanish town of Albuquerque. The Gila (Gileño) Apache established themselves southwest of the Río Grande and the Navajo to the northwest, all with links to a number of groups of Apache who lived in a large area extending from the Southern Plains in what is now the United States to the northern portions of Sonora and Nueva Vizcaya. Close cooperation and coordination between the Apache groups and the Pueblo Indians made possible the great Pueblo Revolt of 1680, which drove the Spanish soldiers, missionaries, and settlers, and the more hispanicized Piro Indians, completely out of the province. Although such alliances rarely proved permanent, a group of Tano and Tewa Indians stayed with the Hopi pueblos. The Tewa-Hopi returned with Fray Miguel de Menchero in 1744 to repopulate Sandía and other pueblos in the Río Grande Valley. The Tano remained with the Hopi, having founded the present-day First Mesa village of Hano. By the early eighteenth century only the Faraone Apache, based in the central portion of the province, to the east of the Sangre de Cristo mountains, remained hostile to the Spanish.

New Mexican officials described Comanche trade visits to the Río Grande villages beginning in 1705, intermixed with reports of their attacks against the eastern Apache and also of the occasional raids carried out on provincial settlements. During the 1720s the Comanche and their Ute allies destroyed the Faraone and Carlana Apache groups and pushed their remnants south and west. The Jicarilla Apache—once trade partners with the northern pueblos and always a threat as raiders from the Southern Plains and Texas Panhandle—settled in the 1740s in the mountains between the Taos and Pecos pueblos. Constant Comanche and Ute attacks reduced them to a fraction of their former strength. The Cuartelejo Apache endured on the Plains longer, but by 1752 they had settled near Pecos, allied with the pueblo

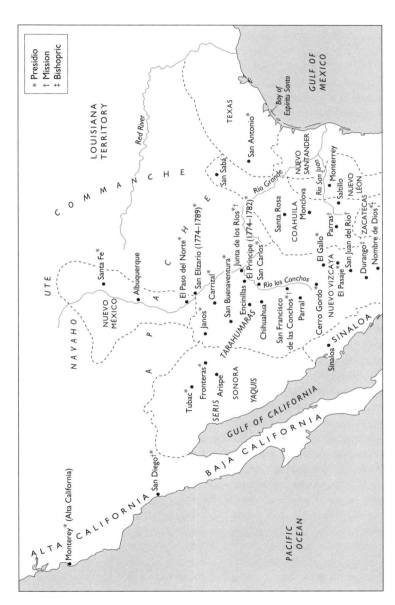

Map 2. The Provincias Internas, circa 1785. *Source:* Adapted from Marc Simmons, *Spanish Government in New Mexico* (Albuquerque: University of New Mexico Press, 1968), xvi.

against the Comanche.[19] The Navajo, an Apache group distinguished by the 1720s in part because they adopted farming, weaving, and sheep raising, began to fight with the Ute over territory. During the 1750s the Ute attacks forced the Navajo from their strongholds near the Río San Juan, northwest of the Río Grande Valley, to new lands in Canyon de Chelly, the Chuska Mountains, and near the Hopi pueblos as far east as Cebolleta Mountain.

By the 1740s the Comanche had begun raiding New Mexico from *rancherías* north and east of the province. The Comanche had become more dangerous due to the firearms, iron axes, and arrowheads they obtained from the French in trade for Spanish horses. During the next decade the Ute broke with the Comanche, forming an alliance with the Jicarilla Apache.[20] Over the next forty years, the Comanche became a threat to the livelihood of every group in the region—Apache, Ute, Navajo, Pueblo, and Spanish settler alike.

European contact with Native Americans brought great changes to the location and livelihood of tribal groups in North America. Complex forces exerted on a huge area—from the French and Anglo-American Old Northwest (the Great Lakes), across the Great Plains, to the Rocky Mountains and the Spanish Southwest—brought about the elaboration of Indian cultures on the High Plains beginning in the eighteenth century. As chapter 1 shows, the historical effect of these cultural changes also altered interethnic social and economic relations within New Mexico.

CHAPTER ONE

"Like a Ball in the Hands of Fortune"
New Mexican Economy through the 1770s

By 1750, Spanish settlers and Pueblo communities had reestablished a network of relationships based upon a relatively stable system of coexistence. Settler and Pueblo Indians functioned within parallel and somewhat autonomous patterns of trade and production. The two systems came into contact frequently: at trade fairs with non-Pueblo Indian groups; through informal barter and judicial proceedings; or when missionaries and provincial officials demanded goods, services, or labor. Each exchange between the Spanish and Pueblo systems of production and distribution could become a potentially coercive relationship, drawing Pueblo goods and labor into the Spanish economic orbit by force. At midcentury, the history of Spanish-Pueblo relations placed limits on expressions of colonial domination, and the provincial economy provided few incentives for extensive economic coercion.

During the second half of the eighteenth century New Mexicans experienced a crisis of such proportions that it threatened New Mexico's very existence as a Spanish province. Only during the disaster of the Revolt of 1680, when the Río Grande Pueblos and their nomadic allies drove the settlers and the most Hispanicized Pueblo Indians completely out of the province, had New Mexico faced anything like these tribulations.

Two blows from outside the province, in the form of Indian raids and epidemic disease, brought the late colonial crisis to New Mexico. From the 1750s to the early 1780s, raids of Spanish and Pueblo settlements by nomadic Plains Indian and Apache groups severely damaged the livelihood of the inhabitants of the province. In 1779 a major Spanish-led military victory over the principal band of Comanche that threatened the province provided hope of a lasting peace for the first time in three decades. New Mexicans had little time to rejoice. Following on the heels of this victory a smallpox epidemic killed a large segment of the New Mexican population.

PRODUCTS AND MARKETS IN
MID–EIGHTEENTH CENTURY NEW MEXICO

The first eighteenth-century trade economy depended on the exchange of goods with nomadic Native groups, such as the Comanche, for materials produced locally by Pueblo Indians and vecinos. Trade fairs formed the basis of internal exchange and the long-distance trade with Chihuahua. At every turn the structure and dimensions of this system faced the limiting factor of a small market, further restricted by the absence of a market structure within the province, the hostile acts of nomadic Indians, and the distance to external markets. Dramatically increased military activity, particularly during the 1760s and 1770s—the "Defensive Crisis," as the historian Oakah Jones dubs the period[1]—shattered the cumbersome trade economy of midcentury.

Trade with the Plains Indians constituted one of the driving forces behind the pattern of trade in the midcentury economy of New Mexico. In 1749 Fray Andrés Varo, who had served as custos of New Mexico, described the workings of the trade fairs: "These Infidel Indians are accustomed to come in peace to the pueblos, and bring buffalo and elk skins, and some young Indians from those that they have imprisoned in the wars that they have among themselves. These they trade to the vecinos, *gente de razón*, Spanish, and Pueblo Indians for horses, mules, knives, awls, clothes, beads, and other things. Sometimes the friar of the mission where they arrive will trade some hides, and if he can obtain in trade some Indian, attach him to the pueblo."[2] In 1769, Governor Pedro Fermín de Mendinueta described the trade fairs as "the nerve that maintains this province with faculties." Since meetings with the Comanche had stopped and those with the Ute occurred rarely, due to hostilities, "one finds the inhabitants in total poverty, which does not permit them to make more than that which they can do themselves, and even this with the pain of appearing so naked and miserable, and more when there is nothing on which to base hope of a remedy, save that the Comanche return."[3]

As Governor Tomás Vélez de Cachupín suggested, the Plains trade stimulated the New Mexicans to carry goods to Chihuahua and Sonora. It also motivated the governor and his alcaldes mayores, who profited from their participation in commerce with the nomadic groups. As one friar put it, when the trading parties arrive, "the fleet is in": "Here the governor, alcaldes, and lieutenants gather together as many horses as they can; here is collected all the ironware possible, such as axes, hoes, wedges, picks, bridles, machetes, and *belduques,* and knives (for the enemy does not lack iron and these other commodities). Here, in short, is gathered everything possible for trade and barter with these barbarians in exchange for deer and buffalo hides, and what is saddest, in exchange for Indian slaves." The goods received from the Plains Indians traded within the province and the *gamuzas,* hides, and chamois found their way to the export market in Chihuahua and elsewhere. Vecinos and Pueblo Indians, as well as the governor and the missionaries, purchased captive Indians. Those retained as servants (*criados*) in vecino households in this manner converted to Christianity and thereby passed from *gentile* (unconverted) status to gente de razón. Many of these people became the basis for the *Genízaro* communities that New Mexican governors settled on the frontier beginning in the 1740s.[4]

Goods entering the province through trade with the Plains Indians complemented the southern trade along the Chihuahua Trail. In between, some of the commodities created by New Mexicans and methods of production followed lines of ethnicity and implied social standing. In the areas of agriculture, animal husbandry, the cultivation of *punche,* and trade in hides, both Pueblo Indians and vecinos contributed to the production of the province. New Mexican river valleys provided a limited supply of good cropland, especially when raids pinned New Mexicans close to their homes. The reports of provincial officials and Franciscan missionaries show that the crops of *maize,* wheat, and beans often bore similar or higher yields than did those obtained in Guadalajara, the agricultural heartland of central Mexico. On the average, New Mexican fields produced as much as one-third more per acre than did Nueva Vizcaya.[5] The long experience of the Pueblo Indians with the climate and soil enhanced the productivity of Pueblo and settler farmers alike.

During the third quarter of the eighteenth century, Pueblo grain harvests surpassed those of their vecino counterparts, due in large part to the greater ability of larger and more compact Pueblo communities to cultivate and defend their fields in common from raids or other dangers. A number of observers remarked at the industry of the pueblo-dwellers, often emphasizing their greater productivity compared with that of the vecinos. In a report on the New Mexican missions written in 1773, Governor Mendinueta described the economic activities of the Natives: "Agriculture comes so naturally to these Indians that their pueblos are the storehouses of all kinds of grain (especially corn). Thither come the Spanish citizens to make purchases, as well as the governor when grain is needed by the presidial paymaster for the troops. . . . They succeed well with their cattle and sheep and with their few horses. . . . They weave *mantas* of wool and cotton for their simple clothing."[6] Of these Pueblo products, only mantas and perhaps some livestock figured in the export trade.

The weaving of certain textiles and the manufacture of pottery distinguished Pueblo from vecino handicrafts during the colonial period: Pueblo men generally wove blankets, and Pueblo women made pottery.[7] Before the arrival of the Spanish, the Pueblos wove rectangular pieces of cloth called

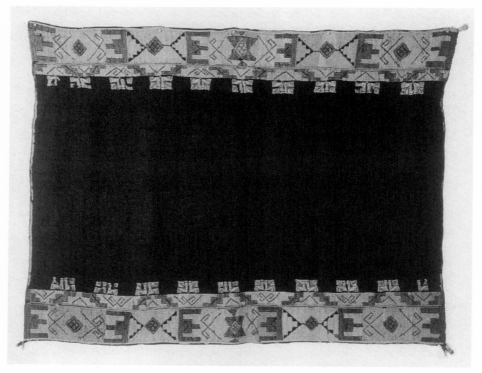

Plate 1. Manta woven with brown undyed wool, embroidered with índigo-dyed handspun and unraveled bayeta yarn, circa 1830, Acoma Pueblo. (Photograph courtesy of and all reproduction rights reserved by Joshua Baer & Co., Santa Fe, New Mexico)

mantas out of cotton and continued to cultivate and weave the fiber through-out the colonial period. With the introduction of sheep in New Mexico by the first Spanish settlers in 1598, Pueblo weavers began to incorporate wool into their textiles. Up to the present, Pueblo weavers have continued to make certain types of traditional textiles, such as those fashioned for ceremonial use.

Plate 1 shows a manta woven on a Pueblo loom. This example came from Acoma Pueblo and probably dates from around the 1830s, although the style had not changed much since colonial times. The manta illustrates the characteristic width of the blanket and the Pueblo and Navajo practice of tying the end of the selvage cords together into a tassel at the corners of the blanket. The substitution of wool for cotton after the arrival of the Spanish did not alter the basic form of the manta or Pueblo weaving techniques.

Pueblo Indians used an indigenous loom on which they strung continuing warp threads vertically and then tensioned them in a wooden frame.[8] The weaver controlled the warp sets using string-loop heddles and a long wooden batten in the shape of a sword blade to separate alternate warps. If need be, the weaver could turn the batten onto its side in order to make room for the weft, which he passed horizontally across the cloth. While adding wefts, the worker used a hand-sized weaving comb made of wood to beat them down. The Navajo had obtained their knowledge of blanket weaving from the Pueblos by the last half of the seventeenth century, and they adopted the vertical style loom because it was simple and easily moved to facilitate their seminomadic lifestyle.[9]

The vertical frame of Pueblo and Navajo looms could most easily accommodate textiles that were wider than they were long, as the manta in Plate 1 illustrates. Pueblo women generally wore a manta as a one-piece dress wrapped around the body under the left arm and fastened on the right shoulder. A narrow sash or woven belt held it in place around the waist, and a second textile often functioned as a manta. The Pueblo-style loom could produce variously sized textiles to fit women and children and to make shirts, breech cloths, and shoulder blankets for men.

The Pueblo weaver of the manta illustrated in Plate 1 used brown undyed handspun yarn for the body of the blanket and embroidered it with *índigo*-dyed handspun wool and red *bayeta* yarn unraveled from a piece of cloth acquired in trade. The geometric designs generally allude to phenomena associated with rain, such as clouds, lightning, or small insects. The small, rectangular shapes that enter the brown central field of the blanket represent tobacco leaves and the prayers that they help transmit to the rain gods.

Vecino craftspeople wove on a horizontal treadle loom of European design, the technology brought into the province during the seventeenth century and still in use today.[10] New Mexicans built the frame of these cumbersome looms out of trunks of ponderosa pine, roughly the size of a large four-poster bed. The warp ran horizontally instead of vertically, as on the Pueblo loom. Long warps could be strung on a horizontal end piece of the frame and unrolled as the weaver worked. The artisan then rolled up the finished material on the end piece on the other side of the frame.

The design of the treadle loom may have affected the width of cloth, but it did not constrain its length. The weaver strung the warps between the dents (teeth) of a reed, which looks like a long, wide comb. This implement served to keep the warps properly spaced. Heddles hung down from a frame above the loom, and the weaver controlled them using a foot treadle, which freed both hands to manipulate the weft. After each pass of the shuttle, a push on the foot treadle raised alternate warps. The reed helped the weaver beat the weft into place. Vecinos produced most of their loom-woven materials out of wool, but occasionally used cotton.[11]

Plate 2 provides an example of a Río Grande blanket woven around 1850,

Plate 2. Río Grande blanket with banded and serrate designs woven with
brown and white undyed wool and índigo dyed wool, circa 1850. (Courtesy of
the School of American Research, Indian Arts Research Center, Santa Fe, New
Mexico, IAF T.445)

but in a style similar to textiles woven on vecino looms since the late eighteenth century.[12] The weaver used hand-spun wool for the warp and weft, and wove the design in natural brown, white, and índigo-dyed stripes, generally referred to as a "banded design" or "*Moqui*" (Hopi) pattern. The stripes have been broken by wider bands of white alternating with serrate designs, probably adapted from "Saltillo-style" *sarapes* woven farther south.

Cloth made in New Mexico on a treadle loom generally had a width of between 22 and 30 inches. Most vecino looms measured about 5 feet in width. Wider looms took more effort to build and proved even more unwieldy; more important, they forced the weaver to move in order to reach all of the textile during production. A loom that produced relatively narrow cloth allowed the weaver to remain stationary while working on the entire length of the loom.

The materials available to New Mexicans for making looms also served to help distinguish cloth woven on them from textiles produced in other centers of weaving in New Spain. Vecinos made all of the articles necessary for the loom out of local materials and tried to avoid employing metal in their construction, as iron proved costly and difficult to obtain. In colonial Mexico, wire or thin metal was used for the dents. New Mexican weavers made reeds entirely out of hardwood, carving the dents as thin as possible and as close together as the wood allowed. Consequently, cloth woven on a vecino loom in New Mexico had warps spaced farther apart than did cloth woven elsewhere in New Spain. This produced heavier cloth that was more suited for the colder New Mexican climate. Blankets woven in Saltillo, Nueva Vizcaya (today in the state of Coahuila), for example, generally had twenty to thirty warps, compared with fewer than ten for those woven on New Mexican looms. Manufactured, wider metal reeds with narrowly spaced dents reached New Mexico before 1890, sent by Eastern merchants over the first railroad lines to arrive in the territory.

In order to achieve the width required for a *jerga, fresada,* blanket, or sarape the weaver sewed two widths of finished cloth together along the length of the finished product. The wearing blanket with a banded and serrated design produced on a vecino loom, illustrated in Plate 2, clearly shows the center seam. The weaver could also make a double width of cloth by layering warps and joining them together at one edge with a common weft. Double-woven blankets display a ridge in the middle of the piece where the weaver utilized one or more pairs of bundled warps.

The vecino preference for the treadle loom stemmed from cultural traditions, the kind of textiles commonly produced, and the desire to increase productivity. The vecino loom lent itself to the production of sarapes and yardage of coarser cloth, such as jerga and *sayal.* Weavers using the treadle loom could produce lengths of woven material far more quickly than Pueblo or Navajo weavers could on an upright loom, as long as they did not incorporate elaborate patterns. Once the weaver departed from plain cloth or a banded blanket design, the comparative advantage in the rate of production on the treadle loom disappeared. Pueblo and Navajo weavers could make Spanish-style narrow pieces of cloth of limited lengths on the indigenous loom, but with much more difficulty. These blankets generally have an unelaborated, banded design, similar to pieces woven on a vecino loom.

During the first system of trade, Pueblo Indians at times took their produce to Chihuahua alongside vecinos, where they traded for products from elsewhere in New Spain or imported from Europe (see Map 2). Nicolás de la Fora, the engineer appointed to accompany the Marqués de Rubí on his inspection of the northern provinces, described the New Mexican commerce with Chihuahua as it appeared in the late 1760s: "The commerce of the inhabitants is limited to a few buckskins or buffalo hides, which they bundle and take annually to Chihuahua. In return they bring clothing for their families. The Indians, too, are in the habit of going after clothing, but usually their women wear the cloth they themselves weave. They weave very fine woolen cloth in patterns of some beauty. From this they fashion blouses, skirts, and capes." In his description of what he saw of the Chihuahua trade, the engineer assumed that Pueblo women wove the cloth, perhaps based on gender roles in the Indian communities with which he was more familiar.

La Fora also mentioned the "blankets, stockings, and embroideries" (mantas, *medias,* y *colchas*) that the vecinos traded in Chihuahua, lamenting the fact that they paid no attention to otter, beaver, ermine, or martin pelts. Governor Mendinueta mentioned some forty Indians from Pecos who secured his permission to accompany the *cordón* to Chihuahua. Unfortunately, they also asked to hunt buffalo "due to the extreme need that they suffered" before joining the rest of the soldiers and vecinos. A Comanche party surprised the group and killed eleven and captured one Indian in the ensuing fight. The other twenty-eight Pecos Indians fled, losing "their poor equipment" in the process. Some of the Pueblo Indian trade occurred as a consequence of having to transport the governor's goods to Chihuahua.[13]

A more detailed picture of the components of the vecino trade has survived in a list of goods sent in 1762 to Chihuahua by a New Mexican merchant, Joseph Reaño. The bulk of the merchandise consisted of livestock: 4 mules and 309 sheep, which he sold for 246 *pesos.* Three Plains Indian captives brought 134 pesos between them. Next in value came 44 hides and 4 cured skins worth 72 pesos, and finally the woven goods: a colcha and 24 medias, which brought 36 pesos. Reaño returned with various types of expensive cloth, including silk, *bretaña,* and material from Cholula and Querétaro. The Reaño inventory illustrates the relative importance of the Plains Indian trade and local manufactures. The most valuable goods, the Plains captives and the hides, came from the trade fairs with the Comanche and other nomadic groups. Livestock also brought a significant return, but Reaño exported a limited selection of vecino woven goods, and those in small quantities. The vecinos also produced sayal, which they carried to market in Chihuahua.[14]

The Pueblos crafted the pottery used by Native Americans and vecinos in the province. Vessels of Spanish origin, trade items from Asia, and export pottery from Puebla and other Mexican sources also found their way into New Mexico during the colonial period. Archaeological surveys of the surface shards at the sites of eight of the northern *presidios* attest to a variety of good-quality wares from Puebla in use in the northern presidios in Nueva Vizcaya, Sonora, and Coahuila, as well as majolica, porcelain, glazed ware from other regions of New Spain, and local unglazed wares. For the most part, however, a vibrant Pueblo pottery-making tradition that dated back a millennium before the entrance of the Spanish served the province's daily utilitarian needs.

Given the highly developed skills of Pueblo pottery makers and the abundant material they supplied, vecinos had little reason to take up ceramic production. Pre-Hispanic trade wares survived and prospered where traditional production fit into European patterns of demand, as they had in specialized regions of pottery production, such as Puebla and Guadalajara. Pottery made by vecinos in New Mexico for export could not have competed with these other suppliers. Charles Carrillo has shown, using archaeological sites and oral histories, that Hispanic village people made unglazed and unpainted pottery during the nineteenth century. He suggests that non-Pueblo production may have begun as early as the 1790s. Nevertheless, vecinos appear to have left pottery manufacture to Pueblo craftspeople during most of the colonial period.[15]

To summarize, the first system of eighteenth-century trade derived most of its impetus from trade between the Plains peoples and the inhabitants of New Mexico. Vecino and Pueblo producers of grain and livestock—and vecino merchants or their agents who had access to goods imported from Europe or New Spain—traded for skins, captives, and buffalo meat. The former two items figured prominently in the New Mexican trade with Chihuahua. Both vecinos and Pueblo Indians produced woven goods for trade in Chihuahua, but before the 1780s these materials formed only a small portion of the goods exported from the province. The Pueblos produced the ceramic wares used by vecino and Indian alike within New Mexico, but no sources suggest that pottery left the province as an export.

PUEBLO INDIAN PARTICIPATION IN
THE FIRST EIGHTEENTH-CENTURY ECONOMY

In the middle of the eighteenth century a series of disputes erupted between the Franciscans and provincial officials concerning the treatment of the

Pueblo Indians in the province. The reports left to us as a result of this exchange describe more fully the role of the Pueblo Indians in the provincial economy during the period of the first trade system outlined in the previous section. In the political battle between the Franciscans and the governor, each party described specific abuses perpetrated by the other and a general system of exploitation of Pueblo goods and labor. The gravity of these charges, and the heated and bitter rhetoric with which the participants fought, makes these allegations seem particularly compelling to the modern reader. The charges clearly resonated with the contemporary officials who were forced to adjudicate the dispute, judging from the copious record made of their investigation into the controversy.

However compelling these allegations seem, the broad limitations on the economy of New Mexico served to limit the practical effect of any economic pressure placed on the Pueblo Indians by vecino actions. The significant contribution that the Pueblo Indians made in the fight against nomadic raiders beginning in the 1760s, and the damage these hostilities inflicted on the New Mexican economy, further weakened the opportunity for extracting goods from the Pueblos by force.[16] The economic position of Pueblo men and women set the tone for social relations between the Pueblo and non-Pueblo communities. A coercive Spanish economic system operated with comparative leniency in the Río Grande Pueblos, making possible peaceful coexistence and closer cooperation during the lifetimes of the generation born at midcentury.

In 1760, nineteen missionaries tended to the spiritual needs of the twenty-one Indian missions; the two padres at Santa Fe served Nambé and Pojoaque. The missionaries received an annual stipend of 300 pesos from the Crown, paid in a lump sum every other year. This money provided the only means with which to purchase items either impossible to obtain or prohibitively expensive in New Mexico. Necessary goods, such as habits, underclothing, religious books, beeswax, and chocolate, entered New Mexico with the annual cordón—provided the stipend reached Chihuahua in time to pay for the purchases ordered by the missionaries. The friars also bore the expense of transportation. In their shipment of 1760, the cost of freighting the goods from Chihuahua to New Mexico alone was 48 pesos, 8 percent of the shipment's total value. As Bishop Tamarón noted, the stipend added a modicum of comfort, but the primary support for the missionaries came from supplies and services received from the Indians of the pueblo in which they resided. Tamarón included a statement from the secular priest Santiago Roibal, who served in Santa Fe, describing the system in general terms: "They sow for them [the friars] 3 *fanegas* [*de sembradura*] of wheat, 4 *almudes* of maize, 2 almudes of broad beans, 2 of vetch; some of them also sow 2 or 3 almudes of chickpeas and 1 of frijoles and their vegetable or kitchen garden. Throughout the year they never lack firewood, which the Indians who serve weekly bring in carts or on their backs. . . . All the Indians give prompt obedience to the commands of the reverend father missionaries."[17]

From the late 1740s through the 1760s secular officials charged that the supplies and services given to the mission father represented a serious burden on the Indians. The controversy stemmed from the report of a *visitador*, Juan Antonio de Ornedal y Maza, appointed by the viceroy in 1750 to review grievances against the Franciscans. To the order, the secular intervention represented a ploy that masked the usurpation of their jurisdiction.[18] Both sides saw important opportunities for political influence within the province at stake in the matter, but the charges and countercharges also produced valuable information about how the Pueblos fit into the vecino sphere of the provincial economy. The available evidence suggests that the pueblos contributed voluntarily to maintain the missionary and that the total burden represented a small portion of the pueblo harvest and labor supply.

In response to charges that the friars forced the Pueblo Indians to produce excess goods, which the missionaries traded for profit, the solicitor general of the Franciscan Order, Fray José Miguel de los Ríos, commissioned Fray Manuel de San Juan Nepomuceno y Trigo to write a rebuttal. In his report of 1754, Trigo described the goods and services that each pueblo provided for their mission. The pueblos planted between 2 and 5 fanegas of wheat for each mission and between a *cuartillo* and 2 almudes of maize. In addition, they provided a bell ringer, sacristán, and two or three boy sacristanes to help in services and to attend to the missionary. A cook, women to grind wheat and maize, men to haul wood, and occasionally a gardener all served the missionary's needs. In the more isolated missions of Laguna, Acoma, and Zuñi, the Indians provided sheep or goats daily for the use of the missionary. The duty of the sacristán included administering this system of weekly rotation, which emphasized the voluntary nature of the enforcement of these obligations.[19]

Fray Domínguez illustrated the degree to which the friars depended upon the goodwill of the Indians when he described the situation at Tesuque: "As for service, there is none at all, since they do not even give the father who visits them a single load of firewood. Even if he asks for it, there is always some petty authority to oppose the gift, for they do not realize that it is not only a minor offering. . . . The missionary overlooks this and other things in order to avoid a breach in harmonious relations." Not only could the Indians decide whether to provide for the mission, they also showed a preference for the system as it stood because it allowed them to limit non-Indian interference in their domestic affairs. When one friar proposed that the pueblo should stop raising his crop and that, instead, each Indian bring him what he wished, "he could not persuade them to leave off planting it, they giving as a reason that when the missionary religious have corn from the field that they [the Indians] plant, and they have none themselves, they apply to the fathers for provisions to relieve their necessity."[20] The response of the Indians reflects a certain level of cooperation and mutual dependence—and perhaps also the feeling that they valued the arrangement as a demarcation of the limit of their obligation to the missionary.

The services owed to the missionary by the Indians varied according to the population of the pueblo and the quality of its lands. Picurís could afford to plant only 2 fanegas and 1 almud of maize, "on which the father gets on badly enough." Santa Ana had a relatively small population and supplied 2 fanegas of grain for the minister, although he provided his own sheep. In contrast, San Juan, which in 1749 had 404 inhabitants to Santa Ana's 379, raised 4 fanegas of wheat for the missionary. What Santa Ana could not provide in wheat it tried to make up with maize, sowing 1 almud to San Juan's cuartillo. The friar at San Juan traded any grain left over for other necessities, probably at Taos. Fray Trigo described Taos as the place "where the other nations [Plains Indians] come to hold their fairs." In the case of Galisteo, the location of the pueblo encouraged a vigorous Plains Indian market in grain, providing the Indians with an incentive to plant larger crops for a greater surplus at the harvest.[21] The minister received only one cuartillo of maize, "but this, with what they sow for themselves, and for 'El Barbaro' [the Comanche] (and store away in great granaries), causes them and the Father to be abundantly supplied with necessities." The report evoked an atmosphere of friendly cooperation between the missionary and the Indians, rather than animosity due to exploitation. At Laguna, the friar provided the Indians with oxen to plow the fields, as well as giving them food and other goods needed until harvest time.

The amount of food and service required to sustain the missions represented, by all indications, a tiny portion of the resources of the pueblos. Unfortunately, no information on the amount of land the Pueblo Indians cultivated during the eighteenth century exists that would allow for an estimate of the total area of pueblo croplands. To give some idea of the small amount of land involved, the four-square-*league* grant that tradition says belonged to each pueblo under Spanish law encompassed 18,000 acres.[22] The area planted for the use of the missionaries by the nineteen pueblos, calculated from the figures mentioned by Father Trigo, totaled about 193 acres of wheat and nearly 4 acres of maize.

A number of other clues also suggest that the land sowed for the mission did not constitute a noticeable burden on Indian food supply. The pueblos planted mostly wheat for the missionary, a crop preferred by the Spanish but not normally consumed by the Indians. Furthermore, the use of a pueblo official to oversee the weekly assignment of servants to the mission and the formal nature of the production of food for the missionary underscored the way in which the Indians used tradition to keep the areas of Spanish contact at a distance from the inner life of the pueblo. Providing for the mission never came to have any meaning as a religious duty; it functioned only as a community tradition, not as a Spanish imposition containing any threat to the cultural values or economic well-being of the Pueblos. As recently as the early 1940s, Santa Ana Pueblo still set aside and cultivated a plot for the missionary. Valencia García, the Indian who worked on the field at that time, had served twice as war chief and as a *koshari,* both powerful Pueblo religious offices.[23] He saw no conflict between his obligation as koshari and war chief to the Pueblo and the work he did to serve the missionary.

THE *"REPARTIMIENTO DE EFECTOS"* IN NEW MEXICO

The economic institutions governing relations between Spanish secular officials and the Pueblo Indians in New Mexico bore close relation to those operating in the rest of New Spain during the eighteenth century. In many parts of Mexico, Spanish local officials and merchants combined to bring the Indian population into the commercial economic system through the forced distribution of manufactured goods in return for Native products desired for Spanish markets. In lieu of a salary, Spanish alcaldes mayores signed contracts with merchants who furnished goods on credit, and the alcaldes then distributed those materials in Indian communities. The alcalde or his agent extended credit to the Indians for commodities valued at exorbitant prices, and in return collected Indian agricultural products or finished crafts. In this manner officials exchanged livestock and finished textiles from Europe and New Spain, along with other goods, for Indian crops such as cotton, cochineal, and Native textiles of cotton or wool. Commentators generally referred to the system as *repartimiento de efectos,* or *repartimiento de mercancías,* translated literally as "distribution of goods."[24]

In 1750, alcaldes throughout New Spain carried on this method of forced commerce in tacitly approved violation of the law: In practice, no other method existed for the recruitment and remuneration of these Spanish officials. The next year the Crown legalized a modified version of the procedure and attempted to regulate it by controlling the prices of the goods distributed to the Indians. The repartimiento system alternated between illegality and official acceptance for the next six decades. Meanwhile, Spanish ministers argued over the generally conflicting issues of how best to draw Indian producers into the commercial economy and how to ensure efficient and economical local and regional government at the same time.[25]

By the late 1740s the charges of the Franciscan missionaries against the commercial practices of the governor and alcaldes mayores had inaugurated a war of accusations between the two parties. The friars held that officials used forced distributions to coerce grain and woven materials out of the Pueblos. The practices described by the Franciscans portrayed the repartimiento system common elsewhere in New Spain, but with regional variations caused by the peculiar economic constraints present in the mid-eighteenth-century New Mexican economy.

In 1756 the Franciscans accused Governor Francisco Antonio Marín del Valle of running a complicated series of repartimientos with the proceeds of the church tithe he collected from the settlers. The tithe owed to the church each year represented 10 percent of each parishioner's annual production, generally paid in kind. The governor sold the grain to the soldiers of the Santa Fe Presidio. He charged the accounts of the presidio soldiers directly and without regard for how much they needed, "placing them in debt in this way so that they were not left with the means even if they wished to get themselves or their wives clothes or footwear of moderate decency." Fray Juan Sanz de Lezaún remarked that "the governors make their largest profits on the tithes; since they have had charge of this tax [in 1744] the country has been even worse off. Formerly the settlers exerted themselves to sow, because the governor bought everything from them in order to supply the presidio, but now it taxes them to be able to sow enough for their own sustenance." If the grain from the tithe did not suffice, the governor or the alcaldes mayores undertook a repartimiento de efectos in the pueblos. Fray Lezaún explained: "When the governor is out of corn, he makes a distribution (repartimiento) of iron hoes, which are worth at most 1 peso, at the rate of 2 fanegas for each hoe, whereas corn is worth by valuation or schedule 2 *reales* [*sic,* read pesos] at most per fanega."[26] According to Fray Carlos Delgado, the governor and his alcaldes mayores

> send agents every year . . . at the time of the harvest, to all the pueblos of the kingdom, under the pretext of buying maize for the support of their households, though most of it is really sold to the nearest villages. The said agents take from all the pueblos and missions 800 or 1,000 fanegas [dry measure], and compel the Indians to transport them to the place where the governor lives [in Santa Fe]. Besides not paying them for the said transportation, they do not pay for the maize at once, and when the date arrives which they have designated for the payment, if the maize is worth 2 pesos a fanega they give them only 1. Even this amount is not in coin or in any article that can be useful to the Indians, but in baubles such as *chuchumates,* which are glass beads, ill-made knives, relics, awls, and a few handfuls of common tobacco, the value of which does not amount even to a tenth of what the maize is worth which they extract from them by force.

Other variations on the theme reflected the different products produced by each pueblo: "To this pueblo [Acoma]," wrote Fray Juan José de Oronzoro of Isleta, "the alcaldes and *tenientes* carry broad knives, axes, wide hoes, and *coas* for the governors, and tear away from the Indians a mutton or a manta for each knife, five or six sheep or mantas for an ax or digging stick, and many times even more."[27]

In addition to the grain disposed of among the vecinos and in the presidio, the governor distributed the wool that he had collected to households in the southern pueblos to card, spin, and weave into "a cloth that here they call sayal, it does not deserve the name of indigenous jerga."[28] In 1750 Fray Lezaún and Fray Manuel Bermejo wrote that Alcalde Mayor Don Antonio Baca distributed to the pueblos the wool from more than 3,000 sheep belonging to Governor Joaquín Cadallos y Rabal, along with that collected in the tithe. They commented, "We do not know how they could have distributed this amount to those poor souls, let alone how they could have brought in enough oxen to carry it." Fray Lezaún elaborated in a report written a decade later that "the wool, which usually weighs about 800 *arrobas* [about ten tons], is distributed among the pueblos so that the Indians may make blankets for the governors; hard after him comes the alcalde mayor and his lieutenant, distributing his own wool." Fray Delgado claimed that the alcaldes "every year make the Indians weave four hundred blankets, or as many woolen sheets. . . . Not even the women are exempt from this tyranny, for if the officials cannot make use of their work in any other way, they compel them to spin almost all the wool needed for the said sheets and blankets."

The repartimiento used to extract grain, sheep, and mantas from the pueblos functioned in a manner similar to that practiced in southern Mexico and elsewhere in New Spain during the same period.[29] Officials distributed cash or manufactured goods and collected Native produce in turn—except that in New Mexico the lack of specie simplified the process. The governors and their assistants evolved the system of distributing wool for weaving into blankets to compensate for the limited amount of trade out of the province. This type of repartimiento transformed one of the materials collected by the tithe into a marketable commodity at the expense of Indian labor. Instead of distributing finished goods on credit and reaping Native manufactures at low prices in return, the official handed out the raw material and collected the benefit of the labor of Pueblo weavers—a kind of coerced "putting-out" system.

Besides making money by chiseling the salaries of the soldiers, the schemes of the governor and alcaldes in the pueblos focused their commercial energies on exchanging Pueblo goods with the Plains Indians. Fray Andrés García of Acoma wrote that "the commerce that there is in this kingdom all redounds to the benefit of the governors and alcaldes and tenientes."[30] "One can come to know their great greed," he said,

> because outside when these fairs take place, [the alcaldes] want the enemy Indians to receive all their horses and at times all those in the hands of the señores governors as well. They strive to sell all their goods, and stop at nothing short of giving Saint James in order to get at those poor souls for their remaining sarapes. . . . The method of trading among the Pueblo Indians is to

give them some knives, and for each one the Indians have to give a mutton. . . .
With this they extract the gamuzas and other skins for their deals and business
agreements in Chihuahua, from where all the silver returns. These extortions
plague the Indians that are in the vicinity of where the Spanish live, because
with the business of the tithes they force the said Indians to transport [them]
a distance of 30 leagues where there are roads that the carts cannot manage.

From an economic point of view, the New Mexican officials used their power
to take over part of the traditional Pueblo trade with the Plains Indians.
The pattern of vecinos appropriating Pueblo production and markets
would reappear in new forms with the revival of trade with Chihuahua after
the Plains alliances.

The Pueblo Indians also owed labor services to the governor and the alcaldes mayores, besides the planting and domestic work that they performed
for the missionaries and the different repartimientos for maize, mantas, and
wool. According to Fray Lezaún, the governor received the services of five
men and five women from the pueblos who arrived at his palace in Santa
Fe every Sunday.[31] Each group labored for a week, hence called *semaneros,*
"the men to haul wood and perform other services, and the women to grind
wheat and corn by hand." Two groups of ten men each, also rotating weekly,
tended the governor's sheep and cattle. The alcaldes divided the services
owed to the governor between the pueblos "upriver"—*Río Arriba*—from
Taos south to Santa Fe, and "downriver"—*Río Abajo*—south from Santa Fe
to Isleta. Herders from the northern pueblos took care of cattle, while those
from the south tended the sheep. Similarly, the governor's household servants came from Río Arriba between Easter and All Saints' Day and from
Río Abajo between All Souls' Day and Easter. In both cases the system of rotating service reduced the burden placed on each pueblo. The alcaldes used
semaneros as well: "the men to till their lands, although they have not sown
lands in their own pueblos, to clean ditches, and to shear the flocks."

As the Franciscan missionaries pointed out, the economic system that they
witnessed operating in New Mexico had the potential to place an unbearable
economic burden on the Pueblo Indians. However, during the third quarter
of the eighteenth century, the difficulty of transporting large quantities of
goods to Mexico, and the increasing hostility of the Plains Indian tribes,
served to limit the intensity of the exploitation of the Pueblos. The constraints on internal commerce also lessened the ability of these practices to
oppress the Pueblo Indians. Until 1778, the Crown maintained only eighty
soldiers at the Santa Fe Presidio, and out of the salaries paid to the soldiers,
the governor absorbed a large portion of this sum through his control of
trade with the presidio. An internal cash market driven primarily by currency provided by the salaries of eighty men, and with restricted access to
markets outside the province, could not provide enough capital to fuel a
particularly coercive system of extracting goods from the pueblos.

Fray Delgado wrote that the repartimiento yielded between 800 and 1,000 fanegas of Pueblo maize.[32] If the governor had sold 1,000 fanegas to the presidio it would have provided 12.5 fanegas of maize (approximately 30 bushels) for each soldier and his family. This amount corresponds quite closely to the 12 fanegas of maize per year that it took to feed a family, according to an estimate made by the bishop of Durango. The governor could also provide an additional amount of grain from the tithes paid in cereals by the vecinos. The 1,000 fanegas of maize taken from the Pueblos through the repartimiento represented less grain than the Pueblos produced annually for the Franciscan missionaries. The Pueblos planted 196 acres (66.25 fanegas de sembradura) of cereals for the friars, which yielded an estimated 1,080 fanegas of wheat and almost 134 fanegas of maize.[33] In contrast, 1,000 fanegas of maize collected by the governors and alcaldes mayores represented the fruit of approximately 80.75 acres of cropland. Even if these crops came only from the Río Arriba pueblos that grew much of the grain in the province, the Pueblo Indians could satisfy the amount collected through the repartimiento without the loss of a large amount of agricultural land.

The repartimiento of wool and the labor services owed to Spanish officials also appear relatively light upon closer examination. Fray Lezaún said that the secular officials distributed 800 arrobas of wool to the Indians for weaving. Fray Delgado mentioned that the alcaldes collected 400 finished blankets annually from the repartimiento. If distributed among the eleven Río Abajo pueblos, the region mentioned by Fray Varo and Fray Bermejo as the most favored by this craft, each had the responsibility for producing about thirty-six blankets, or about one blanket per year from every third or fourth family.[34]

The labor service performed for the missionary and owed by semaneros from the pueblos represented another relatively minor imposition. According to Fray Lezaún, thirty Indian servants worked for the governor at any given time. Each of the eight alcaldes mayores also used an estimated ten semaneros, and the missionaries used about 185 servants. All together, approximately 295 Indian servants left the pueblos each week, or about fourteen persons from each of the twenty-one pueblos. Of these pueblos, only Sandía and Pojoaque had a population of fewer than 200 people, and the latter performed no service for the missionaries.[35] Rotation of servants from the northern and southern pueblos to work for the governor, and the seasonal nature of the agricultural work performed for the alcaldes, served to further distribute obligations and lessen their impact on the labor force of an individual pueblo. Finally, the Spanish officials played no part in distributing the assignments for service within the pueblos: The Indian fiscales handled all such internal affairs.

From the Pueblo point of view, certain elements that conditioned the

Spanish demand for labor and goods served to make an inherently coercive economic relationship less dangerous to the communal life on the inside. The critical need of the Spanish authorities for auxiliary forces drawn from the Pueblos restored the traditional male roles related to warfare and defense from external enemies to their full utility.[36] The war chiefs had never before under Spanish rule been allowed to play such a role of authority and near-autonomy. The governor's dependence on Pueblo warriors to accompany campaigns against the Comanche and Apache and to take part in defensive counterattacks to retrieve captives and livestock also served to allow the male officials of the pueblos greater control over dealings with external authorities who might disturb life within the pueblo. In this light, the ability of the Pueblo fiscales to administer the labor rotation owed to the governor and fiscales takes on added significance. Male leaders sought to regulate the intrusions of the vecino economy so that they did not interfere with Pueblo farming and animal husbandry carried on by both men and women, with weaving, or with pottery making primarily done by women. In this manner the first economic system of the eighteenth century reinforced traditional gendered spheres of activity. It allowed the Pueblos to maintain their production of foodstuffs, ceramics, and woven goods for their own internal use, to satisfy the demands of the Spanish authorities, and to produce items for trade outside the pueblo in return for other goods and materials.

From this perspective, the use of the repartimiento de efectos by the New Mexican governors and alcalde mayores as a last resort to extract goods and foodstuffs from the Indians testifies to the success of the Pueblo officials in preventing the Spanish economic system from fundamentally reshaping internal Pueblo social and economic relations. During the third quarter of the eighteenth century a provincial economy constrained by warfare and a limited export market gave little incentive to vecinos to seek more control over Pueblo trade and production. As chapter 4 will show, from these practices a new pattern of economic coercion of the Pueblo Indians for the benefit of vecinos emerged when, during the following decades, increased exports raised the stakes involved in stimulating production and participating in new markets.

NEW MEXICAN–PLAINS INDIAN HOSTILITIES

The movements of Native American peoples far from New Mexico played an important role in limiting vecino economic power through the 1770s. At the beginning of the eighteenth century Comanche raiders intruded into the Southern Plains, upsetting the balance of territorial claims, alliances, and trade among the existing nomadic Indians groups in the Southwest and beginning decades of tribal warfare and movement of the tribes surrounding New Mexico.

The Comanche emerged as a separate group from the Shoshone people toward the end of the seventeenth century. With iron axes and guns supplied by the French, the Blackfoot and Crow placed continual pressure on the eastern Shoshone bands, forcing them northwest, from the eastern Rocky Mountains above the headwaters of the Arkansas River into the Great Basin. The western bands of the Shoshone chose a different cultural path from that of their eastern relatives, primarily due to their acquisition of horses from the Spanish and the weaponry that the Crow and Blackfoot had used so effectively against them.[37] With the horse, the western Shoshone groups moved to the southeast from the Platte and Black Hills regions onto the Southern Plains, drawn by abundant herds of buffalo, trade with New Mexicans for horses and other goods, and a relative military advantage over neighboring Indian groups.

Unlike the Apache, who used the animals primarily for transportation, the Comanche fought on horseback. In addition, the eastern Apache, particularly the Jicarilla, had learned seasonal farming of squash, maize, pumpkins, and beans from the Pueblo Indians. The modification of their nomadic habits left the eastern Apache extremely vulnerable to the Comanche tactic of staging sudden, effective raids on horseback aimed at stealing horses, women, children, and food. The eastern Apache now found themselves increasingly dependent on the crops they grew, yet they lacked the protection that the adobe pueblos afforded the people along the Río Grande. By the mid–eighteenth century the Comanche had forced the eastern Apache groups out of the area east of the Río Grande Valley, southern Kansas, western Oklahoma, and central Texas.

The Plains peoples and those who lived in New Mexican settlements came together in two zones of interaction: trade fairs and raids. The raids afforded the opportunity to steal livestock and grain and, sometimes, to take captives. However, understanding the dynamics of the Comanche relationship with the Pueblos and the Spanish settlers requires a perspective on the meaning of trade and warfare which differs from that presented in the reports written by Spanish colonial officials. Anthropologists and archaeologists have begun to assemble a picture of Pueblo-Plains interaction in the protohistoric period that emphasizes a mutualistic, almost symbiotic, relationship—one based on trade, raids, and latent competition over certain resources, especially buffalo on the Southern Plains. The basic items of exchange included buffalo meat, fat, and hides from the Plains groups and corn, cotton blankets, and ceramics from the agricultural peoples of the Río Grande Valley.[38]

Two cultural and ecological systems interacted to produce this early Plains-Pueblo relationship. The observations of archaeologists working on Southern Plains sites draw confirmation from the earliest observations of Spanish explorers. Hunting-gathering peoples like the nomadic Plains groups generally produced food at different times of the year than did settled agricultural groups. For those who depended on buffalo and on foraging for varied resources on the Southern Plains, winter and spring could be the most trying seasons. Once a band depleted stores of dried or preserved food, it had to hunt in the very period during which the animals had depleted their fat supplies and therefore afforded fewer calories for the hunter. As a result, the survival of the group might hinge on its ability to move great distances to reap diverse sources for food until the end of spring.[39]

Wintertime could prove difficult for Pueblo groups as well, but the ability to store maize for long periods and the communal nature of their farming meant that a pueblo could often store surplus crops harvested during the previous two or three years. In seasons when crops failed, raiders carried away stored food, or when some other calamity occurred, the affected Pueblos would experience the greatest difficulty during the summer and early fall, between the planting of the crops and their harvest. Hunting also became more constrained at this time because of the labor and care required to grow a successful crop. These differences in the timing of Plains and Pueblo food shortage and surplus indicate that a mutually desirable opportunity for trading Plains meat for Pueblo grain arose during two periods each year: in the spring, before planting and while the Plains peoples had excess meat of less nutritional value; and in the fall, after the Pueblo harvest and when buffalo had achieved their highest fat content and best hides.

The archaeologist Katherine A. Spielmann has argued that during the protohistoric period the difficulty of both penetrating the defenses of the Pueblos and transporting large amounts of grain made Plains groups wary of attacking the Pueblos except under the most dire circumstances and when they lacked meat and hides for trade.[40] Similarly, the ability of the Pueblos to combine maize, squash, and beans provided them with a stable protein source, which they supplemented by hunting in the Río Grande Valley and surrounding areas. Over time, as the population increased and as game near the settled areas became depleted, the Pueblos gained a greater incentive to trade with the Plains peoples for meat and hides. Competition with Plains groups over buffalo ordinarily did not make sense if trade could serve the same purpose. Furthermore, hunter-gatherer groups had reason to discourage Pueblo hunts for buffalo and may have employed coercion as well as trade to protect the source of their trade goods from the Pueblos.

The entrance of the Spanish into the Pueblo-Plains relationship in 1598, on what now became the northern frontier of New Spain, did not immediately disrupt the basic forces in favor of mutually beneficial exchange. However, new goods for trade brought by the Spanish subtly altered the options available to non-Pueblo peoples. During the seventeenth century, before the Pueblo Revolt of 1680, the Spanish governor and his officials found a lucrative form of commerce in the trade of hides and in captives from distant Native American groups. As herds of livestock added to the food resources available in both the Spanish settlements and the Río Grande pueblos, bands of Apache—and later Comanche and other Southern Plains peoples— gained a target that they could carry off in a quick raid more easily than stores of maize. During the second half of the seventeenth century, the diffusion of horses to neighboring non-Pueblo peoples served to make raids more viable as an alternative strategy to trade with the Spanish and Pueblo settlements of New Mexico in times of scarcity.[41] Besides the quickness and range that the horse added to the repertoire of the Plains warrior, the beasts could transport bulkier prizes from a target village or pueblo.

A series of incidents that took place in 1771 illustrate the different perceptions of the Spanish and Comanche on the relationship between trading and raiding. Spanish commentators rarely understood the motivation of the Indians: how a band of Comanche could carry out a furious raid at a pueblo like Pecos and then appear a day or two later at Taos Pueblo expecting to dispose of their goods—even captives—at a trade fair, often the very ones they had just stolen. Spanish officials frequently noted that just after having raided one location the Indians expected welcome at another pueblo to trade as if nothing had happened. Governor Mendinueta remarked that between September 1771 and January 1772, while the Comanche carried out six raids on different locations, they appeared at Taos an equal number of times to conduct trade fairs, offering at one a young Spanish man who had been captured three years previously.

The nomadic and seminomadic groups saw these events from a very different perspective. The settlements had iron tools, weapons, utensils, inexpensive trinkets, corn and other food crops, tobacco, sheep, and, until the early 1770s, horses that the Comanche and Apache wanted. Whenever possible they would trade surplus dried meat, buffalo, deer, and elk skins, and captives taken from distant Indian tribes or from other Spanish settlements. Apache and Comanche societies had what anthropologists call a "nonhierarchical" social structure: no one person or group held status and leadership over the various bands, divisions, or multidivisional groupings. When trade did not suffice, raiding groups formed spontaneously. As Fray Domínguez astutely remarked in his report on New Mexico in 1776, "Whether they are at peace or at war, the Comanche always carry off all they want, by purchase in peace and by theft in war."[42]

Various circumstances determined whether a particular group of Comanche or Apache deemed trade or raids more profitable or convenient. Drought, and the consequent lack of buffalo or other game, made it difficult to accumulate goods for a trade fair. Scarcity brought attacks on the pueblos and Hispanic settlements. So, too, did the disruption caused by conflicts between nomadic groups. The Apache mounted raids against the New Mexican settlements in the 1740s in part because the Comanche and Ute had pushed them out of communal hunting areas that the Apache had long exploited. At the same time, the Comanche attacks on the Pecos and Galisteo Pueblos in the 1750s probably responded to the friendly relations developed between these eastern pueblos and the remnants of the Carlana, Paloma, and Cuartelejo Apache.[43]

Grievances stemming from the trade fairs could also generate hostility between nomadic and settled peoples. In 1754 Governor Cachupín promulgated a list of prices and regulations governing the trade fairs, in an attempt to minimize the misunderstandings that often led to violent confrontations with the Comanche. Like most of the northern provinces of New Spain, New Mexico had very little circulating currency during most of the eighteenth century. Governor Cachupín's list set the price of Plains Indian goods to a fixed equivalent of New Mexican wares. The schedule valued two deerskins and a fanega of maize at 4 pesos each, so on this basis an exchange could take place even if neither party possessed any actual pesos. The system laid down by Cachupín functioned at trade fairs into the 1770s and was renewed, virtually unchanged, by Governor Fernando de la Concha in 1786.[44]

THE "DEFENSIVE CRISIS" OF THE 1770S

Although the intensity of violence between the nomadic Indians and New Mexicans varied considerably over time, between 1750 and the mid-1780s Indian hostilities became the most important single concern that affected the province as a whole. The Comanche harried New Mexico during the late 1740s, until Governor Cachupín negotiated a relative peace during his first term, from 1749 through 1754. Hostilities flared anew during the rest of the decade, calming down again in the mid-1760s during Cachupín's second administration (1762–1767). Attacks from Apache groups, particularly the Gila and Mescalero, occurred sporadically throughout the 1750s and 1760s. Severe drought in 1758 and 1759 contributed to a new cycle of raids, which intensified during the following decade.[45]

From 1772 through 1776 a lack of rain, along with rigorous winters, brought drought and crop failures. When some vecinos near Galisteo spotted a contingent of thirty Comanche in March 1772, they had to use smoke signals to communicate with the teniente of the presidio, since they did not have horses. The Comanche killed two boys and an adult Indian guarding the sheep herd of Santo Domingo, and on the same day they took the horses of the Jicarilla Apache allies who lived between Santa Fe and Pecos, as well as some oxen and horses from neighboring vecinos. The soldiers from the presidio and Pueblo auxiliaries from Santo Domingo could not overtake the Comanche, as the New Mexican horses had grown thin due to heavy snows that prevented foraging for food. Similarly, in the spring of 1774 Governor Mendinueta blamed drought followed by a hard winter for a general shortage of grain and the death of many horses among both the presidio soldiers and the vecinos. In June the governor reported that the situation had worsened to the point that the inhabitants ate toasted cowhide, roots, and herbs to stay alive. Even this meager sustenance showed signs of diminishing. The dearth had taken such a toll on draft animals that Mendinueta worried that not enough would survive to cultivate the fields. That September he linked the resumption of hostilities by the Navajo to the "circumstances of hunger and sterility that afflict the country."[46]

During the late eighteenth century, New Mexicans witnessed new divisions and alliances among the nomadic tribes, suffered drought and dearth, and felt the brunt of repeated raids that led to the Comanche domination of the Southeastern Plains. These factors coincided, and in the process they subjected New Mexico to Comanche, Ute, Navajo, and Apache raids from almost every quarter and on a scale never before experienced. During the height of the onslaught, Antonio Bonilla, a royal inspector who visited the province in 1776, described the situation in New Mexico in his report: "The Comanche commit hostilities from all directions—the Apache from the east and the south, and the Ute and Navajo from the north and the west—to the extent that all the settlements are bordered by enemies and in great danger, because of the thickness of the mountains, and the openings that many have which grant the Indians easy execution of their insults." Figure 1 provides a graphic illustration of the upsurge in Indian hostilities of the 1770s and 1780s, drawn from the extant burial registers from the New Mexican missions and parishes. Between 1700 and 1820, the friars recorded 1,775 deaths that occurred "at the hands of hostile Indians," but the nature of the sources suggests that this undercounts the true number.[47]

The impact of raids on the New Mexican economy went far beyond the casualties from the fighting. Of the deaths recorded between 1700 and 1819 due to "enemy" Indians, more than 60 percent occurred in just two decades, during the 1770s and 1780s. The sheer number and intensity of the raids during this period disrupted the normal activities of the inhabitants of the province. Constant vigilance and warfare wore down both the population and their defenses, especially in the weakest and most vulnerable settlements. The reports that the governors of New Mexico made to their superiors describe each confrontation between Plains peoples and the inhabitants of the province, illustrating the process of attrition and its consequences as they occurred.

In a report covering the three months between June 21 and September 30, 1774, the activity recounted by Governor Mendinueta began with a Comanche attack on Picurís and Nambé pueblos. The raiders stole horses and killed two Pueblo Indians "who were separated, working in the cornfields."[48] A month later, around 1,000 Comanche invaded the province in the vicinity of Chama, "inundating all of that district," killing seven people, taking three

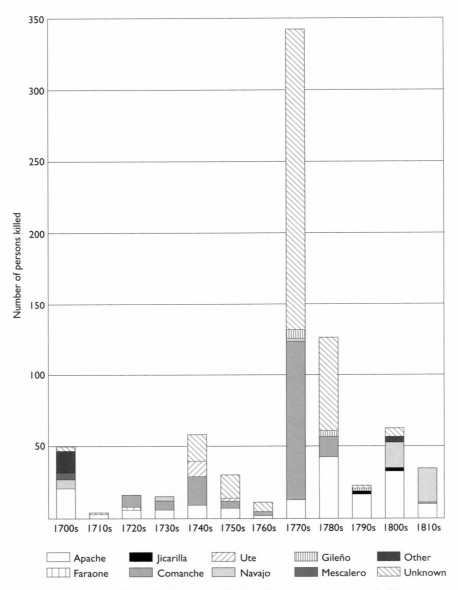

Figure 1. Deaths in New Mexico caused by hostile Indians and recorded in provincial burial records, 1700–1819. *Source:* David M. Brugge, *Navajos in the Catholic Church Records of New Mexico, 1694–1875* (rev. ed.; Tsaile, Ariz.: Navajo Community College Press, 1985), 30–31.

captives, and leaving three men wounded. Then, in mid-August, about 100 Comanche raided Pecos pueblo, where they killed six men and two women and captured seven others. The next day a body of 140 militia, Indian auxiliaries, and troops from the presidio followed the Comanche to their encampment. In the battle that followed, one New Mexican died and twenty-two, including the *alférez* (second lieutenant), received wounds. Mendinueta considered the expedition a success in terms of the number of enemy killed, but the force had to abandon about 200 horses.

During September another troop of about 100 Comanche attacked the plazas and ranches outside Albuquerque. Two vecinos and three Indians died, while the Comanche made off with four shepherds and a large number of horses and killed 400 head of cattle. None of this prevented a fair held at Taos Pueblo beginning on June 27, in which seventy Comanche households brought six captive Indian boys and girls, about 140 animals, two guns, and a large quantity of meat and salt for trade with the assembled New Mexicans. During the same period Mendinueta mentioned three raids by smaller bands of Gileño Apache in the jurisdiction of Albuquerque and Laguna pueblo, causing the death of one vecino and the loss of a number of animals. Navajo raids against Albuquerque, Laguna, and the Keres pueblos killed six Indians, wounded two, and accounted for the loss of cattle, sheep, and horses, both killed and stolen. A force from these settlements mounted two raids against the Navajo and took forty-six prisoners, at a loss of four New Mexicans.

The raiding activities of these three months in 1774 covered much of the province and illustrate the ways in which the hostilities affected its inhabitants. Although only a small number of inhabitants died, the constant hostilities took their toll. The reports from Governor Mendinueta from 1767 to 1777 contain descriptions of 195 separate raids: 106 carried out by Comanche, 77 by Gileño and other Apache, and 12 by Navajo. Taken together, they account for 136 New Mexican Pueblo Indians and vecinos wounded, 94 captured, and 382 dead. At least thirty separate villages and pueblos suffered attacks, some of them many times. The accounts from 1774 and 1775 alone mention more than 1,500 horses and countless sheep and cattle lost to the enemy Indians, and these represent only a handful of raids. All told, the cumulative effect of the raids placed the entire province on the defensive, struggling to survive.

Continued violence, combined with the effect of drought, reduced the Spanish and Pueblo horse herds to the point where the governor concluded that without royal support they could not be rebuilt. On July 4, 1773, a group of some 500 Comanche stole the entire horse herd of the presidio, the vecinos of Santa Fe, and the pueblos of Jémez and Cochití. Reduced to one mount per man, and with many horses extremely thin due to the current drought, a force of soldiers and militia pursued the attackers. Even after managing to retrieve a portion of the stolen herds, the soldiers still could only muster two horses per person instead of the regulation three. Maintaining enough mounts to defend against Indian raids became increasingly difficult. When, on August 10, 1775, the Gileño Apache stole the entire horse herd of Laguna pueblo, the warriors were left to chase their attackers on foot. The situation threatened to leave the province defenseless, and Governor Mendinueta petitioned the viceroy for an emergency appropriation for the purchase of 1,500 horses from Nueva Vizcaya. The governor explained, "when one looks at the horses . . . , isolated by the enemy from trading or raising them, we do not have the tame horses to be able to defend ourselves from the three enemies that surround us. In this regard, excellent señor, if Your Excellency's piety and deep desire to develop this province does not aid it, at the expense of the king, to the number of 1,500 horse if possible, in order to give to this unhappy and valiant population, I fear that the province will arrive at its desolation."[49]

Bureaucratic machinery, complicated logistics, and the drought affecting much of northern Mexico delayed the delivery of the requested horses until the summer of 1777. In his report at the end of 1776, Mendinueta described the difficulties he faced without an adequate supply of mounts to defend against the Comanche, "(an enemy much more terrible than the Apache because of their daring, large number, their ability to gather abundant horse herds, and their knowledge of the entrances and exits of this kingdom) [.] . . . [W]ithout horses with which to follow them, the number of men of the Company that have horses are too few to introduce them only on their own land, [and] they are in this arrangement only a poor defense[.] [W]ith respect to the small flocks of livestock, they are staying in the fields with their herdsmen, the men working in the fields, and all are exposed to the barbarous enemy who know very well how slow we are, and for this one finds them more insolent." In the next year, despite the replenished horse herds, Comanche attacks claimed 127 people dead or captured.[50]

Two elements made the Comanche attacks on the New Mexico settlements particularly frequent and damaging during the 1770s. Severe droughts in 1758–1759 and 1772–1776 affected the ability of the Apache, Ute, Comanche, and Navajo to accumulate goods of their own to trade with the Pueblos and in Spanish settlements.[51] In addition, by the 1750s the Comanche had become the dominant suppliers of horses in a trade network extending northward to the Woodlands peoples who were entering the Northern Plains to hunt buffalo and toward the northwest, following the eastern slope of the Rocky Mountains (see Map 3). Comanche raids on Spanish and Pueblo horse herds intensified during the 1760s and 1770s, fueling the rapid spread of the "horse culture" to the developing buffalo-hunting immigrants to the Plains, such as the Assiniboine, Atsina, Arapaho, Blackfoot, Crow, Dakota, Hidatsa, Mandan, and Salish.[52]

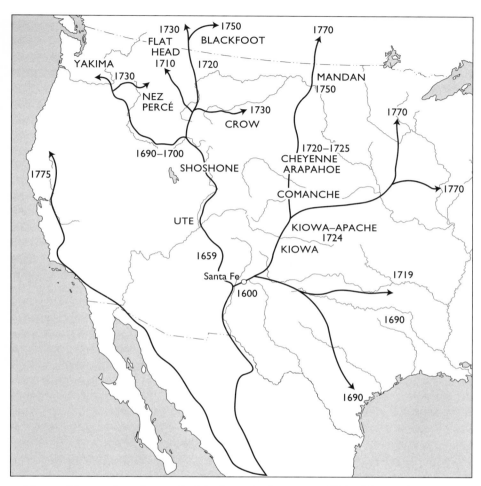

Map 3. The northward spread of the horse in the western United States. *Source:* Adapted from Francis Haines, "The Northward Spread of Horses among the Plains Indians," *American Anthropologist* n.s., 40:3 (1938), 430, fig. 1.

THE EFFECTS OF WAR ON SETTLEMENT PATTERNS

By 1779, the year of Governor Juan Bautista de Anza's victory over the Comanche leader Cuerno Verde (Green Horn), the Indian hostilities had taken such a toll that they reshaped the provincial demography and pattern of settlement (see Map 4). Whole pueblos and settlements disappeared under the

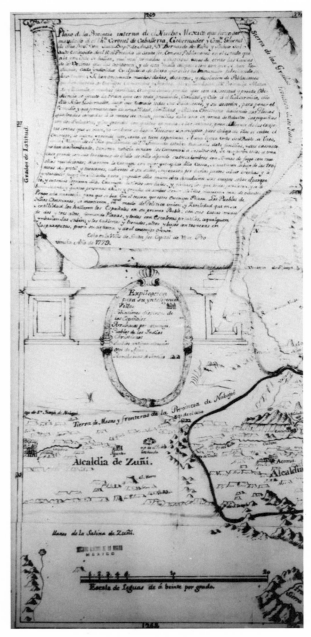

Map 4a. A portion of the Province of New Mexico
as depicted in the map by Don Bernardo de Miera
y Pacheco, 1779. *Source:* AGN: HI 25:2, 283.

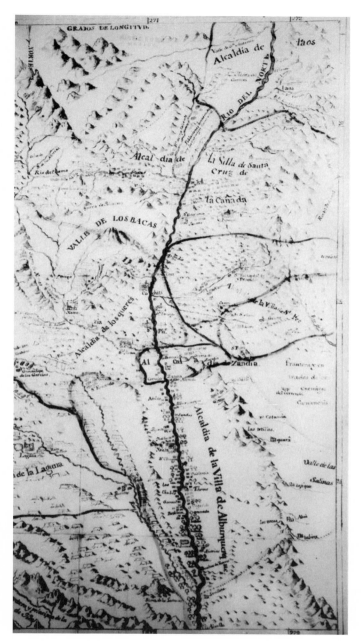

Map 4b. A portion of the Province of New Mexico as depicted in the map by Don Bernardo de Miera y Pacheco, 1779. *Source:* AGN:HI 25:2, 283.

pressure of recurring attacks and the inability of the inhabitants to provide for themselves. The northeastern region in particular, between the Santa Fe area and Taos, bore the brunt of the Comanche raids from 1760 to 1779. The population of Pecos Pueblo, to the southeast of Santa Fe along the Pecos River, declined from 178 to 84 families.[53] Throughout the province, death due to Comanche attacks diminished the population of the Indian pueblos and vecino settlements and forced survivors to flee. Those who remained found their economic activities severely restricted by the constant threat of further confrontations. Fray Domínguez noted in 1776 the effect that drought, combined with constant attacks by the Comanche, had on the Pecos pueblo:

> The Indians have arable lands in all four directions, but only those which lie to the north, partly east, enjoy irrigation. The rest are dependent on rain. These irrigated lands are of no use today because this pueblo is so very much besieged by the enemy, and even those dependent on rain which are at a distance cannot be used. Therefore, but a very small part remains to them. Since this is dependent on rain, it has been a failure because of the drought of the past years, and so they have nothing left. As a result, what few crops there usually are do not last to the beginning of the year from the previous October, and hence these miserable wretches are tossed about like a ball in the hands of fortune.

In the face of the hardship the inhabitants of Pecos were suffering, Governor Mendinueta could give only token aid. He provided the inhabitants with twelve cows, bringing the remnant of their herd to twenty.[54]

A few miles to the southwest of Pecos, Galisteo pueblo suffered a similar decline in population—from eighty to fifty-two families during the same nineteen-year period—and faced destitution. Fray Domínguez noted that the Indians of Galisteo depended even more on rain than did those of Pecos for the cultivation of their fields and consequently found themselves even worse off than their neighbors: "Most of the year they are away from home [in order to find work], now the men alone, now the women alone, sometimes the husband in one place, the wife in another, the children in still another, and so it all goes. Comanche enemies and great famine because of the droughts are the captains who compel them to drag out their existence in this way. The former have deprived many of them of their lives and all of them of their landed property. The latter drives them to depart." As no livestock remained to the pueblo, the governor again came to the rescue. According to Domínguez, Mendinueta lent the Indians seven yokes of oxen for use in planting their crops and to quell talk of abandoning the mission altogether. The effort to save the pueblo ultimately failed, as Galisteo does not appear listed separately in a census after 1779. The inhabitants driven out of their homes by the attacks moved into the larger settlements. Fray Augustín de Morfí described the process as it affected Santa Fe: "In 1744 the settlement consisted of 120 families of all castes, but because of the repeated disaster which it [the region] has suffered, the population has grown to 274 families, with 1,915 souls of all ages, sexes, and conditions. This increase is due to the desertion of the frontier, since the settlers who—harried by the Comanche and Apache—have not perished in the invasions have taken refuge in the capital." The 1821 census of Santa Fe once again included the congregation or "*Partido* de Galisteo," by then reoccupied by vecinos on the site of the abandoned pueblo.⁵⁵

The northern approach into the province ran along a corridor into the heart of the Río Grande Valley between the river and Río del Ojo Caliente. Due to Ute and Comanche attacks on the villages of Ojo Caliente and Abiquíu, Governor Joaquín Cadallos y Rabal in 1748 allowed the settlers in the area along the Ojo Caliente River (now Vallecitos) to move to the west on the banks of the Río Chama. Twenty years later, fifty-three families of settlers returned to Ojo Caliente with a grant issued by Governor Cachupín. Extracts from the San Juan mission book of burials show at least three Comanche attacks between its reoccupation and 1770. Fray Domínguez mentioned in 1776 that the settlement was "now abandoned because of the enemy Indians."⁵⁶ The whole of the area along the Río de Ojo Caliente to the junction of the Río de Chama appears in the 1779 maps of Don Bernardo de Miera y Pacheco with the annotation, "Settlements ruined by the enemy Comanches" (see Map 5).⁵⁷ The elimination of Ojo Caliente afforded raiding parties traveling from the north easier access to carry out raids on Abiquíu, Chama, and the jurisdiction of Santa Cruz de la Cañada.

Many of the small villages and ranchos that had dotted the fertile river valleys on both sides of the Río Grande disappeared during the 1770s. An anonymous census dated 1765 lists population figures for San Fernando del Río Puerco, San Miguel Laredo (San Miguel Laredo de Carnué), and Las Nutrias, all in the central Río Grande Valley around Albuquerque. Domínguez reported that Apache raids in 1772 forced the abandonment of Las Nutrias, a settlement "with good farmlands [that] they used to irrigate from the aforesaid river [the Río Grande]. Cattle and livestock were easily raised here, but the Apache attacked all of it and its people." Carnué, abandoned the same year, also had excellent farmlands (see Map 6). The settlers of Río Puerco, on the other hand, mostly bred cattle because of the scarcity of water in the river before they had to leave their ranchos in 1774 "because of a Navajo uprising" (see Map 7).⁵⁸

By the same token, a number of settlements mentioned by Domínguez in 1776 show up marked by Miera y Pacheco with a small drawing of a ruined

Map 5. Ojo Caliente, a detail of Don Bernardo de Miera y Pacheco's map of the Santa Cruz de la Cañada region, 1779. *Source:* AGN: HI 25:2, 283.

village. The legend of the 1779 maps labeled this symbol as denoting "settlements ruined by the enemies."[59] In the Río Arriba area, Domínguez listed in his report Chimayo and Quemado, to the east of Santa Cruz de la Cañada, and La Hoya, Río Arriba, La Canoa, and Bosque Grande, just north of San Juan pueblo. However, on the later maps these settlements show the ruined symbol or do not appear at all (see Map 5). The Río Abajo area, to the south, fared better toward the end of the decade, but ruined ranchos dot Map 6 on both sides of the Río Grande from Bernalillo south to Sabinal. In addition, Map 7 displays the abandoned settlements and ranches of San Fernando, Guadalupe de los Garcías, Santa Cruz, Cebolleta, Encinal, Ruta de Pino, Portería, Ranchos de Mestas, Ventana, and Nacimiento, in the western part of the province between the Río Puerco and Laguna and to the north. In sum, the 1779 maps of Miera y Pacheco represent remarkable documents that graphically attest to the territorial retrenchment of the New Mexican population caused by the Indian hostilities during the previous two decades.

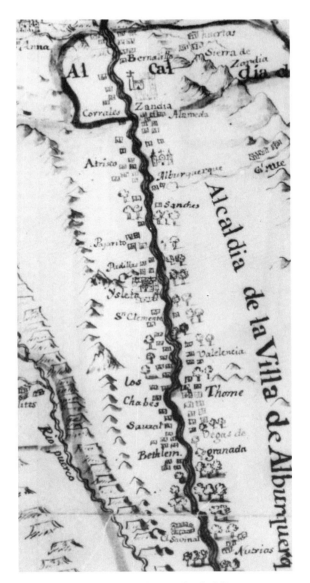

Map 6. A detail of Don Bernardo de Miera y
Pacheco's map of the Albuquerque region, 1779.
Source: AGN: HI 25:2, 283.

Map 7. A portion of the Laguna region and north as depicted in the map by DonBernardo de Miera y Pacheco, 1779. *Source:* AGN: HI 25: 2, 283.

THE EFFECTS OF WAR ON PROVINCIAL DEMOGRAPHY

The years of Plains Indian hostilities served to contain pressures that might otherwise have led to vecino appropriation of Pueblo lands, especially in response to a growing non-Pueblo population. Fear of Indian attack also blocked the settlement of vecinos on new lands north of Taos and along tributaries of the Río Grande. Furthermore, the Plains incursions also restricted access to agricultural land already in use, lowering the availability of usable cropland relative to the population of the Río Grande Valley, especially during the raids of the 1770s. In describing the situation at Abiquíu in 1775, Fray Domínguez wrote, "The enemy [Indians] keep the settlers in such a state of terror that they sow their lands like transients and keep going and coming to the place where they can live in less fear." In some cases the vecinos had to fall back on Pueblo resources due to raids on more vulnerable vecino ranchos. The case of Las Trampas de Taos serves as an example. From 1770 until the late 1780s, the vecinos of Las Trampas de Taos had to abandon their settlement. They built their own compound within the Taos Pueblo and moved in because of the severity of the Comanche raids. In 1772 Governor Mendinueta mentioned that a number of Spanish settlers had relocated to the Pueblo of Picurís for the same reason.[60]

The great calamities of the 1770s—incessant Indian attacks and years of severe drought—had the overall effect of significantly altering the pattern of population growth in New Mexico. Figure 2 shows the change in the Pueblo and vecino populations according to the censuses available between 1740 and 1785.[61] By the mid-eighteenth century, the Pueblo Indian population had stabilized at around 9,000 people, or had declined moderately to that level, depending upon which census one deems most accurate for the 1744–1750 period. After 1760 the Pueblo numbers expanded and contracted in slow cycles for the next three decades. The vecino rate of growth slowed substantially after 1760, reflecting the difficulties brought on by warfare against the Comanche and Apache. The non-Pueblo population grew around 6.3 percent per year between 1750 and 1760, only 0.04 percent per year from 1760 to 1765, and about 1.4 percent annually between 1765 and 1779. According to census information for 1779 and 1784, the vecino population then jumped by more than 16.2 percent per year during that five-year period. Even though the local officials and Franciscan missionaries who recorded the censuses did not classify people at the racial and ethnic interstices of New Mexican society in a consistent manner, the depressing effect of the "Defensive Crisis" on the growth rate of the vecino population emerges clearly from the statistics. The vigorous growth of the period before 1760 slowed dramatically until after the defeat of Cuerno Verde in 1779, and then began a strong and continuous climb until well into the next century.

Differing patterns of settlement and land use affected the vulnerability of vecino and Pueblo populations to the wars during the "Defensive Crisis" of the 1770s. The Pueblo Indians occupied well-ordered adobe towns, settled with defensive considerations in mind. They worked agricultural land and tended livestock communally, choosing the best areas radiating outward from the pueblo center. In periods of heavy pressure from hostile Indians, the pueblo could not use its most distant fields, but at the same time ran

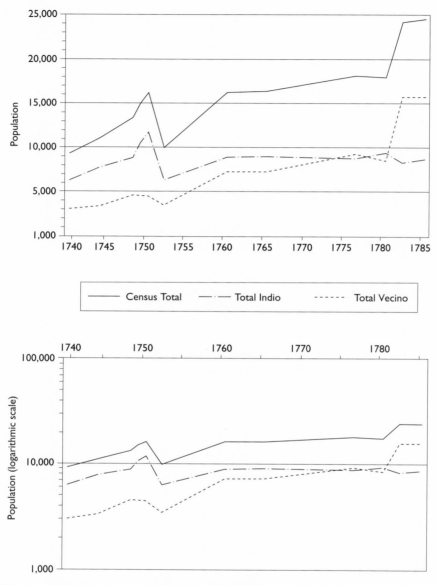

Figure 2. New Mexico population summary, 1740–1785. *Source:* Ross H. Frank,
"From Settler to Citizen: Economic Development and Cultural Change in Late
Colonial New Mexico, 1750–1820" (Ph.D. diss., University of California, Berkeley,
1992), 413–32, table 1.

much less of a risk of suffering a successful penetration of its defenses. In contrast, the vecinos showed heedless determination to settle close to their fields and as far away from the town plaza as circumstances permitted. Communal activities revolved around the church and central plaza, but the settlements often extended for miles in the directions of the best land and the most abundant water. This practice occasioned complaints from almost every visitor, inspector, or official who recorded his impressions of the province. Fray Morfí observed that Albuquerque occupied what would be described as a moderate-sized town but for the vecinos who, "[a]s if fleeing from the company of their brothers . . . withdraw their habitations from one another, stringing them out in a line as fast as they can build them." In consequence, as Morfí put it, "owing to this, they dare not go out and work, or if they do, they become victims of their own folly, since the enemy . . . sweeps through the communities with perfect liberty, on account of their disorderly layout." The Albuquerque Morfí described stretched some 30 miles along the Río Grande.[62]

Governor Mendinueta took the first, bitterly opposed steps toward changing "the fatal situation of this population, which remains indefensible against even the slightest Comanche attack." In 1770 he attempted to congregate the vecinos of Ojo Caliente in a "spacious and defensible place" by proclamation, affectionate persuasion, messages, and fines, all to no effect. The inhabitants preferred to abandon their houses altogether rather than to consolidate them and build a defensible community.[63]

During the same year, the governor tried another tack when the thirteen family heads of San Miguel de Carnué petitioned to abandon their village and return to Albuquerque because "the force of the enemy Indians that one finds today is too great to resist." Mendinueta ordered the Genízaro residents of San Fernando del Río Puerco, along with the vecinos who had left San Miguel de Carnué, to assemble on April 24 in Albuquerque. There the two groups agreed to join together to build a new settlement, "each with lands to work in equality with the rest of the vecinos, and the same in the building of their houses in the compound of the plaza, and enjoy the rest of the site in common." About a month later, on May 27, the ex-residents of Carnué left their new residence at San Ysidro de Pajarito for their recently abandoned one and razed it, under orders from the governor. Mendinueta received a petition from the settlers in March 1774 for permission to resettle the Carnué area, which he refused to grant.[64]

Such drastic measures were adopted in response to the damage done by the enemy Indians. At other times a desperate governor ordered refugees back to their abandoned homes in an attempt to prevent the collapse of frontier defenses. In 1770 Mendinueta ordered the residents who had fled Abiquíu and had scattered themselves throughout the Santa Cruz de la Cañada jurisdiction to return and rebuild their settlement in proper form, with a plaza, streets, and contiguous houses. Four months later, hearing that some of the inhabitants planned to leave the settlement, he ordered Alcalde Mayor Marcos Sánchez to proclaim specifically to the vecinos of Abiquíu that "none dare to abandon it [the said Partido de Abiquíu] on any pretext whatsoever."[65]

Searching for a solution to the problem of defending vecino settlements, Mendinueta called on Viceroy Antonio Bucareli y Ursúa in 1772 to approve a strict regulation that would allow him to congregate the vecino settlements. Without the sanction of the viceroy, Mendinueta knew that he would face trouble from "the churlish types of settlers" who would "populate this Court with complaints." Despite Governor Mendinueta's efforts, very little had changed on this score by 1779, when Miera y Pacheco pointed to the calamities that the dispersed vecino settlements brought on the population in the rubric of his maps of New Mexico. He urged prompt compliance with Governor Anza's recent orders to reduce the larger settlements to a more compact and regular plan. Governor Anza had some success with the reduction of the Albuquerque and Santa Cruz de la Cañada areas, but petitions from settlers to the *comandante general* of the *Provincias Internas* against the restructuring of Santa Fe produced a temporary suspension of Anza's order.[66]

THE ECONOMIC EFFECT OF INDIAN RAIDS

The accounts of soldiers, merchants, and officials also show that the events of the 1760s and 1770s took a heavy toll on the New Mexican economy. They also help to indicate the economic areas that proved especially vulnerable to disruption. Governor Cachupín spelled out the relationship between peace and economic development:

> The conservation of the friendship of this Ute nation and the rest of its allied tribes is of the greatest consideration because of the favorable results which their trade and good relations bring to this province. This is especially true of those settlements dependent upon the *villa* of La Cañada, which without peace, cannot conserve themselves or their neighborhoods, or increase their haciendas engaged in raising cattle, sheep, and horses. Besides, this nation, with its trade in deerskins, benefits the province in such a way that it stimulates in its settlers the disposition to go to La [Nueva] Vizcaya and Sonora to purchase whatever effects they may need for their subsistence and for their families.[67]

The cordones carrying trade goods from the province to Chihuahua and other destinations in northern Mexico frequently drew Indian attacks. Governor Cachupín mentioned a failed assault by the Gileño Apache, which took place in February 1765 on the way to Nueva Vizcaya. In 1769, shortly after taking office, Governor Mendinueta felt forced by the continual movement of Comanche and Apache bands to suspend the annual departure for Chihuahua, "because being that among those who have to leave are found the paymaster of the arms and horses, it would expose everything to total ruin, and for this same reason I find it difficult, almost impossible, to leave in order to visit the Presidio and pueblos of El Paso, since two squadrons of soldiers for my transport and at least three months are indispensable. This is the lack of strength in which one finds the internal affairs of this government." "The nerve that maintains this province with some faculties," explained the governor, "are the fairs or *rescates* with the Comanche and Ute. This commerce having failed completely with the first, and being very infrequent with the second, one finds the merchants in great poverty, since they cannot make more than is given them. . . . [E]ven this [much comes] with the pain of seeing so much bareness and misery, and more when there is nothing upon which to base the hope of recourse save that the Comanche will return to establish their old peace and trade."[68]

The hostilities affected the supply of goods from the Plains for trade with the south and hindered transportation and communication along the Chihuahua Trail. On December 12, 1770, a band of Apache attacked the New Mexican caravan south of El Paso on its way to Chihuahua. The Apache killed one soldier and four vecinos, wounded two people, and made off with 500–600 head of cattle and most of the mules. The lieutenant in charge of the convoy and some of the soldiers and settlers, now almost entirely on foot, pursued their attackers, to no avail.[69]

One of the primary functions of the teniente, who resided in El Paso, concerned the security of the road to Chihuahua. The order naming Don Antonio Daroca Teniente del Paso instructed him to "reorganize the citizens of said pueblo into formal companies . . . and dedicate himself to the maintenance of free communication with the mentioned province [New Mexico]." Apache attacked the caravan from New Mexico on its way back from Chihuahua in early 1773, wounding two soldiers from the escort and driving off some of the straggling livestock. Bonilla reported that in 1774 the teniente mounted an expedition from El Paso against the Apache that resulted in the loss of ten men from the Spanish force and almost all their horses and mules. The disaster brought about the disruption of New Mexico's contact with the south, "cutting for some days the communication and unhappy commerce of the vecinos with the Villa of Chihuahua."[70]

After a particularly violent five months, between April and September 1773, Governor Mendinueta wrote to Viceroy Bucareli:

I submit to your elevated understanding: that it has been seven years during which this province has suffered a continual war with the two nations, Comanche and Apache; and that the little wealth of these poor vecinos consists of products of the countryside where they must maintain themselves; and consequently [they] are exposed to the outrages of so many enemies who in repeated robberies destroy all the grain that [the vecinos] have gathered during this great dearth that is being suffered generally because of the locusts and the drought of last year which continues in the present one to now. From these ghastly circumstances I do not expect any result but that these settlers, lashed by war and hunger, mean to abandon their houses and possessions before seeing the ultimate extermination of their small holdings.

By 1777, drought, raids, and the need to butcher livestock to survive had reduced the herds to the point that Mendinueta issued a *bando* prohibiting the removal of sheep, cattle, and oxen from the province.[71]

The merchants and miners of Chihuahua also recognized the effect that the hostilities had on their prosperity, which depended to a degree on trade with the surrounding provinces. In a petition to Viceroy Teodoro de Croix, Marqués de Cruillas, the deputies of both groups in the *Ayuntamiento* of Chihuahua pointed out that the lack of means to haul wood to the mines, move the metal, or supply necessities to its vassals hurt mining and commerce and also lost revenue for the Crown. By 1771 the ayuntamiento felt the need to put its case more directly:

> Since January of this year to the present [October] the infidels have taken more than 6,000 mules and horses, and killed 120 persons, and this fatality already surpasses those committed during last year. . . . And although [the miners and merchants] have demanded repeatedly, no one has obtained more than good reasons for hope, not more aid than what we have expressed above, since without forces it is impossible to contain these infidels, because [the Indians] have not left [the populace] more to rob than what remains of the mules for the mining trade and cartage, which they will finish off . . . during the rest of the year.
>
> In view of the miserable state of the frontiers of this province [Nueva Vizcaya], the mining that it foments, and the necessary and essential safeguard of the haulage business to Sonora and New Mexico, it is not believable or thinkable that our dearly beloved king and lord would want [the province] abandoned when all of its inhabitants have been and are so loyal and obedient.[72]

The correspondence between the governors of New Mexico and the higher officials and bureaucrats in the government of New Spain leaves no doubt that the Indian hostilities of the 1760s and 1770s had a serious impact on all of the northern provinces, particularly on the economy of New Mexico. Both Indians and vecinos abandoned land needed for agricultural production and animal husbandry. War restricted the opportunity for trade with the nonsedentary tribes and weakened internal economic activity. The danger of attack on the road out of the province made any sustained expansion of external trade difficult.

The stagnation or decline in the rate of population growth during this period reflected the influences of uncertainty and violence. Quantifying the

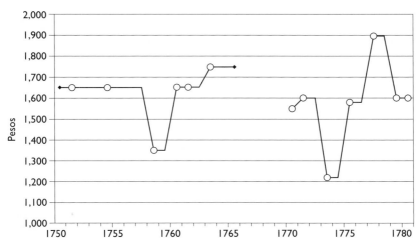

Figure 3. Tithe rentals for New Mexico, 1750–1780. *Sources:* In chronological order, ACD:DZ 3:13, 16R, 67R; 2:12, 24R, 42R; 3:14, 18R, 42R, 97R, 142R; 3:15, 18R, 82R; 3:16, 23R, 65R; 3:17, 24R, 56R; 3:18, 25R, 61R; 4:21, 23R, 41R; 3:23, 28R, 63R, 100R, 139R (bis), 166R, 188R. Tithe rentals for 1766–1769 and 1771–1773 not found in the Durango Cathedral records.

economic effect of a complex set of events—such as Indian raids and the lost opportunities for production due to the threat of attack—poses a more difficult task. Fortunately, information from the records showing the annual fee collected by the Cathedral of Durango for the right to collect the tithe in New Mexico provides evidence that helps to estimate how severely the "Defensive Crisis" set back economic activity during the 1760s and 1770s.

Figure 3 depicts the amount in pesos that the Cathedral of Durango received each year for the contract to collect the tithe in New Mexico, a practice known as tithe farming.[73] As in other ecclesiastical jurisdictions of New Spain, the bishop of Durango depended upon merchants from the northern provinces and officials in New Mexico to actually collect the tithe owed to the church in local products. The *jueces hacedores* of the *Junta de Diezmos* accepted bids for a contract that yielded to the winner the right to collect the tithe for a period of two to five years, in return for a flat fee. The bidder had to take into account not only the intrinsic value of the tithe but also the difficulty involved in collecting it and in transporting the goods to various internal or external markets to realize a profit. Indian attack, decreased production caused by the hostilities and drought, and disruption of trade to Chihuahua, which prevented the sale of the goods collected, all represented uncertainties that lowered the potential value of the tithe.

B. Santiago de Roybal, the ecclesiastical judge of Santa Fe, wrote to the *jueces hacedores* in Durango that Governor Cachupín had bid 100 more pesos than the 1,650 bid for the current year to take over the tithe rental for 1763 from outgoing Governor Manuel Portillo de Urrisola. Cachupín could only undertake this contract because the new governor had asked the Comanche to negotiate a peace. If they continued to make war, reported Roybal, "he cannot give this amount, let alone more, because they [the Comanche] did not leave any livestock, or horses, nor can the vecinos tend to their planting; such force will occur against them, that it will incapacitate this department of the tithe. God would not want but to give us the peace that we used to have."[74]

Fray Morfí also spoke of the rental of the tithe, which in 1778 went to Don Clemente Gutiérrez for 1,895 pesos per year. Don Antonio José Ortiz, the alcalde mayor of Santa Fe, also bid for the contract. He withdrew after refusing to pay Gutiérrez and his brother-in-law (alcalde for the Albuquerque jurisdiction) 200 pesos each and to exempt them from paying the tithe. Due to the Indian hostilities, the Franciscan reported, the total tithe collected amounted to only half of that normally due to the leaseholder. Evidently this state of affairs did not inspire confidence in Ortiz that he could collect the tithe profitably after paying off his competitors.[75] In his decision not to pay the bribes in order to gain the lease, Ortiz's action reflected the gamut of market information available at the time. The system of bidding, which left collection of the tithe in the hands of an entrepreneur, ensured a direct connection between events taking place in the province and the fee paid for the right to collect and sell the tithe.

These examples illustrate the extent to which the method of renting the tithe reflected market forces. Consequently, fluctuations in the value of the tithe rental contract provide a valuable indicator of changes in the economic activity and productivity in late colonial New Mexico. It follows that the amount of the rentals from 1750 to 1780 shown in Figure 3 offers an accurate measure of the relative effect of the Indian wars. The circles in Figure 3 show the beginning of each contract. The large dips in the value of the tithe rental coincide with the nadirs of the province's fortunes against the hostile Indian groups. Interestingly, the two highest years of the rental, 1777 and 1778, may reflect to some degree the delivery of the 1,500 horses that Governor Mendinueta petitioned for in 1775 in order to fight the Comanche and Apache. All told, only five of the thirty years show a rental level above that of 1750.

The day-to-day accounts of Spanish officials responsible for defending the province, the demographic testimony of the maps of Miera y Pacheco, and the records of the New Mexican tithe rentals all substantiate the toll that the "Defensive Crisis" took during the 1760s and 1770s. In cases like Galisteo and Ojo Caliente, the cumulative effect of captives taken, injuries, and deaths due to warfare led to the abandonment of Indian pueblos and Spanish settlements. In quick raids, Comanche and Apache parties kept farmers from working lands at a distance from the Pueblos and vecino villages, stole livestock, and depleted horse herds. In sum, the necessity of defense against Plains Indian attacks sapped energy that otherwise might have gone into securing a better livelihood.

THE 1780–1781 SMALLPOX EPIDEMIC AND THE ECONOMY

Disease had a far more immediate impact on the New Mexican population than did the Indian raids. Smallpox broke out in the province in the late spring of 1780 and reached its virulent peak in January and February 1781. It may have entered New Mexico from either the east or the south. In 1779 a severe epidemic had struck Mexico City, and it could then have followed the lines of transportation and communication north to New Mexico. Even earlier, during 1778, an outbreak of smallpox had moved west from the Indians of the Mississippi River, through Louisiana, and into Texas. Interaction with the nomadic tribes might also have brought this vector of infection into the province.[76]

The epidemic killed many people quite suddenly, but rising birthrates quickly followed the sharp increase in mortality. Shorter lived than the Indian hostilities, the smallpox epidemic brought with it a fundamental change in the demographic structure of the population. Moreover, the reaction of the vecino population to the death and the suffering produced by disease changed the demographic landscape of Pueblo Indians and vecinos. Vecinos emerged from the trauma as the largest group of people in the province, a position they retained until the Anglo-American influx during the second half of the nineteenth century.

The epidemic also served to infuse a modicum of capital into the economy. Smallpox killed New Mexicans, but it generally did not affect their sheep or cattle. Consequently, land and livestock became concentrated into fewer hands and helped to propel the changes in production and increase in trade among vecinos that took place over the next decade. Despite the tragic losses inflicted upon the population, the smallpox epidemic enhanced the ability of late colonial New Mexico to take economic advantage of the period after the 1785–1786 peace treaty with the Comanche and the system of alliances that it helped to forge.

New Mexico had experienced smallpox before, but the epidemic of 1780–1781 wreaked havoc on its isolated people, who had little or no recent exposure to the disease and no medical expertise with which to combat it. Lack of doctors and slow, intermittent communication with the settlements to the south deprived the province of access to even the inadequate medical information available in Mexico. Measures taken by Viceroy Bucareli to control the smallpox epidemic sweeping New Spain had little effect on New Mexico. The practice of inoculating people who had not been exposed with material from an active smallpox sore, variolation, had proved useful in Europe, but in addition to the danger of full-blown infection, the serum tended to spoil during the voyage to America and in the shipment through thinly populated areas.

In a perfect example of Bourbon administrative activism, in April 1785 the Spanish Minister of State José de Gálvez sent 150 copies of a treatise by Dr. Francisco Gil entitled *A Sure Method to Preserve the Pueblos from Smallpox* to the viceroy. Governor Anza received a copy of the work from Comandante General of the Provincias Internas Jacobo Ugarte y Loyola, with a cover letter referring to the "methods which have been practiced with well-known, favorable success in the Province of Louisiana." Along with the book, Gálvez included a paper listing thirty examples of ways to control the disease. In New Mexico the packet did not help matters much, as Governor Anza noted at the bottom of the cover letter: "The examples mentioned in this letter did not accompany it." After the major epidemic of 1780–1781, smaller outbreaks occurred in the province until 1805, when authorities of the Provincias Internas introduced into New Mexico the new process of vaccination developed by the English physician Edward Jenner seven years previously, effectively ending the threat of another large-scale smallpox epidemic.[77]

The 1780–1781 epidemic damaged the New Mexican population much more than any previous outbreak had. Hubert Howe Bancroft estimated that 5,025 persons died in the missions during the two years, which would be almost 28 percent of the entire population as reported by Domínguez in 1777 or by Morfí two years later. Bancroft gave no source for his figure. Information from individual parish burial registers confirms that the epidemic brought with it a high rate of mortality. Fray Andrés Claramonte, missionary of Picurís Pueblo, on the Río Embudo southeast of Taos, listed thirty-six victims of smallpox in 1780. He noted in his burial register at the beginning of 1781, "This year we expected death from the smallpox epidemic." The names of fifty-one vecinos and twenty-eight Pueblo Indians follow this grim comment. Most died in February or early March.[78]

Of the population of 474 vecinos and Indians at Picurís recorded in 1779 by Fray Morfí, 115 people, or more than 24 percent, died during the epidemic years. Taking into account the 29 children born during 1780 and 1781, the population of the Picurís area declined by just over 16 percent during the two years. By the same token, Santa Clara lost 275 persons, or more than 37 percent of the population figure given in Domínguez's census of 1776. About 23.5 percent of the 1,821 settlers of Santa Cruz de Cañada mentioned by Morfí died, adjusted for those born during 1780 and 1781. The population of Pojoaque Pueblo, a few miles north of Santa Fe, declined by more than 58 percent. The epidemic nearly incapacitated the presidial company at Santa Fe. Of the 120 soldiers on the duty roster, 62 were on a mission to Sonora, and of the remaining 58, 27 contracted smallpox. The teniente could spare only one dragoon to protect a caravan leaving for Chihuahua. As a result, the Apache attacked the party and carried off or killed some fifty animals.[79]

As one might expect in a relatively small population spread over a large area, considerable differences appear over the province in rates of mortality as a result of the smallpox epidemic. On average, about 20–25 percent of the populace died during the year, estimating from the available complete sets of baptism and burial records and using the Domínguez and Morfí censuses as starting points.

More significant than the heavy mortality, in the long run, recovery from the epidemic permanently changed the demographic balance between the Pueblo Indian and vecino populations in favor of the latter. The baptism and burial records from the Santa Clara jurisdiction serve to illustrate the relative effect of the smallpox epidemic on the Indian and vecino populations (Figure 4a). After the initial shock of an epidemic, a population normally responds by increasing its birthrate to make up for the loss. In this portion of the province, the birthrate of both populations increased. The vecino birthrate climbed steadily throughout the period, in contrast to the rise in the Indian birthrate, which did not surmount its pre-epidemic rate before 1790. Figure 4b shows the two groups as a percentage change in the population since 1776, as given by Fray Domínguez. In percentage terms, the epidemic hit the vecino population somewhat harder than it did the Santa Clara Indians, but after 1782 the vecino population rebounded rapidly, surpassing its 1776 level in 1787. In 1790 the population of the vecino settlements stood almost 38 percent higher than in 1776; the Pueblo population still showed a decline of more than 11 percent.

Governor Concha noted this demographic phenomenon in 1790 when he appealed to Ugarte y Loyola for a number of new Franciscan missionaries to fill vacancies at various missions. Shortly after the smallpox epidemic, Governor Anza had received permission to reduce the number of missionaries in response to the smaller population of parishioners. He removed the resident missionary from some of the missions and placed them under the purview of a single missionary who worked from a nearby mission. The missionary became the head of a new spiritual jurisdiction. In 1782 Governor Anza made Nambé and Tesuque pueblos dependent on the friar ministering to Pojoaque, San Ildefonso a *visita* of Santa Clara, and placed Jémez under the care of the minister of Zia pueblo. In 1784 Anza added Santa Ana pueblo to the visitation duties of Zia's minister, made Acoma a dependent visita of Laguna, and put Cochití Mission at the head of those at Santo Domingo and San Felipe.[80]

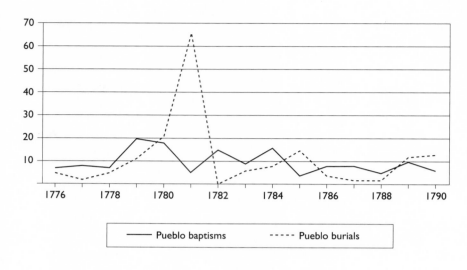

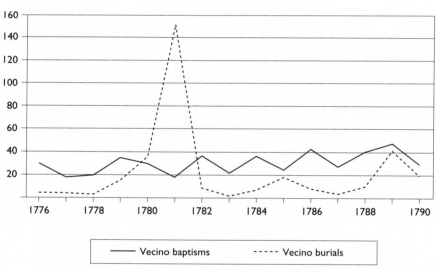

Figure 4a. Santa Clara baptisms and burials, 1776–1790, including the vecino settlements of Chama, Cuchilla, Corrales de Piedra, La Vega, and Mesilla. *Sources:* Santa Clara baptismal and burial registers: AASF:BU Bur-30 (Box 20), 1726–1843; and AASF:BA B–31 (Box 44), 1728–1805.

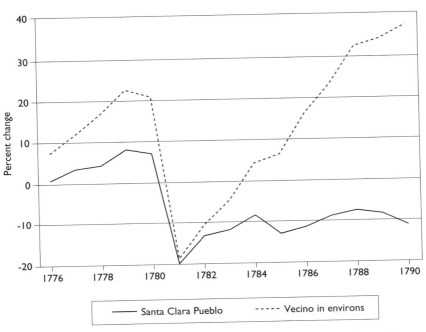

Figure 4b. Population change in Santa Clara, 1776–1790. *Sources:* Santa Clara baptismal and burial registers: AASF:BU Bur-30 (Box 20), 1726–1843; and AASF:BA B–31 (Box 44), 1728–1805.

Only six years later the situation changed greatly. Due to increased population, Governor Concha asked for confirmation of his decisions to separate San Ildefonso from the jurisdiction of Santa Clara, Tesuque from Pojoaque, Santo Domingo and San Felipe from Cochití, and Acoma from Laguna. The governor claimed as justification of his actions in the case of Tesuque and Pojoaque that "the numerous settlers [*vecindarios*] established in their vicinity" made it impossible for one missionary to give Tesuque and the Spanish settlers the assistance they needed. The same rationale pertained to the northeastern Keres pueblos, Santo Domingo, San Felipe, and Cochití, but the increased Indian population, as well as that of the vecinos, caused Concha concern. In Laguna and Acoma the problem stemmed from the population of the Pueblos, who had, by 1782, surpassed their pre-epidemic population, increasing at a faster rate than those along the Río Grande.[81] Overall, the growth of the province's population also shows the emergence of a new vecino majority of the population roughly between the late 1770s and early 1780s (Figure 2). The individual parish records confirm the general timing of the shift to a predominantly vecino population and show the demographic mechanism by which it took place.

The demographic changes wrought by the epidemic ultimately had an effect upon economic conditions within the province. Local church registers confirmed that the disease killed a relatively large number of children and significantly lowered the birthrate of both the vecinos and the Indians during the epidemic years. In Santa Clara, *párvulos* made up more than 42 percent of the Pueblo deaths, while in the vecino villages of the Chama area, the proportion surpassed 59 percent. In the Pojoaque jurisdiction, small children numbered almost 35 percent of the Indian dead and more than 41 percent of the vecinos.[82] At the same time, the epidemic significantly lowered the birthrate of both populations during and directly after its occurrence.

Moreover, the destruction caused by the epidemic struck other communities in the northern provinces and throughout New Spain in ways similar to its effects on the New Mexican population. Mission records show that smallpox struck Indian and vecino populations alike; it generally hit the young and old, and many women of childbearing age, the hardest. The loss of population in different regions averaged between 20 and 30 percent.[83]

In New Mexico the loss of a significant portion of the population in 1781 served to concentrate wealth and helped to provide a basis for increases in production and trade. Since the disease struck just after the harvest, famine did not compound the damage already done by smallpox. With the same area of land to cultivate, fewer people to feed, and more adults relative to the total population, the epidemic should have resulted in a period of overabundance of agricultural products.

The most direct way of testing this hypothesis entails analyzing wills from the late 1770s and 1780s to check for a redistribution of wealth in the aftermath of the smallpox epidemic. Unfortunately, few New Mexican wills of the period survive, which makes the direct tracking of inheritance patterns impossible. However, *cofradías* in New Mexico held assets that they accumulated through the annual dues and charitable contributions of their vecino members.[84] Due to the chronic lack of money in specie, members generally paid their dues in sheep. An audit of the accounts of these cofradías in 1776, and again in 1791, indicates that the flocks owned by the confraternities grew too quickly to have come from membership dues and natural increase alone.

Fray Domínguez recorded the state of the New Mexican confraternities during his visitation in 1776. In general, he gave a pessimistic description. In the case of the Cofradía del Santíssimo Sacramento and the Cofradía del las Benditas Ánimas del Purgatorio in Santa Fe, he doubted that the organizations would survive. The Blessed Sacrament had 173 members, who among them owed 436 pesos in past dues.[85] The confraternity itself owed 500 pesos to Fray Francisco Zarte, who forgave 100 pesos in light of its difficult financial condition. The organization owned 200 sheep, which they rented in *partido* and which brought in 32 lambs annually, not enough to pay for the required observances and related expenses.

When Domínguez wrote, the Blessed Sacrament and the Cofradía de Nuestra Señora del Rosario had been placed under joint administration. Our Lady of the Rosary had 225 members who owed 626 pesos, owed Fray Zarte 533 pesos, and also owned 200 sheep, for which it received the same annual yield as did the Blessed Sacrament. A survey of the holdings of the New Mexican cofradías in 1791, in preparation for the assessment of a 6 percent ecclesiastical contribution to the Crown, showed that the two cofradías held flocks that yielded an annual rent of 750 sheep, almost double their combined capital of fifteen years earlier.[86]

In 1776 the Cofradía de la Santíssima de la Luz, the wealthiest confraternity in Santa Fe because of the patronage of the governor, the presidial officers, and the local elite, owned a large flock of 1,070 sheep. In 1791 the annual rent due to La Luz alone amounted to 1,250 head, surpassing the size of the whole herd of fifteen years earlier. Growth of a similar magnitude took place in Santa Cruz de la Cañada, where the flock of the Cofradía Nuestra Señora del Carmen went from a total of 300 to a yearly interest of 500 sheep. Both Fray Domínguez and the report of 1791 document the yield from the rental of the cofradía's flock and the annual expenses defrayed for the minister, sacristans, cantors, and masses.

Based upon these figures, none of the cofradías mentioned by Domínguez in 1776 could have amassed a flock large enough to produce the rental income recorded in 1791, except for La Luz.[87] The cofradías of the Blessed Sacrament, Poor Souls, Rosary, and Carmen received an increase in capital from new benefactions or donations. These gifts to the cofradías in turn reflected the accumulation of goods by inheritance in the wake of the smallpox epidemic.

The confraternity accounts support the inference that the vecino survivors of the smallpox epidemic of 1780–1781 benefited from the resulting consolidation of property. Did a similar process take place in other provinces in the north? Although many scholars have discussed the effect of disease on Indian and settler populations, on subsistence, and on the process of Indian conversion in the missions, they have not considered the regional economic implications that followed a given outbreak.[88]

Despite the absence of work on the economic effects of epidemics in New Spain, numerous scholars have examined the same issue for epidemics in medieval Europe. The reaction of the English economy to the bubonic plague of 1348 provides a useful framework for comparison with what occurred in late colonial New Mexico. The sudden loss of somewhere between one-quarter and one-third of the English population lowered the price of agricultural goods because fewer mouths remained to be fed. At the same time, shortages of laborers created pressure for higher wages and raised the cost of manufactured goods. In fourteenth-century England, the peasant farmers owed labor services to and held their land from noble or ecclesiastical landlords, so they could not bargain freely. Even so, they benefited from the pressure placed on the great landowners to pay more to laborers in order to keep them on their estates, a consequence of the population decline brought by the plague.[89] In distinction to the villeins of late medieval England, eighteenth-century New Mexican farmers did not participate in any labor market that recorded the value of their services after 1781. The underlying economic principle, however, remains the same: Fewer workers using the same amount of land and physical resources reaped a benefit in the form of increased production of food and other goods.

The parallel between the New Mexican epidemic of 1780–1781 and the economic effects of the Black Death suggests that the smallpox epidemic served to concentrate capital at the moment when the province began to reestablish relatively free communications with Nueva Vizcaya over the Chihuahua Trail, and settlers began to open up new agricultural land with less fear of nomadic Indian attack. In New Mexico in 1781, as in England in 1348, disease did not affect sheep, cattle, horses, or draft animals. Livestock, tools and implements, and other durable goods remained for the use of the heirs of those who succumbed to the epidemic. In England this effect of the plague on the economy appears to have brought with it a per capita increase in agriculture output.[90] Chapter 4 presents the evidence for a similar burst of productivity in New Mexico.

By 1785 the period of the "Defensive Crisis" had ended for New Mexico. Officials of New Spain's colonial government orchestrated campaigns, punitive raids, and alliances against the nomadic Indians during the 1770s. Soldiers, provincial militia, and Pueblo Indian auxiliaries in New Mexico helped return some measure of control over the province to New Mexican officials and to its inhabitants. New Mexicans survived their twin afflictions—Indian warfare and smallpox—and in the process began to integrate the vecino population into the larger political and economic changes affecting northern Mexico. Officials representing the policies of the Bourbon government attempted to play a more active role in shaping the development of the northern provinces. Chapters 2 and 3 explore these changes and the response within New Mexico to policies coming from northern administrators and from Mexico City.

TRANSFORMING HISTORY INTO CULTURAL MEMORY

Ultimately New Mexican vecinos emerged from the "Defensive Crisis" with new economic possibilities and the seeds of a cultural transformation from settlers to citizens. However, the ordeals of the previous decades had left a mark on more than a generation of New Mexicans who had matured in an environment of Indian warfare, drought, and epidemic disease. So potent were the memories of this time that in the 1930s, residents still called a stormy night or day of blizzard "a day of the heretics," referring to the preference shown by the Indians for launching raids during poor weather.[91] Vecinos continued to acknowledge the lasting effect of the period of Indian attacks by reenacting critical moments in folk plays, tales, and sayings.

One important traditional play, *Los Comanches,* which is still performed at year's end in a number of villages, dramatizes the period of Comanche hostility using historical elements drawn from the two most significant campaigns against the Comanche of the 1770s.[92] In 1774, Captain Don Carlos Fernández won a victory against Cuerno Verde and his Comanche on the Staked Plains, near the present town of Antón Chico, New Mexico.[93] *Los Comanches* depicts Fernández in command of the New Mexican forces, along with his officers, Don Toribio Ortiz, Don José de la Peña, and Don Salvador Rivera. Accompanying these military figures, Barriga Dulce (Sweet Belly) provides comic relief and a satirical commentary on events as they unfold. Cuerno Verde leads the Comanche, represented by the chieftains Oso Pardo, Cabeza Negra, Lobo Blanco, and Zapato Cuento. In the play, the two sides face each other on horseback, each character making speeches to his counterpart with great bravado in preparation for battle. The play ends with the death of Cuerno Verde, an event taken from the famous battle won by Governor Anza in 1779.

The drama attests to the impact that the 1760s and 1770s made on the cultural consciousness of the province. In it the Comanche, and, indeed, all of the gentile Indians, threaten the honor of the province. In his comments during the battle, Barriga Dulce plays upon his gluttonous character while pointing out the deeper significance of the Comanche wars for the New Mexicans:[94]

> *Captain:* I will not lose sight of you
>   inhuman, Indian traitor.
>   You will die by my hands:
>   Die! Die! Cuerno Verde! *(¡muera muera!)*
> *Barriga Dulce:* Grind, grind my companions *(muelan, muelan)*
>   why have they gone from me?
>   Follow them, my good bakers
>   so that I may ask for two payments:
>   For you [Comanches] the battle axe,
>   and for me the corn cakes,
>   the grains and the cactus,
>   the sweet pudding and those *reales.*
>   Also, the chile and onion

with all of these little herbs
that are cooking in the big pot
we will be well protected.
Run, you wild idiots [the Indians],
cry to your captain.
If they don't feel grief,
by blows they must mourn.

To Barriga Dulce, the defeat of the Indians meant that he could line his belly with greater ease. He shows little interest in the pious, chivalric speeches offered by the Spanish officers prior to the battle. With his uncouth parody of the Spanish captain, Barriga Dulce voices the underlying concerns of vecinos still struggling to survive, their economy crippled and their province besieged by enemies.

CHAPTER TWO

"If We Should Lose
New Mexico a Second Time"
Bourbon Reform, Indian Policy,
and the Alliances of the 1780s

The king of Spain, Carlos III (1759–1788), and his ministers began to change the economic and bureaucratic relationship between Spain and its American colonies in order to assert more active control and to increase royal revenues. These actions are referred to as the Bourbon Reforms in order to distinguish them from the style of royal government practiced by members of the Hapsburg line, before the French Prince Philip de Anjou became King Philip V of Spain (1700–1746). By the 1770s the Bourbon officials had begun to apply new measures to the provinces on the northern frontier of New Spain.

Although the Bourbon Reforms produced important and well-documented changes in the political and economic structure of New Spain and its colonies throughout the Americas, the effect that the activist bureaucratic approach of the Bourbons had remains the subject of much debate. This chapter contains an overview of major Bourbon initiatives applied to New Spain and the form they took in the northern provinces. Along with new taxes and administrative structures to extend royal control, beginning in the 1770s the Spanish government provided the direction and financial support to combat the Apache, the Comanche, and other hostile Native groups over the expanse of the northern frontier of New Spain. New Mexico became the focus of a largely successful strategy to contain and reduce the danger that hostilities posed to the mining and commercial centers of northern New Spain and to the economic development of the region.

THE BOURBON REFORMS

The initiatives of Spanish officials in late colonial New Spain, David A. Brading reminds us, had everything to do with the search for "profit and

65

power."[1] Appointed in 1765 by Carlos III as visitor general of New Spain, José de Gálvez spent the next six years innovating and reorganizing colonial government and then became minister of the Indies (1776–1787). Although royal functionaries had introduced measures of bureaucratic overhaul and other reforms throughout most of the century, in a little more than two decades Gálvez implemented initiatives that fundamentally altered the dynamics of the imperial relationship with New Spain. By carefully attacking accretions of power and monopoly, the Bourbon state worked to remove obstacles to its control over critical elements of the colonial society in order to improve production and efficiency and to ensure access to a portion of the revenue.

In 1778 Gálvez ended the monopoly that the *consulado* of Cádiz had on imports and exports to the Spanish American colonies. His decree of *comercio libre* freed trade from the extra cost and control that the Cádiz merchants added to imports and exports. Eventually, merchants in Mexico established their own independent consulados in Veracruz and Guadalajara.[2]

Gálvez also applied his penchant for large, structural changes in the colonial economy to the silver-mining sector in Mexico. In the eighteenth century, the ore dug from silver mines had to go through a complex chemical process in order to extract the silver. For lower-quality ore that could not be smelted, the operators added mercury in proportion to the amount of silver they expected to extract. Through a lengthy process of mixing, the mercury amalgamated with the silver, and then the refiners washed off the extraneous material and heated the amalgam to free the silver. During the late colonial period, the mercury used in American silver mines came from the Almadén Mine near Córdoba, Spain. The Crown distributed mercury as one of its royal monopolies, from which it profited and through which it could exert some control over the development of the silver-mining industry. Bourbon administrators brought in German experts to renovate Almadén, and the resulting increase in efficiency doubled the annual output of mercury. Gálvez used this boon to encourage the silver-mining sector in New Spain. Beginning in 1775, he cut the price of mercury in half and increased the supply exported to Mexico, at the expense of Peru and other areas of silver production.[3]

Bourbon measures of reform, exemplified by comercio libre and the subsidy of silver mining, appeared to increase trade and economic activity in New Spain. Lower production costs spurred investment in new mines and reclamation of marginal ones, and silver production rose dramatically in New Spain, especially in the regions from Zacatecas to Mexico City and in the northern provinces of Nueva Vizcaya and Sonora.

Commercial activity released by the Bourbon fiscal reforms, together with general transatlantic economic conditions, also had a profound effect on rural agricultural markets. Economic changes in Mexico during the second half of the eighteenth century began to bring smaller economic units together into thriving interregional economic systems. In his study on the Guadalajara region, Eric Van Young has supplied a sophisticated picture of how the mining booms at Guanajuato, Bolaños, and Rosario stimulated demand for foodstuffs in the region. The good fortune of the mine owners and workers also had the effects of raising the price of grain and increasing the value of cultivable land.[4] With additional money available for investment in haciendas, landowners took back land they had rented to tenants in order to farm it directly, using wage laborers. Many of the successful hacendados spent large sums on improvements in order to increase the production of wheat and maize to supply the demand created by workers in the silver mines and the expanding urban market. The process also increased the supply of wage labor by driving tenant farmers off the land and raised tensions with Indian communities over communal property.

A number of other hacienda studies, such as Brading's analysis of large-scale agricultural production and markets in the Bajío, support a picture of dynamic regional webs of trade and commerce maturing during the late colonial period.[5] The textile industry in Querétaro and the system of cochineal extraction in the Oaxaca region, for example, owed their rapid growth in the late colonial period to the stimulus provided by vigorous markets in Mexico City and other distant regional urban centers.[6]

Judging from the revenues reaped by the Spanish Crown from New Spain, the Bourbon Reforms appear to have been quite successful. Bourbon administrators met increased economic activity with more taxes and rationalized bureaucracies to collect and remit them efficiently. Beginning in the 1750s, royal administrators began to construct procedures for collecting state revenues directly, rather than renting out the right of collection to the highest bidder. Gálvez applied the *alcabala,* a tax on goods moved between jurisdictions, to a number of important towns in Mexico in 1776, and then to the whole colony. Royal monopolies governing the manufacture and sale of tobacco, gunpowder, pulque, playing cards, and an official lottery required an army of salaried or commissioned officials in order to administer them in each jurisdiction. Royal mints collected the tax on silver production and profited as well from striking coins. All told, revenues collected by the royal treasury increased dramatically during the last quarter of the eighteenth century. The treasury accounts show an increase from 10−15 million pesos per year during the 1780s, to 20−30 million in the 1790s, and to 40−60 million in the first decade of the nineteenth century.[7]

Assessing the larger issue of the nature of economic growth in late colonial New Spain and the effect of the Bourbon Reforms poses a more difficult problem. Despite the demonstrable examples of increased activity in specific areas of the economy and regions of the colony, scholars have voiced skepticism that the late colonial economy generated the kind of growth and productivity that provided the resources needed by Mexican society to improve the standard of living for the bulk of its population. In his massive study of economic data from the Bourbon period Richard L. Garner concluded "that growth did not translate into development."[8]

THE REFORMS IN NORTHERN NEW SPAIN

The northern provinces of New Spain may well show that the Bourbon Reforms brought them both growth and development. These regions also experienced population growth and the formation of new regional economic centers like those seen elsewhere in Mexico during the Bourbon period (Map 2).[9] Chihuahua and Durango in Nueva Vizcaya, Saltillo in Coahuila, and, to some extent, the administrative town of Arispe in Sonora became commercial hubs for regional markets. The economic influence of the major market systems in central Mexico toward the end of the eighteenth century, coupled with the growth of settlements and mining enterprise in Nueva Vizcaya and Sonora, began to penetrate other areas that had been only marginally or locally connected to commercial markets. New Mexico, devoid of silver mines during the colonial period, also felt the quickening of economic activity.

Whatever one concludes for the more densely populated areas of central Mexico that had spent longer periods under Spanish control, the goals and effects of Bourbon government in the north differed considerably. From the start, military defense of the north engaged the attention of Bourbon reformers. By the 1750s missions, settlements, and outposts along the entire northern frontier, from the Gulf of Texas to the Gulf of California, called on Spanish officials to bolster the military defense of the region. The Apache raids that plagued New Mexico also struck deep into Sonora and Nueva Vizcaya, threatening the mining industry and the regional markets that Bourbon officials hoped to encourage. Direct confrontation proved useless. In 1768 Colonel Domingo Elizondo began a three-year campaign against the Apache in Sonora at a cost of more than 600,000 pesos, to little or no avail.[10]

Even before any of Gálvez's innovations reached the northern provinces, Carlos III sent the Marqués de Rubí to personally inspect the system of defensive garrisons that the Crown had established in 1729. Rubí recommended an extensive rearrangement of the line of presidios that stretched from Sonora to Texas. Growth, shifts in population centers, and new patterns of warfare brought in large part by Comanche movement into the northern provinces required the construction of new presidios and the relocation of some of the old ones. Bourbon administrators included the bulk of Rubí's recommendations in the *Reglamento* of 1772. The new regulations called for fifteen presidios spaced about 125 miles apart and for a limited number of mobile *compañías volantes*. Extensive guidelines covered the military equipment, training, uniforms, and other preparations called for to adequately defend the northern provinces.[11] In the aftermath of the costly failure of previous offensive campaigns, Rubí's strategy called for a flexible defensive perimeter that could respond to many situations.

The second unique aspect of Bourbon interests in the north involved active intervention to increase the Spanish population in the most sparsely settled areas. The earliest of these projects brought a small number of families in 1731 from the Canary Islands to San Antonio de Béxar. There they supplemented the presidio soldiers and their families assigned to protect the Franciscan missions in the Province of Texas. The expense and difficulty of relocating even these few settlers ultimately made this an impractical model to follow.[12]

Under Gálvez, the plans for the Spanish settlement of Alta California in 1769 combined concern over Russian and English designs on the northern California coast, interest in populating a new frontier region, and a wider view toward fomenting regional economic growth. Once established, Gálvez envisioned, the presidio population and the mission economy would form the nucleus of a thriving province that could trade with Sonora and New Mexico.[13]

Finally, although the Bourbon government imposed the fiscal reforms, royal monopolies, and taxes on the north in the same way as it had elsewhere, officials often paid attention and took action when local merchants and other groups complained that these policies hurt their economic opportunities. Treasury officials raised the alcabala charged in the Saltillo district in 1777 from 2 percent to 4 percent. In 1778 the tax went up to 6 percent, and the merchants complained to the treasury that the assessors had forgotten to apply a special exemption for Saltillo due to its status as a frontier town. Most of the other northern provinces successfully petitioned for at least a temporary exemption from the alcabala or received a reduced rate. Resistance could also prove a useful tactic in the north, at times protected by distance and bureaucratic inertia. Saltillo residents ignored Comandante General Teodoro de Croix's order that they come up with 12,000 pesos to raise and outfit a militia for their district in 1779 and that they pay another 6,000 pesos annually to maintain it. In response, Croix lowered the initial assessment to 7,000 pesos and collected only 4,000 pesos for the militia's maintenance.[14]

Bourbon officials often identified economic problems particular to the north and thought about possible solutions. When Gálvez arrived in 1768 to visit the mining districts of Ostimuri (in southeastern Sonora), he realized that not enough money circulated to pay the workers in specie and arranged for officials to place 200,000 pesos in coin in circulation. Unfortunately for Gálvez, even this amount did not counteract the economic forces that drew circulating money out of the province. Officials tried to send tax receipts out of the province in ore instead of refined silver or coin, and they proposed that a regional repository be built in Guadalajara or Chihuahua to keep money in circulation in the north. Not until the comandancia general moved to Arispe after 1783 did authorities approve the construction of a regional treasury in Sonora.[15]

BOURBON INDIAN POLICY AND NEW MEXICO

The record of Bourbon interest in New Mexico belies the impression often given by historians that the officials of New Spain took little direct action on behalf of the province during the colonial period.[16] On the contrary, concern over the possibility that Comanche and Apache attacks would destroy the viability of the settlements in northern New Spain prompted Bourbon officials to make unprecedented investments in the region, deploying soldiers, purchasing military equipment, and building presidios. Without a developed mining industry, New Mexico never had the economic clout of Sonora or Nueva Vizcaya. As it happened, many of the military campaigns undertaken to protect the north centered on New Mexico. The geographical position of the province, north of the line of provinces from Texas to Sonora, placed it in the center of the activity as Comanche bands moved into the Southwest and displaced Apache and other nomadic groups from their homelands. For a brief time in the 1770s, New Mexico's location and the perceived experience of its population in warfare made it a logical choice for Bourbon attempts to deal with Apache and Comanche hostilities. The fruits of this policy, the Comanche-Spanish alliance of 1786, proved a perfectly timed catalyst for the development of a new provincial economic system in New Mexico during the decade that followed.[17]

The liberation of northern New Spain from the constant attacks by nomadic Indian groups took a concerted effort, planned, directed, and financed by the highest officials of the Provincias Internas. This effort placed New Mexico at the center of a strategy designed to control Indian attacks along the entire northern frontier, from Texas to Sonora. The plan combined military campaigns, to force the Comanche and other groups to lay down arms and form an alliance against those who remained intractable, with fiscal reforms designed to promote trade and economic growth in the frontier provinces in order to strengthen them internally. In addition, the terms for peace with the nomadic peoples included generous amounts of food, clothing, and other trade goods, as gifts in return for their continued good behavior. As chapter 4 will show, the production of goods for the "gratificación de los indios gentiles de paz" stimulated provincial industry in New Mexico and provided the impetus for further economic expansion.

In Croix's 1781 report to his superior, Gálvez, he expressed the strategic importance held by New Mexico in the battle to pacify the northern frontier:

> From the pueblo of El Paso there intervenes to the north a desert of more than 100 leagues to the first establishment of New Mexico. For this reason, and for the reason that this province is advanced beyond the rest of my command, without other communication with Nueva Vizcaya except by caravans that annually cross the above mentioned desert, it depends for its defenses upon the presidial company at Santa Fe of 110 units, and upon the strength of its settlers, Indians, and Spaniards.
>
> Its conservation is so important that if we should lose New Mexico a second time, we would have upon Vizcaya, Sonora, and Coahuila all the enemies who now invade that province.[18]

The policy designed to hold New Mexico and stem the Indian attacks elsewhere along the northern frontier had taken clear shape in Chihuahua during the autumn of 1778, at the last of three Councils of War convened by Croix. The governors and presidial captains of Nueva Vizcaya and the governor of Coahuila attended, along with the departing governor of New Mexico, Mendinueta, and his replacement, Anza, who came with frontier experience gained in Sonora and during the establishment of the first missions in Alta California.[19] The council decided that an alliance with the Comanche against the Gileño and Lipan Apache represented the best chance for peace. They believed that a combination of military action and the promise of gifts and open trade could secure such an alliance.

The strategy decided upon by Croix in 1778 consciously placed the responsibility for success in bringing the Comanche into line upon the decisive action of the New Mexican governor. Despite the damage it sustained during the 1770s, New Mexico represented the only province in direct contact with the Comanche that had sufficient people and resources to mount any serious campaign against them. In 1777 the contingent of soldiers at the presidio in Santa Fe represented a force larger than that stationed at any other presidio in Coahuila, Nueva Vizcaya, Sonora, California, or Texas.[20] Most of the presidios had a total force of 57, and only San Antonio de Béxar, with 81 soldiers, came close to the 110 stationed in New Mexico. As the comandante general pointed out in his 1781 report to Gálvez, the province served as a buffer for Nueva Vizcaya, Sonora, and Coahuila and as the pinion for sustaining or continuing Spanish settlement to the north.

The governor of Texas had his hands full keeping the Comanche and Lipan Apache from destroying the already battered Spanish missions and settlements. In 1777 the non-Indian population of Texas totaled slightly more than 3,100 people, too few to help augment the small force of soldiers in the presidios. Sonora, which had a larger non-Indian population than did New Mexico in the 1770s, suffered a rebellion of the Seri Indians in 1777, which Anza had quieted for the moment but which prevented the province from lending any major assistance for the proposed action against the Comanche.[21]

Croix's plan originally called for an increase of 1,800–2,000 soldiers in order to undertake the coordinated campaigns needed to hold off the Apache and put pressure on the Comanche to make peace.[22] Not only did the comandante general find it impossible to obtain the proposed new soldiers, but a royal order of February 20, 1779, directed him to eschew war in favor of diplomacy wherever possible in meeting his objective. In the short run, Croix managed to raise an additional 580 troops, 120 of whom he prised out of the viceroy for use in Sonora to put down the Seri rebellion. Croix distributed the remaining soldiers to the presidios: each received nineteen men, with the exception of Santa Fe, which was given thirty-five. In addition, Croix appointed Anza, fresh from his successful handling of the Seri crisis in Sonora, to the governorship of New Mexico to replace Mendinueta, for he believed that the province would need a leader with proven skill and experience in order to move against the Comanche.

Despite the difficulties encountered in devising a plan, the strategy endorsed by the council of war in 1778 soon produced results in New Mexico. Under the guidance of the experienced campaigner Anza, a force of 85 soldiers from the Santa Fe Presidio, 203 militia, and 259 Indian auxiliaries left Santa Fe on August 15, 1779, to head toward the Comanche strongholds north of Taos (in what is now southeastern Colorado). Along the way, 200 Ute and friendly Apache joined the expedition, agreeing to divide any spoils equally, with the exception of captives taken by individuals. The group took a Comanche ranchería by surprise and learned that the bulk of the Comanche warriors had gone to raid Taos and were expected to return shortly. Anza led his men toward Taos and defeated the main Comanche fighting force as it returned from the raid.[23] The Comanche leader of the ranchería, Cuerno Verde, his eldest son, and a number of his most respected warriors perished in the battle, and the expedition returned to Santa Fe after taking 139 Comanche captives. Anza did not sign a treaty with the Comanche leaders until the end of February 1786, although a disposition in favor of peace emerged on the part of sizable Comanche bands beginning in 1779 and became even clearer after 1783.[24] In less than one month Anza's campaign had gained New Mexico respite from the province's most dangerous enemy and had opened the way for a Spanish-Comanche alliance against the hostile Apache.

A number of factors converged in the mid-1780s to bring the Spanish and Comanche together in an alliance against the Lipan and Gileño Apache and to emphasize the commercial side of Comanche relations instead of raiding. The passing of Louisiana from the French to the Spanish at the end of the Seven Years' War as a part of the Treaty of Paris reduced the market for Comanche booty in the villages of the Pawnee and Wichita on the Kansas and Nebraska prairie. The French withdrawal from North America also ended the easy flow of French trade goods that the Comanche trading partners had purchased with the material gained from raids on New Mexico and Texas. Furthermore, the growth of horse herds among Native peoples throughout the trans-Mississippi West by the 1780s had begun to lessen the demand for horses that the Comanche obtained in one way or another from Spanish missions and settlements in Texas and from the vecinos and Pueblos in New Mexico. The Spanish offer of gifts to the Comanche accorded well with the changing circumstances of trade on the Southern Plains. As Pedro Vial and Francisco Xavier Chaves reported after their negotiations with the eastern Comanche, "in the end, their temper does not cease to be ambitious and greedy, but [they are] friendly if they are given what is equivalent to the pillaging, thefts, and hostilities that they may make when at war."[25]

The smallpox epidemic of 1780–1781 also struck the Comanche, perhaps carried from New Mexico or brought west from contact with the Osage or other groups to the east. Both may have reached the Comanche on the Plains between the Santa Fe and Natchitoches, where in 1785 Vial and Chaves reported that "[s]ince smallpox so devastated them, this nation has been greatly reduced. Nevertheless, there may be nearly 2,000 men at arms, and there are many women and children."[26]

The loss of a good portion of the Comanche leadership in 1779, closely followed by the destruction wrought by the smallpox epidemic, considerably lessened the frequency and intensity of raids on New Mexico. In addition, Croix and his successor, Felipe de Neve, increased the military pressure on the Comanche in Texas. The strategy led to a series of meetings with Comanche captains beginning in July 1785, with an eye toward negotiating a peace agreement.[27] In the treaty document signed by Anza and the Comanche captain Ecueracapa, the parties agreed to abide by five articles governing the end of hostilities and the formation of a permanent alliance. The comandante general, in keeping with the Spanish policy of attempting to elevate Ecueracapa over other Comanche captains, made clear that he expected the agreement to govern the Comanche in Texas and Nuevo Santander as well as in New Mexico.

The Spanish officials also undertook to guarantee peace on the part of the Ute in return for an end to the Comanche-Ute enmity that stemmed from their break during the 1750s. The confirming resolutions of the comandante general again emphasized the broader application of the alliance throughout Comanche territories by promising to mediate disputes with the Pawnee in Louisiana, now a Spanish colony, and by requiring the Comanche "to keep peace with all the Indians who may be friends with the Spaniards." The Comanche agreed to follow the orders of the governor of New Mexico in his prosecution of the war against the eastern Apache in that province and in Texas. In return, they secured the right of free passage to Santa Fe and to attend regular trade fairs in Pecos Pueblo. The New Mexican governor promised to regulate these trade fairs in order to prevent fraud and other abuses that could lead to reprisals.

The Comanche peace of 1786 formed the crowning piece in a system of treaty and alliance that freed New Mexico from the burden of more than three decades of Indian warfare. By the time of the alliance, the new viceroy, Bernardo de Gálvez, had refined Spanish strategy in the north to bring the full measure of diplomatic, military, and economic resources available to him to align the Indians who were willing to make peace with the Spanish against the Apache bands who remained hostile. As Gálvez explained in his instructions to the comandantes generales of the two newly created northern administrative divisions: "I am very much in favor of the special ruination of the Apache, and in endeavoring to interest the other tribes and even other Apache bands in it, because these Indians are our real enemies in the Provincias Internas; they cause its desolation and are the most feared because of their knowledge, cunning, and warlike customs acquired in the necessity of robbing in order to live."[28]

The peace was the cornerstone of Gálvez's strategy: Using the prospect of access to trade with the Indian pueblos and vecinos at established trade fairs, gifts of desirable trade items, and the implicit threat of an allied war against intransigents, Spanish officials forged a series of agreements that put New Mexico's adversaries at peace with Pueblo and vecino inhabitants— and with each other. Negotiations between the Comanche and Ute peoples closely followed the diplomacy surrounding the Comanche-Spanish peace, leading to a treaty agreed upon in early March 1786.[29] On March 22 Governor Anza arranged a conference with the Navajo in order to begin the process of trying to lure them away from their fifteen-year alliance with the Gileño Apache. By the end of June, the Navajo had promised to show "subordination and fealty" to the Spanish king and to cooperate in expeditions against their recent Gileño allies. During the session in which Governor Anza proposed the terms of the treaty, Comanche representatives addressed the council to promise retribution should the Navajo fail to live up to their word.[30]

In 1787, campaigns led by General Juan de Ugalde in the Pecos River region against the Lipan and Mescalero Apache led to an alliance, signed in 1788, with the principal Mescalero chief. By 1790 most of the Gileño bands had undertaken to settle near the Spanish presidios due to the combined pressure brought to bear on them by the various Spanish-Indian alliances and campaigns. The Jicarilla Apache too made peace with the Spanish, the Comanche having driven them from their old territory on Jicarilla Mountain during the 1780s. By the mid-1790s they depended largely upon the protection of the Spanish. In addition, between 1789 and 1794 a considerable body composed of various Apache bands settled in the area between La Cebolla and Socorro on the Río Grande, encouraged to go the way of the Navajo and Jicarilla with the help of Spanish seed and provisions given for farming. Although many of these Apache began to abandon their new sedentary life in the mid-1790s, the previous decade of negotiation, treaty, and trade had broken the cycle of Apache-New Mexican violence.[31]

The decade of the 1780s brought New Mexico into an era of relative peace for the first time since midcentury. Although the province continued to experience occasional raids, nothing close to the frequency and magnitude of the Comanche and Apache raids of the 1770s occurred during the next three decades. At the end of 1787, Comandante General Ugarte y Loyola gave an account of hostile Indian activity during the previous year and a half. Indians had killed 18 New Mexicans, compared with 127 during the single year of 1778.[32] Until the last years of Spanish colonial rule, the alliance system erected to protect the northern provinces from Plains Indians hostility gave the inhabitants of New Mexico respite from the burden of their own defense and freed the energies and resources they needed to improve the quality of other aspects of their lives on the frontier of New Spain.

CHAPTER THREE

"This Type of Commerce Cannot Remedy Itself"

Obstacles to Economic Growth in New Mexico and the Bourbon Response

POWER AND PELICANS

On March 22, 1775, Governor Mendinueta received a request from Viceroy Bucareli, asking him, on behalf of the king, "in the case that one finds in this kingdom any pelicans, [to] conduct to Spain those which can be obtained in some moderate number."[1] The viceroy directed the governor to pay careful attention to documenting any expenses that the collection of pelicans might incur and to advise him even if no pelicans could be found in the province.

King Carlos III stocked his royal zoo in Madrid with birds and animals collected from all the lands under Spanish dominion, including elk from New Mexico. In 1765, 1774, 1779, and again in 1782, the New Mexican governors arranged for the capture of small groups of elk and their transportation to Mexico City for eventual shipment to Spain. Commenting on his visit in 1774 to New Mexico, Don Pedro Alonso O'Crouley mentioned seeing this "particular species of sorrel-colored deer" in Madrid at Buen Retiro Park.[2]

A few months after the initial inquiry, in August 1775, Governor Mendinueta replied to Viceroy Bucareli that pelicans did not live in New Mexico. No further mention of the species appears in the Spanish documents relating to the province.[3]

The episode illustrates several aspects of the relationship between New Mexico and the higher levels of government in New Spain toward the end of the eighteenth century. Although New Mexico existed at the end of long and often tenuous lines of communication, the Spanish government in Mexico and Madrid nonetheless could exercise true power and authority in the province. During the second half of the eighteenth century, the Bourbon King Carlos III (1759–1788) began to implement a multitude of fiscal, economic, and political reforms that rejuvenated state power and control over the colonies. These policies shaped the development of New Mexico more actively than at any time since the reconquest of the province. Beginning with the reorganization of the system of frontier defenses in 1772, the Crown initiated an unprecedented program of investment of money and people in the northern provinces. The Spanish government used its resources on the northern frontier to impose peace on the hostile Indians that plagued Spanish settlements, either by employing force, offering trade, or crafting a policy that combined both strategies.

Establishing peace with the Indians represented only the first step toward the implementation of one of the fundamental goals of Bourbon policy that underlay its actions. In New Mexico, as in other parts of New Spain, the Bourbon government sought to rebuild Spanish power by reforming the machinery of state and encouraging economic growth in ways that would enhance Bourbon control over fiscal resources.[4] From this perspective, the order from Spain through the viceroy and the other bureaucratic intermediaries directing Governor Mendinueta to search the province for pelicans becomes emblematic of the kind of power that Bourbon Spain could project into the far corners of its possessions. Carlos III had such power and control that he could send an order directing the governor of New Mexico to collect elk for the royal zoo. On the other hand, every province had to respond to the king's request for pelicans whether they lived there or not. At times the Bourbon government proved itself a rather crude instrument for fashioning policies that could foster the economic development of its colonies.

TO TAX OR DEVELOP? THE BOURBON DILEMMA IN NEW MEXICO

Besides keeping New Mexico from collapse under the constant attacks by hostile groups of Native Americans, the architects of Bourbon policy faced another problem on the northern frontier. In the midst of the effort and financial burden needed to carry on war with the Comanche and Apache raiders, the administrators of royal policy had to fit the northern provinces into the larger fiscal and governmental reforms designed for New Spain. Because of the very cost of the military strategy in the north, officials always felt the temptation to enforce rigorously the newly created Bourbon state monopolies in order to recoup at least a portion of that expenditure. On the other hand, settlers, merchants, and provincial officials argued consistently that the collection of revenue of any kind by the state would only add to local and regional economic troubles. They held that, given the distance of the most northern provinces from the centers of mining and commercial activity and the devastation to local economies caused by Indian raids, attempts to produce revenue in the far northern provinces would dampen economic activity and in the long run increase the financial burden on the royal exchequer.

New Mexico provides an excellent illustration of the dilemma faced by Bourbon reformers. The settlers in the province had persevered in the midst of one of the harshest periods of hostile Indian raids. They had survived without the economic base possessed by the mining districts in Parral, or those around Chihuahua or Durango, and yet New Mexico still possessed a substantial population of settlers and "Christian" Pueblo Indians who could bear the new monopoly taxes. The issues surrounding the administration of the tobacco monopoly (*estanco de tabaco*) in New Mexico reveal the concern that local officials expressed over matters that affected the provincial economy, shared increasingly within higher levels of the government of New Spain.

The cultivation and distribution of tobacco became one of the state monopolies established by Gálvez during his inspection of New Spain (1765– 1771). Under Gálvez, a new department of the *Real Hacienda* held responsibility for contracting for tobacco from growers in the only districts authorized to cultivate the commodity: Orizaba, Córdoba, and Zongolica (on the Gulf side of the Continental Divide in central Veracruz).[5] The monopoly also ran factories that manufactured cigars in Puebla, Mexico City, Querétaro, Orizaba, and Guadalajara, and from these locations it distributed the finished product throughout New Spain.

On November 26, 1765, the viceroy directed Governor Cachupín to establish the tobacco monopoly in New Mexico. Instructions from the director of the tobacco monopoly in New Spain explained how to set up the necessary account and provided guidelines for its administration. The viceroy enclosed sample bandos for the governor's use to inform New Mexicans that they could no longer grow tobacco and that they had to purchase their tobacco products from the state monopoly.[6]

In an extremely informative and cogent report, Governor Cachupín explained how the extension of the tobacco monopoly to the province would harm the New Mexican economy. He first described the general factors that limited New Mexico's trade with Chihuahua, namely the great distance and fear of attack by Apache raiders. The annual journey to Chihuahua provided the only opportunity for inhabitants of the province to buy necessary provisions for their families, trading their produce and handiwork for goods that could not be obtained in New Mexico. Because of the limited access to the New Mexican market afforded by a single annual convoy to the south and back, few merchants served the interior of the province. In addition, New Mexico also lacked a mining sector that might have stimulated the region's economy, as it had elsewhere in northern New Spain. As a result, the province suffered from a general lack of currency, which meant that commerce within New Mexico involved barter in native commodities. For instance, a person with a deerskin worth roughly 2 pesos might trade it to a provincial merchant for a *manojo* of tobacco.

On the other hand, New Mexicans did not barter gamuzas, since these buckskins represented the only commodity that brought a sure profit in Nueva Vizcaya and Chihuahua. The average gamuza sold for 2 pesos in hard currency and sometimes commanded prices as high as 18 or 20 reales.[7] In fact, Governor Cachupín maintained, the bands of "barbarous" Indians liked the clothing so much that they formed a principal item of trade in an area that extended about 600 miles beyond the New Mexican settlements. The attacks of these erstwhile trading partners had hurt the production of gamuzas, severely limiting their supply.

According to Governor Cachupín, any possible advantage to the coffers of the Real Hacienda gained by the introduction of the tobacco monopoly into New Mexico would be nullified by the lack of circulating currency in the province. The costs involved in converting New Mexican goods commonly accepted in trade into specie would leave less money for the purchase of tobacco. "It does not appear to me," wrote Cachupín, "that this would have the beneficial consequences that are anticipated."[8] The El Paso region, the southern portion of Cachupín's jurisdiction, produced wine and aguardiente as its principal commodity by value. Cachupín argued that the settlers incurred high costs in transporting these beverages and marketing them in Chihuahua. To combine these with the added cost of transporting and distributing tobacco in the northern reaches of New Spain would bring "much bother and little benefit to the Real Hacienda."

The governor then addressed the proposal to establish a factory in Chihuahua, pointing out that even if production in the north would hold down the cost of tobacco, there still would be no way of getting it into New Mexico except by the annual convoy from New Mexico to Chihuahua. Some settlers would purchase tobacco for their own use, and others would buy it to barter for goods within New Mexico, but the higher price that tobacco could command in New Mexico would again be more than offset by higher costs for its transport, the administration of the monopoly, and the difficulty of dealing with payment in kind.

The tobacco monopoly required that the governor suppress the cultivation of punche, a native variety of tobacco whose origin remains somewhat obscure and which the inhabitants of New Mexico used "as a supplement to the small portion [of tobacco] that has always entered from commerce of Chihuahua." Cachupín claimed that punche had come originally from Córdoba and Orizaba but that in New Mexico it had "degenerated" and become extremely strong.[9] The governor explained that the grip that smoking held over the settlers made them tolerate punche. They also needed the crop to trade with the Plains Indians, especially the Comanche. The Pueblo

Indians grew punche for the same reasons, and Cachupín argued that the Pueblo economy would feel the loss of this crop even more keenly. He also pointed out that the government would have a more difficult time enforcing the prohibition among the Indians because they harvested punche in the mountains and planted it among the maize plants in their fields. Hoping that the viceroy would respond to his arguments and reverse the order, Governor Cachupín nevertheless promised to publish a bando prohibiting the cultivation of punche in March 1766, as soon as the inhabitants traveling with the convoy returned from Chihuahua.[10]

Governor Cachupín showed a sincere interest in protecting the limited avenues of economic activity that existed within his province. In fact, in this report the governor appeared to set the foundation for arguing later on that, after having complied with his orders and prohibiting cultivation, regulating the production of punche in New Mexico had proved impossible. Cachupín's successor, Governor Mendinueta, made this very case to the new viceroy a year and a half later. After recapitulating many of the arguments advanced by Cachupín, Mendinueta wrote,

> For these same reasons [already given], it may not be possible to make effective the prohibition against the planting of their tobacco, punche, by the vecinos and the pueblos of converted Indians for their respective consumption; and it becomes doubly impossible to regulate in the one or the other the disposition to make gifts with the tobacco of their crop to the barbarous nations or to exchange it with them. . . . Since the publication of the orders prohibiting the planting, according to your Excellency's superior mandate at the beginning of the past year '66, the greatest dissatisfaction is evident.
>
> This proclamation, despite compliance to it, particularly on the part of the vecinos, has resulted in there not being at the present time any tobacco for their use. They have had to avail themselves of the weed *mata* from the Taos and Pecos [Mountains], and the punche from the Pueblo Indians. The latter, because they were not the most obedient to the proclamation or because of their economy, put aside the previously mentioned crops, having had sufficient for their own needs, and find themselves in a position to provide, although meagerly, for the satisfaction of the vice of these inhabitants, who at present do not hesitate to smoke any herb that they believe acts as a substitute for tobacco.

To add insult to injury, Mendinueta pointed out that the vecinos had brought no tobacco back from Chihuahua during their last journey because of a shortage in that city. "Your excellency will discern," Mendinueta continued, "the general discontent that is to be feared because no provisions of a palliative nature are forthcoming to minimize the dangers incident to the prohibition of tobacco planting. This discontent necessitates a silent, polite dissimulation in order to prevent further exasperation and requires that the inhabitants be supplied in the accustomed manner." Mendinueta ended his plea for New Mexico's exemption from the prohibition of punche cultivation by reminding the viceroy that the punche crop was too small, and the province too distant, to form any threat to the operation of the tobacco monopoly in other areas. In addition, the poverty of the province, its exposure to hostile Indians, and the defense that the citizens provided at their own expense constituted further reasons that justified special treatment.

By all indications, New Mexicans continued to grow punche openly after this series of official exchanges. Fray Morfí included punche as one of the crops collected in the provincial tithe, and the New Mexican tithe records indicate a mounting yield between 1796 and 1806.[11] Governor Fernando de Chacón noted that in 1803 everyone grew tobacco and that even most of the missionaries smoked it and took it in powder.[12] Official scrutiny of the situation continued as well. In March 1784 the comandante general of the Provincias Internas, Pedro de Neve, wrote Governor Anza complaining that "the vecinos and Indians consume an herb that they call *oja* or *mata.*" Neve ordered Anza to prohibit the consumption of the herb, to remove it from the fields, and to inform the inhabitants that they must buy the tobacco from the government shops, "so that they do not cheat the income [of the monopoly] with the foul use of the herb." The next month Neve suspended his order for the destruction of the "wild tobacco" crop, "considering now that this action could have grave difficulties in the present constitution of those pueblos, and Indians [*Naturales*] ... with the exception of ordering the Troop and vecindario of this villa [Santa Fe] to take care to purchase that which they consume from the *Real Estanco;* and prohibiting the vecinos from taking it [punche] to the south, and the Indians when they go by horse, because of the bad example that it sets in those lands that are generally provided on the account of the Real Hacienda."[13]

The implementation of the tobacco monopoly in New Mexico demonstrated the process of compromise, negotiation, and obfuscation that met the attempts of higher officials to extend the new Bourbon fiscal policy into the far northern reaches of New Spain. The response of local officials in New Mexico to the unwelcome effects of this broader policy on their jurisdictions differed little from the tactics used in other parts of New Spain. In Oaxaca, for example, during the two decades after Gálvez wrote his *Plan de Intendencias,* the local alcaldes mayores and their business agents and financiers from Mexico City combined to oppose the abolition of the coercive repartimiento system of cochineal and cotton-textile production.[14] Significantly, throughout the dialog concerning the fate of punche and mata in New Mexico, the ramification of the tobacco monopoly for the health of the native economy consistently underlay all discussion of policy.

The successful efforts of a progression of New Mexican governors in preventing the suppression of punche cultivation, to the prejudice of tobacco-monopoly revenues from the region, held some measure of irony. In the 1770s the profits from the tobacco monopoly in the northern provinces became one source of revenue for the maintenance of both the presidio in Santa Fe and the New Mexican missions along the Río Grande. Prior to 1773, all funds for the presidios along the northern frontier came from the treasury in Mexico; thereafter, the treasuries at Guanajuato and Durango sent a portion of their annual surplus to meet part of the expenses of the presidios, and much of these funds came from revenue brought in by Gálvez's new taxes and monopolies.

NORTHERN MONETARY AND FISCAL PROBLEMS

The occasional success of New Mexicans in opposing the perceived effects of Bourbon policy on their provincial economy did not alter the structural obstacles they faced. Fray Juan Augustín de Morfí wrote in 1778 that "[M]oney doesn't even circulate in the interior of the kingdom, and in the settlements around El Paso scarcely at all. Business is conducted by barter with the merchants trading things from Spain and Mexico, and receiving in return from the natives and [Spanish] citizens [of New Mexico] their own local products. . . . These things constitute the principal part of this defective and corrupt trade."[15] This unflattering appraisal of commerce in New Mexico, like other similar complaints, caught the attention of Spanish officials implementing the Bourbon administrative reform of the government of the northern provinces in the 1770s. The policy of Spanish officials on the northern frontier encompassed more than just creating a strategy to contain and pacify the Plains Indians in order to prevent them from invading the mining regions and population centers of Nueva Vizcaya and Coahuila. Spanish officials took action to implement a policy designed to stimulate regional commercial enterprise and encourage the development of local economies. When they made the financial arrangements in order to establish the new line of presidios as outlined in the Reglamento of 1772, administrators showed sensitivity to the complaints that officials throughout the northern provinces had voiced: the lack of circulating currency and the difficulty of developing and sustaining commercial activity.[16] The officials in charge of governing the Provincias Internas, from the provincial governors up to the viceroy, responded by attempting to manage the fiscal affairs within their jurisdiction with an eye toward maximizing the beneficial effects of royal funds on the economy.

Besides redrawing the line of presidios stretching along the northern frontier of New Spain, the Reglamento of 1772 attempted to build a financial base for the new defensive system, taking advantage of the revenue produced in the provinces by the royal monopolies established by Gálvez during the same period. With this in mind, between 1772 and 1785, officials at all levels of the Bourbon government in New Spain worked to construct a fiscal system that could provide a steady source of income to meet the expense of the presidios and the companies of troops in the north. At the same time, these officials sought to maximize the benefit that royal investment in the defensive perimeter could have on the provincial economy as a whole.

The problem of lack of specie in the north, of which the governors of New Mexico continually complained, also presented problems for the financial arrangements that accompanied the Reglamento.[17] In May 1773, shortly after officials had begun to implement the new system, the fiscal reported to Viceroy Bucareli that a survey of the frontier treasuries revealed a shortage of funds. This meant that the treasury could not make the payments for the fixed expenses of the presidios to the *habilitado*. Under the Reglamento, the Real Hacienda had the responsibility of meeting the payroll and expenses promptly every six months. The treasurers of San Luis Potosí and Durango said that they could not send funds to cover the expenses of the presidios unless they first borrowed the money from another regional treasury. As the fiscal explained, "in reality in their territories there is not more than one or the other of limited resources, and these are needed in order to give drafts to their merchants, the rest suffering a general inactivity for the depression that the merchants are in, and the decadence in which one finds mining."[18] If pressed, the treasury at Durango could only come up with 2,000 pesos, but these funds were due the Church, as Don Ignacio Lino had just made a payment on his successful bid for the ecclesiastical tithe. At the same time, the *Cabildo* of the Durango Cathedral owed at least 14,000 pesos in its next payment to the Real Hacienda.

Some of the provincial treasury officials reported that the treasury would have to solicit the necessary amount from wealthy merchants and settlers in its jurisdiction in order to supplement existing funds, make up the anticipated presidial payment, and pay the expenses associated with its transport. In return the treasury would guarantee an early repayment of the loan. The provincial treasuries of the north could not provide the resources needed by the presidios unless the treasury in Mexico contributed the lion's share. As it turned out, only the Durango treasury contributed directly to the support of the presidios in the years following the Reglamento (*see Figure 5*).[19]

In general, the commitment to the defense of the northern perimeter of New Spain also represented an enormous infusion of money that had potential economic benefits throughout the region. From 1773 to 1798, between 100,000 and 440,000 pesos per year left the Durango treasury for the *presidios internos*. The officials of the treasuries of Mexico and Durango earmarked almost 18.5 million pesos for the northern frontier between 1770 and 1810. More than 12.5 million of this amount was allocated before 1786. The Durango treasury sent money to the *Real Caja* of Chihuahua, and together they acted as a funnel for money provided by the richer regions farther south, especially Guanajuato and Mexico.[20]

Officials at all levels understood the potentially useful role that royal

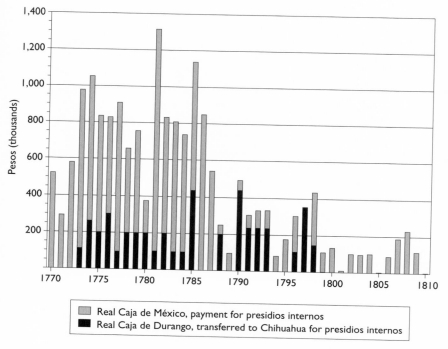

Figure 5. Expenditures for presidios internos from the treasuries of Mexico and Durango, 1770–1811. *Sources:* John J. TePaske and José and Mari Luz Hernández Palomo, *La Real Hacienda de Nueva España: La Caja de México (1576–1816)* (Colección Científica Fuentes, 41; Mexico City: Instituto Nacional de Antropología e Historia, 1976); and John J. TePaske and Herbert S. Klein, *Ingresos y egresos de la Real Hacienda de Nueva España* (Colección Fuentes; Mexico City: Instituto Nacional de Antropología e Historia, 1986).

expenditures in support of the line of presidios could play in the creation of a strong regional economy. In a report concerning payment policy for the frontier military posts, Antonio Bonilla, secretary to Comandante General Croix, discussed the way in which the method of purchasing supplies for the presidio companies perpetuated the lack of specie by allowing it to leave the region: "But if the idea is that money circulate in these internal provinces, so that commerce, mining, and agriculture flourish, the subject is encouraged, and the royal rents increase; we conclude in consequence, that the departure of the paymasters to Mexico, far from being advantageous, is very prejudicial."[21] At the center of the deliberations of colonial officials regarding changes in monetary policy and financial procedures lay the interrelated problems of security and the lack of money in circulation, issues crucial to the development of commercial investment and activity. In the Council of War held in Chihuahua in 1778, the assembled officials focused their discussions on fiscal options they could institute to benefit the northern provincial economies.

In one of the meetings held in July, the council discussed Comandante General Croix's plan to use the money collected by the Administration of Tobacco in order to finance the payment of the soldiers stationed in the presidios of Nueva Vizcaya, the compañías volantes, and the presidial troops at Santa Fe.[22] In considering their options, the officials encountered two related problems. With too little money circulating in the north, the comandante general and the provincial governors had to consider whether the transfer of funds would have an impact on trade transactions. Implementing the plan to finance the presidial troops ran into another difficulty caused by the combined effect of a recent recoinage of the Spanish peso and the scarcity of specie on the northern provincial economies. As a Bourbon measure to maximize revenue, the Crown lowered the content of a *mark* of silver and began minting "new money" at the beginning of 1772. Every mark of silver minted produced an extra three-tenths of a real after the devaluation; a mark now produced 69.6 reales instead of only 69.3. Because of the scarcity of specie in the north, much of the trade took place by exchanging goods instead of through cash purchases. Barter and the hoarding of silver coin contributed to the sluggish circulation of what specie did exist. Consequently, the old coinage had penetrated so deeply into the northern provincial economies that, at the end of 1778, the fiscal felt forced to exempt Nueva Vizcaya and New Mexico from the deadline set for the exchange of old pesos for new coins.[23]

All of these considerations weighed on the officials trying to fix the system for funding the northern presidios. The plan that they devised depended upon extending the system of collecting revenue that the Bourbon government had instituted so that funds could be redistributed to the northern provinces and allowed to circulate. Generally, the administrator of a government franchise such as the tobacco monopoly remitted the revenue collected in the north to the central treasury in Mexico City in the form of a *libranza,* a bill of exchange drawn by a merchant or official on funds deposited elsewhere. The corresponding person or institution in Mexico City redeemed the bill in specie paid to the bearer upon its presentation.[24]

The officials participating in the War Council recommended that some part or half of the tobacco revenues be assigned to it for payment of military expenses and that the rest be remitted to Mexico "in money of the old coinage, which would contribute immensely to its extinction." Using the tobacco revenues collected in Durango to pay for the compañías volantes in Nueva Vizcaya and the presidio troops stationed in Santa Fe would not help extract the old coinage from the north. It did, however, prevent the remittance of money earned by the tobacco monopoly from further draining the province of coin. While the council agreed that this provision would not help the shortage of currency, it would at least ensure that any new money that did circulate would be of the current coinage.

The War Council surmised that many of the economic difficulties of the region stemmed from the fact that

> the money of the old coinage circulates among the populations of Nueva Vizcaya without penetrating into the neighboring provinces, nor in the province of New Mexico, since there are no revolving business transactions, nor dealings that they use, and since in those provinces little or no money enters. Those posted at Santa Fe spend the money on horses, materials, and consumer goods in order to provision the troops, and to trade or barter for the grains and fruit that the land offers, as soon as the official supply officer receives it in the treasury of that town; this type of commerce cannot remedy itself until [it has] the opportunity to occur for other attentions that they would prefer in that distant territory.[25]

To help stimulate the economy and aid commerce, Comandante General Croix and his officers also offered another fiscal recommendation calculated to help money circulate within the provincial economy. They revived a proposal of Don José Rubio, the previous comandante general, to allow the city treasury of Chihuahua and the Real Caja of Durango to accept deposits of money from merchants, issuing in return a corresponding libranza without charging a premium. The libranza would be drawn against the royal treasury of Mexico, Guanajuato, or Durango. Whenever possible, the treasury at Chihuahua would give the merchants libranzas from Guanajuato and Durango, drawn against Mexico. The council agreed that the Chihuahua and Durango treasuries should abide "by only the quantities that the merchant enters in money of the new coinage, not the old one, and that the treasury [of Chihuahua], just like the royal officials of Durango, give the libranzas accurately drawn against the treasury and officials of México, without carrying a premium for the merchants."

The plan to allow Chihuahua to issue libranzas would provide a number of important financial benefits. By drawing all the libranzas on treasuries in other provinces, the plan would allow for the transfer of funds between the northern provinces in a manner less costly and dangerous than physical transport, at the same time keeping specie in circulation through the constant expenditures by the provincial treasuries. Libranzas would provide much-needed letters of credit for merchants who sold goods in Nueva Vizcaya and New Mexico that had been purchased farther south. Merchants from Mexico City or other commercial centers who wished to purchase goods in the north could present a libranza drawn on the Durango or

Chihuahua treasury and receive coin, increasing the supply of money in the north. In addition, the holder could endorse a libranza and turn it over to another party before being presented to the person responsible for making good the warrant. To the extent that libranzas could be used in this manner to make purchases in Nueva Vizcaya or New Mexico before they were returned to the place on which they were drawn, the plan offered by the War Council could increase the effective supply of currency available to commerce in the region.[26]

The recommendations of the Council of War addressed directly the economic problems facing the northern provinces beyond those created by the raids of nomadic Indians. Over the next decade, Spanish administrators implemented most of the council's recommendations or worked to devise other solutions to the problems it had identified and discussed. The use of libranzas as proposed by the council, however, became standard practice more by force of circumstances than through deliberate implementation.

In March 1785 Miguel Francisco de Arroynde, the administrator for the tobacco, gunpowder, and playing-card monopolies in San Juan del Río, the district north of Durango, wrote to the agent and accountant for the royal rents, saying that he could not send the money collected to Chihuahua because no one could travel the roads due to a serious drought and the consequent scarcity of pasturage.[27] Moving the specie to Chihuahua would expose it to great risk, which led Arroynde to suspend the shipments until such time as he could assure their security.

Arroynde invited the officials in Durango to give *libramientos* drawn against the Cuencamé funds in his care. The agent and the accountant for the royal tobacco rents, Juan Baptista de Ugarte and Vicente de Muro, agreed with Arroynde that specie should not be transferred between treasuries, adding that the revenue of the monopoly decreased because the hacienda owners did not like having to pay in specie. As a result, "without doubt [the hacienda owners] bring great delay in the resulting circulation and in the introduction of the money in this treasury and of that in the general [treasury]." Ugarte and Muro recommended that treasury officials in the north make use of libranzas in order to increase the circulation of money in the region: "[R]unning the administrations with the liberty that [they had] until now, taking place from Mexico or Guanajuato, they distribute the freight directly and make their payments adapting as best they can; that if [payment] will be in libranzas, it facilitates a faster circulation of the revenue, and the public will remain being helped with the money collected in the estancos, which revolves by the purchasing power of the particular persons through their libranzas, promoting their commerce with more extent, and also in consequence augmenting the contribution to those treasuries." The suggestion of Ugarte and Muro, while an innovation in the procedure of the Real

Hacienda, simply reflected a business practice already considered the life-blood of the great merchant houses based in Mexico City.[28]

The officials of the tobacco monopoly referred the matter to the fiscal of the Real Hacienda, who incorporated the proposal into his report concerning various measures relating to the northern frontier. "The principal object of this proceeding," wrote the fiscal, "is to establish a constant and well-ordered method to provide help to the Provincias Internas with what they need annually, granting additional funds *when they appear fair, and necessary to this viceroyalty.*"[29] The fiscal recommended that Acting Comandante General José Antonio Rengel and *Intendente* Pedro de Corvalán order timely reporting from the provinces of Nueva Vizcaya, Sonora, Coahuila, Texas, New Mexico, and the Californias. This would allow them to budget expenditures and arrange for the transfer of funds by shipping specie or by drawing libranzas against the revenues from the royal monopolies. In addition, the fiscal examined the merits of the proposal for the extension of libranzas to merchants and businessmen, pointing out the problems he encountered and recommending regulations to forestall them. The fiscal recommended that Rengel and Corvalán compare the difficulties that he outlined with "the utility that results to the Royal Treasury and in the local areas in not exporting their funds with large and dangerous transports, incurring freightage; obstacles that are currently inevitable. It would be advantageous to the revenue to fund a proportion of libranzas in all areas, and none can be more secure, than those which are issued against those royal treasuries."

Meanwhile, the drought of 1784–1787 prevented the operation of the usual arrangements for transferring funds between the northern provinces. In June 1785, Accountant Muro of the tobacco monopoly in Durango wrote that he could not redeem a libranza for 5,000 pesos drawn upon the tobacco revenues by the administrator at Somberete. The "hunger and lack of the most necessary foodstuffs" for both men and mules made the transport of the money in specie impossible. The directors of the tobacco monopoly immediately forwarded Muro's letter to Viceroy Gálvez, asking him to resolve the issue as he judged best. In October, Comandante Rengel outlined the new regulations for issuing libranzas for Gálvez's approval. Merchants and other recognized private individuals could deposit funds in nearby reales cajas in return for libranzas drawn on distant ones. Treasuries that normally had large surplus revenues would remit funds to Mexico, unless a region experienced a scarcity of money in circulation due to the extraction of specie by commercial activity or for other reasons.[30]

The use of libranzas by merchants doing business in the north began very soon afterward, encouraged by the establishment in 1785 of a new Real Caja in Chihuahua. Comandante Rengel had already reached an agreement at the end of 1784 that the tobacco, gunpowder, and playing-card monopolies would remit their revenues to Chihuahua for payment of the troops assigned to the presidios. However, the real change in the fiscal situation in the north came with the new policy extending the use of libranzas. Figure 5 shows a dramatic reduction after 1785 in the amount of money transferred from Durango and Mexico to Chihuahua for the expenses of the presidios. Comandante General Jacobo Ugarte y Loyola next ordered a transfer of funds from Guanajuato to Durango in 1787, amounting to 200,000 pesos, for the payment of the presidial troops by the officials in Chihuahua for the next year. In his request, he cited as his justification the scarcity of circulating money currently felt in Chihuahua and the report of 1785 from Rengel to Gálvez.[31]

The importance of the extension of the system of libranzas to commerce in the north becomes clear when one examines the protest elicited by moves to change the policy during the next few years. Upon arriving in Chihuahua in 1788, Ugarte y Loyola found that the merchants refused to deposit their money in the Real Hacienda in exchange for libramientos because the office there would not disburse funds fairly without charging a percentage for the service.[32] The "extremely useful" practice of allowing merchants libranzas without charge, argued the comandante general, allowed for the payment of the troops, avoided risks to the funds, and saved money on transport, "lessening as well by this simple method the extraction of money in public circulation that is so necessary, and of such great importance for the transactions of the subjects, and with the relief of those, benefiting the royal treasury." Ugarte y Loyola asked Viceroy Manuel Antonio Flores to "remove the obstacles that impede or obstruct the effect of this concept, with prejudice to the Real Hacienda and the public."

Four years later, members of the merchant's guild of Chihuahua, all of whom were officials or military officers in their own right, petitioned the comandante general to order the treasury of Chihuahua to resume issuing libranzas without restrictions to qualified merchants. Three of the petitioners, Don Pablo de Ochoa, Don Pedro Ignacio de Irigoyen, and Don Diego Ventura Márquez, had contracted for the provision of the presidios and compañías volantes for 1791.[33] They complained that the officials of the Chihuahua treasury misinterpreted a recent directive of Viceroy Conde de Revillagigedo II, confirming the decision of the previous viceroy. Viceroy Flores had allowed libranzas only to merchants who held the presidio supply contract, and then only for the amount sent by the presidio paymasters to pay for the goods they ordered. After 1791 the duty of supplying the presidios reverted back from merchants to the paymasters themselves. The members of the merchant guild in Chihuahua suddenly found themselves barred from receiving libranzas for money deposited in the treasury, which they relied upon to fulfill their financial obligations elsewhere.

The merchants again recounted the benefits of the system for the region:

libranzas saved the Crown the cost of materials and transportation needed to ship money from Guanajuato and other places to pay the troops; and the merchants saved the same costs associated with remitting specie to Mexico to maintain their credit, not to mention money lost by robbery along the way. "[T]he more money that leaves these dominions," they wrote, "the greater the shortage becomes, as is the case, the dangers of which would be averted by giving the Real Hacienda the corresponding libramientos, considering that this [province] is a closed port, in which more money neither enters nor circulates than that which His Majesty provides for the salaries of the troops." Comandante General Pedro de Nava forwarded the petition to Viceroy Revillagigedo II, agreeing with the merchant guild that libranzas promoted the broader economic interests of the region and recommending that the matter once again be settled in their favor.[34]

Between 1770 and 1811 the treasury accounts show that officials earmarked 25.6 million pesos for the defense of the Provincias Internas. Figure 6 illustrates the aggregate annual expenditure and the amount dispersed by each treasury. Although the amount of money going to New Mexico does not appear separately in the treasury accounts, the payments to the presidial soldiers in Santa Fe, to missionaries, and for other expenses in New Mexico provide a rough estimate. These sources suggest that the Bourbon treasury expended around 2 million pesos in New Mexico during the same period, about 7.8 percent of the total amount spent on the presidios internos.[35] Even with the expenditures for gifts to the newly allied Indians called for in the treaties, peace and the system of alliances significantly reduced royal expenditures after 1785. In addition, the establishment of the provincial treasury at Chihuahua, combined with the extension of libranzas, served to reduce dramatically the amount of money transferred from other treasuries to Chihuahua for maintenance of the line of presidios (see Figure 6).

The tremendous investment made in New Mexico, documented by the colonial archives, underlines the importance of the province in the military and economic strategy of the Spanish Crown in the late eighteenth century. In addition, the care taken by Spanish officials to consider the economic impact of their fiscal decisions demonstrates a surprising degree of conscious support for the development of the far north. The innovation that allowed merchants to deposit money in Durango and Chihuahua in return for libranzas drawn on Mexico City provides a case in point. Merchants and citizens alike had difficulty obtaining hard currency and credit in colonial Mexico, and particularly in the Provincias Internas. By extending the use of libranzas in northern New Spain, officials kept specie in the northern provinces and at the same time eased access to credit. Furthermore, while the libranzas remained in circulation on their way to redemption in Mexico City, they served to increase the total amount of money in circulation in the north. "This type of commerce cannot remedy itself," wrote the Council of War in Chihuahua

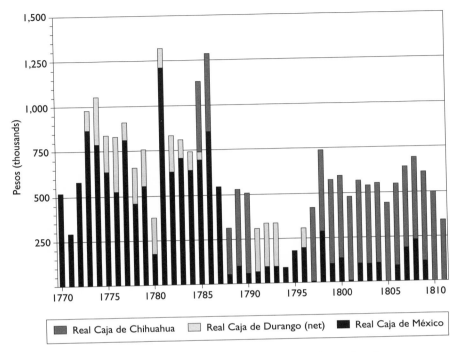

Figure 6. Total estimated outlay for presidios internos and associated expenses, 1770–1810. *Source:* John J. TePaske and José and Mari Luz Hernández Palomo, *La Real Hacienda de Nueva España: La Caja de México (1576–1816)* (Colección Científica Fuentes, 41; Mexico City: Instituto Nacional de Antropología e Historia, 1976); and John J. TePaske and Herbert S. Klein, *Ingresos y egresos de la Real Hacienda de Nueva España* (Colección Fuentes; Mexico City: Instituto Nacional de Antropología e Historia, 1986).

in 1778 concerning the problem in New Mexico. Bourbon officials listened and took action.

PRESIDIO SUPPLY AND THE BOURBON RESPONSE

In September 1768 Thomas Madrid and Francisco Esquibel, teniente and alférez of the company of the Royal Presidio of the Villa of Santa Fe, wrote to Comandante General Teodoro de Croix: "[C]onsidering that the governor told you that it was impractical to pay our salaries in money, since it does not run or exist in this country, and that for us it is impossible to subsist in service without the almost daily and necessary supplies—as much for our persons as for our families—we supplicate the aforementioned governor that attending to our need it will serve you to order him to administer to us the necessities in the same proportion as before."[36]

For more than 100 soldiers and their families living at the Santa Fe Presidio, and the hundreds stationed elsewhere in Nueva Vizcaya, Sonora, and Coahuila, the shortcomings of the system that brought supplies to the presidial companies constituted a most serious matter. Men like Madrid and Esquibel complained about not receiving supplies at a fair price or receiving inadequate ones when paid in kind. Such issues prompted action on the part of those in charge out of genuine concern for the welfare of these citizens and because Bourbon officials saw the problems that they described as manifestations of the larger economic issues they faced in the Provincias Internas.

Spanish officials viewed the limited economic development of the northern provinces as a product of two related problems. The issue of how to get money into the northern provincial economies, and how to keep it in circulation, led to changes in the financing of the military effort and to the extension of libranzas to northern merchants with money to deposit in the regional treasuries. The other problem concerned arranging public expenditures so that a greater portion of the money went toward the purchase of locally produced goods, which in turn would help to develop and expand local markets. The largest portion of annual royal expenditures went to pay the salaries of the soldiers based in the northern presidios that defended the perimeter of northern New Spain. Consequently, after 1772 Spanish officials in charge of the Provincias Internas attempted numerous reforms of the supply system for the northern presidios. They took these steps with the goal of ensuring that a greater part of a soldier's *situado* remained in his hands so he could buy goods that would stimulate the local and regional economy.

The motive for the official interest in reforming the supply system did not follow from an entirely altruistic concern for the welfare of the presidial soldier. Although the total payroll for the troops on the frontier rose rather consistently—largely due to the expansion of the garrisons for the presidios, the addition of the compañías volantes, Indian auxiliaries, and supplies for militia—the income of the individual soldier shrank just as consistently. In 1701 a regular soldier on the frontier received 450 pesos per year, a figure reduced to 365 in 1724, to 290 in 1772, and down to 240 pesos in 1787.[37] Besides attempting to direct the money paid by the Crown in salaries toward the purchase of goods that would contribute to the northern economy, royal officials had an interest in seeing that the finances of the presidial troops did not affect their morale and hinder the performance of their duty.

Supplying the soldiers in the presidio presented a problem for officials from the beginning of the eighteenth century.[38] Due to the distance of the presidios from market centers in which the soldiers could purchase their necessities, they received the bulk of their salary in goods given by the captain of the company or governor of the region. The official in charge of supply, often in collusion with a local merchant, purchased basic supplies of food, clothing, and goods that could not be obtained within the region and deducted a portion of each soldier's salary to pay for the materials. This practice led to widespread price gouging and subjected the soldiers to numerous deductions for uniforms, clothing, and other goods, leaving them in debt. In New Mexico, Governor Ignacio Flores Mogollón found himself in jail in 1715, charged by his successor with having deducted sums from the salaries of the soldiers in the Presidio of Santa Fe for overvalued goods and then having tried to sell them the same merchandise.[39]

Changes in the rules governing the supply of the presidio companies covered by the Reglamento of 1729 and subsequently did little to help the situation. Not until the inspection of the Marqués de Rubí in 1768 did Spanish officials seek to do anything about the basic problem: The soldiers had no control over the disposition of a large portion of their salary. Fray Lezaún wrote in 1760 that, of the 400 pesos the Crown provided in salary to the soldiers in New Mexico, the governor deducted 150 pesos for clothing of the poorest quality and paid the rest in other supplies; "whether they want them or not, they must take them."[40] While a fanega of maize normally sold for 2 silver pesos in the province, the governor asked the soldiers to pay 3.5 pesos in silver. The troops saw the prices of other staples similarly inflated.

After Rubí submitted his report in 1768, the viceroy ordered that the governor pay the presidial salary in cash rather than goods. This solution led directly to the problem of how to furnish specie to the governor so that he could pay the troops. Due to lack of funds in the regional treasury, Mendinueta had paid for the goods to supply the presidio in 1767 and 1768 through the good offices of a prominent vecino of Santa Fe, Don Joseph González Calderón. Because of the viceroy's recent order, the soldiers received one-half of the situado for 1768 in reales and the rest in necessary foodstuffs and clothing. Shortage of cash and the fact that some of this material came from Chihuahua in any case forced the governor to report his inability to comply fully. With no payment forthcoming for Calderón, and with arrangements for the salaries due in cash for 1769 pressing, Governor Mendinueta wrote Comandante General Croix that "there is no one in this land who can supply 500 pesos in reales or goods." Governor Mendinueta petitioned for an exemption of the order to pay the soldiers in currency due to the general lack of specie available in the province, proposing instead to pay them in "products of the land." He included letters in support of his request written by the teniente and alférez of the company. Calderón received his payment before Mendinueta's letter left the province, and the governor added that Calderón had agreed to continue the arrangement for two more years. Croix agreed to the governor's request for exemption from paying the situado in specie a few months later.[41]

The Reglamento of 1772 reorganized the line of presidios that protected the northern provinces, but it also attempted to provide a source of money to meet the expenses of frontier defense and sought to place that money in the hands of the soldiers. Beginning in 1773, a captain or governor could no longer participate in the supply of the troops.[42] Each presidio elected its own habilitado, who had the responsibility for ordering the supplies requested by each soldier. The habilitado picked up one-half of each soldier's pay every six months at the nearest provincial treasury, in order to provide the officer with the finances necessary to negotiate with merchants for the best prices when making the presidial purchases. The treasury of Chihuahua disbursed the payroll for the presidios in Nueva Vizcaya and New Mexico.

The Reglamento also standardized deductions taken from each soldier's remaining salary: 10 pesos for the *fondo de gratificación;* about 90 pesos for the *fondo de retención;* and 25 pesos per year until the soldier accumulated 100 pesos for his retirement. The paymaster paid the balance of each soldier's salary account in cash at the end of the year. As the Reglamento also reduced the regular salary to 290 pesos, in theory each soldier had 165 pesos at his disposal after all of the deductions. Of this he collected 20 pesos, and the remaining 145 pesos went to the habilitado for the purchase of provisions ordered by the soldier. As Comandante Inspector Hugo O'Connor pointed out after he implemented the new regulations, even though the soldiers received less in salary, more money circulated in the local economy as a result of the 2 reales per day paid in cash to each of the troops. This situation stood in contrast to the previous system, in which no soldier saw a peso and most ended their service in debt.[43]

The new system of provisioning the presidios soon showed its flaws. Comandante General Croix inspected the frontier presidios in 1777 and found widespread neglect of the procedures mandated by the Reglamento of 1772. The habilitado did not secure the presidio funds in a locked box, seldom kept the soldiers' accounts in order, and rarely performed audits or kept track of the distribution of provisions. Some of the paymasters yielded to the temptation of gambling or other misuse of the money entrusted to them when they arrived at a large market town with one-half of the annual wages of the presidial company. Furthermore, few habilitados used their purchasing power to negotiate the lowest price for goods bought for the company, preferring to give their business to a single merchant. As a result, Croix found that five of the presidios had amassed a combined debt of 15,000 pesos, and some of the habilitados from companies in Nueva Vizcaya had declared bankruptcy, leaving the soldiers in debt and without adequate provisions.[44]

In order to end the problems and abuses found in the supply efforts of the habilitado, Croix began in 1781 to experiment with a system of provisioning the presidios based upon contracts entered into with private merchants. Unlike the habilitado, who could not charge more than the wholesale cost of merchandise at Chihuahua plus a 2 percent commission and freight costs, private merchants who bid on the supply contracts could pass on prices at or above retail unless competition forced margins lower. Manuel de Urquidi, a member of the consulado of Chihuahua, won the contract for 1782 for the provision of San Elizario in Nueva Vizcaya. Despite fears that the prices charged for goods would exceed the amount that the payroll would bear, in 1783 Croix expanded the program to six presidios, agreeing to three-year contracts for individual Chihuahua merchants, all members of the Chihuahua guild.

Upon assuming the viceroyalty in 1785, Bernardo de Gálvez once again brought attention to the problem of the supply of the presidios. The next year, in his instructions to Ugarte y Loyola, Gálvez expressed his dissatisfaction with both of the existing supply procedures. He asked for a report from Colonel Don Juan Ugalde, the commandant for military affairs, "upon the delicate matter of managing the business affairs of the troops, discussing with me the best method, that up to now has not been found in the paymasters, who have incurred numerous bankruptcies, nor in the contractors; for I have learned that some do not fulfill the contracts, and others absorb the only free commerce with which the provinces can prosper."[45] In spite of the complaints against contractors mentioned by the viceroy, Comandante General Ugarte y Loyola met with the same six Chihuahuan merchants who held contracts for 1783–1786, just before their supply obligations expired. The merchants refused to lower the prices charged to the troops, claiming that the current margin of profit left to them was so low that they would rather not renew the contracts than lower prices any further.[46] The rejection forced Ugarte y Loyola to allow the habilitados from the presidio companies to purchase the supplies for 1787, while he solicited bids for the following year.

The events of the next four years illustrate how far Spanish officials responsible for the Provincias Internas would go in their attempts to improve the welfare of the region and its soldiers. At the same time, their efforts ultimately failed to reform the contract system of supply. Despite the best of intentions, the structure that the Bourbons created in order to achieve fiscal control could not mobilize the resources needed for an effective intervention in provincial economic affairs.

Francisco de Guizarnótegui, a consulado member who had held the supply contract for the presidio at Carrizal, also submitted a bid to Ugarte y Loyola for the provisioning of a number of the northern garrisons. Compared with the innovative use of libranzas as a way of easing the chronic deficiency of money in circulation, the Guizarnótegui episode yields a more complex picture of the motives and methods of the Bourbon officials governing the northern provinces. Short of providing the soldiers on the frontier with higher salaries—the true root of the supply problem—inspectors, comandantes generales, and viceroys tried virtually every fiscal and administrative means at their disposal. They attempted to fix a problem that seemed to them to combine both their ultimate military success against the hostile Indians and the efficient management of public investment that would encourage the development of a stronger regional economy in the north. While they did not succeed in influencing the supply system in accordance with their goals, their actions illustrate the constructive intent and commitment behind policies that had more effect in other areas.

Guizarnótegui offered to supply the seven presidios in Nueva Vizcaya, the four compañías volantes, and the presidio of New Mexico for five years. He agreed to charge the troops the cost of goods purchased at the retail price in Mexico City, plus the customary 4 percent commission charged by agents for purchases in central Mexico. To win the contract, Guizarnótegui had to pay a premium. He agreed to a 2.5 percent commission for goods from Michoacán, and the total cost also included expenses incurred for freightage (at a 20 percent discount), alcabalas, and losses in transit. In order to fulfill his obligations on time and at the agreed upon rate, Guizarnótegui asked to receive the list of goods requested by the companies one year in advance, from which he would make an estimate of the cost of the order. After approval of the estimate, the treasury in Chihuahua had to deliver the full amount to Guizarnótegui in libranzas payable in Mexico City. This would allow him to take advantage of seasonal markets and regional commercial fairs at Veracruz, Jalapa, Puebla, and Querétaro and to purchase the merchandise at the best price in advance of the date of delivery.[47] Only when Guizarnótegui had delivered the goods to the presidio or, if desired, to the habilitado's escort in Chihuahua, and only after he had paid taxes on the goods, would he bill each company for the purchases made on its account and settle any outstanding balance on either side.

In a competing bid, twelve merchants of the Chihuahua consulado argued that the contract Guizarnótegui proposed would ruin the economy of the Nueva Vizcaya and New Mexico. They offered a two-year contract, during which they would purchase goods through agents from the same regions as Guizarnótegui and deliver them to Chihuahua. The cost charged to the troops would reflect the purchase price, commissions, excise tax, and freightage. Agents from the presidios could purchase produce directly from Michoacán or from the merchants in Chihuahua, which would save about 4 percent over what Guizarnótegui would charge.

The auditor, Pedro Galindo Navarro, evaluated the two bids and the arguments made in their support. In his report to Ugarte y Loyola he discussed the proposed contracts in the light of two objectives: to provide the troops with supplies at the lowest possible price in order to improve and maintain their fitness for service, and to use the payroll in such a manner that it would aid the economy of the northern provinces.[48] The auditor rejected the argument of the merchant group that the income lost to them by giving the contract to Guizarnótegui would have an adverse impact on the economy of the province. The amount of money spent on the troops in 1787 totaled 303,480 pesos, about two-thirds of which they expended on staples such as food, livestock, and other items produced in the region, rather than on goods bought from the commercial houses of Chihuahua and other market centers. This money, argued Navarro, would in time naturally circulate through the hands of merchants and would not be affected no matter which party won the contract to supply the presidios.

As for the remaining third, calculating the return to the merchants on 121,363 pesos at even as high a rate as 11 percent profit, the total would come to less than 14,000 pesos. Dividing this potential profit among the twelve merchants making the bid, the auditor calculated that the amount that they would lose was too insignificant to cause any real hardship. Following this reasoning, Auditor Navarro preferred Guizarnótegui's bid to that of the Chihuahua group because the contract ran for three more years, included a low, fixed rate for transportation of the merchandise, and promised to deliver the goods to the presidios if desired by the habilitado. He recommended to Ugarte y Loyola that he accept Guizarnótegui's bid.

In choosing the bid of Guizarnótegui, the comandante general decided to actively involve the Bourbon government in developing the northern economy. Under the previous systems, a soldier advanced half of his salary to the habilitado in anticipation of his purchases, and the private contractors relied on their own credit when buying goods. The contractors recouped their costs by selling the goods at the prevailing retail prices in Chihuahua, far higher than those of Mexico City. In effect, Guizarnótegui's proposal shifted the burden of providing credit when making purchases from the contractor and the individual soldiers to the royal treasury. In a manner analogous to the extension of libranzas to northern merchants, this arrangement constituted a subsidy of the entire supply system by the Spanish government in the interest of freeing the purchasing power of the individual soldier so that it could more effectively stimulate the local and regional economy. Furthermore, where previous contractors and the habilitados had to assume the risks involved in transporting the goods from their points of purchase to Chihuahua, Guizarnótegui bargained to have the presidios cover all losses and the time and expense of the escorts needed to transport the merchandise. In essence, the Spanish Crown subsidized a portion of Guizarnótegui's operations.

Comandante General Ugarte y Loyola accepted Guizarnótegui's offer on February 17, 1787, and shortly thereafter authorized the treasurer at Chihuahua to issue libranzas for 80,000 pesos to Guizarnótegui, payable in Mexico City.[49] At that point, the terms of the contract that required action on the part of the Crown's officials collided with the Bourbon financial controls adopted in order to control government expenditures. The *Real Ordenanza de Intendentes* signed by the King Carlos III in December 1786 placed all functions relating to finance, the military, and judicial affairs under the supervision of regional administrators called intendants. Nueva Vizcaya fell under the jurisdiction of the intendant of Durango. In committing the treasury at Chihuahua to provide Guizarnótegui with the money he needed in advance in the form of libranzas, Ugarte y Loyola had arguably overstepped his authority, even though he had operated according to the Gálvez instructions of just a few months earlier. When the comandante general sent a report of his actions to the *Real Audiencia* in Mexico City notifying them of the contract and the impending redemption of the libranzas, the audiencia sent the matter to the Real Hacienda and ordered a full investigation of the contract and Ugarte y Loyola's jurisdiction. Until the disposition of the case, the Real Hacienda suspended payment on the 80,000 pesos that Guizarnótegui held in libranzas.

Between the audiencia, the intendant of Durango, Viceroy Flores, and Comandante General Ugarte y Loyola, it took more than three years to resolve the Guizarnótegui case. In the meantime, Guizarnótegui made the purchases required by the companies using his own credit, without the benefit of either money in advance or a valid contract. In consequence, the merchant houses in Mexico charged him 9 percent interest until the troops received their salary the following January, instead of the preferred rate of 5 percent that he had to pay on the balance thereafter. Guizarnótegui added the extra amount to his invoices, and although the habilitados did not protest at the time, when the treasury finally paid for the 1788 deliveries, it deducted the extra interest charges of 14,000 pesos from the bill.

From this point on, matters did not improve for Guizarnótegui. On his way to deliver the first order of goods to Chihuahua in December 1787, and just outside the city, a band of Apache attacked, wounded him, and took 1,500 pesos' worth of merchandise. For this loss Guizarnótegui received no reimbursement, although the contract stated that the government should bear the risk of loss during transport while under protection of a military escort. In addition, Guizarnótegui's agent in Chihuahua, Justo Pastor de Madariaga, received 21,000 pesos from the treasury in Chihuahua before the audiencia suspended payment on the contract. After sending 10,000 pesos to Guizarnótegui in Mexico City and purchasing more than 30,000 pesos' worth of goods from Michoacán with the addition of money raised from Guizarnótegui's store in Chihuahua, the intendant of Durango ruled that the entire amount had required his prior approval. In order to pay back the treasury in Chihuahua for the 21,000 pesos already spent, Guizarnótegui again had to sell material from his own store in October 1788.

Finally, the assessor of the Real Hacienda ruled that the comandante general had acted within his rights, and in September 1788 Viceroy Flores provisionally approved the contact with Guizarnótegui, pending final approval from the king. Carlos III died the following December, delaying any final confirmation still further. Guizarnótegui received reimbursement for the first deliveries nine months after the fact, and then not enough to cover his purchases in Mexico City alone. Ugarte y Loyola suggested that, by guaranteeing the annual subsidy of the troops for the 1789 orders, Guizarnótegui might reduce the premium paid for his purchases in Mexico City, but the contractor felt that lack of definitive approval from the viceroy would make such a guarantee worthless. Guizarnótegui bought his supplies under the same terms as before. Upon making his deliveries in January 1789, the habilitados from the presidios paid only 21,561 pesos on a balance of 134,982 pesos. The remaining 108,421 pesos were due the following July, when the troops received the second half of their salary, but Guizarnótegui only collected 2.5 percent on the balance and had to pay the full 5 percent premium to his creditors in Mexico City. The following year proved slightly better, because the viceroy approved 40,000 pesos prior to Guizarnótegui's purchases, but without a larger amount forthcoming in advance the presidios saw little improvement in their final bill.

At least partially in order to make up the profit of which this bureaucratic labyrinth had deprived him, Guizarnótegui resorted to various devices that did not help his position in the eyes of the authorities. In the invoice presented to the Presidio of Santa Fe covering the deliveries for 1788, Guizarnótegui included interest at 9 percent for the full year instead of the four months that had elapsed between his purchases in October 1787 and the payment received in February 1788. Guizarnótegui charged 18 reales per arroba for freight instead of the 16 reales mentioned in his contract; furthermore, he also sold identical goods more cheaply to a local merchant than to the soldiers. The next year Guizarnótegui not only included in his invoice the 9 percent interest charge for the entire year but also extended it to cover the 9 percent purchasing commission as well. An official from the Presidio of Carrizal made this accusation and added that many of the goods were not of the quality ordered.[50] Complaints that Guizarnótegui had delivered goods of inferior quality prompted an extensive review of his merchandise, resulting in a comparison of the prices charged by other merchants in Chihuahua.

Governor Concha wrote in 1789 that the pay of the soldiers from the Presidio of Santa Fe "was sufficient to maintain themselves without indigence," hardly testimony to the success of the new system. According to the governor, "the apparent advantages of the contracts [with Guizarnótegui] absorb everything, and not even one-half a real enters in specie. In the statement for this year [1789] (the invoice of which I do not think very truthful, paying attention to the comparison with other people who similarly came from

Mexico and brought suitable goods), 14,000 pesos of goods were included, and with a surcharge of 4,000. This disaster forces the soldier to consume all that he has only to clothe himself poorly, and necessitates his working and personally cultivating his own land in order to eat."[51] Concha requested that the viceroy give this problem his highest consideration.

After another review by the newly appointed auditor of the Provincias Internas, Comandante General Ugarte y Loyola allowed the full interest expenses incurred by Guizarnótegui in 1787 while making the purchases for the 1788 deliveries. Even though Guizarnótegui had operated without sufficient funds paid in advance, and without a valid contract, Ugarte y Loyola limited reimbursement for the 1789 and 1790 contracts to a 5 percent premium. For the two remaining years of 1791 and 1792, Guizarnótegui could charge no premium on any goods paid for upon delivery to the presidio habilitados.

Guizarnótegui had seen enough of the business of supplying the presidios after Ugarte y Loyola's ruling of April 1790. Nine members of the consulado of Chihuahua accepted a contract to supply provisions for the presidios in 1791, and at terms far more costly to the soldiers than those given by Guizarnótegui. The companies bore the cost of the 9 percent premium for credit, 4 percent purchasing commission, excise taxes, and packing and freight costs and still had to provide escorts for the merchandise during the journey to Chihuahua.[52]

The travail of Guizarnótegui demonstrates a conscious decision at the highest levels of Spanish colonial administration to provide a fiscal and administrative solution to the inadequacies of supply to the northern presidios. The episode also shows the obstacles to the effective implementation of Bourbon policies inherent in the new articulation of Spanish administrative power in the northern provinces. Like the king's request for New Mexican elk for the royal zoo, reform of the supply system proceeded from the center along a descending hierarchy of command and responsibility. Reform involved trying out different proposals to fix identifiable problems and achieve rational goals with improved efficiency. The response of Bourbon officials to the difficulties of maintaining currency in circulation in the Provincias Internas followed a similar pattern. The analogy holds for the military response of the Bourbon government to the "Defensive Crisis" of the 1770s. A regional plan administered, supported, and coordinated centrally did have a substantial influence on the alliances made by the Spanish with neighboring Native American groups.

As long as the system performed as expected, Bourbon authority achieved meaningful results in the north. When administrative measures did not have their intended effect, Bourbon officials had little time for rethinking their larger strategy, but they did have an interest in local and regional solutions to the problem. The protest of the New Mexican governors prevented the Bourbon governments from enforcing their prohibition of punche cultivation in New Mexico. Regional officials in Chihuahua and Durango had success in offering solutions for financing the presidios and extending libranzas to northern merchants. The overriding interest in promoting economic development in the Provincias Internas among officials like Comandante General Croix and his successors served to add some flexibility to the system. Like the request for pelicans broadcast throughout the northern provinces, the broad strokes of Bourbon policy flowed in one direction, but when the governor of New Mexico responded that pelicans did not live in New Mexico, at least the viceroy listened.

IN SEARCH OF INTERREGIONAL TRADE

Spanish officials thought that many of the difficulties that plagued the New Mexican economy would disappear if the settlers could trade with the Spanish provinces near New Mexico. In the late 1790s a report to the administrators of the tithe in Durango expressed the belief "that if this province [New Mexico] had neighboring provinces for the facility of its commerce, because of the hardworking character of its inhabitants and the abundance of the land, as much in livestock as in wool and cotton, it would be without dispute the most thriving province in America."[53] During the last quarter of the eighteenth century, New Mexican governors attempted to open new roads between New Mexico and other provinces in order to provide additional avenues for commercial activity. From 1776 to 1809, Spanish officials mounted explorations to provide access from New Mexico west to Alta California, southwest to Sonora, and east to Texas and Louisiana (see Map 8). With an eye toward the economic development of the north, provincial governors and the officials of the Provincias Internas supported these exploratory expeditions.

In 1747 Fray Juan Miguel Menchero, along with the captain of the El Paso Presidio, Alonso Victores Rubí de Celís, undertook the first exploration from New Mexico in the direction of Sonora.[54] Although the campaign did not have much success against the Gileño Apache, the Spanish did reach the headwaters of the Gila, Mimbres, and San Francisco Rivers, near the present border between New Mexico and Arizona. In doing so, Menchero and Rubí de Celís demonstrated the potential for a permanent route between New Mexico and Sonora. Somewhat later, the governor of Sonora, Francisco Antonio Crespo, took up the idea of finding a suitable route to New Mexico. In 1774 he proposed to the viceroy that he authorize an exploratory expedition. Governor Mendinueta of New Mexico received a copy of this request and responded, suggesting two possible routes for a road and concluding: "The distances are not great, nor would there be much difficulty in promoting communication between New Mexico and Sonora, provided the Apache

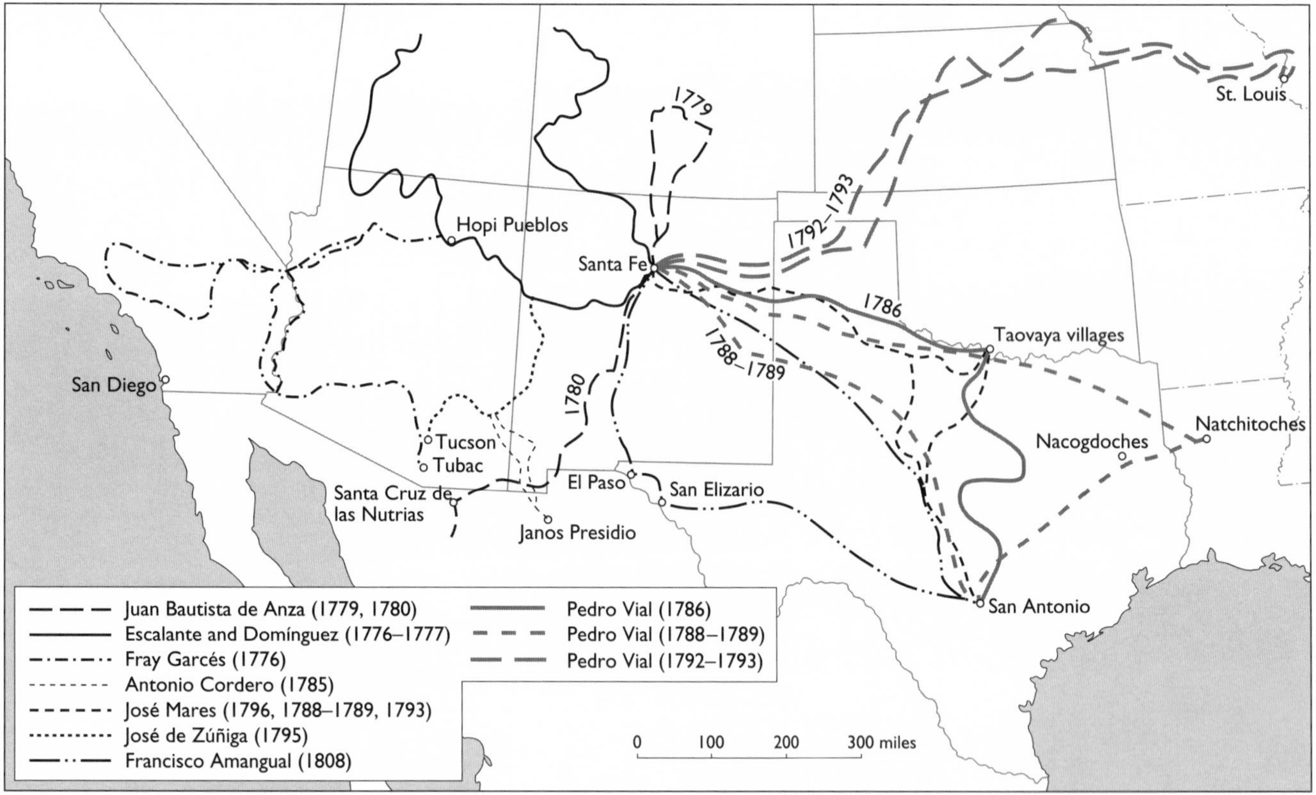
St. Louis
1779
1792–1793
Hopi Pueblos
Santa Fe
1786
Taovaya villages
1788–1789
San Diego
1780
Natchitoches
Nacogdoches
Tucson
Tubac
El Paso
San Elizario
Santa Cruz de
las Nutrias
Janos Presidio
San Antonio
Juan Bautista de Anza (1779, 1780)
Escalante and Domínguez (1776–1777)
Fray Garcés (1776)
Antonio Cordero (1785)
José Mares (1796, 1788–1789, 1793)
José de Zúñiga (1795)
Francisco Amangual (1808)
Pedro Vial (1786)
Pedro Vial (1788–1789)
Pedro Vial (1792–1793)
0
100
200
300 miles

Map 8. Northern interregional explorations, 1770–1800. *Source:* Adapted from Warren A. Beck and Ynez D. Haase, *Historical Atlas of the American West* (Norman: University of Oklahoma Press, 1989), map 19 ("Explorations, 1772–1792").

did not interfere. But if these are at war, seldom if ever could citizens from one or the other provinces get through because whatever commerce there might be established would be so small that a sufficient number of people could not be gotten together to risk it."[55] Apache hostility or other considerations must have intervened, for Crespo did not launch his proposed search for a route to New Mexico.

The next expedition to explore the issue also originated from Sonora, but without the financial support of the Crown. In 1776 Fray Francisco Garcés left the Mission of San Xavier de Bac, just southeast of Tucson, on one of a number of exploratory trips to make contact with the Hopi Pueblos in northwestern Arizona near the New Mexico border (see Map 8). He reached the Hopi that summer but, finding them unreceptive to proselytizing, returned to Sonora after sending a letter to the missionary in Zuñi Pueblo with an Acoma Indian who had taken refuge at Hopi. Garcés recounted the lack of courtesy that the Hopi had displayed toward him and wrote that he planned to return with gifts, Christian Indians, and troops from Sonora. Garcés also had commerce with New Mexico in mind when he wrote: "We shall have a means of communicating with one another by the establishment of a presidio on the Colorado [River], and also send cattle from that province [New Mexico]. And it may be possible to make trade with Sonora safe, because the Apache who can prevent it are friends with the Yumas and Jomabas, who, I believe, may soon have [missionary] fathers."[56]

The same year, Fray Atanasio Domínguez and Fray Silvestre Vélez de Escalante began an expedition from Santa Fe to Monterey in newly settled Alta California. Proposing the ambitious project to Governor Mendinueta, Fray Escalante explained that it would "facilitate the most useful establishment of some presidios and missions in the vicinity of the Gila and Colorado Rivers, the passage by land to Monterey, the reduction of the Moqui [Hopi Indians], and the commerce of these provinces [New Mexico] with those of Sonora and California."[57] The journey of Escalante and Domínguez lasted almost a year and a half (see Map 8). Their party covered a huge swath of territory, circling through portions of Arizona, Utah, and Colorado before returning to Santa Fe. Governor Mendinueta had decided to supply the expedition with provisions and materials in the hope that Domínguez and Escalante could open a road to Alta California.

Upon the return of the expedition, Bernardo de Miera y Pacheco expressed in his letter to the king his encouragement for continuing the effort to interconnect the region: "The basic and fundamental principal for securing the good success of that proposed [further exploration] is in the development of the Port of Monterrey [*sic*, Alta California] with the other settlements and the immediate transportation to these, by sea along the coast of Nueva Galicia, with all that is necessary for good colonization. And I suppose it to be truly the will of Your Majesty for the facilitation of transit and communication from the two provinces of Sonora and New Mexico with the ports that are populated and those to be settled on the coast of California. One finds this necessary to supply the settlements and the soldiers of those presidios with cattle, sheep, and horses."[58] In arguing the merits of their exploration to the king, Miera y Pacheco and Escalante appealed to the larger regional vision of Gálvez, of which the recent foundation of the missions and future growth of communities in Alta California formed a crucial part.

The highest officials of New Spain focused their attentions on the project of opening up the northern provinces to interregional trade. In 1774 Juan Bautista de Anza, then a lieutenant colonel serving in Sonora, journeyed along the Gila River from the Sonoran Presidio of Tubac to Monterey in northern California, accompanied by thirty-five men. A report written two years later by the royal engineer, Miguel Costanzó, considered the possibility of supplementing the lines of communication between the northern provinces. The *Camino Real* ran northward from Mexico City to Chihuahua, then branched out to the other provinces in the north. Costanzó estimated that 375 common leagues lay between Santa Fe and Monterey in northern California.[59] The most direct line from the Presidio of Tubac to Santa Fe measured 243 leagues, but in practice a road would require a journey of at least 300 leagues due to the winding Gila River, the need to circumvent Hopi lands, and the difficulty of the terrain. The royal engineer compared this proposed route with the road that already linked Mexico City to Chihuahua: the distance from point to point was 320 leagues, yet the Camino Real was 400 leagues long.

With this information in hand as he assumed his position as comandante general in 1777, Viceroy Bucareli outlined his concept of connecting the northern provinces in his instructions to Croix. The New Mexican capital of Santa Fe, he explained, occupied the same latitude as the famous port of San Francisco in northern California, just garrisoned by the king's soldiers the previous June. The king had given him the responsibility of establishing communication with the new colony and exploring the terrain between Alta California and Sonora, "so that giving all the possessions of the king a hand, they would be able to aid each other reciprocally, and not remain ignorant of what we have so close by." Bucareli stated that Anza's successful expedition of 1774 had persuaded him that these plans remained feasible. Anza's proven record of dealing with hostile Indians in Sonora and carrying out pathbreaking expeditions won him appointment as governor of New Mexico the following year—over the objection of Croix, who wanted him to continue his work in Sonora.[60]

From the beginning of his tenure as governor, Anza planned an expedition to forge a route and stimulate trade between the province under his charge and Sonora. At first he conceived of the subjugation of the Hopi

Pueblos as the first stage in establishing a road to Sonora, following the lead of Fray Menchero and Fray Garcés. The chances of success seemed propitious in 1779, due to a two-year drought that had left the Hopi in dire straits. During the early part of the next year Anza led an expedition for the relief of the Hopi. He had hoped to use this opportunity to establish contact with the troops based in Sonora at some point between the two provinces. He also intended to construct a new road using 100 militia recruited from among the New Mexican settlers. Croix suspended the expedition because the Crown lacked the resources with which to pay the settlers whom Anza wished to use. Instead, Anza had to content himself with providing the Hopi with food and with returning to New Mexico with about 200 Hopi refugees, whom he resettled in the province.[61]

Events outside New Mexico made the opening of a shorter road from New Mexico to Sonora more important. In 1779, settlers in San Ildefonso de Cieneguilla in western Sonora discovered huge placers of gold, providing a major boost for the existing mining activities in the area. A number of New Mexican settlers wished to travel to Sonora, either to try their luck at mining or to sell New Mexican products to prosperous miners. By November, Anza found himself responding to a request from Croix regarding support for an expedition to Sonora. Anza asked that troops from Sonora prepare to meet his men on the New Mexico side of the Río San Fernando, following the path that Fray Menchero had used in 1749. He also requested a salary of 3 reales per day for 100 militia or settlers, as well as for two soldiers from Anza's old company in Sonora. Croix replied that the treasury could not afford to pay a salary to those who participated in the expedition but that Anza should try to recruit settlers to go at their own expense, writing that "perhaps [avoiding the expense] could be achieved if benefit should accrue to the settlers of that province [New Mexico] from the outlet for products by bringing them to Sonora." By May 1780 Anza informed the comandante general that he had problems with the settlers he had recruited for the journey. Eighty people had volunteered from the jurisdictions of Albuquerque and Santa Cruz de la Cañada, but many of them had become so impatient to reach Sonora that they had left the province illegally, in advance of the expedition.[62]

In order to reach Sonora, caravans leaving New Mexico followed the Chihuahua Trail to El Paso, then turned southwest onto a trail that ran into the plains of Nueva Vizcaya.[63] Below the present New Mexico border and south of the Hatchet Mountains, the road branched either south to the Presidios of Janos and San Buenaventura in northwestern Nueva Vizcaya or northwest back into New Mexico. The latter route crossed San Luís Pass between the San Luís and the Animas Mountains and finally proceeded southward down the Guadalupe Canyon to the Sonoran Presidio of San Bernadino (1775–1780). At this point travelers turned south to reach Arispe, the residence of the comandante general, and the town of Fronteras. Alternatively, they could proceed westward to reach the northern outposts of Tubac and Tucson on the Pimería Alta.

Anza planned to explore a new route, one that promised a considerable reduction in the distance to Sonora, instead of attempting to find another path through the mountains south of the Hopi pueblos or trying to find the old path used by Fray Menchero through the valley of the San Francisco River (see Map 8). On November 9, 1780, the governor headed south, accompanied by the vecino convoy to Chihuahua and a combined force of 55 vecino militia, 36 Indian auxiliaries, and 60 troops from the Santa Fe Presidio. At Socorro the contingent separated. The convoy, met by an escort of 40 troops sent from El Paso, continued south to Chihuahua. Anza's party turned west. Proceeding south and west around the Black Range and Mimbres Mountains, the party aimed at the Presidio of Santa Cruz de las Nutrias near the headwaters of the San Pedro River, seeking to cross the Chiricahua Mountains. After forty days and 221 leagues of travel, Anza reached the El Paso–Sonora road just at the Janos Presidio in Nueva Vizcaya. Clearly disappointed, Croix wrote to Gálvez that he would "arrange matters at the end of the current year [1781], with the hope that a direct road may be found, short and passable, to open convenient and sure communication between the two provinces."[64]

Despite the intention to renew the project during 1781, neither Croix nor Anza attempted any further expeditions to connect New Mexico and Sonora directly. The smallpox epidemic that reached its worst stage in January and February 1781 probably contributed to this delay. Encouraged by Anza, now military governor of Sonora, in October 1788 Capitán Manuel de Echeagaray of the Sonoran Presidio of Santa Cruz set off on a campaign against the Gila Apache, with the intention of probing possible routes to New Mexico. Echeagaray arrived at the pass over the Mogollón Mountains leading from the San Francisco River toward Zuñi pueblo, known from the Menchero expedition, but the party had to turn back because it lacked supplies.[65]

Two other leaders, Governor Concha, who replaced Anza in New Mexico, and Enrique de Grimarest, the military commander of Sonora after Anza's death in 1788, both showed continued interest in exploration, but neither succeeded in bringing plans to fruition. Finally, in 1795 Echeagaray, now in charge of military operations in Sonora, chose Captain José de Zúñiga of the Presidio of Tucson to lead an expedition. Zúñiga succeeded in reaching Zuñi pueblo over the same route that Echeagaray had been forced to abandon seven years earlier. Comandante General Nava of the western Provincias Internas then wrote to the viceroy about the route, recommending further work on the trail so that it could be used for trade between the provinces. He estimated that a pack train could make the journey to Zuñi in twenty-two days and to Santa Fe in another fourteen. The length of the road opened by Zúñiga compared favorably with that of the old road already in use through El Paso, but the provincial authorities never developed it sufficiently to change the itinerary of the settlers and merchants who traveled between Sonora and New Mexico during the remainder of the colonial period.[66]

The quest for a viable direct trade route from Sonora to New Mexico represented one of a number of ambitious explorations with the goal of connecting New Mexico more easily with other parts of New Spain. In addition to the Domínguez-Escalante attempt to reach Monterey in 1776, the governors of New Mexico, Texas, and Louisiana combined to finance four separate expeditions between 1786 and 1793, three of them led by Pedro Vial, a remarkable explorer, diplomat, trapper, and trader of French extraction (see Map 8).[67] In 1786, Vial traveled from the mission at San Antonio de Béxar in Texas to Santa Fe, a journey that took him almost eight months. The next year Governor Anza commissioned José Mares to use Vial's diary to refine and shorten the route as he traveled back to San Antonio. After a little more than two months, Mares arrived in San Antonio in October 1788, having essentially followed the path taken by Vial. On his return, Mares attempted to travel directly from San Antonio to Santa Fe, instead of along the established but more circuitous route by way of a group of Taovaya Indian villages on the Red River. This expedition meant traveling over considerably more difficult terrain, and Mares took more than three months to return to Santa Fe. Vial expanded the journey in 1788–1789, traveling from Santa Fe to Natchitoches before arriving in San Antonio. He then completed the triangle by journeying directly from San Antonio to Santa Fe.

Three years later, Viceroy Revillagigedo II authorized, and Governor Concha of New Mexico financed, an expedition led by Vial "to open direct communication with our settlements in Illinois, . . . dependencies of the province of Louisiana." Vial traveled from Santa Fe to Saint Louis in just under four and one-half months, including six weeks during which the Kansas Indians held him and his two companions captive. Not until 1808 did Spanish authorities undertake another major trail-blazing expedition. Governor Antonio Cadero y Bustamante of Texas sent Francisco Amangual, with a large contingent of about 200 men, to Santa Fe from San Antonio. Amangual completed his journey, returning down the Chihuahua Trail to El Paso, from there to the Presidio of San Elizario, and back to San Antonio.[68]

From the proposal of Governor Crespo of Sonora in 1774 for a new route to New Mexico, to the last Spanish colonial expedition by Amangual in 1808, officials at all levels of the government of New Spain supported the investment of manpower and resources in order to establish commercial connections between New Mexico and the other provinces on the northern frontier. Like the fiscal reforms and the changes in presidial supply of the same period, the trail-blazing expeditions formed part of a larger strategy to encourage and develop economic activity within the northern provinces. The impetus for their planning and execution came less from viceregal or commandant levels of authority than from provincial governors, such as Anza, who realized that by establishing an interconnecting network they could increase the markets for provincial goods throughout the region. Assessor Pedro Galindo Navarro reported to Croix in 1780 that Anza felt that a Sonora–New Mexico road would "encourage backward settlers," since "trade circulating between both provinces would put an end to the grievous and dishonest trade that until then has been carried on with the province of Nueva Vizcaya; that besides the advantage that would be secured by there being less distance and smaller freightage, the settlers could buy effects from Europe more reasonably, and could avail themselves of opportunities to furnish labor for silver mines."[69]

Although these expeditions demonstrated that Sonora could prove closer than Chihuahua as an outlet for New Mexican trade and that caravans could also reach settlements in Texas and probably Alta California, the opening of a new trail could not, in and of itself, establish a market for New Mexican goods. When the opportunity existed, New Mexicans sold their agricultural products and livestock in exchange for money or other goods imported from central Mexico or Europe. In general, the northern provincial markets outside Nueva Vizcaya and the presidio communities had limited money or goods to offer enterprising New Mexican vecinos and merchants.

The few years of rich silver finds in Sonora in the late 1770s and early 1780s, however, coincided with New Mexico's first period of relative freedom from Comanche engagements. The appearance of mining settlements produced sudden demands for livestock and woven goods and thereby created an overland trade with New Mexico. New mines, and the migration of families to work them, stimulated trade and opened markets in ways that the new roads alone could not accomplish. The projects to open new roads and encourage interregional trade that provincial governors and viceregal officials had underwritten did not make New Mexico "without dispute the most thriving province in America," as the report to the officials of the Durango Cathedral had predicted. Increased interregional trade, on the other hand, did contribute to the New Mexican economic boom described in chapter 4.

VICEREGAL SUPPORT FOR PROVINCIAL PROJECTS

The efforts of Bourbon officials to bring the Provincias Internas into closer contact with each other marked a shift in which the Spanish government became more involved in matters perceived likely to produce direct economic benefits for the region. Once the Bourbon Reforms were under way in the northern provinces, it became clear that in order for each region to benefit from the bureaucratic and fiscal changes, administrators would have to adapt them to local needs. Accordingly, Spanish officials seemed more responsive to proposals from provincial governors requesting that the government improve specific aspects of the New Mexican economy. Requests from two New Mexican governors—one in the 1760s, the other in the 1780s—illustrate the significant change in attitudes toward direct involvement in projects that accompanied Bourbon policy in the north. After the peace and alliances of the 1780s, Bourbon administrators met suggestions for public projects with interest and, at times, financial support. In contrast, in 1762 the officials dismissed a proposal to build a gunpowder factory in New Mexico as an inappropriate decentralization of the system of royal monopolies.

The proposal to build a gunpowder factory in New Mexico began in response to news of events far from the daily affairs of the province. In a letter to Viceroy Joaquín de Monserrat, the Marqués de Cruillas, Governor Cachupín acknowledged having received a bando announcing Spain's declaration of war against England in 1762 as part of the Seven Years' War (known as the French and Indian War in the American colonies). The governor complained, however, that nearer to home New Mexicans had problems obtaining muskets for their defense. "Equally," he wrote, "they have difficulty providing themselves with the corresponding gunpowder, and only once in each year, when they leave in the month of November for the villa of San Felipe el Real de Chihuahua, 200 hundred leagues from this capital, for the sale of their goods and hides that they take out of this province, do they buy scarcely any gunpowder because their limited resources do not permit it and because of the high price that they encounter."[70] In a separate letter, Cachupín explained that although the official military supplier in each region had the responsibility of storing gunpowder for the troops' use, the great distances that separated the factory in Mexico City from each of the presidios prevented the gunpowder monopoly from effectively supplying New Mexico. To remedy this situation and to help the provincial economy, Cachupín suggested that the viceroy build a gunpowder factory in El Paso, within his New Mexican jurisdiction.[71] The El Paso area, he maintained, had the correct proportion of saltpeter, sulfur, and coal, all of the best quality for the manufacture of gunpowder. In addition, the governor pointed out that from El Paso the monopoly could easily supply Nueva Vizcaya, Sonora, and the interior of New Mexico. This location would prove more convenient to the mining regions of the north, which used gunpowder to blast the ore from the earth before extracting the gold or silver.

If the viceroy replied to the request of Governor Cachupín for a new gunpowder factory, no record of his response remains in the major archives of New Spain. More to the point, Viceroy Monserrat did not order an investigation of the merits of Cachupín's proposal, and the El Paso gunpowder factory did not receive the kind of careful consideration that similar projects would command a quarter-century later.

In contrast to the proposed gunpowder factory, the response in the late 1780s to a proposal to construct a *cuartel* in Santa Fe shows that Bourbon officials had begun to realize that local initiatives might best serve their regional economic policies. Like the gunpowder proposal, the idea was promoted to his superiors by the governor of New Mexico. Governor Concha wrote in 1787 to Comandante General Ugarte y Loyola, asking for permission to resume the plan to resettle Santa Fe in a more compact form, based upon the plan developed in 1772 by Governor Mendinueta.[72] Comandante General Croix had initially suspended and then in 1781 reinstated Governor Anza's order to relocate the inhabitants of the capital, but the Comanche invasions and the smallpox epidemic had interrupted execution of the plan. Afterward, the new opportunities brought by peace and the alliance with the Comanche encouraged the settlers to ignore the plan entirely.

At the same time, Governor Concha renewed the request of his predecessor to build a cuartel near the Presidio of Santa Fe. Governor Anza had made the original request in 1780, soon after his victory over Cuerno Verde, and at that time the presidial troops had offered to contribute more than 2,000 pesos from their fondo de retención toward their new quarters. Some of the troops, said Concha, lived 3 miles from the presidio. When an emergency occurred, the captain of the presidio could only notify these soldiers by sending runners out to shout the alarm among the dispersed homes. Housing the soldiers together in barracks, the way other presidios had already, would allow greater control in military situations. It could also "unite" Santa Fe and would help to prevent soldiers from reacting to some small incident that could shatter the peace with the recently allied nomadic Indians. Concha suggested rather pointedly, "Your Grace knows better than myself that the capital must be respectable, and that its ruin drags down the entire province." Comandante General Ugarte y Loyola recommended Concha's proposal for a cuartel to Viceroy Flores, adding: "I anticipate that it could be carried out as proposed, and that in time it would little by little give form to the settlement [of Santa Fe] without seriously disturbing the vecinos."[73]

After the viceroy and the comandante general approved the plan to build the cuartel in January 1788, there remained the twin problems of where to build it and how to pay for its construction. Governor Concha first considered proposals to locate the building at Analco, one of the districts within Santa Fe, or on land outside the town in the direction of Santo Domingo pueblo. He rejected the first location because it was too far from water and pasturage. In addition, it would have cost 2,000 pesos to purchase the existing vecino houses. The Santo Domingo and Santa Clara Indians, however, had planted crops on the second proposed site, and they refused to give up the land voluntarily. Instead, Concha proposed to build the cuartel in back of the governor's house in the center of Santa Fe, where he would have to compensate only three vecinos, albeit some of the capital's richest residents.[74] This he would do by offering them land elsewhere in exchange for their houses.

In July 1788 Ugarte y Loyola authorized Concha to begin cutting the wood and gathering supplies for construction while he worked out a proposal to finance the project for the approval of the viceroy. The comandante general found 2,000 pesos that had been set aside in 1772 to build the outpost at Robleado—but never used. Ugarte y Loyola made available to Concha from the treasury in Chihuahua another 1,995 pesos left over from the construction of the Presidio of San Sabás. The 3,995 pesos allocated represented just under half of the total cost for constructing the cuartel, estimated at 8,000 pesos. Concha then instructed Vicente Troncoso to act as his agent, to travel with the convoy to Chihuahua, and to arrange for supplies. Concha also charged Troncoso with drawing up contracts with craftsmen who were needed for the construction but who could not be found in New Mexico. In addition, Concha asked Ugarte y Loyola to find a mason, "perhaps one that could have been condemned in one of the *obrajes;* those that we have here serve very poorly."[75]

By the middle of 1789, Governor Concha had to petition the comandante general for more funds. He reported that the workers had completed one side of the compound, containing 33 houses, and had made 30,000 adobe bricks. The cuartel workers received a monthly salary and a daily food ration. The governor paid part of the salary in kind with goods imported from Mexico. To pay those who provided the grain and vegetables for the workers, Concha needed 1,000 pesos in cash. Furthermore, the owners of the houses expropriated to provide space for the cuartel now demanded money instead of the land that Concha had originally offered. The governor blamed his predecessors for this "embezzlement," having granted land enough "so that today there are not two *varas* of land without an owner in the entire province." To finish construction and to pay the owners, Concha requested another 2,000 pesos. Accordingly, instead of paying 2,000 pesos to a number of smaller house owners in Analco, the governor placed a little more than 370 pesos into the hands of three of the wealthiest families in the province.[76]

Governor Concha also sought to justify to his superior the need for a cuartel that was larger and more costly than those in some of the other presidios. Almost all of the soldiers who served in New Mexico, he claimed, came from the first families of the country or were descended from the original conquistadores of New Mexico. These men habitually enjoyed comfortable and well-made houses, so the cuartel had to meet their high standards. If the new accommodations proved uninviting, more than half of the troops would ask for their licenses [in order to request transfers], and replacements would take place here, but with "Genízaros and people of bad quality, and worse habits with whom it would be difficult to arrange it so that they work with the good ones who remained, and in the future none of the class of the first would enter to serve." Ugarte y Loyola appeared to accept these arguments, and the explicit appeal to ethnic hierarchy, and made a request for 3,000 pesos for the cuartel in Santa Fe—which the viceroy approved.[77]

Not surprisingly for a large public project, the cuartel was still under construction in 1790. The governor had anticipated that it would be completed in 1790, but in November he informed the comandante general that heavy rains during the previous summer had delayed construction and had destroyed about 8,000 adobe bricks that had been prepared in the spring. No doubt precipitated by the elements, the soldiers had moved into 98 of approximately 105 houses even though many must have been in various stages of completion. Construction continued until October of the following year, raising the cost of the barracks to more than 9,200 pesos instead of the estimate of 8,000 pesos made years earlier. The treasury of Chihuahua had paid the 6,995 pesos authorized by Ugarte y Loyola. In the end, Governor Concha provided 538 pesos from his own funds, his officers contributed another 366 pesos, and the soldiers of the presidio gave up 1,000 pesos from their fondo de retención to help make up the shortfall. The remaining sum came from selling leftover oxen, tools, and goods in order to supply wages for the project.[78]

The plans drawn by the engineer Juan de Lagaza Urtundúa (Figure 7) shows the building as it looked shortly after its completion. The drawing indicates that 101 two-room houses formed the walls around the grounds of the cuartel. The sergeants lived in larger houses, which made up three of the corners of the cuartel. The entire structure measured about 1,000 feet (360 varas) on its north and south sides. The present Palace of the Governors formed the southeast corner of the earlier compound. The cuartel held thirty-three houses on the west side and thirty on the east. The entire length along the east and west sides totaled 1,200 feet (440 varas). In 1807 Zebulon Pike described the general appearance of the finished cuartel from his experiences while he was a captive of New Mexican Governor Joaquín Real Alencaster: "In the center [of Santa Fe] is the public square, one side of which forms the flank of the soldiers' square, which is closed and in some degree defended by round towers in the angles which flank the four curtains: another side of the square is formed by the palace of the governor, his guard-houses."[79]

The construction of the cuartel in 1788–1791 represented a significant investment in the New Mexican local economy, even though Spanish officials did not undertake the project for that reason. Viceroy Flores and Comandante General Ugarte y Loyola based their decision on military grounds. Bourbon officials built new presidios throughout the Provincias Internas during the last quarter of the eighteenth century. Beginning in the 1790s, engineers and other officials drew up plans to build cuarteles for presidios

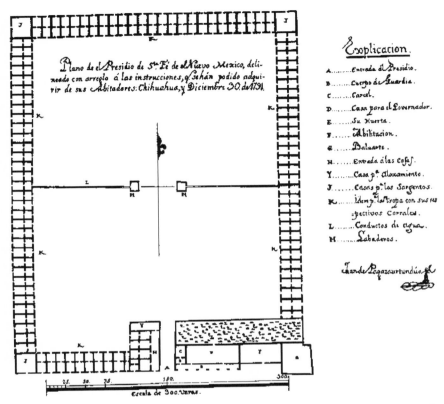

Figure 7. Plan of the cuartel, Presidio of Santa Fe, 1791. *Source:* Plano del Presidio de Santa Fe del Nuevo México . . . , Chihuahua, December 30, 1791, AGN: PI 161: 4, 51, shown in Archivo General de la Nación, *Catálogo de ilustraciones* (Mexico City: Centro de Información Gráfica del Archivo General de la Nación, 1979), 1:67, no. 159. Illustrated in Marc Simmons, *Spanish Government in New Mexico* (Albuquerque: University of New Mexico Press, 1968), xxii.

or outposts in San Francisco, Alta California, and Nuevo Santander y Nuevo León.[80] The project in Santa Fe, however, provides an opportunity to assess just how such projects stimulated the local economy.

During the spring of 1789, Governor Concha ordered that any unemployed vecino or Genízaro man between the ages of fourteen and fifty could be required to work on the cuartel. All of those who did not own land, those who did not rent farmland, and those who were not in the service of a landowner had to report to the local alcalde mayor. The governor received a list from each jurisdiction of the laborers who qualified for selection. Upon the recommendation of the alcalde, those who presented themselves voluntarily would receive preferable assignments.[81]

Governor Concha recognized the direct economic benefit generated by this public works project. In his order, Concha wrote that choosing men for employment "by means of a salary according to one's application and assigned work could contribute to the maintenance and subsistence of their families." The record of salaries beginning in May shows that around forty men worked on the construction crew during the months of active construction. Of the 9,214 pesos spent on the building, about half went for wages. Except for the skilled workers, the laborers received most of their wages in kind. The governor had arranged to import desirable goods from Mexico for this purpose, and in addition distributed corn and vegetables.

The wages paid to workers by the project encouraged key areas of the local economy. They also stimulated markets and production by providing an infusion of currency. More than 74 percent of the money raised for the cuartel went toward paying cash wages or to purchase goods and materials that came from New Mexico. Presidio officials bought oxen, large amounts of maize and vegetables, and pottery made by the neighboring Pueblos. They also contracted for building materials and furniture to adorn the new quarters. Furthermore, although the presidio paymaster paid a good deal of the wages in kind, he spent more than 40 percent of the cuartel's total budget on goods and services that he purchased with cash in the form of silver. As silver began to circulate in the hands of vecinos, their economic activities began to create new markets and extend commerce within the province.

The governor justified the next project in purely economic terms. In the same report of 1788 in which Concha discussed the progress made on the cuartel, he asked Viceroy Flores to consider establishing an obraje in New Mexico that would encourage and develop one of the cottage industries already flourishing among vecinos:

> The women weave cotton and wool more perfectly than in Spain. The abundance of the later class or kind, and the supply of water and firewood that lend itself to this town [Santa Fe], could facilitate the establishment of a complete obraje for the manufacture of *paños* and other woven goods. From the end of October when the harvest is gathered to the beginning of May when one starts to sow, all of the people are inactive and scarcely leave their house because of the increase of the snow and the extreme cold. This exact time could be invested in spinning and weaving, by means of which they could clothe themselves with little cost, supply the company what is necessary for its consumption, and would gain some money which they barely know.

Concha apparently conceived of the obraje as a means of organizing the existing vecino weavers and providing the training and expertise needed to improve the quality of New Mexican woven products.

Concha's interest in starting an obraje in New Mexico followed the establishment of obrajes during the 1780s in both Chihuahua and Durango. With the approval of Comandante General Ugarte y Loyola, the municipal council of Chihuahua purchased an obraje in 1786 from a prominent local merchant, Don Manuel de Urquidi, for 5,500 pesos.[82] The council ran the business, using the labor of convicted criminals until 1810, when the disturbances associated with the Hidalgo rebellion apparently affected both the supply of wool and the demand for the finished textiles produced in the obraje.

Viceroy Flores wrote Ugarte y Loyola regarding the New Mexican governor's request, noting that the project could be useful and asking him to provide information about any undertaking like this that had been attempted in the past. He also asked about any royal order concerning such a project that could help Flores determine its merits. A month later, Ugarte y Loyola replied that, in his opinion, building an obraje in Santa Fe would not prove effective at the present time, mostly due to the cost of setting up the enterprise. Ugarte y Loyola referred the viceroy to the proposals of Bachiller Miguel Hernández Hidalgo and of Don Martín Mariñelarena and Don Manuel de Urquidi to establish the obrajes in Durango and Chihuahua, respectively. The Supreme Council of the Indies had approved of the project in Durango, with the limitation that the obraje produce coarse textiles that would not compete with commerce coming from Europe and that Mariñelarena and Urquidi put up the required investment money. Bachiller Hidalgo had advanced 50,000 pesos of his own funds in 1784 to start the Durango obraje. Accordingly, Ugarte y Loyola had no objections to doing something similar in New Mexico, as long as funds could be found. The viceroy referred the matter to the fiscal of the Real Hacienda, Ramón Posada, who wrote: "The respondent considers that [the obraje project proposed by the governor of New Mexico] would be very helpful to the progress of the commerce and industry of that province, but it has a serious difficulty: that [the proponents] lack models, teachers, implements, and all of the necessary funds that they would not be able to defray on the account of the royal treasury, nor is there a fund, or the means which by they could be remitted." The fiscal concluded that Viceroy Flores should tell Governor Concha that a license could be granted for an obraje if he could find an interested person to finance its construction. The viceroy agreed with this pronouncement and conveyed his decision to the comandante general, who in turn notified Governor Concha.[83]

While the officials responsible for the Provincias Internas became more interested and involved in the economic progress of the region, in 1788 they stopped short of providing the resources needed for a project justified only by the beneficial effects it might have on the New Mexican economy. However, in 1803, on behalf of the consulado of Veracruz, Comandante General

Nemesio Salcido asked for extensive information regarding the economy of the province. A similar request made in 1788 to Governor Concha had elicited his proposal to build an obraje in New Mexico. Governor Chacón's response reopened the entire matter. Chacón again pointed out that the vecinos took up all sorts of crafts due to both necessity and natural industry and that their products suffered only from their lack of knowledge and proper training. In the conclusion of the report, the governor noted that "the province is not really as poor as is normally supposed and that its natural decadence and depression consists of the lack of promotion and instruction in agriculture, commerce, and the arts." In fact, the governor had already arranged for some skilled artisans to assist in improving the production of crafts in the province. In 1798, at least two spinners formerly condemned to the obraje at the Hacienda of Encinillas arrived in New Mexico to help educate people in the local textile industry.[84]

This time the comandante general and his superiors took action. Shortly after Governor Chacón's report, the Real Hacienda contracted two master weavers, the brothers Juan and Ignacio Ricardo Bazán, to move to New Mexico to teach their art to the vecinos. However, Ignacio Ricardo fell ill in Durango, so the Bazán brothers did not reach New Mexico until March 3, 1807; once there, they stayed for at least seven years.[85] During the service of the Bazán brothers, woven goods became one of the leading exports of late colonial New Mexico. Although the success of the industry did not depend on the two master weavers from central Mexico, in his report on New Mexico Pedro Bautista Pino, the provincial representative to the Spanish Cortes of 1812, singled out the contribution the Bazán brothers made to weaving: "Within recent years we have witnessed the introduction of fine looms for cotton by an expert sent there by the government. Although I call this fine weaving, I do so in reference to that which was formerly woven, for this fine cloth is hardly better than coarse goods in comparison with the fine materials from China, with which we are all familiar."[86]

The obraje proposal of Governor Concha and the eventual contract with the Bazán brothers afford a good vantage point from which to view the Bourbon efforts to aid the New Mexican economy. Spanish officials showed a sincere interest in the projects the governor promoted to develop the provincial economy. They agreed with local assessments that New Mexicans needed to develop attractive goods for export that in turn could help them extend the province's participation in economic activities throughout the Provincias Internas. Spanish officials had little difficulty supporting public projects such as the new cuartel, which might indirectly invest in the local economy. On the regional level, Bourbon officials followed the same logic in response to regional problems like the scarcity of specie and tight credit in the north and the problem of presidio supply. However, when asked to invest directly in local projects that purported to address the central problems of the New

Mexican economy, Bourbon officials demurred. Faced with the choice between starting an obraje or contracting for the services of two master weavers to instruct vecinos, the Spanish government preferred to fine tune the existing system. Even so, government support for provincial projects, such as it was, did have a beneficial economic effect.

ASSESSING THE BOURBON REFORMS IN NEW MEXICO

Curbing the raids of Indian groups on the frontier represented only one aspect of the Spanish struggle to protect the portions of Nueva Vizcaya, Coahuila, and Nuevo León that possessed mining wealth and significant populations. Bourbon officials consciously and energetically pursued a wide variety of fiscal and administrative policies—even ones requiring direct action and investment—calculated to foment growth within the northern provinces. Spanish officials combined military action with a new interest in actively developing the economy of the north, both to aid in its long-term defense and, ultimately, to produce growth and revenue for the region and the Real Hacienda. On a regional level, government officials and local elites worked to modify established fiscal policy to increase the availability of credit and bills of exchange in order to accommodate commercial transactions. Bourbon officials also showed a keen awareness of the effect that the royal expenditures used to defend the north could have on the local and regional economy and a willingness to use fiscal and administrative measures to increase the benefits of their investment.

New Mexico received specific attention from colonial officials, due to its relatively large population, its perceived capacity for economic growth, and the success that New Mexicans had against the Comanche and Apache under the leadership of Governors Mendinueta and Anza. The decisions and policies of the late colonial regime did not always bring success. Despite their intentions, the Bourbon state could not overcome problems introduced by bureaucratic inertia and inadequate resources. Against the background of these institutional difficulties, Spanish officials struggled with questions of which actions might best aid the economy and general welfare of New Mexicans.

Alongside the prominent role that New Mexico played in the military strategy for protecting the northern provinces, regional and local officials and administrators made a conscious commitment to use the resources of the Bourbon state to guide further economic development in the region. Bureaucratic and administrative solutions to vexing questions about taxation, the circulation of money and credit, and the role that military procurement played in the economic health of the northern provinces occupied the energies of people at all levels of the Bourbon government. Their concern for correcting what they saw as the key impediments to economic development in the region illustrate at once the sincerity of Bourbon policies in the north and their limitations in solving large, complex, and intractable problems. Nonetheless, Bourbon actions to defend the north and to manage state resources and monetary policies with an eye toward their effects on the regional economy provided part of the foundation for the New Mexican economic boom that followed in the 1790s.

CHAPTER FOUR

New Mexican Economic Development, 1780–1820

After the mid-1780s, respite from constant raids and the system of New Mexican alliances with the Comanche and other Plains peoples made possible the settlement and, at times, the resettlement of land that the previous era of hostility had rendered inaccessible. For vecinos, the opening of new lands proved fortuitous given Governor Concha's complaint in 1789 "that today there are not two varas of land without an owner in the entire province." During the 1790s, vecinos began a process of applying for grants to unsettled lands upon which to found new villages. The established centers of the vecino population provided families of settlers who began to build new villages along the river valleys, the areas that afforded fertile, irrigatable land. Settlements radiated outward from the more densely populated "source" settlements, expanding the vecino territory around Taos, Abiquíu, into the Mora Valley, and south and west of Albuquerque—a process that continued for almost a century.[1] An expanding vecino population eagerly absorbed new areas for agriculture and livestock. As a result, vecino villagers increased the production of foodstuffs and crafts, fuel for a boom in economy activity in the province.

New Mexico's good economic fortunes began just as most of New Spain experienced one of the worst droughts and subsequent famines of the century. Due to lost harvests in the central Mexico and the Bajío beginning in 1783, the scarcity of maize and other foodstuffs and the unusually high prices caused widespread starvation and loss of life. The administrator of the royal monopolies at San Juan del Río (north of Durango) could not send his remittance due to lack of food for his mules (see chapter 3). The famine of the mid-1780s provided one of the reasons for extending the use of libranzas in the Provincias Internas. The price of cereals at the *alhóndiga* in Chihuahua reached 7.5 pesos per fanega in May 1787, and wheat brought a peso less.[2] In

1786, the worst year for the Bajío, the price of maize in Guanajuato stopped a little above 5 pesos a fanega. Drought and dearth did not visit New Mexico in 1783–1787, as it did in Nueva Vizcaya; nor did it appear in 1789–1791, when it struck the province's new Indian allies.

By the last decades of the eighteenth century the internal economy of New Mexico operated as a vast system for extracting foodstuffs and commercial goods for export. The system complemented the annual trade caravan to Chihuahua and the other southern destinations. In his economic report of 1803, Governor Chacón made a distinction between the export trade to Chihuahua and the various types of commercial activity carried on inside the province:

> The internal commerce is carried out by twelve or fourteen merchants who are neither licensed, nor are they very intelligent in this department. Of these, only two or three do business with their own capital. All that the rest handle or introduce into the province is signed for [on credit], and in the same vein they distribute or sell [the goods] from one year to the other. This results in not paying back the money more than once a year, and with much loss and arrears in the collection of the credit accounts because they normally distribute [the goods] among the poorest people and at excessive prices. [This is] making more difficult the lack of money in circulation that has begun to be known for the last three years in the province. This situation still exists to a large degree, and in particular [among] the [Pueblo] Indians who do not value anything in money.[3]

In his description Chacón contrasted the merchants engaged in the repartimiento de efectos from the hundreds of people who participated in the annual trade with Chihuahua. He also acknowledged an even greater distinction between the participants in the overland trade and a large number of less fortunate vecinos, and especially the Pueblo Indians. Of the vecinos who operated inside the province Chacón wrote: "The rest of the citizenry are so many traders who are continually dealing and bartering whatever goods that they have to hand, from which redounds substantial work for the territorial justices, who mediate in their contracts, [made with] much malice, deceit, and bad faith."

A few years earlier, in 1797, Chacón provided a more illuminating discussion of the social and economic divisions that commerce had created within New Mexican society.[4] The most numerous and opulent citizens lived in the district of Santa Fe. Regarding those not attached to the presidio, Chacón found "generally such poverty among the inhabitants that . . . they survive by virtue of connections, relations, spongers and servants, who help and provide most of them with the necessities." Among the people of substance Chacón numbered scarcely four who fit the role. Those who call themselves merchants, according to the governor, "are not, in so much as they have no license and what they really practice is the occupation of traveler. They must tour all of the province to sell their merchandise, and in this they invest four or six months of the year, and the rest in tilling the land that they possess. [Then] they make the trip to this capital in order to take their fruits and return to provide themselves newly, since without doing this it would be impossible to subsist." The repartimiento had not disappeared from New Mexico with the advent of the second commercial system. In fact, new economic opportunities brought by expanding production and a receptive market outside meant that enterprising New Mexicans could take up commercial practices previously reserved for the governor and alcaldes mayores.

Governor Concha gave an example of the emerging commercial repartimiento in an economic report written in 1788 for Viceroy Flores.[5] New Mexican merchants typically purchased in Chihuahua a vara of wide bretaña for 10 reales in silver and a vara of another type of cloth for 2.5 reales. They then distributed both types of cloth to their clients on credit at the standard price of 2 *pesos de la tierra* per vara. The peso de la tierra generally equaled one-fourth of a peso or 2 reales in silver. The price of the cloth at the time of distribution made it appear that the two types of merchandise were of equal value, but the merchant assigned a value to the goods brought by a client to satisfy his account at a level that ensured a profit on each transaction. "At first glance," said Concha, "this enormous difference in price seems to be an encumbrance for these merchants. That is not the case, however, because the knowledge and management that guides them [the merchants] makes it so that the distribution of their goods is the mode that produces for them great advantages." Compared with the repartimientos of midcentury illustrated in chapter 1, merchants by the 1780s profited less by coercion than through mastery of a complicated system of barter.

Vecinos who lacked land or capital could not participate directly in the new commercial system. As a consequence, they faced a loss of economic independence and social status during the late colonial period. As Governor Chacón had observed in 1797, subject to high prices and the repartimiento de efectos, the poorest vecinos often fell into debt and servitude, making it difficult for them to escape their lowly economic position. The landless entered or continued in debt peonage, became day laborers, or contracted to raise sheep for a percentage of the flock's increase. Those with land for the most part remained small farmers or ranchers.[6]

Governor Chacón pointed to the social transformation that economic growth had brought to the province at the beginning of the nineteenth century. The social effects of late colonial commercial development in New Mexico form a crucial link between changes in the provincial economy and the cultural self-definition of vecino society. A growing population created goods for its own consumption and for the export market and gave impetus to a New Mexican economy that brought with it profound changes in the social ordering of economic tasks. As New Mexicans expanded the quantity and diversity of the materials they exported, the major areas of economic activity became more closely tied to products made or controlled by the vecino population.

Two related developments, both new to the second commercial system, determined the form that Pueblo participation in the vecino economy took during the decades of economic growth. Beginning in the 1780s, vecino weavers started to produce large quantities of textiles, developing a distinctive regional style very different from the traditional Pueblo Indian manta. At the same time, with the renewal and expansion of the export trade in the 1780s, Pueblo Indians no longer accompanied vecinos in the annual caravan to sell their own produce in Chihuahua. As these economic developments occurred, they began to alter the traditions and methods of producing textiles and pottery within the pueblos. Heightened demand for exports fundamentally changed the economic relationship between the Pueblo Indians and vecinos by the close of the eighteenth century.

By the turn of the nineteenth century, when Pueblo Indians participated in the internal economy of the province, the goods they produced passed through the hands of vecino merchants and middlemen on their way to markets in Nueva Vizcaya, Sonora, and elsewhere. The process of excluding Pueblo Indians from direct participation in the export trade lessened their incentive for creating a surplus of goods for export, but, at the same time, the demands of the market increased the pressure for harnessing the productivity of the Pueblo and vecino populations. As a result, vecinos employed methods of economic coercion, long in use in other parts of New Spain, to extract goods from the pueblos when they did not respond to the incentive of the market.

Ultimately, social interaction between Pueblo Indians and vecinos became a casualty of the structural changes in the New Mexican economy. The story of blankets and pottery, the two major products of Pueblo manufacture involved in the New Mexican export economy, link the economic development of the late eighteenth century to the cultural transformations described in chapter 5.

THE ECONOMIC BOOM AND
THE SECOND EIGHTEENTH-CENTURY TRADE ECONOMY

The first commercial system of the eighteenth century depended on two separate but interacting economic spheres of production. Until the 1770s the Pueblo Indians formed the greater part of the population, harvested a larger surplus, and created the bulk of manufactured articles that formed the basis for trade within and outside the province. They participated in the vecino economy in a number of ways. Both vecinos and Pueblos had trade interests in common with the Comanche and other nomadic tribes. Pueblo men also played a part in the annual convoy to Chihuahua, trading their produce for manufactured items alongside the vecinos. The Pueblos also involuntarily supplied a portion of their produce and labor through the repartimiento and other exactions to the other economic sphere dominated by vecinos. Nevertheless, the bulk of Pueblo economic life remained outside vecino commercial activity. Apart from the ventures of the governors and alcaldes mayores to supply the Santa Fe Presidio with grain grown in New Mexico and to export surplus products to agents in Chihuahua, the vecino population produced cereals, livestock, and woven goods for exchange at the trade fairs. Hides, buckskins, Pueblo and vecino textiles, and livestock made up the bulk of the New Mexican export economy.

As long as hostilities with non-Pueblo peoples did not stop the trade fairs and annual caravans out of the province, the system continued to function. During the 1760s and early 1770s, raids by the Comanche and Ute frequently took place within a few days of the trade fairs. Nevertheless, commerce at trade fairs and exports continued. By the middle of the 1770s, however, intensified warfare had virtually stopped trade with the Comanche, and Apache activity constantly endangered communication with Chihuahua. During the period of constant fighting the Plains trade did not cease altogether, but after the wars ended in the 1780s, it never regained its earlier importance in the commercial system.[7] The large amount of trade goods given annually by Spanish authorities to the Comanche and other allied nations after 1786 may have made the trade fairs somewhat less critical as a supply source for these Indian groups.

Out of the trading system that had adapted to war, smallpox, and population growth through the 1770s emerged a second system of trade and commerce, one that would dominate economic activity for the next two decades. For the vecinos, goods produced in New Mexico replaced hides and buckskin as the leading exports after livestock. The increasing quantities of material exchanged, the change in the mix of exports, and the wider territorial markets that New Mexicans and their goods penetrated all attested to the expansion of the vecino economy in new directions. These changes within the vecino economic sphere did not leave the Pueblos untouched. The development and growth of the second commercial system toward the end of the century set in motion a reordering of the economic relationship between vecino and Pueblo Indian producers, with significant social implications for both peoples.

Expanded trade with other provinces outside New Mexico, in contrast to that of the 1760s and 1770s, marked one manifestation of the new provincial economy. A few months after he left the province, in December 1760, Bishop Tamarón wrote that the annual convoy for Chihuahua left with about 200 New Mexicans, instead of the 500–600 who usually made the journey. Many who generally traded in the south stayed home, due to the fear of Comanche attack. With the abatement of hostilities in the mid-1780s, herds of livestock that the raids of the previous decade had depleted began to recover substantially. Vecino ranchers also proved eager to expand exports to Chihuahua. Even while Governor Anza and the Comanche leaders negotiated their peace and alliance in early 1786, Comandante General José Antonio Rengel proposed increasing the frequency of the expedition to Chihuahua from one to two trips per year. Apparently Governor Anza felt the move premature, and the next year the new comandante general, Jacobo Ugarte y Loyola, suspended the second convoy.[8]

Nonetheless, in 1787 Governor Concha estimated that about 30,000 pesos' worth of "woven belts, livestock, fruit, [and] textiles of wool and cotton" went to Chihuahua. A Franciscan report of 1794 on the New Mexican missions estimated that 15,000–20,000 sheep left the province annually for Chihuahua, "and even more, having had years when one saw as many as 25,000 leaving." Juan Ysidro Campor, appointed to review the prospects for increasing the New Mexican tithe, reported in 1797 that exports did not fall below 20,000 sheep even in the worst year.[9] Vecinos consumed double that amount inside the province, and if they had a large enough market for wool in Chihuahua, they could shear another 60,000.

In fact, the number of sheep exported continued to grow during the next decade. In his report written in 1803 for the Consulado of Veracruz, Governor Chacón said that 25,000–26,000 head left New Mexico for Nueva Vizcaya and the other presidios each year. Sheep from New Mexico proved an attractive commodity in Chihuahua because they sold at a discount due to their condition after the long journey over the Chihuahua Trail. Merchants purchased them "in order to fatten them here [in Chihuahua] for one or two years during which time they always shear them promptly, and if they are compelled to cover the tithe they respond that they do not pay because they purchased [the sheep] with the wool." New Mexican *churro* sheep also generally yielded three times as much wool as did the sheep native to Nueva Vizcaya.[10]

Demand for New Mexican goods in the south proved so strong that in August 1800 an unscheduled caravan to Chihuahua "was made use of by the settlers to extract 18,784 sheep and 213 head of cattle, with other various goods consisting of wool and pelts." Zebulon Pike reported that by 1806 the caravan left twice a year, once in February and again in the autumn. That year Comandante General Nemesio Salcedo established a new trade fair held in December for the express purpose of "fomenting the commerce of New Mexico." After a good deal of discussion between Santa Fe and Chihuahua, Salcedo ordered the trade fair to commence on December 18–23, 1806, at Valle de San Bartolomé. Lieutenant Pike, using the information he had gathered about New Mexican commerce from his captors in 1807, estimated that New Mexico sent about 30,000 sheep annually to Chihuahua.[11]

Larger quantities of exported sheep and the demand for more frequent trade expeditions outside New Mexico represented manifestations of expanded production within the province and the increasing profitability of the export market. Governor Chacón estimated that the combined values of exports from New Mexico, including El Paso, had in 1803 reached 140,000 pesos annually. Provincial officials convened at Santa Fe in 1805 to discuss measures for further improving the economy. In their report, the participants estimated that if the royal treasury had collected the alcabala in New Mexico, the average value of the taxable goods exported to Chihuahua during the previous five years would have yielded revenues of 50,000–75,000 pesos annually.[12] Even though the figure for 1803 included income from wine and aguardiente from El Paso, all the sources show the rising value of exports. This in turn reflected an expanded selection of goods and a larger and more widely distributed market.

The dimensions of the New Mexican export market had broadened considerably by the early years of the nineteenth century. The 1803 report of Governor Chacón listed oxen, sheep, woolen textiles, some raw cotton, hides, and pine nuts. More than 500 settlers took part in the caravan that year, about one-third of them heading for Sonora, Coahuila, and the smaller presidios. The rest journeyed farther into Nueva Vizcaya, stopping at Chihuahua; some went on to Durango. Governor Alencaster wrote in 1808 that about 700 vecinos from New Mexico, "among them the most interested in trade and commerce, and many of the well-to-do in goods of the country," had come to Chihuahua.[13]

A greater variety of woven materials represented the biggest difference in the commodities that vecinos brought to sell in Chihuahua, compared with those marketed before the 1780s. Fray Morfí mentioned blankets, colchas, and medias, as had Nicolás de la Fora a decade earlier. Elsewhere Morfí described mantas, sayales, paño, a good quality plush, and "colchas, which in their variety of design and beauty of color are much better by comparison than those of Puebla and San Miguel El Grande, which are so widely used in New Spain." Chacón, in his economic report of 1803, identified most of these textiles as products woven on the looms of vecinos.[14] The weavers "produce, on narrow loom combs, bayetas, *sarga*, fresadas, sarapes, sayal, and jerga. . . . From cotton they make a kind of manta of twisted cord more closely woven and stronger than that of Puebla, and textiles for altar cloths and stockings." The proliferation of types of products woven on the Spanish loom underscores the increasing importance of New Mexican textiles to the second trade system.

On the other side of the commercial route, the documents show that, beginning in the late 1770s, New Mexican textiles had become integrated into the larger economy of Nueva Vizcaya. In 1777, Paymaster Joaquín Peru used woolen stockings from New Mexico to pay soldiers from the Chihuahua and

San Elizario Presidios. The records of prominent merchants operating in Nueva Vizcaya, such as Don José Antonio Iribarren, contain stockings and other New Mexican goods. Fresadas from New Mexico also appear in the inventories of Don Juan José Zambrano, head of the largest and wealthiest house of commerce in Durango, suggesting that these goods played a significant role in the interregional economy. Materials from the traditional Plains Indians fairs of New Mexico, such as hides, still appeared in Chihuahuan transactions, but less frequently. Lieutenant Pike saw "wrought copper vessels of a superior quality" made by vecinos accompanying his convoy to Chihuahua.[15] As New Mexican exports became a part of the network of commercial trade throughout northern New Spain, by the 1790s the province's exported products began to look increasingly similar to those generally produced in Nueva Vizcaya.

Sales of wool by New Mexican merchants, made possible by expanded internal production and safer trade routes, demonstrate the formation of stable commercial ties. In 1793 the Ayuntamiento of Chihuahua signed a contract with Don Miguel Ortiz of Santa Fe for him to deliver 800 arrobas (more than 10 tons) of wool to the municipal obraje the following year. The council offered a purchase price of 21 reales per arroba, provided that the amount of black wool did not exceed 30 arrobas. Since an arroba of wool generally brought 12 reales in New Mexico, Ortiz stood to make a good profit, even taking into account the freight costs. The next year, the Chihuahua obraje expanded its purchases of New Mexican wool to include a contract with Don Diego de Montoya for delivery of 200 arrobas in 1794 as well as the renewal of the Ortiz contract on the same terms as before. The Chihuahua obraje also purchased smaller quantities of New Mexican wool that arrived Chihuahua as a part of the annual New Mexican caravan. Alum from New Mexico, used in fulling textiles, also appears in the inventory of the Chihuahua obraje.[16]

These examples indicate economic activity on a scale and organization not seen in the mid-eighteenth century. At the same time that Montoya entered into the contract with the Chihuahua obraje for wool, Governor Concha made plans for his retirement from New Mexico due to poor health. The terms of the new joint enterprise reveal the productive power of the New Mexican economy in an unusually direct way.[17] Concha appointed Don Francisco Manuel de Elguea as his attorney. Elguea had already served as alférez of the presidio in Chihuahua. Using Elguea's services, Concha set up a "company of livestock, sheep, and cattle" with Don Phelipe Gonzales de Cosío, the administrator of the Real Hacienda of Encinillas. Subsidized by public funds, the hacienda housed convicts who, among other things, labored in a public obraje weaving textiles.

The new company planned to take advantage of the demand for sheep, cattle, and wool in Chihuahua. The Encinillas hacienda, located about

45 miles north of Chihuahua, afforded easy access to the region's major markets. To begin the company, Concha pledged to supply it with 6,666 head of sheep, "of all classes and ages," and 400 cattle. In October 1794 Concha delivered the livestock to Encinillas, where they joined the 1,111 sheep already owned by Cosío. Several months later the two men signed a contract that set up the company for a term of five years. Cosío took charge of caring for the animals, shearing them, and selling the wool, as well as bringing the livestock to market. The company would charge the expenses related to maintaining the herds, including any loss of animals, to the two investors, according to the size of the flock each investor had contributed, one-seventh to Cosío and the rest to Concha. At the end of the five years, the principal contributed by Concha, valued at 6,838 pesos 6 reales, would be returned. Any profit they would divide into five equal parts, three-fifths paid to Concha for his considerable investment and the rest to Cosío, "in recompense for the application, care, and hard work that he will have had in the direction and management of the company, keeping the accounts, and other things that will happen."

Where did the governor of New Mexico acquire 6,666 sheep and 400 cattle to set up a business that would provide for his retirement? From 1787 through 1793 Concha had rented the right to collect the church tithe throughout New Mexico from the Bishopric of Durango (see chapter 1). The vecinos, however, paid their share of the tithe in kind. As a result, over time Concha had ample opportunity to accumulate the herds he needed to capitalize his operation with Cosío at Encinillas in 1794.

The archbishop of Durango shared Concha's understanding of the opportunities afforded by New Mexico's integration into the northern regional economy. Concerned about the stagnant rentals from New Mexico, El Paso, and Chihuahua during the 1790s, the tithe judges of the Durango Archbishopric undertook an investigation in 1797 as to why the value of tithe rentals had lagged behind the growth in population. The investigator, Campor, confirmed that New Mexico's economy had recently flourished, buoyed by direct export of sheep from the province to Chihuahua, Sonora, and the presidios. Campor believed that the New Mexicans could expect increased gains since, "with the peace gained, this province has growth, not only of sheep, but horses, and mules as well." As proof, the investigator pointed out that for the last five or six years the troops from New Mexico were no longer forced to purchase horses and mules from the haciendas in Valle de San Bartolomé.[18] Despite the depressed value of the tithe itself, the economy of the province generated a surplus of commodities that fed a growing export trade. Campor estimated that at least 20,000 head of sheep left New Mexico, not to mention the 40,000 "that in this time are consumed in that province, being the meat most common. We may guarantee without hyperbole," he added, "that in a year they [will] have a harvest of another

60,000 head, [but] that limited by the low value of 4 reales each that they bring there, they must produce only 3,000 pesos in tithes."

Campor also reported that Concha had done very well indeed from 1787 to 1793. During his years of renting the tithe, Concha never cleared less than 8,000 pesos after expenses. In order to capitalize on the economic strength of the province the investigator recommended that the tithe judges hold an open auction for the rental, as the church had done in the past, rather than to continually award it to the governor. Campor described the financial dealings of Concha as the prime example of the problem with allowing the governors to control the tithe since, "at the time that they retire they take from that province all of the movable goods that they have obtained from the tithes to sell them in the province of Sonora or Chihuahua, and then do not pay attention to whether [the sheep are] pregnant or not, which makes the industry diminish. This happened with the last governor, Don Fernando de la Concha, when at his retirement from that province [New Mexico] he took more than 30,000 pregnant[19] sheep to those [provinces] outside." It would seem that a number of these sheep made it to the Hacienda de Encinillas to further improve the ex-governor's financial future. Moreover, the episode shows that the perception of New Mexican economic growth was widely shared both within and outside the province.

The new enterprise of Governor Concha points to the relationship between the tithe rental and the collection of the actual tithe in produce from vecino farmers and ranchers, and it suggests how both link directly to the remarkable growth of the New Mexican economy beginning in the 1780s. Figure 8 depicts the rental history of the tithe in pesos and on a logarithmic scale for a more accurate visual representation of the change in rental value. While the value of the tithe rental grew by almost 19 percent from 1760 to 1784, it jumped by 525 percent between 1784 and 1820, an annual increase of 14.6 percent compared with 0.65 percent for the earlier period.[20] Since the value of the tithe rental should bear some relationship to the annual production of New Mexicans, the growth in the rental value after 1788 suggests a more dynamic economy. However, if the New Mexican economy also experienced some inflation during this period, then the increase in the peso value of the tithe rental also reflects the declining value of the peso relative to New Mexican goods. The question then becomes, how do we know that the increase in the tithe rental does not represent only the effects of population growth and inflation, rather than greater productivity on the part of New Mexicans?

Historians of colonial Mexico have argued that inflated prices for basic foodstuffs became a major problem for a large portion of the population toward the end of the eighteenth century.[21] Several factors came into play: the effects of population growth, particularly in central Mexico; changes in the strategies that haciendas followed in order to maximize profits; and the in-

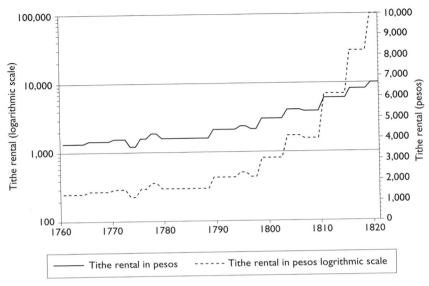

Figure 8. New Mexico tithe rentals, 1732–1819. *Sources:* ACD:DZ 3:13, 16R, 67R
(1750–1751); 2:12, 24R (1752); 3:12, 42R (1753); 3:14, 18R, 42R (1754–1755);
3:15, 18R, 82R (1756–1757); 3:16, 23R, 65R 97R, 142R (1758–1761); 3:17, 24R,
56R (1762–1763); 3:18, 25R, 61R (1764–1765); 4:21, 23R, 41R (1770–1771);
4:23 f., 28R, 63R, 100R, 139R (bis), 166R, 188R (1773–1779); ACD:DZ 1801,
1R (1800); 1802, 1R (1801–1802); 1803, 1R (1803); 1804, 1R (1804); 1806, 1R
(1805–1806); 1807, 1R (1807); 1808, 5 folios, 1R (1808); 1808, 10 folios (1797–
1801, 1799–1803, 1802–1806, 1805–1809, 1810–1814, 1811–1815, 1815–1819,
1820–1824); 1810 (1810–1811); ACD:VA 30–57 (1781–1801).

creasing production of silver. Combined, these phenomena led to large fluctuations in the price of maize and wheat, in addition to an underlying trend
toward higher prices.

For New Mexico, the change over time in the prices of the principal staples
—maize, wheat, and sheep—show the effect of inflation on the value of the
tithe rental. Changes in the prices of major foodstuffs can then be used to indicate the portion of the value of the tithe rentals caused by inflation, instead
of a change in productivity.[22] Following this technique, Figure 9 compares
the percentage change in the population of the province with the percentage change in the value of the tithe rental after accounting for inflation. Before the "Defensive Crisis" of the 1770s both the provincial population and
the value of the tithe rental grew steadily and in a closely related, parallel,
fashion. During the 1790s, however, the productivity of vecinos outpaced the
growth in population by a wide margin. Around 1800 the growth in population and tithe rental value began to resemble once again the relationship

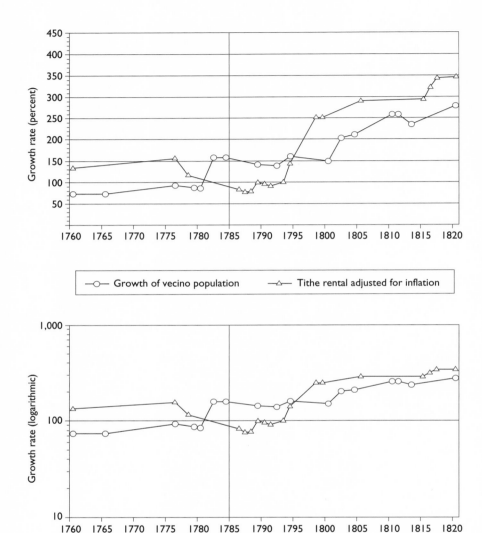

Figure 9. Growth in value of tithe rental relative to vecino population, New Mexico, 1760–1820. *Source:* Ross H. Frank, "From Settler to Citizen: Economic Development and Cultural Change in Late Colonial New Mexico, 1750–1820" (Ph.D. diss., University of California, Berkeley, 1992), 196, fig. 15.

that had existed prior to the decades of warfare, drought, and disease. Used in this manner, the evidence from the tithe provides an independent confirmation of the tremendous economic transformation of New Mexico at the end of the eighteenth century.

As the entrepreneurial interests of Governor Concha have demonstrated, the behavior of individuals in various positions of opportunity and the new strategies they began to use reflected the economic growth taking place within the province. The cessation of war with the Comanche, Ute, and Apache, a growing population, and renewed exports in the 1780s and 1790s coincided with the appearance of a new entrepreneurial attitude among New Mexicans. One illuminating episode occurred during a mission of Vicente Troncoso, an officer from the Santa Fe Presidio assigned by Governor Concha to lead an expedition to return an imprisoned Navajo chief to his people.[23] The story began in October 1787, when a Navajo leader named Antonio "El Pinto" entered Isleta Pueblo with an unauthorized trading party. In view of the recent alliance between the Spanish officials and the Navajo, and to prevent misunderstandings that might endanger peace, trade fairs could only take place with advance preparation, including a proper license from the governor. The alcalde at Isleta arrested El Pinto and brought him to Santa Fe, where Governor Concha imprisoned him. Responding to pleas from other Navajo chieftains, and recognizing a chance to garner some goodwill and learn more about the Navajo rancherías, Concha decided to release El Pinto under a Spanish escort.

The report of Troncoso describing his journey, his reception by the Navajo, and his observations of the erstwhile enemy affords a rich picture of late-eighteenth-century tribal life among the Navajo. When Troncoso saw the textiles produced by the Navajo, his response transcended that of a dedicated officer engaged in a delicate diplomatic mission for his superior.[24] He saw Navajo women weaving "sarapes, *tilmas, cotones,* stockings, sashes, and other materials for their clothing and for sale." In addition, Troncoso admired "the small vessels or *jícaras* that they call Navajosas." Immediately this New Mexican soldier thought of commercial opportunities. In a deviation from the official recounting of the daily events he observed, Troncoso described the Navajo weaving:

> These well-deserved praises that I gave without flattery cause much pleasure among all of the gathering. And even better received was the proposal that I made to them for their benefit and to better stimulate this labor with the interest that it will generate for them, . . . that their sarapes being so worthy even to the officers of the presidio, they should make all that they can until the convoy [to Chihuahua] departs. Then they should deliver them to me that I might remit them [to Chihuahua], sell them, and with the proceeds bring back spun wool yarns in good colors so that with these [the Navajo] can make them more

attractive and command higher prices and of equal utility. My ideas seemed very good to them, remaining to be executed.

No record shows whether a venture to market sarapes ever went any farther, but the incident nicely connects the sense of new commercial opportunities on the part of New Mexican vecinos to forces generating cultural change on the part of indigenous peoples. Troncoso's remarks proved prophetic in one respect. Within a dozen years, the Navajo achieved general recognition for their "frieze, blankets, and other weavings of coarse wool," which they regularly exchanged at trade fairs in New Mexico and elsewhere.[25]

As for the Navajo vessels, Troncoso apparently did attempt a commercial venture. He described the "Navajosas" as "pretty and useful, much valued not only in the Provincias Internas, but even in Mexico, as I will prove with letters from persons who have placed orders for them from me." In his drive to realize the economic possibilities of the era, Troncoso's natural reaction to Navajo material culture exhibited the heightened spirit of enterprise that characterized the new commercial foundation of the New Mexican economy.

PRIMING THE PUMP:
THE "EXTRAORDINARY EXPENSES FOR PEACE AND WAR"

All told, the most effective economic aid offered by the Bourbon government to New Mexico revolved around the defense of the province. The salaries of the troops and officers, at times amplified by reforms in the supply system, provided a continuous if not adequate source of money that served to sustain local and regional economic activity. In addition, programs financed by the Real Hacienda in the late 1780s provided infusions of additional funds at precisely the moment when the New Mexican economy could most profit, since peace with the nomadic Indian groups afforded better access to transportation and communication both within and outside the province. The construction of the cuartel in Santa Fe represented one such endeavor that pumped funds into New Mexico. On a larger scale, funds given by the Spanish government to secure and maintain the Indian alliances functioned as a colonial experiment that directly stimulated important sectors of the province's economy.

Toward the conclusion of the talks leading to the treaty between the Spanish and the Comanche, Comandante General Ugarte y Loyola approved the establishment of an Extraordinary Fund for the purpose of purchasing gifts for the Indian treaty partners. Beginning in 1787, he requested 6,000 pesos per year "for all the extraordinary attentions of this province."[26] The following year the expenditures on the "Indian Allies" totaled almost 12,000 pesos.

Each year the governor of New Mexico sent a full account of how he had managed the "extraordinary expenses of peace and war," along with receipts for each transaction.[27] A substantial portion of the goods given to the allies came from outside the province. The governor provided many of the Comanche, Navajo, Ute, and friendly Apache allies with sets of clothing, complete with shirt, trousers, vest, blankets, brightly colored capes, hats or headdresses, and sometimes ceremonial silver medallions. The New Mexicans also gave tobacco, cigars, hoes, pipes, candles, needles, *piloncillos*, bits for horses, and all sorts of cloth brought from Europe and other parts of New Spain.

In addition, a substantial portion of each year's funds went to New Mexican vecinos for the purchase of goods and materials and in payment for the labor needed to manufacture and assemble these purchases and transport them to the Indians. New Mexicans provided sheep and other livestock, meat, maize, beans, bread, tortillas, salt, and some wheat for consumption — all products of local farmers and ranchers. The Comanche and the other allied groups smoked New Mexican punche in large quantity, in addition to tobacco brought from Mexico. Vecino craftspeople provided woolen stockings and a variety of blankets, textiles, and cloth to supplement the material imported from the south.[28] Two vecino tailors, Juan Rafael Pineda and Pedro Rendón, made a good portion of the wardrobes given to the Indian allies out of both local and imported materials, presumably with the aid of assistants. The Extraordinary Fund also paid for the transport of goods and materials from the province to the Indian rancherías, for the salaries of interpreters, gunsmiths, and guides, and for other incidental expenses related to the tremendous effort made to "gratify" the Indian allies.

In addition to these gifts, the governor of New Mexico undertook two programs to help the allies obtain food and shelter. In 1787 Governor Concha ordered his lieutenant, Don José Maldonado, to oversee the building of a new pueblo on the Río Napestle (Arkansas River) for one of the Comanche groups.[29] New Mexican soldiers and vecinos carried out the construction of this settlement from July through November 1787, transporting the bulk of the necessary materials and provisions from within the province. More significant in terms of impact on the allies, large numbers of Comanche, Jicarilla Apache, and Navajo survived periods of intense famine by eating New Mexican grain and meat, especially during the summer of 1789 and the spring and summer of 1790. The receipts throughout the period from 1786 to 1791 attest to the dire situation experienced by many of the neighboring Plains Indian bands: "Value of 80 fanegas of maize to rescue the Comanche nation from the extreme necessity in which it finds itself, according to the personal representation of their general, accompanied by 130 individuals. Today, 30th of June, 1789. Concha." Spanish officials delivered at least 320 fanegas of maize alone to Indian rancherías between March 1789 and August 1791.[30]

The expenditures of the Extraordinary Fund not only aided Indian groups outside the province but consistently stimulated the sectors of the

New Mexican economy that would hold the greatest promise for economic development over the ensuing two decades. Some of the profit from the goods that officials purchased in Chihuahua to give to the Indian allies remained in the province. In addition, for laborers, provincial farmers, ranchers, vecino weavers, tailors, and other craftspeople and artisans, these purchases provided additional demand for their products and services. Between 1786 and 1804, the Extraordinary Fund purchased well over 72,000 pesos' worth of goods to dispense to the Spanish allies. During the period from 1786 to 1791, the accounts of the fund show that the governor used slightly under one-quarter of the money under his control for direct purchases of goods and services within New Mexico.[31]

Figure 10 illustrates the trend of the total expenditures from 1789 to 1793 and the portion of the funds dispersed in New Mexico from 1789 to 1791. The large proportion of goods purchased within New Mexico in 1786 reflects the need to substitute provincial products for ones that New Mexicans would ordinarily import. By 1787, New Mexican officials could make arrangements for the shipment of large amounts of material from the south over the Chihuahua Trail, a journey now made considerably safer due to the Comanche peace. The jump in the portion of the fund spent in Chihuahua or farther south after 1787 provides a glimpse into the significance of the reopening of the trade route to New Mexico.

Provincial officials who made the Extraordinary Fund purchases did not provide consistent descriptions of each charge in the accounts they submitted to the comandante general. Consequently, the receipts do not yield a complete inventory of New Mexican products and services purchased for the Indian allies. Figure 11 provides a rough guide to the provincial economic activities that were supported by the gifts made to the allies by grouping the items in the fund receipts according to major categories of expenditure. The agriculture and food category includes maize, pinole, bread, other foodstuffs, and agricultural products such as punche. Livestock and meat comprises sheep, cattle, and oxen, as well as horses. Work done by tailors, armorers, carpenters, and other tradespeople in order to provide gifts to the allies such as textiles, leatherwork, and pottery falls under crafts and products. The final category consists of the salaries and commissions paid for labor and services performed by scouts, Pueblo auxiliaries, interpreters, merchants, and millers, for transporting goods, and for the construction of the pueblo on the Río Napestle.

The significance of the expenditures within New Mexico from the Extraordinary Fund lay not in the amount of money brought into the province but in the stimulus it provided to key sectors of the economy. During the first six years, expenditures from the fund for buying New Mexican goods and services totaled less than the amount spent by the Spanish government to run

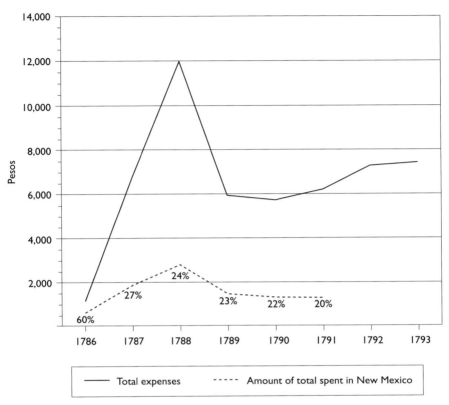

Figure 10. "Peace Expenditures," Extraordinary Fund, Province of New Mexico, 1786–1793. *Sources:* Of 1786 data, AGN: PI 67:1, 32R–34V; 65:1, 259R–261V; and 67:1, 36R–76R. Of 1787 data, AGN: PI 67:1, 112R–120V; 65:1, 268R–278V; and 67:1, 84R–109V and 122R–198R, V. Of 1788 data, AGN: PI 67:1, 203R–214V and 228R–390V. Of 1789 data, AGN: PI 67:1, 216R–223V, 224R, and 391R–473R. Of 1790 data, AGN: PI 67:1, 488R–497V and 500R–595V. Of 1791 data, AGN: PI 204:15, 337R–341R and 342R–419V; and AGN: HI 427:8, 1R–4R. Of 1792 data, AGN: HI 427:8, 5R–8V. Of 1793 data, AGN: HI 427:8, 9R–12R.

the New Mexican missions for one year.[32] Nevertheless, the money went to vecino households and artisans, upon which New Mexican economic productivity depended.

The New Mexican census completed in 1790 serves to illustrate the effect that government-sponsored purchases had begun to have on specific areas of production. The census recorded information on the occupations of a large number of family heads of vecino households in Santa Fe and

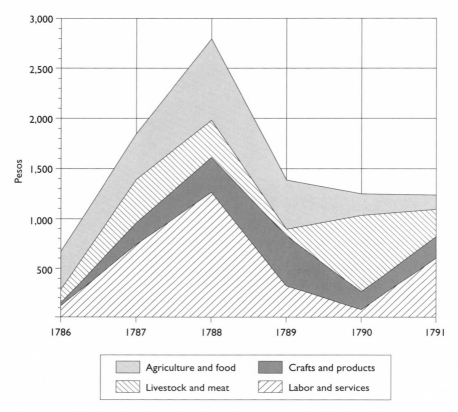

Figure 11. Distribution of goods and services purchased within New Mexico, using the "Peace Expenditures," Extraordinary Fund, 1786–1791. *Sources:* Of 1786 data, AGN:PI 67:1, 32R–34V; 65:1, 259R–261V; and 67:1, 36R–76R. Of 1787 data, AGN:PI 67:1, 112R–120V; 65:1, 268R–278V; and 67:1, 84R–109V and 122R–198R, V. Of 1788 data, AGN:PI 67:1, 203R–214V and 228R–390V. Of 1789 data, AGN:PI 67:1, 216R–223V, 224R, and 391R–473R. Of 1790 data, AGN:PI 67:1, 488R–497V and 500R–595V. Of 1791 data, AGN:PI 204:15, 337R–341R and 342R–419V; and AGN:HI 427:8, 1R–4R. Of 1792 data, AGN:HI 427:8, 5R–8V. Of 1793 data, AGN:HI 427:8, 9R–12R.

Albuquerque who identified themselves as artisans.[33] By 1790 these two centers of population reported 7 masons, 14 blacksmiths, 16 tailors, 39 shoemakers, 41 carpenters, and 169 weavers.

As a proportion of the population, many more New Mexicans worked as artisans during the last decade of the eighteenth century than did their counterparts in Nueva Vizcaya, a province much more closely connected to the larger economy of colonial Mexico. The difficulties New Mexicans experienced with the Apache and Comanche had served to encourage artisans inside the province to produce items that vecinos could not import with the consistency or in the quantity desired. The effect that this situation had on craftspeople in New Mexico becomes clear in a comparison between the New Mexican communities of Santa Fe and Albuquerque and the most populous areas of Nueva Vizcaya: Durango, Chihuahua, Parral, San Juan del Río, and Nombre de Dios (see Table 1). The New Mexican towns contained a population equal to about 11 percent of that in Nueva Vizcaya, but they contained more than 35 percent of the total number of artisans reported in the 1790 census. If the number of artisans listed for Santa Fe and Albuquerque represented all of those in New Mexico, the province still had more than 22 percent of the artisans recorded for the whole of Nueva Vizcaya in 1790, and only about 18 percent of the population. The 1790 census shows that New Mexicans made up the great majority of the people who produced textiles, almost 72 percent. A large number of New Mexicans appear in the census as "carders," "spinners," and "weavers," terms that distinguish a thriving cottage industry from the *obrajeros* working in the towns of Nueva Vizcaya.

The occupational information provided by the 1790 census shows that the areas where New Mexican artisans abounded corresponded to those stimulated by the large purchases made by Spanish officials of materials for the "allied Indians." Spinners, carders, weavers, tailors, shoemakers, blacksmiths, and silversmiths all benefited as they produced the goods purchased by the Extraordinary Fund. Similarly, the construction of the pueblo for the Comanche on the Río Napestle and the cuartel in Santa Fe contributed to the number of carpenters and masons working in the province. Of the artisans mentioned in the 1790 census, only the musicians and singers did not receive money from the fund in the 1780s and 1790s. Those who played a direct role in the success of the alliances with the Plains Indian groups, the artisans, farmers, ranchers, and laborers, formed the basis for the more intensive pace of economic development in New Mexico during the next quarter-century.

The history of the alcabala, the Spanish sales tax levied on commercial goods during the late colonial period, shows how the official concern for the economic welfare of New Mexico had changed since the 1760s in the face of a quickening of economic activity. Bourbon administrators continued to tailor fiscal policy to the special economic conditions found there.[34]

As in the case of the tobacco monopoly, the application of the alcabala to northern New Spain represented a Bourbon addition to the tax burden. In contrast, the alcabala affected all aspects of commerce between the province and other parts of New Spain, not just the tobacco trade. At the very beginning of the colony, in the contract issued in 1595 to Don Juan Oñate authorizing the conquest and settlement of New Mexico, the Crown had exempted New Mexico from the alcabala for at least twenty years. In 1775 the government of the Provincias Internas decided to apply the alcabala to

TABLE 1   Comparison of Household Occupations, Nueva Vizcaya and New Mexico, 1790

	Nueva Vizcaya							New Mexico			
Occupation	Durango	Chihuahua	Parral	San Juan del Río	Nombre de Dios	Total, 5 Jurisdictions	Total, Nueva Vizcaya	Albuquerque	Santa Fe	Santa Fe and Albuquerque as a Percentage of 5 Nueva Vizcaya Jurisdictions	New Mexico as a Percentage of Nueva Vizcaya
Silversmith	3	12	3	0	0	18	36	2	1	14.3	5.6
Blacksmith	19	14	10	11	6	60	142	4	10	18.9	2.9
Painter	3	1	1	0	0	5	8	0	0	0.0	0.0
Tailor	40	42	19	12	11	124	231	9	7	11.4	3.8
Carpenter	28	24	16	17	14	99	183	28	13	29.3	13.4
Shoemaker	70	27	21	2	6	126	239	26	13	23.6	9.9
Mason	9	2	2	0	0	13	24	4	3	35.0	15.3
Hatter	5	1	2	1	0	9	10	0	0	0.0	0.0
Weaver	10	16	0	6	4	36	66	167	2	82.4	71.8
Singer	12	9	4	0	0	25	25	1	1	7.4	4.1
Musician	12	6	3	0	0	21	23	7	0	25.0	24.0
Barber	6	4	3	0	1	14	33	1	0	6.7	3.1
Total	217	158	84	49	42	550	1,020	249	50	35.2	22.7
Population	11,122	10,416	5,193	11,226	7,528	45,485	124,151	1,347	3,656	11.0	18.0

SOURCES: Lista de los Oficios Mecanicos en la Nueva Vizcaya, Francisco Josef Urrutia, AGN: HI 522:38, 278R; Census of Nueva Vizcaya (1790): Fuerza Total de cada Jurisdiccion de la Provincia . . . , Francisco Josef Urrutia, AGN:HI 522:38, 269R; Census of New Mexico (1790): Report of the general visitation and census of the pueblos, Governor Fernando de la Concha, September 11–December 9, 1789, RHUN 2:40.

all material purchased in Chihuahua bound for New Mexico.[35] Governor Mendinueta protested the action immediately, just as Governor Cachupín had done a decade before. In his appeal to the comandante general, he argued that the government should suspend collection of the tax due to the added hardship it placed on New Mexican settlers already hard-hit by Indian raids. This petition went to the assessor of the comandante general, Pedro Galindo Navarro, who agreed with Mendinueta. The assesor pointed out that the alcabala would also affect goods taken down the Chihuahua Trail from New Mexico, adding the 2 percent sales tax to their price. The higher price would hurt both the consumer and the profits from sales made by the settlers from New Mexico, who already faced great obstacles in carrying on any commerce with the south. After deliberation on the matter, Comandante General Croix suspended the alcabala for New Mexico for two more years.

The sparse records of the collection of the alcabala in northern New Spain show that payment of the tax began in New Mexico and El Paso del Norte at the end of 1780, a little over a year after the defeat of the Comanche by Governor Anza. The province paid the tax, at least in theory, until Governor Chacón secured a new exemption in 1796 for ten years.[36] In contrast to the earlier suspension, when Governor Mendinueta argued that the alcabala would make a bad situation even worse, officials in the 1790s thought in terms of protecting and enhancing an already blossoming trade between the provinces. The ten-year period of freedom from the alcabala represented a conscious decision by the government to forgo revenue in favor of encouraging commerce between New Mexico and the Chihuahua region. Thus, in one area where the government had the power to directly promote economic growth—by levying and collecting taxes—Spanish officials heard the arguments of the New Mexican governors sympathetically, and they proved their commitment by moderating fiscal policy.

Despite the limits that Bourbon officials placed on policies designed to stimulate the economy of the Provincias Internas, and the problems they faced in carrying them out effectively, the efforts of the Spanish government had an impact on the direction and pace of economic activity during the last decades of colonial rule. In the case of New Mexico, the general benefits of peace with the Comanche and other Indian groups complimented Bourbon efforts to improve the function of the fiscal machinery. Taken together, their specific attempts to stimulate economic activity in the region helped to smooth the way for the rapid expansion of trade and increased productivity in the province beginning in the late 1780s.

"IMAGINARY MONEYS" AND THE CREATION OF A MARKET ECONOMY

In addition to the increasing productivity and territorial expansion of the New Mexican population, the evolution of a more stable market for goods and services and a heavier reliance on currency for common transactions, all hallmarks of a developing internal economy, marked another component of the late colonial economic picture. Driven by a larger population at home and increased trade outside the province, and influenced by regional policies toward trade and finance (discussed in chapter 3), New Mexico developed a rudimentary market structure to complement its changing economy. This development proceeded in three stages. In the first period, from the 1760s (for the purpose of this discussion) into the 1770s, New Mexicans based exchange on simple barter, which reflected the lack of connection between the province and the larger regional economy. A transition period followed, extending from the 1770s into the 1790s, in which settlers tried to reconcile economic growth, increasing yet uncertain economic links with the south, and the existing system of barter. The use of local monetary denominations, the "imaginary moneys" described by Fray Atanasio Domínguez and Fray Juan Augustín de Morfí, exemplify the economic adaptations of this period. The third period, beginning in the 1790s, marked the conversion to a commercial, money-based economy driven by a more intensive and extensive economic connection with the developing regional economy of northern New Spain.

In 1766 Governor Cachupín prepared a report on the New Mexican economy for the viceroy in which he argued that the absence of currency, combined with an imperfect regular internal market for goods, limited commerce to forms of barter among vecinos, Pueblo Indians, and Plains Indian trading parties.[37] Cachupín described the annual New Mexican convoy to Chihuahua that enabled vecinos to exchange native produce for goods from elsewhere, the general lack of merchants from the south bringing produce up the Chihuahua Trail, and the lack of circulating currency within the province. "This need and deficiency," the governor wrote,

> obliges the inhabitants to conduct their internal commerce in barter and exchange of one good for another, the price of each good being established and regulated from the early times. The same [obtains] with clothes, as in the meats, grains, and skins, and all the rest that are used in the land, so that in barter there is no voluntary alteration [of the value]. And in this disposition that one finds established, this government runs and subsists, so that in the barter of one deerskin already prepared, which is worth 2 pesos being of a thick type, a merchant of this land gives a manojo of tobacco without distinction as to quality, that is the current [value]; and the other goods [function] like this, respectively.

Even those who had some currency, such as the soldiers of the presidio in theory, followed the tariff of prices originally set by Governor Cachupín in their dealings (discussed in chapter 1). In 1773 Governor Mendinueta described the abundance of grain that the Pueblos harvested, from which vecinos purchased what they needed, "as well as the governor when grain is needed by the presidial paymaster for the troops. Prices are uniformly established throughout the province."[38]

Documents from the 1760s and 1770s show few money values assigned to goods, and those that do appear reflect the relatively fixed values for the price of staples mentioned by Cachupín and Mendinueta. From 1760 into 1770s, then, this informal system of barter prevailed. During the 1770s, due to the increased economic activity of the burgeoning vecino population, the continuing lack of specie, and the changes in the monetary policy of the Real Hacienda, the barter system became more elaborate by evolving a number of "imaginary moneys," which reflected different levels of participation in the regional market-oriented, money-based economy.

Discussions of the New Mexican economy during the late colonial period ordinarily rely heavily on the description of trade and the examples Morfí provided in his two reports on New Mexico that sought to explain the functioning of the colonial economy during the late 1770s.[39] At this time Morfí served as a consultant to Comandante General Croix.

The complaints of Morfí about the practices of merchants in New Mexico have received an interpretation that has completely obscured their significance for understanding the system he criticized. Morfí's examples are included here in order to explain the problems with their current interpretation and to demonstrate how they document an important stage in the economic reorientation of the New Mexican economy.

The merchants from Spain and Mexico, "not content with the monopoly by which they oppress the settlers," concocted four types of "imaginary moneys":

1. silver peso (*peso de plata*), worth 8 reales;
2. peso of enterprise (*peso de proyecto*), worth 6 reales;
3. old peso (*peso antiguo*), valued at 4 reales; and
4. peso of the land (*peso de la tierra*) or common peso (*peso de común*), worth 2 reales.[40]

In Morfí's view the merchants manipulated these fictitious denominations to their benefit:

(14.) . . . A length of ordinary cloth which is called a *judía* costs the merchant 6 pesos. A settler needing to clothe himself buys it at a peso per yard, giving in place of pesos, pints of liquor. The piece, having 32 yards, costs him 32 pints of liquor. This miserable fellow then later goes to buy a pint of liquor at the house of the same merchant who sold him the cloth for common pesos [de la tierra]{worth 2 reales}. But now the merchant tells him in all honesty he must sell the liquor by the silver peso {of 8 reales}, which results in the merchant getting in the long run 32 pesos {silver} for the original price of the cloth.

From that, 6 pesos 4 reales {silver} are deducted for handling and losses of liquor, leaving him a profit of 25 pesos, 4 reales. The merchant makes collections at the end of the year [for goods bought on credit].

(15.) But as this amount is not received in cash, it is charged to the account of the buyer against his future harvest of corn; this is an example of the usual way sales are made {since few silver pesos circulate}.[41] Corn by the sack [*costal*] is worth one old peso, (that is, 4 reales), and contains half a bushel [*fanega*] of grain. On account of that, 25 pesos 4 reales {in silver} buy 25.5 bushels. These are then sold to the presidial troops of San Elzeario, Príncipe, and Carrizal when they go to El Paso to purchase supplies of grain. And ordinarily they pay the merchant 20 reales [per bushel] which means that he has made 64 pesos on that in the course of a year if the figuring begins with his original cost of 6.5 pesos. On both the settler who sold him the grain and the soldier who bought it from him, he made a profit.

(16.) If the cloth is not sold for liquor but is immediately exchanged for grain, it has another price. By the yard it is not worth a common peso (that is, 2 reales), but rather an old peso of 4 reales. This being the price of a half fanega of corn, 32 yards of cloth, 32 stockings, or 16 bushels, when sold {outside of the province} each at 20 reales, bring 40 [silver] pesos of 8 reales on an original investment of 6 pesos in cloth. . . .

(19.) Indeed, with this profitable business, [it seems] the merchants are getting rich, although that doesn't keep them out of harm's way. At the very least they ought to have something to show for what their wealth adds to the province. But the painful fact is that in spite of some large returns all are in miserable shape and none can show more than 500 pesos in coin [*en reales*] on hand. They are truly puppets of the Chihuahua merchants, from whom they get credit to run their own businesses and to whom they must repay with products of the country. The Chihuahuans, who know perfectly well the ins and outs of that business, overcharge for the goods they sell and knock down the prices on what they buy so that there is scarcely any margin with which the New Mexicans can pay the freight and still support themselves even at a poverty level. Since they have no alternative, they are forced to accept rules laid down in Chihuahua.

Hubert Howe Bancroft first commented on this passage, revealing much more about his views on the backwardness of the New Mexican economy than about the system Morfi actually described:

The beauty of this system was that the traders always bought for the cheap pesos and sold for the dearer kinds, all being "dollars" to the Indians. . . . Another system of swindling commerce was the habitual selling of goods to be paid for in future products. Thus, for a little seed grain 6 fanegas were promised at harvest; or for a bottle of brandy in holy week a barrel was exacted. . . . While the settlers and pueblo [*sic*] Indians were always in debt to the traders, the latter in turn were debtors to or agents for Chihuahua merchants, who thus monopolized all the profits, and nothing was left for New Mexico, except for certain traders, who as alcaldes mayores exercised their political authority for private gain.[42]

Bancroft passed judgment on certain elements that formed a normal part of colonial government throughout the Spanish possessions in America. The trail of debt payable in goods leading from New Mexican individuals, to merchants, to agents in Chihuahua or Mexico represented nothing new or insidious in an agricultural and stock-raising economy that did not have access to a ready, circulating medium of exchange. Until the largely unsuccessful Bourbon attempt to place the officials serving in the provinces on salaries in the 1770s, arrangements to distribute goods to families and individuals provided a large portion of their income.[43] Commercial agents provided the goods to the officials on credit and expected payment from the profits collected in this manner. New Mexicans created the system to reconcile the value of bartered goods within the New Mexico with prices set by the export economy. Bancroft mistook Morfi's description for evidence of financial decadence and corruption.

Bancroft's appraisal of the business practices of the merchants in New Mexico and Chihuahua has exerted continued influence on the interpretation of Morfi's report. Max L. Moorhead wrote, "The dire financial entanglement in which the New Mexicans became enmeshed was due in some part to their ignorance, but mainly due to a shortage of currency and the unscrupulous policies of the merchants at Chihuahua."[44] Morfi's "illuminating commentary," in Moorhead's opinion, explained that because of the lack of specie "trade in New Mexico was reduced to mere barter, but this simple method of transaction was extremely complicated by a quadruple standard of values which was imposed by the merchants of Chihuahua for purposes of pure extortion." His work on the Chihuahua Trail represents the standard point of reference for subsequent works touching on the colonial New Mexican overland trade.[45]

Fray Morfi sought to explain economic practices that arose suddenly, during a period of rapid change, and that had no contemporary analogy elsewhere in New Spain. Spanish officials both within and outside the province shared Morfi's observation that the New Mexican trade depended on the Chihuahua market and needed to be freed from this economic constraint based on location. Morfi's examples, however, do not shed light on the monopolistic practices of the Chihuahua merchants; nor do they support the conclusion that the system of imaginary moneys related to the natural influence of the Chihuahua market on New Mexican commerce. If one analyzes the examples more closely, they demonstrate a method of integrating an internal economy based on barter with a commercial export market only imperfectly accessible due to distance and Indian hostility.

On further study, Morfi's example in paragraph 14 represents a relatively

TABLE 2   Summary of the Transaction Described by Fray Juan Augustín de Morfí in Paragraph 14 of "Account of Disorders, 1778"

Transaction	Silver pesos	Common pesos	Cost (reales)	Sale (reales)	Profit (reales)
Merchant bought cloth	6	[24]	48		
Settler traded for liquor	[8]	32		64	(16)
Settler purchased liquor	32			256	
Handling and loss	0.5		4		
Total (reales)			52	256	204
Total (pesos)			6.5	32	25.5

SOURCE: Fray Juan Augustín de Morfí, "Account of Disorders, 1778," in *Coronado's Land: Essays on Daily Life in Colonial New Mexico,* ed. and trans. Marc Simmons (Albuquerque: University of New Mexico Press, 1991), 135–36.

simple transaction (see Table 2). For a cotton cloth of 32 varas in length (about 30 yards) that cost 6 silver pesos, or 48 reales, a settler paid in liquor valued at 32 common pesos, or 64 reales. At this point, the merchant had made an unrealized profit of 16 reales, or 2 pesos; but, instead of silver, he still held 32 cuartillos of aguardiente. He then sold his liquor at 1 peso, or 8 reales, per pint, four times his cost. Morfí focused on the substitution of pesos de la tierra for silver pesos instead of on the transaction itself, but, as the summary shows, the merchant in the end made 25.5 pesos on an investment of 6.5 pesos. The merchant faced the difficulty of obtaining capital, carried the charges, and bore the risk involved in holding and trying to sell goods in a province under attack by hostile Indians. Recall the effect that these variables had on the profitability of Francisco de Guizarnótegui's attempts to supply the northern presidios during the 1780s (see chapter 3). Under the circumstances, the eventual profit earned by Morfí's hypothetical merchant does not seem to reflect an undue exploitation of his clientele.

Notice that in this example, the price of the goods does not change, just the composition of the peso used in their valuation. These prices still reflect the old schedule of values originally set up in the 1750s by Governor Cachupín. The merchant offered the cloth at 1 peso de la tierra (2 reales) per vara and the liquor at 1 silver peso (8 reales) per cuartillo. The changing value of the peso represented the mechanism used by the merchant to translate the customary barter value of local goods in New Mexico into their equivalent value in the regional market. After all, the merchant ultimately had to realize his profit in money, and generally that could happen only outside New Mexico in places such as Chihuahua, Durango, or the northern presidios. Fray Domínguez explained the system in these terms in 1776, a few years before Morfí gathered the information used in his report: "For the present, in order that these pesos may be completely understood, I shall

TABLE 3   Summary of the Transaction Described by Fray Juan Augustín de Morfí in Paragraph 15 of "Account of Disorders, 1778"

Transaction	Silver pesos	Old pesos	Cost (reales)	Sale (reales)	Profit (reales)
Merchant held liquor (net)	25.5		52	204	
Settler traded for maize	[25.5]	52	52	204	
Merchant sold to troops	63.75			510	
Total (reales)			52	510	458
Total (pesos)			6.5	63.75	57.25

SOURCE: Fray Juan Augustín de Morfí, "Account of Disorders, 1778," in *Coronado's Land: Essays on Daily Life in Colonial New Mexico,* ed. and trans. Marc Simmons (Albuquerque: University of New Mexico Press, 1991), 136.

say that they are pesos in name only, for actual coins do not exist; and that they weigh as much as the ring of the word. The only sound so many pesos make comes down to the fact that 50 of them may be worth 6 or 8 real ones, and this value is estimated from the effects in which payment is made."[46] Later, Domínguez explained further, "When I discussed the Third Order . . . I promised a brief statement, or explanation, of the pesos of this land in terms of things used in trade." He then listed the values of a number of goods in local pesos.[47] In contrast to Morfí's view, Domínguez understood that the mechanism existed not for the purpose of cheating New Mexican clients but to mediate between the value of goods in a barter economy and the equivalent value in the money economy outside the province.

Paragraph 15 of the description completes the example, clearly demonstrating the translation of the barter values to the money values of the external regional market (see Table 3). The merchant held his potential profit in the form of 25.5 cuartillos of liquor. His clients paid after the harvest at a rate in maize valued at 1 old peso (peso antiguo), or 4 reales, per fanega of maize. This price represented the value of maize from the schedule that Governors Cachupín and Concha mentioned and also appears as the price of maize in the reports of Fray Lezaún and Fray Domínguez.[48] The merchant then sold his corn in El Paso to the troops from the presidios in northern Nueva Vizcaya at the price of 2.5 silver pesos per fanega. Finally the merchant realized his profit in money, reaping almost nine times his original investment of 6.5 pesos. Once again, the money paid for maize by the troops had nothing to do with the substitution of silver pesos for old pesos. In New Mexico, the merchant paid the current price for the maize based on the tariff of trade prices established in 1754 by Governor Cachupín (discussed in chapter 2). The merchant made money by selling the grain in a commercial market hundreds of miles outside New Mexico, where it brought a higher price due to regional market conditions.

TABLE 4   Summary of the Transaction Described by Fray Juan Augustín de Morfí in Paragraph 16 of "Account of Disorders, 1778"

Transaction	Silver pesos	Old pesos	Cost (reales)	Sale (reales)	Profit (reales)
Merchant bought cloth	6	[12]	48		
Traded settler for maize	[16]	32		128	(80)
Merchant sold to troops	40			320	
Total (reales)			48	320	272
Total (pesos)			6	40	34

SOURCE: Fray Juan Augustín de Morfí, "Account of Disorders, 1778," in *Coronado's Land: Essays on Daily Life in Colonial New Mexico,* ed. and trans. Marc Simmons (Albuquerque: University of New Mexico Press, 1991), 137.

The third example provided by Morfí underscores the distinction between the use of the imaginary money to translate from barter prices and the profit made by buying and selling goods (see Table 4). The merchant bought the cloth and traded it for grain, without first trading it for liquor. As the summary below shows, when he sold his produce to the presidial troops, he made less profit because he turned over his inventory one less time. The intermediate stage in the first example, in which the merchant traded the cloth for liquor, served to add to the value of the original investment.

In 1788, Comandante General Ugarte y Loyola explained the function of the peso de la tierra to Viceroy Flores in terms that showed that he, too, understood the true nature of the system. Trade for foreign and Mexican goods in Chihuahua prevented vecinos from returning to New Mexico with specie. Lack of circulating currency, "and the necessity of having it, substituted the imaginary, or peso de la tierra, with which the contracting parties assign a value known among themselves to the goods that they give and receive there in barter. The same, and the decadence peculiar to any similar system, one always finds on whatever land whose active commerce becomes inferior and passive."[49]

The Morfí report holds a clue to the genesis of the peso antiguo. The settler who paid for his cloth or liquor in maize had to arrive at an equitable exchange using the schedule created in 1754 by Governor Cachupín to regulate trade between New Mexicans and the Comanche and other Native groups. Fray Lezaún, in 1760, reported that "corn is sold at a regular price which does not rise or fall; it is 4 pesos de la tierra, equivalent to 2 pesos of silver." However, after 1772, the peso that set the value of bartered goods became obsolete due to the revaluation of the peso and its subsequent recoinage (discussed in chapter 3). While the new 8 real coin, peso de plata, began to circulate, officials referred to the old coinage as "pesos antiguos." An interim point in the conversion from peso to peso antiguo appears in an anonymous report written in 1773, just after the recoinage: "The pesos at the project price (pesos al precio al proyecto) correspond to that [peso] of 6 reales in silver. Pesos at the old prices (pesos a precios antiguos) are worth 4 reales. The prices of pesos of the land are equivalent to 2 reales of silver, and in this way their trades take place."[50] During the 1770s, with the old peso disappearing from circulation along with the general shortage of specie, New Mexicans continued to use the old schedule to exchange their goods within the province, as Morfí described in his report. The peso antiguo became an imaginary money used to translate the goods on the official schedule into equivalent values using the new silver peso.

The origin of the peso de proyecto remains obscure. It seems to have functioned as a method of repaying credit on the old peso with interest, as its name, peso of enterprise or project, implies. In any case, I have found no actual example of its use in colonial records, and no information other than the mention above and that of Morfí.

The report of Fray Domínguez on the missions of New Mexico in 1776 provides insight into the origin of the peso de la tierra. Just as the peso antiguo defined the value of goods exchanged in trade, the peso de la tierra functioned to translate the schedule of payments for church services—principally marriages, baptisms, and burials—into local produce. New Mexico received a tariff of religious services from Bishop Don Benito Crespo during his 1730 visitation of the province. All charges appeared in pesos, but the bishop instructed that the religious could collect fees in reales "or their equivalent according to the prevalent custom." Domínguez explained the regional custom that had developed in his report on the missions. For baptisms, New Mexicans offered three "regional pesos in chile or seeds or something else instead of the customary christening fee." In addition to calibrating payment in goods using pesos de la tierra, local custom in New Mexico dropped a number of traditional charges included in the schedule. Marriages between Españoles cost 33 pesos and 1 real, while those among the lower classes cost 10 or 12, but in neither case at that time did the parties have to pay the *arras*, probably because of poverty and the difficulty in obtaining specie. Except for similar payments for a mass at burial, all the other fees on the schedule lapsed in New Mexico. The fees listed by Domínguez appear similar to those listed by the missionaries in 1750 in a document explaining how the friars valued the obventions collected at that time.[51]

The cost of marriages and burials listed by Domínguez in regional pesos doubled the amount in reales that appears on the schedule left by Bishop Crespo. For each peso on the schedule, parishioners gave 2 pesos de la tierra worth of acceptable goods. Since the ecclesiastical tariff used the old pesos, after the recoinage pesos de la tierra appear in Morfí's report with a nominal value of 2 reales. As Domínguez's description of the mission finances makes clear, translating the local pesos into reales consumed a good deal of effort.

In addition, the peso de la tierra did not always hold a consistent value in relation to the real or silver peso. An explanation of the peso de la tierra appears in a 1791 report and reiterates the connection between the common
and silver peso, as well as the manner in which the device related to the collection of ecclesiastical fees.[52] The pesos of the land, wrote the friar, "are not
adaptable in any other province. It is a species of barter or exchange that one
esteems as money, or circulating currency, and that all value for their purchases or sales since silver does not circulate in this province. Of these pesos,
one must be able to take some for 4 reales of silver, and others that have an
intrinsic value of scarcely 1 real of silver. With this type of peso one pays the
obventions of the father ministers."

In this description of the monetary system as it functioned in 1791, one
may already see the effects of the introduction of specie into the province
resulting from increasing trade with Chihuahua and other markets, as well
as the general economic quickening within the province. The report lists
several New Mexican products and their equivalent value in silver pesos
or reales. One can compare the price of goods in common pesos, and their
value in silver, given in Domínguez and in the 1791 report (see Table 5).[53]
The relative silver peso values of the same goods, and the relative value of
the peso de la tierra to the silver real, have changed according to the importance of the goods in the export trade. In most cases, the prices of commodities as expressed in pesos de la tierra remained the same in 1791 as they
had been in 1776. The cattle and the oxen, which figured less prominently
in the export trade, gained value relative to the 1776 price in silver, in part
reflecting the need for draft animals in an expanding agricultural economy.
These two commodities also showed the least alteration in the historical
2 : 1 ratio of value between the peso de la tierra and the silver real. On the
other hand, the goods most in demand for the export market—sheep,
woolen textiles, tobacco, and chile— underwent a significant alteration in
their value in silver after 1776 and radically disturbed the relationship between the peso de la tierra and the silver real. The connection of these commodities to an outside market based to a large extent upon money had begun to distort the structure of the imaginary money that New Mexicans used
to translate barter values into prices in silver.

The records of the expenses for provisions during the building of the barracks in Santa Fe show that a similar two-tiered structure for prices had extended to internal markets as well by the end of the 1780s.[54] The ledger lists
the monthly purchase of vegetables in pesos de la tierra for the maintenance
of the laborers. The rate of conversion for vegetables from pesos de la tierra
to reales held constant at 3 reales and 5 *granos* from April 1789 through
October 1791. Other necessities, such as maize, wheat, mules, and oxen, the
master purchased in cash without having to translate from an imaginary

TABLE 5   Comparison of Peso de la Tierra Values,
New Mexico, 1776 and 1791

New Mexican item	1776, pesos de la tierra	1776, reales (silver)	1791, pesos de la tierra	1791, reales (silver)	Ratio: 1791, pt:real	Ratio: reales, 1776: 1791
Oxen	25	50	25	56–64	.45–.39	.89–.78
Cow	20	40	20	48	.42	.83
Sayal	n.a.	—	1	1	1	—
Sabanilla	2	4	1.5	1.5–2	1–.75	2.6–2
Chile, 1 string	2	4	2	2	1	2
Punche, 1 manojo	n.a.	—	2	3 or less	<.67	—
Woolen blanket / gamuza	n.a.	—	2	8	.25	—
Sheep (carneros)	4	8	4?	6	.67?	1.33

SOURCES: For 1776 data, Fray Francisco Atanasio Domínguez, *The Missions of New Mexico, 1776*, trans. and ed. Eleanor B. Adams and Fray Angélico Chávez (Albuquerque: University of New Mexico Press, 1956), 245; for 1791 data, ACD:VA 44:116, 19R.

currency. These records show that, in Santa Fe at least, an internal market had developed for products like maize, wheat, mules, and oxen but not for vegetables.

Spanish officials distinguished between the system of imaginary money and the commercial connection between the markets of New Mexico and Chihuahua. In 1788 Governor Concha described the function of the peso de la tierra as translating between the internal and external prices of both imported goods and New Mexican products brought to Chihuahua. In his summary of Concha's report for the viceroy, Ugarte y Loyola explained:

> The disproportion that exists at present between the one and the other [imaginary and real pesos], according to the judgment of the governor, even when arising in part from the excessive prices at which the vecinos of the abovementioned province purchase in Chihuahua, ought not to be blamed directly on those merchants of that city [Chihuahua]. These assign the value of their merchandise that the particular circumstances establish in each land, vulgarly known as current prices (*precios corrientes*). The variation of these [pesos de la tierra] depends immediately on those [current prices] and are not subject to a resolution of the government.

Stimulation of the economy of Chihuahua provided the answer to the difficulties of the New Mexican trade. According to the comandante general, "without fomenting the first, the second cannot progress, even when one applies regulations conducive to its particular prosperity."[55]

Sonora also had alternate "precios corrientes" due to lack of money in specie, even though mining formed the backbone of the provincial economy. Once cast into bars, gold and silver had to go to the nearest Real Hacienda to be assayed, taxed, and minted into coin. Ore often left the province in the hands of merchants for use in satisfying their debts or to purchase new goods. Merchants charged the miners 9 reales' worth of ore for every peso of goods purchased. If customers provided the refined metal, the merchant also discounted its value, depending on which refining process had been used.[56] Officials consistently criticized merchants for gouging customers in order to pad their profits, just as Morfí did in his description of the "imaginary moneys" in New Mexico. In Sonora, too, the commercial practice probably made more economic sense than officials gave it credit for. Someone eventually had to transport heavy ore to a refiner, pay refining charges, transport the metal in bars to a treasury, and pay the royal tax of 10 percent. Under the circumstances, a 19 percent premium in the case of ore, and 10–15 percent for bars, seems reasonable. The practice demonstrated the desperation of the merchants for something that worked like money, rather than a propensity to arbitrarily fix prices.

Shortly after 1791 the peso de la tierra disappeared from the financial terminology of colonial New Mexico, a case of good money chasing out the imaginary. The king authorized *donativos* at various times of emergency, such as during the war with England at the end of the eighteenth century. The list of goods contributed by the New Mexican citizenry in 1799 no longer had to be translated from any system of imaginary money in order to be exchanged for specie. All told, the province contributed 6,171 pesos, 1 real, and another 2,218 pesos, 6 reales, and 6 granos in a large assortment of goods that Don Miguel Ortiz transported to market in Chihuahua. Governor Chacón, in his report of 1803, also indicated that New Mexico had of late seen more specie in circulation. He blamed the poorly financed merchants for "making more difficult the lack of circulation of money that for the last the years this province has begun to know."[57] Even the nomadic Indian groups began to take an interest in money by the end of the eighteenth century. Lieutenant José María Cortés, a military engineer who toured the northern provinces during the 1790s, commented in his report of 1799 that the Ute, Apache, and Navajo used to ignore money when they came upon it in a raid. "Today," he wrote, "they are learning that money makes everything possible. . . . So sure and so convinced are the Indian allies of this knowledge . . . [that] the first greeting which they make to whomever approaches them is to ask for a real or a half."[58]

Clearer evidence still of the complete conversion to a money economy comes from an account book of the Santa Fe Presidio. This ledger recorded all transactions in the common account of the presidial company from April 1805 to December 1835.[59] The soldiers began the account so that they could use their purchasing power to reduce living expenses and to share them more equitably. In contrast to the predicament that presidial soldiers faced during the supply crisis of the 1770s and 1780s discussed in chapter 3, the development of a money-based internal economy by the turn of the nineteenth century made such a strategy possible. The company purchased sheep for a herd, maintained at common expense. The soldiers shared the cost of purchases of horses and, at times, blankets and grain. In addition, the troop sold the wool shorn from the presidial sheep herd and put the proceeds back into the account.

Sales of wool, *abrigos* made from the wool of the presidial flock, and some grain, plus receipts for hauling supplies and transporting goods using teams of oxen and mules purchased in common, enabled the account to weather the first few years of relatively sizable deficits. Beginning in 1809 the common account showed a small year-end surplus. Unlike the one previous profit realized in 1806, when the administrator of the account distributed 1 real and 2.5 granos to each soldier, the surplus remained in the common fund. After 1811, with the exception of one year (1814), the account saw a remarkable increase in surplus funds at the end of each year. The excess money in the account dried up immediately after 1820, and during the year in which Mexico declared independence from Spain the common fund lost more than 716 pesos, ending the year in debt for the first time since 1808. It took another three years for the fund to regain solvency, but never did it return to the level of profitability seen in the middle of the previous decade. The healthy growth of the fund after 1805, due to the skillful exploitation by the soldiers of new markets both within and outside the province, bears comparison with the increase in the real value of the tithe rental during the same period. Both attest to the dramatic growth and development of the New Mexican economy during the last decades of colonial rule.

VECINO USURPATION OF THE PUEBLO TEXTILE TRADE

By 1790 the constraints upon vecino ability to wield economic power over the Pueblo Indians had vanished. The vecino population had surpassed that of the pueblos two decades earlier and continued to grow at a faster rate. This demographic shift and the Spanish alliance with the Comanche lessened the need for Pueblo-vecino cooperation and understanding. Furthermore, whereas limited and difficult access to external markets from within New Mexico at midcentury had discouraged economic pressure for Pueblo products, the boom of the 1790s reversed the process as a means of drawing the Indians fully into the Spanish economy. These changes had predictable consequences. In the hands of the vecino economic elite and provincial officials, the second commercial system tightened its grip on Pueblo foodstuffs and manufactures. In addition to extracting goods and services through the repartimiento de efectos and other coercive practices, vecinos ended direct

Pueblo participation in the export trade and took over some areas of traditional production.

Governor Chacón observed in his economic report of 1803 that each year the Pueblo Indians produced an abundance of grain and other commodities:

> The great part of the inhabitants are little applied to farming, in particular the Spanish and castes, contenting themselves with sowing and planting precisely what is [needed] for their sustenance. In years of scarcity like the present, they experience great want. . . . On the contrary, the Indians of the pueblo, who comprise one-third of the population, work great fields which they cultivate in common. . . . With this practice and the harvest that they save every year, they never feel the effects of hunger. Furthermore, they apply themselves to the cultivation of gardens, orchards, and vineyards [in El Paso]. In the same way they are most likely to take pains to profit by the planting of cotton, with which they manufacture mantas for their own use.

Lieutenant Pike also left New Mexico with the impression that the Pueblo Indians accounted for much of the production of the exported handicrafts. His hosts told him that the journey to Chihuahua and back took five months, and he listed "rough leather, segars [*sic*], a vast variety and quantity of potter's ware, cotton, some coarse woolen cloths, and blankets of a superior quality." As an American, Pike had an eye for the relationship between economic function and social status in Spanish culture. He noted: "All those manufactures are carried on by the civilized Indians, as the Spaniards think it more honorable to be agriculturists than mechanics."[60] This sentiment did not proceed entirely from Pike's Anglo-American sensibilities. Although vecinos produced all of these "manufactures" except pottery, Pike grasped that many of the exported items came from the pueblos. At the same time he aptly expressed the dominant social attitude of the emerging vecino elite, who insisted on distinguishing themselves from the lower classes.

The official repartimiento still functioned at the end of the eighteenth century, although no longer for the personal profit of the governor. In his instructions to his successor, Governor Concha explained to Fernando Chacón that the governor had to obtain horses from the Pueblo Indians in order to keep the soldiers of the presidio supplied: "The only way that one can collect horses cheaply and of good quality is to order the commissioner to have supplies delivered from the presidio store of the kind that the Pueblo Indians use and with these tour all of the districts. In these [pueblos] there is much breeding of horses, and in that of Taos and Pecos there is a considerable portion which the natives barter to the Comanche nation."[61] As an alternative, the commissioner could visit the Comanche rancherías in the company of an interpreter and "in exchange for goods as well, purchase them firsthand." From the point of view of Governor Concha, the involuntary distribution of goods from the presidio stores in exchange for Pueblo Indian horses represented a legitimate mode of purchase. For the Pueblos, the repartimiento functioned as an openly extractive system that pulled Indian products into the vecino economic sphere.

The sarapes, fresadas, abrigos, and different kinds of cloth (sarga, *sabanilla,* jerga) that vecino weavers produced by the turn of the nineteenth century, in addition to the stockings, colchas, and some woolen cloth made earlier, represented the metamorphosis of an industry in response to economic change and the formation of a new tradition of craft production in New Mexico. The 1790 census listed ninety-seven weavers, thirty-eight carders, and sixteen spinners, in addition to fifteen tailors. According to the census takers, Genízaros did a good deal of the carding, but vecinos performed nearly all of the weaving and spinning.[62]

The ninety-seven weavers listed in the 1790 census represented only a portion of the labor force at work in the burgeoning weaving industry. Although textiles woven on a vecino loom appear quite different from those made on a Pueblo loom, as discussed in chapter 1, it does not follow that only non-Indians used Spanish-style looms during the late colonial period. Vecinos, whether counted as weavers in the 1790 census or not, used servant or slave labor in order to take advantage of the increasing demand for woolens. Between 1770 and 1810, at least 751 non-Pueblo Indians received baptism in New Mexico, and the church records have not survived from this period for all jurisdictions.[63] Criados were widely distributed to households throughout the province and placed in servitude to work as farmers or domestics. Of these, at least 179 came from Hopi villages or Navajo rancherías that produced their own textiles. The experience of at least some of these slaves, in addition to Indians who married outside the Pueblo or left for other reasons, must have provided the labor that produced woven goods on vecino looms by the 1790s. A suggestive example comes from the disposition of the estate of Don Antonio José Ortiz and his wife, Rosa Bustamante. Ortiz died in 1806 a wealthy merchant, local official, and prominent religious benefactor. When his wife passed away eight years later, her will mentioned, "220 sarapes made from this year's wool crop." Such a quantity of blankets indicates that a sizable weaving workshop, if not an obraje, prospered among the Ortiz enterprises.[64]

The generation of weavers documented in the census of 1790—vecino, servant, and slave alike—developed a distinctive type of sarape woven on the traditional Spanish-style treadle loom. Scholars in the twentieth century have named this sarape the "Río Grande" blanket. Early Río Grande blankets, woven of long-staple, New Mexican churro wool, carried banded designs along the width of the blanket. Weavers normally used the colors provided by the natural white and browns of the wool, as well as blues from índigo. Some examples of Río Grande blankets have índigo, yellow, madder, reddish brown, and green vegetal and mineral dyes. Governor Chacón mentioned in 1803 that vecino weavers used both índigo and brazilwood "imported from outside," although samples of yarn tested with colors thought to come from "brazil-stick" probably came from a natural dye of local manufacture.

At around the same time, Río Grande blankets appeared with adaptations of complicated designs, such as large center medallions and repeated interlocking diamond motifs borrowed from elsewhere in New Spain, perhaps in conjunction with the arrival of the Bazán brothers.[65] The Río Grande blanket in Plate 2 has this type of "Saltillo design," named after the style made popular by merchants at the annual trade fair held in Saltillo, Nueva Vizcaya (today in the state of Coahuila). Fancy blankets or sarapes produced in New Mexico on a Spanish-style loom around the time of Chacón's report would have looked much like this example.

Vecino weaving occupied a preeminent position in the export economy of the second commercial system. In 1794 Custos Cayetano José Ignacio Bernal compared the burgeoning weaving industry with vecino agriculture hampered by "little application to the work" and lack of water:

> In matters of industry one finds things arranged well enough, and taking root more every day. It is limited to working with wool that they shear in this province, making fresadas, sarapes, woolen stockings, etc., which they take out [of the province] to sell in Nueva Vizcaya, Sonora, etc., for prices so low at present that, although they do not take out the cost of transport, [this amount figures] as much as or more than the principal. Before, they used to sell a fresada for 4, 5, or more pesos, and now they cannot find anyone to give 10 reales for them. The most ordinary sarapes used to bring at least 2 pesos, and today for the best they give 5 reales. The stockings used to be another part of this commerce that they make very well, and with which the greater part of the vecindarios of the province, who are the poor, clothe themselves. The common ones were sold [outside the province] for 9 pesos a dozen; in the present year the highest that a dozen has been valued at has been 3 pesos, and the price has dropped in this manner for fine stockings, and all other woolens. Because of this loss, this province will begin to lose its principal branch of commerce and industry.[66]

As Governor Concha recommended before, and Governor Chacón would echo in his report of 1803, Fray Bernal suggested increasing the quality of vecino production by introducing weaving masters and new equipment as the best medicine to prevent further decline. The poor market that vecinos faced in the mid-1790s recovered by the end of the decade, and the vecino weaving industry continued to grow.[67]

Even at its ebb, the situation of vecino textile production compared favorably with the state of Pueblo weaving in 1794, according to Fray Bernal. The men of the Tewa pueblos (Tesuque, Nambé, Pojoaque, San Juan, Santa Clara, and San Ildefonso) wove only a few woolen blankets, "in order to clothe their women" and for ceremonial purposes. The northeastern Keres pueblos (Cochití, San Ildefonso, and San Felipe, but Bernal includes Santa Ana and Zia) and Jémez fared somewhat better. These pueblos planted and harvested a small amount of cotton, which they worked and wove into blankets along with the wool from their flocks. In addition to weaving mantas to clothe their women, the Tewa "sell them to the Indians of the other nations who, although they know how to weave, do not do so because of laziness or because they do not have wool since they are not good at raising sheep." They also traded mantas with the Genízaros, probably at Abiquíu. Fray Bernal distinguished these blankets from the longer, woolen ones of vecino manufacture, describing the Pueblo style as "a type of wide scapular that they call cotones." Fray Diego Turado and Fray Ramón Gómez wrote more bluntly about the Río Arriba pueblos, "These Indians have no industry at all, because although they know how to weave mantas of wool with which they clothe their women, they do not make them due to their great laziness and laxity, but purchase them from others."[68] Only the western pueblos, Zuñi, Laguna, and Acoma, produced larger numbers of woolen mantas, "because those pueblos have more sheep and are generally the most industrious Indians."

Governor Chacón's description of New Mexican commerce at the turn of the century took care to distinguish the export trade from internal commerce and the production of the Pueblo Indians. Although he did not explicitly describe the process that made Pueblo products available for export, the report leaves the impression that the internal repartimiento and exchange with vecinos served that purpose. The lists of New Mexicans making alcabala payments for 1781 and 1783 show no Pueblo Indians, and the entries for 1811 and 1817 give no indication of Pueblo participation, although the latter two sources do not list all of the individual participants.[69] In the mid-1780s Governor Anza attempted to explain why the Pueblos did not participate directly in the export trade, as they had during the first commercial system:

> The development [of goods of the country] at present has advanced but little. I hold that this is due to the difficulty or impossibility of enterprise because the region finds itself separated from all of the Provincias Internas by more than 200 leagues with the inevitable increased risk [associated with distance]. Since the province does not contain in its territory appreciable yields that attract outside people, most of their [Pueblo Indian] consumption is that which they produce, although one observes the progress of the same [production] limited to some sheep, weaving of wool, and skins which the gentiles provide,

in this way furnishing the [Pueblo] Indians with what they need. For their extraction [from the province] the Indians would run into the difficulty of the small profit of their sale (which the Spanish experience) and the obstacle of the high costs that originate in the distance mentioned.[70]

A decade later one could add to the reasons provided by Anza that the proliferation of the vecino production of textiles had deprived the Indians of their most salable items in Chihuahua.

The renewed opportunity for long-distance trade provided the incentive to favor textiles made on vecino looms over Pueblo cloth because weavers using the treadle loom could produce large amounts of woven material with greater efficiency. Hence, when enterprising vecinos took control of textile production and exports to Chihuahua and elsewhere in northern New Spain, it signaled a shift from extracting the product of Pueblo labor through the repartimiento de efectos, to utilizing the service of Pueblo men and women, detribalized, intermarried, or exiled, and the servitude of Genízaros to produce woven goods within the expanding vecino economy[71] The new commercial order served to divide economic functions between the relatively privileged merchants, agents, and traders who created the export market and the common vecino, Genízaro, Casta, and Pueblo producers. Both Chacón and Pike described and commented on this important social consequence of economic development in late colonial New Mexico. Furthermore, the reorganization of textile production by vecinos and their servants set the stage for undisguised slaving raids against Navajo and other non-Pueblo Indians after 1821, when Mexican independence and the Santa Fe trade with Saint Louis renewed commercial opportunities for the export of blankets once again.[72]

The textiles that the western pueblos (Zuñi, Laguna, and Acoma) still produced in the 1790s entered the vecino market through repartimientos of the type explained by Chacón or through barter with local vecinos. With demand for Pueblo weaving eclipsed by vecino production, pottery remained the Pueblo product that still held economic value for the long-distance trade.

ECONOMIC COERCION AND CHANGE
IN THE PUEBLO CERAMIC TRADITION

The economic forces brought to bear on creating exportable commodities toward the end of the eighteenth century also altered the production of pottery, the other major Pueblo manufacture during the colonial period (see Map 9). Changes in shape, design, and pottery-making techniques demonstrate the power of the commercial forces unleashed by the new economic system.

At midcentury, during the first commercial system, pottery formed one of the goods extracted from the pueblos through the use of the repartimiento.

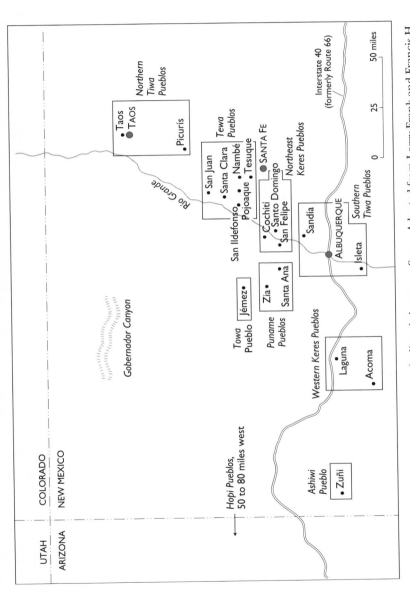

Map 9. The Pueblo pottery-making area, by linguistic group. *Source:* Adapted from Larry Frank and Francis H. Harlow, *Historic Pottery of the Pueblo Indians, 1600–1880* (Boston: New York Graphic Society, 1974), 3–4 ("Pueblo Indian Pottery-making Areas").

Fray Pedro Serrano wrote in 1761 that the alcaldes did not enter the pueblos except to force the Indians to weave, to barter, "or to gather pots, plates, jars, jugs, etc., or for services and oppressions for the profit of the governors." Governor Chacón described Pueblo pottery production in 1803: "The craft of potter [produces] ordinary crockery as well as pots, cooking pots, stew pots, bowls, etc. The women of the pueblos practice it without using a wheel, but by hand with the patience that is their way. Afterward they fire it with manure, without using any ingredient for a glaze because of lack of knowledge of this material."[73] Although archaeological and documentary evidence establishes that Pueblo pottery formed a common part of vecino households during the eighteenth century, Fray Morfí made first mention of it as an exported commodity. Writing in 1778, he included the export of "small quantities of pottery" among the goods that merchants brought to Chihuahua from New Mexico as a part of "this defective and corrupt trade." Later in the same report he said that the merchants "buy from the poor Indians inside this province, they being the only ones who have any surplus of sheep, buckskin, blankets, cloth, and pottery." Forty years later, Pike noted that a "vast variety and quantity of potter's ware" made by the pueblos left the province for southern markets.[74]

Although historical sources indicate that Pueblo Indian pottery left the province as part of the trade to the south, they do not describe what type of pottery New Mexicans exported. Unfortunately, collections of Pueblo pottery do not contain any examples found in northern Mexico that could have come from New Mexico during the late colonial period. The scanty archaeological work on the late colonial presidios and administrative centers in northern New Spain has shed little light on the question. The archaeologist Rex E. Gerald published a description of the pottery shards found at eight northern Mexican presidio sites, but of these only Janos, Carrizal, and El Príncipe functioned after 1781. The Carrizal and El Príncipe samples that he analyzed consisted only of decorated shards collected on the site's surface and yielded no evidence of pottery from the Río Grande pueblos.[75]

Without further archaeological investigation of the northern Mexican centers that traded with New Mexico during the 1770–1820 period, one can only speculate about the specific types of pottery mentioned in colonial New Mexican documents. Pueblo potters fashioned vessels for carrying water and larger storage jars to hold grain and other foodstuffs. Plates 4–6, 8, and 9 illustrate examples of smaller Pueblo jars, and Plates 12–14 show storage jars, all made at various times in the eighteenth and early nineteenth centuries. Although New Mexico produced large quantities of maize and wheat, these commodities found their market within the province and among Comanche, Apache, and Navajo neighbors, not in Chihuahua or in the northern presidios. Furthermore, vecino merchants would have found storage jars too heavy and unwieldy to export from New Mexico.

Utility wares, such as bowls, plates, and cups, appear in quantity at the sites of the presidios in northern New Spain. They comprise Spanish majolica, foreign porcelain, wares from Puebla and other sources in New Spain, and a large amount of coarse, unglazed pottery, presumably of local origin. Utilitarian wares from New Mexico would seem to have been either too expensive to transport over the Chihuahua trail when compared with local ceramics or not fine enough to compete with manufactured pottery imported into the north. Most likely, small and medium-sized decorated bowls and jars made up the Pueblo Indian pottery types in demand for use in Chihuahua and the northern presidios. These pottery types had no locally manufactured equivalent and represented an attractive, less-expensive alternative to items imported from elsewhere in Mexico.

Although archaeological work in northern Mexico has not yielded evidence of the ceramic trade mentioned in the documents, production for export to the south had a dramatic effect on the technique, shape, and decorative style of Pueblo Indian potters. The period from 1750 to about 1810 forms perhaps the least understood of the waves of dramatic change that punctuated pottery production in the New Mexican pueblos since the arrival of the Spanish. During the relatively short span of a few generations, important alterations in shape, decorative designs, and production techniques took place at an extraordinarily rapid pace across most of the pueblos with active ceramic traditions.

Plate 3 illustrates the dramatic changes in the shape of pottery that took place in each the four groups of pueblos that represent the principal pottery-making traditions.[76] As Plate 3 shows, current scholarship based on stylistic and archaeological information dates the new pottery types at various points during the 1760–1820 period. In each case, the late-seventeenth- or early-eighteenth-century shape has a low, short bulge accentuated by a decorative band that marks or frames this distinctive feature. Plate 4 shows an example of a Puname Polychrome jar, a style made at Zia Pueblo before 1750. The characteristic bulge is framed below by the unslipped underbody and above by the two thin, black lines enclosing the red cloudlike design. Below the bulge, the bottom of the vessel fans upward and outward to form a pronounced overhang caused by the lip of the mold that the potter used to hold the coiled clay while fashioning the bottom section. Above the bulge, the walls slope up in a graceful, elongated curve ending in a small lip. Red and black matte paint on a cream-colored slip (hence polychrome) makes up the decoration on the upper portion of the vessel.

Puname Polychrome gave way to a transitional style named San Pablo Polychrome in the evolution of pottery production at Zia and Santa Ana

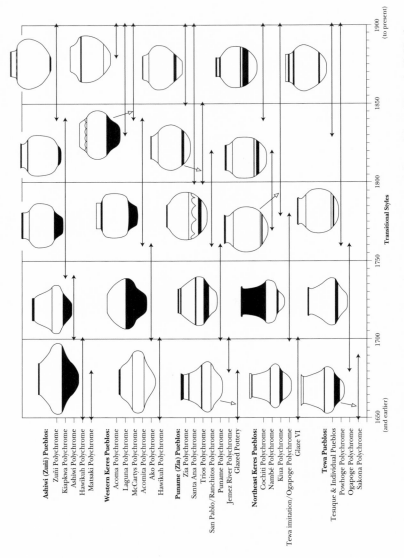

Ashiwi (Zuñi) Pueblos:
Zuñi Polychrome
Kiapkwa Polychrome
Ashiwi Polychrome
Hawikuh Polychrome
Matsaki Polychrome

Western Keres Pueblos:
Acoma Polychrome
Laguna Polychrome
McCartys Polychrome
Acomita Polychrome
Ako Polychrome
Hawikuh Polychrome

Puname (Zia) Pueblos:
Zia Polychrome
Santa Ana Polychrome
Trios Polychrome
San Pablo/Ranchitos Polychrome
Puname Polychrome
Jemez River Polychrome
Glazed Pottery

Northeast Keres Pueblos:
Cochiti Polychrome
Nambé Polychrome
Kiua Polychrome
Tewa imitation/Ogapoge Polychrome
Glaze VI

Tewa Pueblos:
Tesuque & Individual Pueblos
Powhoge Polychrome
Ogapoge Polychrome
Sakona Polychrome

1650 (and earlier) — 1700 — 1750 — 1800 — 1850 — 1900 (to present)

Transitional Styles

Plate 3. Chronology of Pueblo pottery types, circa 1650–1900+. *Source:* Adapted from Francis H. Harlow, "Glaze-Matte Transitions in Pueblo Pottery" (unpublished book manuscript, 1983), 12. (Courtesy of Francis H. Harlow)

Plate 4. Puname Polychrome jar. Height 11.5″. (Photograph by William Acheff; private collection, with permission)

Pueblos (see Plate 5). The bulge became the entire midbody of the vessel, but a separate section with its own design area still marked the position it held in the earlier Puname example. Instead of a gentle slope above the bulge to the rim, San Pablo Polychrome exhibits a markedly rounded shoulder that curves back to join the short rim, as if the earlier bulge had simply migrated upward.

Plate 6 shows the completion of the transition from the Puname style into the shape that distinguished individual pueblo pottery styles by the mid–nineteenth century. This example of a Trios Polychrome jar produced at Zia Pueblo illustrates the continued evolution of the rounded midsection until no evidence of the Puname-style bulge remained in either the shape or the decorative scheme. In addition, the neck has become firmly integrated into the shape, sloping up and slightly inward from the slight shoulder to the mouth of the jar. Plate 3 shows a similar evolution taking place in the shape

Plate 5. San Pablo Polychrome jar. Height 10.5″. (Photograph by William Acheff; private collection, with permission)

of pottery from the Tewa and northern Keres region, the western Keres Pueblos, and Zuñi.

Unlike their predecessors, Pueblo transitional wares reflect the shape of ceramic wares commonly imported into the Province of New Mexico in the late eighteenth century. Mexican ceramic centers such as Puebla made blue-and-white vases and jars in the style of Chinese imports and exported them to markets all over New Spain. The chocolate jar shown in Plate 7 was collected in New Mexico and illustrates the high, rounded shoulder and short, vertical neck typical of talavera ware. These same features also represent a distinctive feature of the Pueblo transitional wares developed in each of the major pottery-producing Pueblos.

Pueblo pottery fashioned during the second half of the eighteenth cen-

Plate 6. Trios Polychrome jar, Zia Pueblo. Height 10.25″. (Photograph by William Acheff; private collection, with permission)

tury also underwent a general change in the style of the designs painted on the outer surface of the vessel. The Puname Polychrome example in Plate 4 has a design made up of stepped cloud designs and feather motifs arranged in a formal relationship of four panels around the top half of the jar. Vertical diamond bands within framing lines edge each panel, and inside the red stepped clouds tipped with black feathers come together in a V-shape that divides the panel into three design elements. Double black lines above and below carefully frame the entire upper body of the jar, setting off the interlocking motifs. The pretransitional style at Acoma, Ako Polychrome (Plate 8), dates from before 1750 and exhibits the pronounced midbody bulge also typical of the Puname type. It also exhibits the old-style decorative program. Like the Puname example, the Ako design has two bands filled with cloud and feather designs, the upper band divided into four formally arranged panels, each broken up into smaller, interlocking trapezoidal sections and all bounded by framing lines.

Plate 7. Chocolate jar, Puebla, Mexico, eighteenth-century tin glaze, blue-on-white talavera ware. Height 13.375″. (Photograph © Blair Clark; all rights reserved; courtesy of the Museum of International Folk Art, Santa Fe, New Mexico, catalog no. A.69.45.17)

Plate 8. Ako Polychrome jar. Height 11.5″. (Photograph by William Acheff; private collection, with permission)

Ako Polychrome evolved into a transitional pottery style named Acomita Polychrome. Plate 9 shows that in Acoma and Laguna Pueblos the changes in shape toward a round body, high shoulder, and narrow lip at the end of a short neck mirror the Puname–San Pablo progression. The painted decoration on the Acomita Polychrome jar has abstracted and stylized the tightly ordered Ako cloud and feather motifs. The artist still repeated design elements around the vessel, but the elements float freely on the cream slip that forms the background and have taken over the lower band of decoration apparent in the Ako style. The design element has also become more elaborate and complicated in the process. The same abstraction of the formal cloud and feather motifs and their elaboration into a complex schema of design elements accompanied the progression from Puname Polychrome to the later San Pablo and Trios styles (Plates 4–6).

Plate 9. Acomita Polychrome jar. Height 10.5″. (Courtesy of the School of American Research, Santa Fe, New Mexico, catalog no. 2797/12)

Once again, to understand the changes in decoration that mark transitional Pueblo pottery, one must look at contemporary developments within the vecino visual world. New Mexican vecino artists began to produce their own religious art for the first time starting in around 1790. Although earlier in the eighteenth century immigrants from Spain and Mexico and some of the Franciscan missionaries crafted religious art during their residence in New Mexico, at the same time they openly regarded such works as inferior substitutes for contemporary religious art produced in Spain or Mexico that the province could not afford to import.

Hide paintings and statues of saints made in New Mexico by Franciscan missionaries and some imported religious art did hang on the walls of eighteenth-century churches and missions, but the inventories of the period before 1790 show a general lack of decoration. The descriptions of religious furnishings do not mention frescos, large altarpieces, or chapels decorated with any type of coherent visual expression of the Catholic faith, items considered essential to religious observance and the proper education of the laity. In contrast, a striking movement began in the 1790s to refurbish and redecorate religious buildings and to endow new chapels within the churches and missions. These physical manifestations of invigorated vecino religious activity reached full stride in the early nineteenth century. A few decades later, church officials visiting New Mexico demanded the destruction of the earlier provincial attempts to surmount the effect of poverty and isolation on their places of worship, preferring the recently established style of religious art produced by vecino artists.[77]

Plate 10 shows the altar screen of the mission church at Laguna Pueblo as it looked in 1940. An unknown artist, designated the Laguna *Santero,* painted the images of the saints and the surrounding decoration on gesso-covered wooden boards. The Laguna Santero decorated churches and altarpieces in New Mexico between approximately 1795 and 1808 and represented the beginning of a vecino artistic tradition of major importance to the religious life of late colonial New Mexicans.[78] During his brief career in New Mexico, the Laguna Santero developed a provincial interpretation of the baroque elaboration found in the art and architecture of churrigueresque churches of the Bajío and elsewhere in late colonial New Spain. From this beginning, his vecino contemporaries and successors developed a unique New Mexican style of religious art during the late eighteenth and early nineteenth centuries.

The elaborate vegetal decoration, the drooping foliage covering the front of the altar, the flowers, roundels, medallions, and decorations framing the pictures of saints all suggest a direct source for the new motifs used in the transitional types of Pueblo pottery. Rather than absorbing specific designs directly from the non-Pueblo materials at hand, Pueblo potters applied a process similar to that used by Mexican baroque artists who altered the traditional Spanish decorative forms by elaborating them into intricate surface decorations. In so doing, Pueblo artists created elements resembling the patterns, volutes, medallions, and other intricate shapes that appeared on imported Mexican jars and vases and the wall decoration of altar screens in contemporary mission churches. Consider the floating red-and-white forms in the Acomita example shown in Plate 9. The formal cloud and feather motifs of the Ako Polychrome have relaxed and incorporated the swirling, rounded shapes floating on the white-slipped background, similar in its strategy of elaborating surface decoration to contemporary vecino and Mexican decorative styles. In the San Pablo Polychrome example of transitional ware from

Plate 10. Interior of the Laguna Mission Church, facing the altar, 1940. (Photograph by Max Barnett, Taylor Museum; courtesy of the Taylor Museum of the Colorado Springs Fine Arts Center, Colorado Springs, Colorado, negative 1519)

Zia Pueblo (Plate 5), the spaces inside the panels contain stylized clouds and feathers now made up of irregular, rounded shapes resembling vegetal forms. The Trios Polychrome (Plate 6) continues the development of design elements along these lines, approximating the elaborate plantlike decoration found in vecino religious art such as the Laguna Mission Church altarpiece (Plate 10).

Why did such an explosion of Pueblo innovation and change occur during the late eighteenth century in centers of pottery production remarkable for their "conservative" yet continually evolving tradition?[79] The new commercial system of the late colonial New Mexican economy provides the key to interpreting these changes in the material culture of the Pueblo Indians. The Pueblo weaving tradition became economically marginalized by a burgeoning textile vecino production, yet otherwise continued within the Pueblos largely along traditional lines. In contrast, the stylistic and technical changes in late-eighteenth-century Pueblo pottery suggest that Indian craftspeople felt economic pressure intense enough to change their pottery-making traditions in order to produce for a non-Indian market.

The pottery made by the Tewa and northeastern Keres pueblos, located in the center of the populated region of the province (see Map 9), illustrates the dramatic changes in pottery-making technique, as well as the evolution of shape and design, that marked the late-eighteenth-century transitional wares elsewhere. This region produced Ogapoge Polychrome during roughly the first half of the eighteenth century.[80] The particular example shown in Plate 11 comes from Gobernador Canyon, a region occupied by refugees from the pueblos during the reconquest and into the early eighteenth century. The distinctive bulge above the molded base curves gently up and inward to a slightly flared lip forming a shape comparable to that of the Puname and Ako types. The stepped cloud designs and feather motifs make up the majority of Ogapoge decoration. Even the sunflower or medallion composed of feathers contains an abstracted, stepped design as its stalk.

At some point during the second half of the eighteenth century, the Ogapoge style evolved into a style termed Powhoge Polychrome, here exemplified by the storage jar in Plate 12. This storage jar, most likely from San Ildefonso Pueblo, shows the exaggerated bulge typical of Ogapoge Polychrome now transformed into a large, almost spherical midbody, divided by a boundary between the red-slipped underbody and the decorated upper section. Potters working in the Powhoge style reversed the two bands of decoration found in Ogapoge Polychrome: The lower band held the major design elements, leaving only a narrow band of decoration just below the rim. However, the most striking part of the transformation appeared in the elements of the painted designs. The artist abstracted the traditional feather, cloud, and other motifs, building them into other patterns that threaten to

Plate 11. Ogapoge Polychrome jar. Height 11.5″. (Courtesy of the University of Colorado Museum, Boulder, Colorado, catalog no. 381)

obscure their origin. In addition, the formal geometrical motifs found in the Ogapoge designs have become more relaxed and rounded; the feathers appear to grow in a bunch out of their cloud-pedestal. Compare, for example, the flowerlike shape formed of feathers in the Ogapoge jar in Plate 11 to its Powhoge counterpart in Plate 12. The feathers now appear in the abstract, producing a sunburst medallion filled with an elaborate starlike pattern made up of scalloped, triangular design elements. With Powhoge Polychrome, the black-painted areas also begin to appear thin and watery.

Plate 12. Powhoge Polychrome storage jar. Height 15.75″. (Photograph by William Acheff; private collection, with permission)

The Cochití and Santo Domingo pueblos developed a variant of Powhoge Polychrome called Kiua Polychrome, distinguished by the thicker red band separating the upper and lower sections of the pot and by the extremely small neck at the rim.[81] The changes in shape and design also reflect those that took place in Powhoge Polychrome.

A number of alterations in technique accompany the transition from Oga-poge to Powhoge and Kiua Polychrome. Around 1800 Kiua potters abandoned the painstaking tradition of finishing their vessels by polishing them with a smooth, rounded stone before firing to give them a hard, even surface. Instead, they covered the outside with a bentonite slip applied with a buckskin rag or a piece of fleece. The surface of the fired pot appeared streaked and coarse as a result, as is especially apparent in the lighter portions of the

Plate 13. Kiua Polychrome storage jar, Cochití Pueblo. Height 19″. (Photograph by William Acheff; private collection, with permission)

Kiua storage jar shown in Plate 13. When viewed close up, a striking difference appears between the stone-polished pot, yielding a smooth, glossy veneer with uniform crazing, and the soapy, striated rag-polished surface, often with tiny, blistering craze marks. Archaeological excavations at San Antonio de las Huertas (about 18 miles northeast of Albuquerque and around 6 miles due east of Bernalillo) in the early 1980s demonstrate that this change took place around 1800.[82]

The output of some pueblos also shows evidence of sloppier execution in the decoration or firing of their works. Nambé Pueblo represents a particularly important example because a decline in the general quality of its output can be directly connected to its importance as a center of pottery production for trade to other pueblos and the vecinos until about 1830. Contemporary sources commented on the ceramic production of the Tewa pueblos, notably Tesuque, Nambé, and Pojoaque. In 1794 Fray Bernal wrote: "Particularly in the Tewa nation, the women labor harder than the men, and their common work is to make things of pottery, by hand and without any instru-

Plate 14. Nambé Polychrome storage jar. Height 16.6″. (Photograph by Bernard Lopez; collection of Francis H. Harlow)

ments whatever. [They make] large jars or large pitchers for water, pots, bowls, tubs, plates etc., but all very coarse and with little consistency. They sell them or barter them to obtain food, vegetables, etc." A related report noted that these pueblos traded pottery to the vecinos for food. The Nambé storage jar in Plate 14 illustrates the characteristics associated with the period of increased production: haphazard execution of the design, an irregular, lumpy shape, and a soft, thin, easily eroded, rag-polished slip. Archaeological sources confirm the impression of heightened production for the vecino market provided by the documents. The excavation of a trash pit at San

Antonio de los Poblanos, a vecino site in the north valley of Albuquerque, yielded large Powhoge Polychrome storage jars and water jars from the Tewa pueblos, demonstrating that the Pueblos of the middle Río Grande provided ceramic wares for a large part of the province.[83] Other imperfections appear with uncharacteristic frequency in some of the same transitional pottery types. Note the large smudge marks on the Kiua storage jar shown in Plate 13. Fire clouds posed a constant threat during firing, caused by pieces of fuel that touched the surface of the pot during the process. This storage jar received more than its fair share of smudges.

In the transition of Zuñi Pueblo pottery from Ashiwi to Zuñi Polychrome (see Plate 3), a phase sometimes called Kiapkwa Polychrome, developments in form and decoration follow that of the Ako–Acomita evolution. Kiapkwa and Acomita pieces generally show an important break with past styles of Ashiwi and Ako Polychrome, respectively, moving toward thicker, heavier walls, less well crafted shapes, and a slip of poorer quality compared with the preceding types.[84] Like the change in the Kiua Polychrome to a rag-polished slip and the degeneration of workmanship found in Nambé Polychrome, all of these developments point to intensified levels of production around 1800.[85]

One can discern three major trends in the late-eighteenth-century transitional styles of Pueblo pottery, all linked to contemporary economic changes in northern New Spain and New Mexico. The shape of pottery vessels evolved from the low bulge that defined Ogapoge, Puname, Ako, and Ashiwi Polychrome styles, to transitional types that have a large, almost spherical midbody, generally ending in a shoulder that meets a short neck. The pueblos replaced clouds, feathers, and other formal design elements with complex abstractions, less formally organized decorative spaces, and new active, stylized shapes. Finally, in a number of pueblos the new types exhibited a marked degradation in the quality of their output consistent with increased production for trade.

Connecting Pueblo pottery production to an expanding colonial export economy accounts for many of the similar alterations in form, design, and technique that appear in Pueblo transitional wares of the late eighteenth century. Parallel changes in the tradition of ceramic production took place in each of the pueblos, roughly between 1780 and 1820. An expanding vecino population, increases in productivity, the beginnings of a money economy, and a resurgent export market helped to create New Mexico's second eighteenth-century commercial system. Within the fabric of the new economy lay many of the institutions and mechanisms of coercive extraction found earlier, now no longer as effectively curbed by the structural deficiencies of the economy or by the need to concentrate on cooperation against a common Plains Indian enemy. In the case of textiles, the availability of subservient labor to expand production of woven goods within vecino households substituted for labor coerced from the pueblos by the repartimiento. For pottery, the demand for exports and the lack of a viable substitute for Pueblo ceramics increased the vecino incentive to use the same time-honored techniques more vigorously. The vecino usurpation of the Chihuahua trade after 1785 and the replacement of Pueblo textiles with the Río Grande blanket and other woven goods produced by vecinos illustrate a trend in the vecino economic response to the new economic forces emerging in New Mexico at the end of the eighteenth century.

The late colonial transition in historic Pueblo pottery took place within the context of this charged economic atmosphere and reflected a concentration of forces strong enough to alter the social and cultural fabric of the Pueblo peoples. The changes in ceramic shapes, design elements, and production techniques that occurred in the pueblos from 1780 to 1820 represented powerful manifestations of the social and cultural sea change brought about by economic growth. The nature of the transformation of the traditions governing Pueblo pottery making and weaving—shaped by Hispanic tastes and economic currents—attested to the growing dominance of vecino society in late colonial New Mexico. Carrying with them potent seeds of social change, these economic forces engendered a newly defined sense of vecino culture, increasingly expressed through new forms that will be examined in the next chapter.

CHAPTER FIVE

Creating Vecinos
Cultural Transformation

The creation of a vecino culture in New Mexico, based on an experience and a worldview distinct from those in other areas of contemporary New Spain, arose as a cultural product of the economic developments of the late colonial period. The impetus for this transformation came from a growing vecino population, increased productivity, and the spurt of long-distance trade that sparked the economic boom in New Mexico. New Mexicans began the process of evolving from settlers laboring for survival on a difficult frontier to citizens living in a social and cultural context they had worked to create, in 1598, as soon as Juan de Oñate established the first Spanish towns in New Mexico. It started anew when Diego de Vargas reestablished the settlements a century later, after the Pueblo Revolt had driven the Spanish out of the province. However, development toward self-definition never occurred as rapidly or with such far-reaching consequences as in the 1780–1820 period. New Mexicans began to establish the core of what made them citizens at the end of the eighteenth century.

The economic and demographic developments that shaped New Mexico during the last decades of Spanish colonial rule directed and deepened social and cultural change and reorganized the dynamic of social and cultural relationships within the province. Through the increased yield of agricultural products, livestock, and finished goods that could be exported, vecino prosperity influenced the forms and techniques of craft production. Economic linkages with the rest of New Spain through interregional trade brought about new expressions of Spanish cultural forms, rearticulated by vecino hands. Like the development of the Río Grande style of blanket, vecino santeros and carpenters created unique provincial interpretations of Mexican religious imagery and forms of domestic furniture.

Population and commercial expansion in the province between 1780 and

1820 formed the basis for a mature and self-confident vecino generation in the process of developing an ethnic identity—as the "citizens" of the province of New Mexico. The same changes that manifested themselves in the creation of new forms of social behavior and religious expression worked to privilege Spanish and vecino components of this emerging identity and increasingly define them in contrast to the cultural practices and communities of Pueblo Indians. By the 1790s, success of the vecinos at dominating the social and economic life of the province attracted the Franciscan missionaries and led them away from their traditional defense of Pueblo Indian lands and other prerogatives. In turn, the Pueblos reacted to economic coercion and social subjugation with new and sophisticated forms of cultural resistance.

TRANSFORMING PUEBLO INDIAN–VECINO RELATIONS

Colonial marriage records provide striking evidence of the process of self-definition taking place within vecino society. By the 1780s the male:female ratio among vecinos had dropped to somewhere around 87 to 94 men per 100 women, the result of losses during the preceding decades of fighting and of increased vecino intermarriage with Pueblo women and Plains Indian captives. Compared with the sex ratio in the jurisdiction of Durango during the same period, New Mexico had a far higher percentage of women among its population. Work done by Ramón Gutiérrez using *diligencias matrimoniales* from the New Mexican missions—the investigation required by canon law in order to ensure that no impediments to marriage existed— shows that the age difference between spouses at first marriage decreased significantly at the same time.[1] Both phenomena indicate that the demographic profile of New Mexican vecinos had evolved from that of a young frontier population of settlers to a more stable and mature society at the end of the eighteenth century.

The census records also show a new concern with ethnic divisions of the population during the 1760–1800 period. Ethnic classifications based on the product of mixed marriages appear in the New Mexican documents from the early years of the province, but their usage underwent a marked change toward the end of the eighteenth century. After 1760, the ethnic designations of respondents appear in increasing number in the records of the diligencias matrimoniales. In addition, for the first time the investigating friar consistently included in his report ethnic labels denoting the offspring of mixed marriages, such as *Color Quebrado, Coyote, Lobo,* and *Mulato.* This change reflected two trends: the increasing frequency of endogamous, cross-ethnic marriages encouraged by a quarter-century of close proximity and collaboration due to the Plains Indian threat; and a heightened sensitivity to racial designations, at least on the part of the missionaries responsible for recording the censuses.[2]

Two changes of great significance to the understanding of late colonial New Mexican society took place corresponding to the period of rapid growth in vecino economic activity. During the last decade of the eighteenth century, vecinos and Pueblo Indians for the most part stopped intermarrying. At the same time, interest in mixed-race classifications that so preoccupied officials and missionaries in the 1760s and 1770s began to disappear.

Gutiérrez, in his investigation of the diligencias matrimoniales, divided the marriage population into vecinos, Indios, and Castas and tested the association of bride's and groom's racial designations against a model assuming the random selection of a mate.[3] He found that the partners of marriages represented in his sample expressed a marked preference for a spouse from their own racial category through the 1760s. This association decreased dramatically through the 1770s and into the 1780s, when spouses appeared to marry with little regard for ethnic status. Beginning around 1790 the trend reversed, and by the early 1800s the statistic used for demonstrating marriage preference indicates that virtually all couples married within their own ethnic group.

Additional analysis of the data collected by Gutiérrez confirms that vecinos chose fewer Pueblo Indians in marriage and shows that the change took place after the 1780s. Figure 12 includes all marriages recorded in the diligencias matrimoniales in which Gutiérrez identified at least one of the spouses as a Pueblo Indian. From the point of view of the Pueblo marriage partners through the 1780s, the diligencias show a very large percentage of exogamous marriages, but since the friars could only investigate impediments to marriages made with partners outside the Pueblo, only a small number of total Pueblo marriages became subject to investigation. Figure 12 shows that the percentage of marriages between Pueblo Indians and vecinos declined substantially after 1789, even as the number of total marriages with at least one Pueblo partner went up. After 1800 the number of Indians marrying a partner from another pueblo rose markedly, perhaps in lieu of outside marriages to non-Pueblos. Consequently, Franciscans conducted more diligencias matrimoniales covering Pueblo marriages.

Simultaneously, the proliferation of ethnic classifications found in the diligencias starting in the 1760s had disappeared almost entirely by the end of the century. Similarly, many census documents that had counted vecinos, Indios, and Castas in the 1760s through 1780s listed only two classifications, "Indios" and "vecinos y Castas," or just "vecinos" (or "Españoles"), later in the century. As in other parts of New Spain, the self-designation of racial status in marriage documents had rendered such labels increasingly inaccurate during the eighteenth century.[4] When asked by missionaries to identify their race at baptisms or marriages, respondents often replied in ways calculated to improve their status in the eyes of Spanish society. In New Mexico, the new currents of economic activity added to the incentive for passing from Color

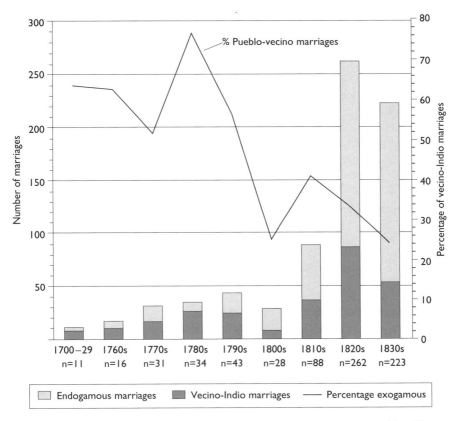

Figure 12. Vecino-Indio marriages as a percentage of those represented in diligencias matrimoniales, New Mexico, 1700–1839. *Source:* Table showing place of residence at marriage, by decade, courtesy of Ramón Gutiérrez, University of California, San Diego, compiled from AASF:DM.

Quebrado, Coyote, Lobo, Genízaro, or other Castas to vecino or Español through self-identification. For Pueblo Indians, however, lack of interest in the system of classification or Franciscan missionaries who assigned racial status based on residence in a Pueblo served to increase the differentiation between Indios and vecinos.[5]

The New Mexican response to the Revillagigedo census of 1790 presents a notable exception to the trend toward fewer ethnic labels, made more significant because of the tendency of scholars to emphasize this particular census in their research. Spanish officials conducted the 1790 census throughout New Spain, and nearly complete responses from New Mexico survive.[6] The census organized the populace according to six racial classifications, including designations not often found in other colonial documents from New Mexico of the same period. Printed census forms and instructions sent to New Mexican officials from Mexico in preparation for a consistent enumeration throughout New Spain caused the racial categories to appear or reappear suddenly in 1790, and they did not necessarily reflect contemporary local practice.[7]

The mixed-race classifications in use in New Mexico during the third quarter of the century—Genízaro, Casta, Color Quebrado—became incorporated during the next generation into the vecino label. The collapse of the terms describing mixed-race peoples into one non-Indian group left a bipolar system that resembled the early-eighteenth-century distinction between vecinos and Naturales, before the elaboration of mixed-race classifications. "Vecino" indicated one's Spanish settler neighbors, and "Natural" signified the "uncivilized" Pueblo Indians before conversion. However, while the old terms represented different racial groups, their meaning at the end of the century signified a distinction in cultural terms. The redefined category of vecino, or Español, now encompassed hispanicized Genízaros and Castas.[8] Labeling groups by a set of primarily cultural, rather than racial, characteristics underscores the significance of this period in the transformation of frontier society in New Mexico. After three decades of cooperation and intermarriage between Pueblo Indians and their neighbors, vecinos at the end of the eighteenth century had begun to fashion their own cultural identity, defined in large part in contradistinction to that of the Pueblos.

The movement of ethnic markers in New Mexico differs in interesting ways from what researchers have found in other areas of northern New Spain. A number of scholars agree that the racial categories understood in central Mexico broke down in northern communities and that provincial communities created new ethnic identities from the categories previously ascribed to them by others. However similar the process, the nature of the changes depended largely on the economic and cultural contours of the locality. Cynthia Radding has shown in the Sonoran highlands that the policy of *reducción*, reducing the scattered villages to larger communities, created a period of flux in ethnic categories. Uprooted Pima and Opata migrated to non-Indian villages, where they supplied their labor and worked to gain vecino status. At the same time, settlers encroached upon Indian villages and mission lands to expand their herds and fields. Other groups of seminomadic Indians also moved seasonally in and out of the villages to trade and to work at harvests. These movements, each in its own way tied to Bourbon policy, formed vecino communities by a steady process of accretion. Mining, and to a lesser extent agriculture, combined with the effect of the reducciones, provided a strong pull toward social integration in Sonora.[9]

All of these elements existed in late colonial New Mexico in some sense:

Pueblo Indian outcasts and some who married outside the pueblo formed a steady stream of new Casta or Coyote members of vecino communities; vecino encroachment on Pueblo lands intensified beginning in the late 1780s (discussed below); and Genízaros, slaves, and semi-nomadic groups of allies and refugees had increasing contact with both Pueblo and vecino communities. In contrast to Sonora, Pueblo Indian cultural boundaries and Bourbon economic forces each worked to reinforce a process that made Pueblo Indians marginal to vecino society and subjected them to somewhat indirect forms of vecino economic exploitation but that still afforded them a measure of cultural autonomy.

Vecino cultural change brought with it a hardening of socially constructed racial-ethnic distinctions into class lines. Spanish folktales collected in New Mexico appear to illustrate this development further. In one story, a wealthy young man saw Beatrice, the daughter of a count, while attending Mass, and they fell madly in love with each other.[10] When he applied to her father to ascertain his chances of winning her, the count replied that custom made the gap between their social positions too much of a barrier for any hope of success. When the count next saw his daughter talking to the young man he had her placed at night in a convent under orders of strict silence. Her lover tried to help her escape, but the count, having been forewarned, appeared suddenly to stop them. In the exchange of blows that followed, the father fell and the man fled, believing that he had killed the count.

After going to war and becoming a captive of the Indians, a young Coyote[11] woman named Sicay chose the young man as her husband. Although she lived with the Indians, Sicay had refused ever to marry an Indian, in deference to the Spanish blood of her mother. Together they planned to flee to the Spanish, but the Indians apprehended them and placed the husband in prison. Meanwhile, Beatrice persuaded her father to let her marry her exiled lover, and she dressed herself as a man in order to lead the troop attempting his rescue. Beatrice freed her lover, and together they killed the old witch who had imprisoned Sicay. When Sicay greeted her husband with joy, he refused to embrace her: "You no longer want me?" asked Sicay. "No, no longer, because my first love has come," said the young man.

The Indians in the tale appear to be a strange combination of Pueblo and Plains; the Spanish fight them, yet among these Indians lived a priest who counseled Sicay, encouraged her engagement to the young man, and joined them in a Catholic marriage. Ultimately, an advantageous marriage with a woman of high Spanish birth took precedence over a properly consummated marriage with a beautiful half-Indian woman. The folktale embodies the social preferences of vecino society in the late colonial period. Beatrice, the wealthy young man, Sicay, and the full-blooded Indians represented, in descending order, the ranks of New Mexican social hierarchy by the first decade of the nineteenth century.

SANTOS AND FURNITURE:
NEW FORMS OF VECINO CULTURAL EXPRESSION

Population growth and economic development in New Mexico had a direct influence on the components of vecino identity that emerged at the
end of the colonial period. Beginning in the 1780s, vecinos suddenly expanded their repertoire of forms for cultural expression and acquired new
channels for the social articulation of a self-confident, distinct Spanish sub-
culture on the northern frontier of New Spain. A vecino religious movement
emerged at the end of the eighteenth century, characterized by santos and
by the renewal and expansion of cofradías, including the foundation of
La Hermanidad Nuestro Padre Jesús Nazareno, commonly referred to as *Los
Penitentes*. Vecino craftsmen began to produce images of saints for the missions, chapels, and churches around 1790, complementing a movement to
rebuild and decorate religious edifices.

Given the expansion of the vecino population at the end of the eighteenth
century, one would expect to find a contemporary surge in the construction
of churches and other religious buildings in New Mexico. As settlers from
the established areas of vecino settlement founded new villages, they built
churches and chapels, often without any way to obtain an ecclesiastical license and almost always without a resident priest. Due to a chronic shortage of secular priests, in new villages, as in the older settlements, the friar
from the nearest pueblo mission attended to the sacraments and the occasional Mass when convenient. When Bishop Don José Antonio de Zubiría
visited New Mexico in 1833, he authorized more than thirty licenses for
new churches, chapels, and oratories in all parts of the province.[12] Pedro
Tamarón y Romerál in 1760 had conducted the last visitation of New Mexico made by a bishop of Durango. Since Fray Atanasio Domínguez's visitation occurred in 1776, many of these buildings had functioned without the
benefit of official sanction. Among others, Bishop Zubiría issued licenses
to the church at Ranchos de Taos, begun by the late 1780s, the church of
Nuestra Señora de Guadalupe in the plaza of San Fernando de Taos, the
chapel also dedicated to the Guadalupe in La Cuesta, near San Miguel del
Vado, and the church of the Santuario del Señor de Esquipulas at Chimayo,
constructed around 1816. Vecino communities built between 1780 and
1820 period represented almost all the religious edifices that Bishop Zubiría
licensed during his visitation.

In addition to the construction of new religious buildings needed to keep
up with an increasing laity, vecinos undertook a program of reconstruction
and refurbishment of long-standing structures on a scale not seen in New
Mexico since the reconquest. A portion of the attention lavished on existing
churches and on new chapels and oratories came from the hands of vecino
santeros, who established at this time a new artistic tradition in the province.

Architectural evidence and documents describing construction and dedication attest to the tremendous activity undertaken between 1780 and 1820 to erect, rebuild, repair, and decorate religious structures. Important support and patronage for many of these projects came from members of the emerging vecino commercial elite involved in the trade with Chihuahua.[13]

Don Antonio José Ortiz provides an outstanding example of the natural links between provincial economic development and the cultural enrichment that followed. Ortiz came from a well-established vecino family. His great-grandfather, a sergeant from Zacatecas, moved his family of six and entered the province with Governor Vargas.[14] His father served as teniente in the Presidio of Santa Fe. In April 1750 he married Gertrudis Páez Hurtado, daughter of Vargas's teniente general, Juan Páez Hurtado. Born in 1734, at the age of 20 José Antonio married Rosa Bustamante, the daughter of Don Bernardo de Bustamante y Tagle, who served as lieutenant governor in 1722–1731 under his close relative, Governor Juan Domingo de Bustamante. Ortiz rose to prominence in Santa Fe in the 1770s, becoming patron of the fiesta held by the Confraternity of La Conquistadora in 1772 and, after 1776, perpetual majordomo of the organization. The money that Ortiz lavished on religious donations came from a profitable career as a merchant and public official. In 1778, as alcalde mayor of Santa Fe, he attempted unsuccessfully to win the tithe contract for New Mexico.

A glimpse of Ortiz's commercial activities in the trade to Chihuahua appears in the alcabala records for 1783. He paid the tax on fifty sarapes, which he carried in the annual convoy from New Mexico.[15] Two years later he successfully bid for the tithe and held it for the 1785–1786 biennium. At that time he held the title of captain of the Santa Fe militia in addition to his position as alcalde mayor of the villa. When Governor Concha wrote his instructions to his successor in 1794, he commended Alcalde Mayor Don Antonio José Ortiz as the man "in whom resides the necessary knowledge of all of the inhabitants." He recommended that incoming Governor Chacón seek the advice of Ortiz on the appointment of future alcaldes mayores.

Beginning in the 1790s and until his death in 1806, Ortiz provided patronage for a number of projects of religious renewal.[16] Before 1797, work funded by Ortiz had begun on a new chapel dedicated to San José attached to the parish church of San Francisco in Santa Fe. As portions of the church had deteriorated almost to ruins, Ortiz had the structure renovated. He had already repaired and refurbished the Rosario chapel attached to the parish church, the San Miguel chapel in Santa Fe, and the mission church at Pojoaque Pueblo, close to his ranch. In 1798 he petitioned the bishop of Durango for permission to build an *oratorio* near his house, due to his poor health. He received the license for an already finished oratorio the following year. At the same time, part of the parish church collapsed, and Ortiz undertook to repair the damage. By 1804, work had progressed to the point

that the structure awaited *vigas,* when lightning struck. The disaster forced
Ortiz to begin the project again. This time he tore down the existing walls
and had the church considerably enlarged. In the early years of the nineteenth century, Don Antonio also constructed a second private chapel at his
ranch at Pojoaque.

Ortiz's patronage illustrates the natural connection between the New
Mexican economic boom and the late-eighteenth-century renewal of provincial religious buildings. However, the cultural ramifications of religious
patronage ran even more deeply, encouraging the development of a direct
religious expression of the late colonial vecino experience. Don Antonio
again provides a fine example. Ortiz supplemented his considerable program of construction with gifts of interior decoration and furnishings calculated to make the buildings more attractive and serviceable to meet the
religious needs of his family and the Santa Fe community. In a letter to the
bishop of Durango in 1805, he listed some of his donations: "The sanctuary
and high altar [of San Francisco] have been renewed by me, also the chapel
of Nuestra Señora del Rosario and the chapel of San José, in which Your
Lordship has granted me the privilege and grace to have, all, from their
foundations to their conclusion, sanctuary, and other ornaments have been
placed by me. The sanctuary of the chapel of San Miguel outside the parish
I made myself. I have given various jewels to the parish church, not only
in adornment but in services to the Mission of San Diego at Tesuque; I have
made the principal sanctuary at the Mission of Nuestra Señora de Guadalupe."[17] The ornaments and adornments mentioned by Ortiz link his patronage to a corpus of santos made by the Laguna Santero, one of the earliest and most influential saint makers working in New Mexico.

Other documentary sources and inscriptions on the works confirm that
Ortiz commissioned the altar screen for the sanctuary in the chapel of San
Miguel, a large *reredo* in the mission church at Pojoaque, an altar screen in the
chapel of San José in the Santa Fe parish church, and similar "adornment"
for the sister chapel of Nuestra Señora del Rosario. Similar stylistic elements
indicate that the artist who crafted the altar screen in the San Miguel chapel
in Santa Fe also fashioned altar screens at Laguna (Plate 10), Acoma, and
probably those at Zia and Santa Ana. The alcalde mayor of the Laguna district, Don José Manuel Aragón, commissioned both the Laguna and Acoma
altar screens, and Vitor Sandoval and his wife, Doña María Manuela Ortiz,
donated the ones at Zia and Santa Ana. Both groups of patrons had a connection to Don Antonio José Ortiz. Second cousins María Manuela Ortiz and
Don Antonio belonged to the same wealthy Ortiz family.[18] The will of Don
Antonio José Ortiz mentioned forty-eight cows due to him, at the time in
the hands of José Manuel Aragón as the result of a partido. Patronage from
the Ortiz family and business associates who were equally active in the second commercial economy accounted for the completion of the known al-

tar screens carved and painted under the artistic direction of the Laguna Santero. Scholars have named this anonymous artist after the altar screen he completed in the Laguna mission church, his last and best-preserved monumental work.

The Laguna Santero worked in New Mexico from approximately 1795 until about 1808, judging from documents, inscriptions found on panels, and dates supplied by a dendrochronological analysis of wood used by the artist.[19] The short span of his career in the province and the fully formed style apparent in the earliest of his works has led to the suggestion that Antonio José Ortiz contracted with an artist from Mexico who returned there a few years after the death of his primary patron. Despite the brevity of his activity in New Mexico, the Laguna Santero bridged the gap between style and technique current elsewhere in New Spain and an artistic expression in harmony with the needs and sensibilities of vecino society. Although perhaps not a vecino by birth, he created an original New Mexican vocabulary of religious imagery that continued to evolve long after the end of his active career in the province. During this period of fourteen years or so, the Laguna Santero completed at least eight major commissions for Ortiz, Aragón, and Sandoval-Ortiz, and in addition left a number of *retablos,* paintings on hide, bas-reliefs made of gesso, niches for statues, and a group of *bultos.* Recently, restoration of the church at Santa Cruz de la Cañada reclaimed an altar screen made by the Laguna Santero, and he also may have worked on the church of San Francisco at Ranchos de Taos, at least for a time. The Laguna Santero established a workshop of painters, wood carvers, and carpenters to execute commissions under his direction. At the same time—and in much the same vein—the government of the Provincias Internas took the suggestions of Fray Morfí, Governors Concha and Chacón, and others and contracted with the Bazán brothers to heighten the quality of the vecino weaving industry in New Mexico.

The artistic production of the Laguna Santero established a number of stylistic interpretations of the baroque tradition of New Spain that directed the development of a provincial industry, producing religious images for churches, chapels, oratorios, private homes, and Penitente meeting places during the succeeding generation.[20] In general, the Laguna artist translated the complicated architectural structure and exuberant decoration of eighteenth-century Mexican religious furnishings into a simplified form carved in the soft woods available in New Mexico (principally pine and cottonwood) or painted on a flat surface in two-dimensional perspective.

In carving and painting the altar screen at Laguna (see Plate 10) the artist brought together a number of innovations begun in earlier works to create a unified provincial style. The architecture of the altar screen blends three-dimensional, carved, and painted Salomonic pillars with painted, flat boards forming arches to create niches for the display of the patron saint, San José, in the center, flanked by Santa Barbara and San Juan Nepomuceno (Nepo-mucene) on the right and left, respectively. In the earlier altar screens made for San Miguel Chapel and the mission church at Pojoaque, the altar screen forged a similar architectural space meant to house either sculptures of saints or oil paintings imported from Mexico, or occasionally from Spain. These al-tar screens conformed to the basic design and function of their contempo-rary counterparts in Mexico and Spain. Beginning with the altar screen at Zia, and gaining maturity with the works at Acoma and Laguna, the santero began to supply the saints in addition to the architectural frame. The Laguna Santero painted the figures of the saints on wood panels and inset them within his decorated frames in the traditional manner as if they were sepa-rate works imported from Mexico or Spain. Scholars have postulated that the Laguna master also fashioned bultos to serve as the focal point for his altar screens, but apparently no large figures have survived.[21]

The integration of the picture of the saint and the Spanish tradition of elaborate architectural frames for santos altered the function of the screen, merging the two elements into a single visual unit. The image of the saint now included a large frame made up of decorative conceits in a complimentary style, instead of a separate structure designed to set off the central image in contrast to its elaborately ornamented architectural space. Unifying the simplified baroque elements and the central religious image in a single, con-sistent form created one of the basic ingredients developed by the succeed-ing vecino santo tradition. The concept appears in individual retablos with saints depicted in gesso as a bas-relief associated with the Laguna Santero or his workshop, and it took on new life in the hands of indigenous vecino san-teros who followed. In replacing the scarce and highly valued piece of im-ported religious art with the picture or statue of a saint made by his own hand, Laguna Santero also expressed the self-confidence of the new vecino laity in their own provincial forms of religious expression.

The Laguna Santero translated other aspects of prevailing Mexican ba-roque styles into forms that communicated in two dimensions, eschewing the complication of three-dimensional perspective. In the Laguna panel, the robes of the figures of the Trinity that form the *remate* and that of San José below appeared as a simplified version of the swirling, naturalistic movement and detail that provided sentiment to Mexican baroque painting. As a result, the figures seem to lack mass, and their clothes appear merely decorative, rather than adding emotion to the scene. The faces of the saints also lack the intense baroque naturalism that gave them emotive power in contemporary Mexican painting. Instead, the Laguna Santero provided his subjects with a sense of solemn detachment. Only the eyes of the saints pierce the two-dimensional space, searching for those of the viewer. Finally, the decorations that fill most of the remaining space have become two-dimensional patterns and emblems instead of the exuberant baroque foliage that typified Mexican artwork. The frescolike painting on the side walls at Laguna seem like a patterned tapestry, although they still resemble the plant motifs sculptured on the exterior walls at the entrances of the cathedrals of Chihuahua and Durango, or even the more elaborate growth decorating the Retablo Mayor of the chapels of San Pedro and Los Arcángeles in the cathedral of Mexico City.[22]

The demand for religious images among a growing vecino population created an indigenous santo industry before the turn of the nineteenth century. The Laguna Santero provided a coherent artistic style adapted to New Mexican conditions and a workshop of followers with some training gained from the master. The career of santero Don Pedro Antonio Fresquis also began in the 1790s, creating santos in a style independent of influence from the Laguna Santero. Fresquis represented one of the earliest vecino craftsman catering to a popular, rural demand for religious images. His work often drew directly on imagery from popular European prints and engravings imported throughout New Spain. Fresquis painted with thin, flowing lines and the precision of a draftsman. He rendered the conventional perspective found in his printed models to flat, two-dimensional form to create the illusion of space by using cross-hatching and other techniques borrowed from Spanish and Flemish prints. Before the identification of Fresquis as the artist responsible for this style, his technique provided the title "Calligraphic Santero." The wide range of religious subjects that Fresquis depicted, and the iconography he drew upon, attest to the influence of imported materials. Another early santero, known as Molleno, worked in the early nineteenth century. Molleno probably received his training as an apprentice of the Laguna Santero.[23]

The innovation of the Laguna Santero and Pedro Antonio Fresquis in developing a vecino language of religious imagery occurred through a process that George Kubler called "form-splitting" (*Formenspaltungen*) common elsewhere in colonial Latin America and in Europe during the Middle Ages. The term, introduced by the German art historian Adolf Goldschmidt in 1936, referred to artists using other artifacts, instead of nature, as models for new art. Form-splitting describes the transmission and translation of fashions current in the metropolitan centers to distant regions. Kubler provided the example of "the tendril-like proliferation of Plateresque scrollwork in provincial hands, when we compare Acolman with Yurutia in Mexico," as a New World equivalent to the process that took place in medieval art described by Goldschmidt. The early New Mexican santeros also employed form-splitting as a means of adapting styles current elsewhere in New Spain. This phenomenon accounts in large part for the aspects of santo form and style that appear to derive from the seventeenth or early eighteenth century, or even from medieval Spain, instead of contemporary Mexico.[24]

Despite the emphasis on an itinerant folk tradition of New Mexican santeros in much of the literature, the beginnings of the vecino santo industry relied heavily on commissions from wealthy patrons or newly established communities to fashion larger altar screens and individual bultos and retablos for the furnishing of religious buildings. Religious patronage of the arts functioned in a manner similar to that of Mexico City or a provincial capital, albeit on a smaller scale. Fresquis painted a major altar screen for the church at Truchas around 1818, and he received a commission from the family of Antonio José Ortiz for a wooden collateral for the Rosario chapel mentioned above. He designed the work to house the statue of Nuestra Señora del Rosario, known as La Conquistadora in New Mexico, held to have first been brought to the province by Fray Alonso de Benavides in 1623 and again by Governor Vargas during the reconquest. Documents also mention work— no longer extant—executed at the churches of Santa Cruz de la Cañada and Chimayo. Molleno completed the altar screen in the side chapel dedicated to Nuestro Señor de Esquipulas at the Church of San Francisco, Ranchos de Taos, between about 1815 and 1817, and may also have painted the original main altar.[25]

The Rosario and Ranchos commissions demonstrate the continuing connection between the vecino elite and the early development of the santero tradition and the passing of the mantle of innovation from the Laguna master to native vecino craftsmen. Although smaller, individual retablos and bultos became common during the next generation, catering to a truly popular demand for religious images and patrons of fewer means, larger projects proved an important source of support for santeros well into the nineteenth century. The numerous altar screens commissioned from nineteenth-century santero José Rafael Aragón (working dates circa 1820– 1862) appear in religious buildings throughout the Río Arriba region. Examples include the pueblo mission of San Lorenzo de Picurís (completed by 1826), the private Durán chapel at Talpa, near Taos (1838), and a public chapel in Córdova, near Santa Cruz de la Cañada (1834–1838).[26]

The secular brotherhood of Penitentes also emerged in New Mexico during the last decades of the Spanish period. Very little information exists to shed light on the origin or precise date of the beginning of La Hermanidad de Nuestro Padre Jesús Nazareno. The religious movement arose in New Mexico between 1776 and 1833, when Bishop Zubiría made specific mention of the "abuses" of corporal penance practiced by the cofradía at Santa Cruz. The Penitente organization grew in the context of a general resurgence of confraternities in the province.[27] The Penitente emphasis on reliving the suffering and redemption of Christ—taken to the extent of elaborate rituals of flagellation and the reenactment of the Passion—represented a popular religious movement whose spiritualism and iconography exemplified the articulation of this powerful, self-confident, vecino worldview emerging from the changes and ordeals of the preceding half-century.

The development of the New Mexican santo at the end of the eighteenth century coincided with the establishment of vecino techniques and styles of furniture production. In addition to providing religious structures with devotional imagery and decoration, the transformation of forms and styles from elsewhere in New Spain also took place within the domestic setting of vecino homes. Assigning dates to vecino furniture remains difficult because fewer documents, inscriptions, or groups of works representing individual styles survive for utilitarian goods than do records of church renovation or the commission of altar screens. Although provincial wills and inventories show that settlers produced some furniture throughout the eighteenth century, no documents describe the way it looked in any detail. In contrast to surviving examples of Franciscan styles of religious imagery that preceded the blossoming of the art of the santero, no New Mexican furniture known today can be confidently dated before the late eighteenth century.[28]

The earliest examples of New Mexican furniture that survive represent another node on the roots of late colonial vecino material culture. Like the innovation of the Río Grande blanket style and associated textiles and the establishment of a native santo-making tradition, vecino furniture production at the end of the eighteenth century constituted a resurgent craft that also responded to New Mexican demographic change and economic growth. The argument presented here rests on three observations: Most of the items of early furniture mentioned in wills and extant examples came from wealthy families likely to patronize carpenters and to commission furniture as a means of displaying status; the process of rendering Mexican furniture prototypes and decoration into a vecino aesthetic form operated in a fashion similar to that of the development of santos; two innovative vecino furniture types exist, the New Mexican framed chest developed late in the late eighteenth century and the *harinero,* from the early nineteenth century and directly linked to expanding agricultural production.

Descriptions of vecino households by American visitors after the opening of the Santa Fe trade with the United States in 1821 emphasize the sparseness of the domestic interiors of most New Mexican homes.[29] Josiah Gregg, an American who first entered New Mexico with a trade caravan in 1831, wrote a dozen years later that:

> The immense expense attending the purchase of suitable furniture and kitchen-ware, indeed, the frequent impossibility of obtaining these articles at any price, caused the early settlers of northern Mexico to resort to inventions of necessity, or adopt Indian customs altogether, many of which have been found so comfortable and convenient, that most of those who are now able to indulge in luxuries, feel but little inclination to introduce any change. Even the few pine-board chairs and setees [*sic*] that are to be found about the houses are seldom used; the prevailing fashion being to fold mattresses against the

walls, which, being covered over with blankets, are thus converted into sofas. Females, indeed, most usually prefer accommodating themselves, *à l'Indienne,* upon a mere blanket spread simply on the floor.

Gregg responded to the relative indifference of New Mexicans to furniture compared with contemporary Anglo-American households.

Nonetheless, late colonial wills and private inventories show that both native-made and imported pieces of furniture had significant value. Wooden chests, the most frequently mentioned type of furniture, received values of 2–12 pesos in wills from the 1780–1820 period. The wills containing the most furniture pertained to the estates of the wealthier families of the province, always closely connected to the second commercial economy. Don Clemente Gutiérrez died in 1785 as one of the richest men in New Mexico. He made his fortune in the Chihuahua trade, after emigrating from Aragón, Spain. Gutiérrez held the tithe contract for New Mexico from 1779 until the year before his death. He left an assortment of furniture that had adorned an eighteen-room house: two trunks and nineteen chests and boxes of various kinds, six chairs, five tables, two beds, four benches, three *armarios,* and a desk from Michoacán. Of the twenty-one chests, boxes, and trunks, six came from Michoacán. In contrast, Tomasa Benavides died in 1762 leaving only one piece of furniture, a chest. The probate record attested that the "deceased had always been a poor woman."[30]

Don Manuel Delgado died in 1815 without having made out a will. Delgado had become a wealthy merchant also involved in trade with Chihuahua and had served in the military for more than thirty years. His estate included twenty-five pieces of furniture, not including forty-one stools, which may have formed part of his commercial inventory. All of this material apparently came from New Mexico, as the only mention of imported furnishings concerned six washbasins from Michoacán. One year earlier, Rosa Bustamante swore out her will in Santa Fe in front of her notary and the required witnesses. Bustamante, the widow of Antonio José Ortiz, patron of the Laguna Santero, assigned to her heirs two writing desks, twelve stools, two or three tables, two sofas, and a wardrobe. Three of the estates that contained furniture belonged to alcaldes mayores, pointing to the link between provincial posts, wealth, and family status.[31]

Given the social status of the families most likely to possess furniture in any quantity, one might expect vecino craftsmen to rethink Spanish furniture types in provincial terms in much the same manner as did the New Mexican santeros. Plate 15 shows a chest made in New Mexico for the storage of household goods during the late eighteenth or early nineteenth century. The carpenter made this piece, called a board chest, by joining four panels together with dovetail joints and attaching the bottom board to the edges of the sides with pegs.[32] The construction differed very little from that of Span-

Plate 15. New Mexican board chest, late eighteenth or early nineteenth century. 23.6″ × 50.8″ × 22″. (Photograph by Mary Peck; courtesy of the Museum of International Folk Art, a unit of the Museum of New Mexico, Santa Fe, New Mexico, A.82.10–1 [NMF #31])

ish or Mexican boxes. Some board chests retained a proportional scheme of one-half vara squares for either end of the box and two for the front and back, making them one vara wide. The arrangement of the decoration followed Mexican guild requirements for borders and divisions of Roman molding and proportional design elements.

Various features identify this chest as unmistakably New Mexican. Lacking hardwoods in the province, the pine boards used in furniture construction could not have taken the elaborate, deeply-carved designs in relief used in chests from Spain.[33] Instead, the New Mexican craftsman chose one traditional motif carved in low-relief as an emblem for each panel, framed by a simplified border pattern. Rosettes, stylized vines in the upper center panel, regardant lions, and pomegranate motifs all hail from the Spanish and Moorish decorative tradition but appear in a patterned, two-dimensional form. The process paralleled the relationship of the Laguna Santero's decoration to that found on contemporary Mexican churches. A number of extant board chests exhibit an exterior painted in bright colors, emphasizing another connection between vecino furniture and santo production. The similarity in baroque motifs used on furniture and santos has become the basis for dating early examples. Finally, due to limited access to iron, the artisan kept the use of metal hardware to a minimum, reserving it for the latch, simple hinges, and strap iron reinforcements of the corners for added strength in some pieces.

Plate 16. New Mexican framed chest, late eighteenth or early nineteenth century. 27.6″ × 33.5″ × 15.8″. (Photograph by Mary Peck; courtesy of the Millicent Rogers Museum, Taos, New Mexico, MRM 1967–3–53 [NMF #465])

Board chests, such as the one in Plate 15, often sat on wooden stands to protect the bottom from rotting and to provide some protection against rodents. Late in the eighteenth century vecino craftsmen developed framed chests with legs that built the stand into the structure of the piece. One example appears in Plate 16. The frame required eight horizontal rails and five vertical stiles, four at the corners and one dividing the front, center panel.[34] The artist secured the elements of the frame by using mortise-and-tenon joints, pinned with a wooden peg instead of a nail. Four or more panels fit inside the framing rails to form the sides, which the artist then decorated with chip-carved gouged designs in relief. While this type of decoration did not have the elegance or sophistication of the heraldic figures found on the chest in Plate 15, the design concept remained similar to furniture made

Plate 17. New Mexican harinero, late eighteenth or early nineteenth century. 26″ × 71.1″ × 33.1″. Made by the Valdez family. (Harwood Museum of the University of New Mexico, Taos, New Mexico, 1980.0083 [NMF #10]; photograph by Mary Peck; courtesy of the Museum of International Folk Art, a unit of the Museum of New Mexico, Santa Fe, New Mexico)

outside the province. The bottom panel slid between the lower rails, and pegs gave it additional strength and stability. Because the mortise-and-tenon frame bore the load of the contents instead of the dovetailed joints of board chests, framed construction suited chests made for heavy objects, such as grain.

The extension of the stiles of a framed chest downward to create short legs represented a particular characteristic of furniture made in the north of Spain, particularly in the regions of Asturias and Navarra. Although similar in concept, the long legs with angled braces found on New Mexican framed chests, such as the piece in Plate 16, represented another New Mexican innovation. The uniqueness of the extended legs on framed chests has led to the suggestion that a carpenter came from these parts of Spain and influenced local techniques or that vecinos copied an imported specimen. In either case, New Mexicans lengthened the legs without regard for Spanish tradition.

Of the framed chests that currently reside in museums and private collections, eighteen samples of the type shown in Plate 17 display such great similarities in form and design that they probably came from the same workshop or community. Information regarding provenance that has accompanied a number of these pieces points to a source from the Río Arriba region, in the vicinity of Taos. The chest in Plate 17 came with documentation that allowed Lonn Taylor and Dessa Bokides to identify the carpenter as a member of the Valdez family, a part of the generation that resided in 1790 in the vicinity of La Joya (present-day Velarde). The Valdez family may have operated a workshop for the production of furniture in the Velarde area, again similar to the workshop run by saint makers such as the Laguna Santero. Workshops represented a method of increasing output while maintaining quality and hence assumed some of the functions of the craft guilds found in other parts of New Spain.[35] The identification of at least one Valdez family carpenter also dates this innovative and uniquely vecino woodworking style to the end of the eighteenth century.

The framed chest in the Velarde style pictured in Plate 17 once had diagonal braces reinforcing long legs like the piece in Plate 16. The legs have been shortened and the braces cut off, but diagonal traces of the supports remain on the bottom rail on either side of the center stile. Larger chests like this piece served to hold grain or flour and appeared as harineros in wills and inventories. The earliest documented mention of an harinero occurs in the will made in 1804 by Manual Mares of Santa Fe. At his death in 1815, Manuel Delgado owned two harineros. The wills of the 1780s do not mention this type of chest—not even in the lengthy inventory of the estate of Clemente Gutiérrez, who died a far wealthier man than Delgado.[36]

The harinero represented a new form of chest, making its appearance by the first decade of the nineteenth century, just as increased New Mexican agricultural productivity created surpluses that required storage year around. Because of the weight of flour or grain and the need to prevent spoilage by mice and other pests, carpenters resorted to more elaborate and complicated joinery. Slats that fit into mortises in the bottom front and back rails often gave additional strength to the bottom panels. An harinero generally had four panels at each end, and twelve to sixteen panels could make up the front, depending on its size. Because of the dimension and weight of the boards, the artisan hinged only a central panel that became the lid, or the front portion of the top as shown in this example. Harineros were the largest pieces of furniture used in vecino houses, and possession of one or more of them attested to the owner's status and prosperity.[37] Vecino craftsmen also made tables, chairs, cupboards, wardrobes, and other kinds of furniture at the turn of the nineteenth century using the same framed technique.

However, if one hypothesizes that the framed construction of furniture represented a new technique introduced at the end of the eighteenth century and adapted for use with chests meant to hold heavy loads, the extension of the corner stiles of the frame would serve as a substitute for the separate wooden stands generally made for board chests. Legs added directly to board chests could not have held the weight of a heavy load, since without stiles they did not form a structural part of the box. The frame provided the bottom of board chests with additional support while raising it above the floor, making redundant a separate stand to accompany a board chest. Legs that formed part of the structure of a framed chest presented a logical replacement for the board chest stands, and they also saved materials and labor. Although the framed chest clearly followed carpentry practices standard in Mexico at the time, the idea of fashioning long, built-in legs to keep the chest off the ground used by vecino artisans may well not have originated in northern Spain.

The board chests with relief carving (Plate 15) exhibit such a different method of construction and design from other documented early New Mexican furniture, and framed chests in particular, that they call for some explanation. Heraldic designs carved in relief on the board chests contrast with both chip or gouge carving and the raised panels cut in geometric patterns common on most framed chests. After reviewing extant chests from all periods, Taylor and Bokides suggest that the board chest may have derived from inexpensive military furniture, representing a Río Abajo style different from that of the Río Arriba framed chest. They also suggest that the large number of chests from Michoacán that appear in colonial inventories might refer to a form of the board chest.

New Mexican carpenters showed a remarkable ability to adapt Spanish furniture-making tradition to meet the tastes and needs of vecino patrons at the end of the eighteenth century. The evidence from the inventories of the period appears to confirm the impression gained from looking at the material record, although one cannot rely on either source alone: that more furniture entered vecino homes, and that most of it came from the hands of vecino craftsmen.[38]

The redefinition and expansion of three important vecino craft industries—textile weaving, santo making, and the production of furniture—occurred at the end of the eighteenth century as a part of the fundamental transformation of the New Mexican economy. The florescence of these forms of vecino material culture signaled a wave of cultural change sweeping through all aspects of vecino society. On one hand, the development of vecino material culture received nourishment from, and contributed directly to, the creation of a diverse and active market system within New Mexico and greater commercial interaction with provincial neighbors. On the other hand, changes in material culture fed the transformation of facets of colonial lifeways and society, helping to propel a fundamental redefinition of the vecino perception of their own society.

The vecino culture and society that emerged through two generations of demographic and economic change provided powerful incentives that dramatically altered the position of both the Franciscan missionaries and the Pueblo Indians. In each case the tide of change worked to marginalize those groups, but in very different ways.

REORIENTING FRANCISCANS TO A VECINO CULTURE

At the end of the eighteenth century the Franciscan missions in New Mexico differed from the mission systems in neighboring provinces in northern Mexico in significant ways. Unlike the missions of Alta California, and to a lesser extent in Texas and the Pimería Alta, the mission system in New Mexico sat relatively lightly on the Pueblos during most of the eighteenth century, both in terms of the economic demands made on the Indians, discussed in chapter 1, and in the pressure for cultural change placed upon them by the Franciscans, discussed below. In contrast to other areas of northern New Spain, competition and enmity between missionaries and secular officials over control of the Indians grew less, instead of greater, toward the end of the eighteenth century. Where the secularization of the missions became an issue during the early nineteenth century in Alta California and Texas, or occurred due to Indian abandonment and pressure from settlers to occupy mission lands, secularization of the Franciscan missions in New Mexico never became a serious point of contention.

Before the turn of the nineteenth century, changes in the economy, cultural framework, and population of the new Spanish society rendered the original role of the Franciscan missions irrelevant and reoriented the interests of the missionaries toward those of the New Mexican settlers. The waning of the mission influence in New Mexico at the end of the eighteenth century did not occur because of official neglect or lack of missionaries to maintain the system. Long before secularization, or before the last Franciscan left the province, the system was peaceably overcome by the vibrant vecino society that late colonial prosperity had engendered.

During the 1750s and 1760s the Franciscan missionaries leveled serious charges of abuse and exploitation of the Pueblo Indians against the governors and alcaldes mayores of the province. If the reports of the Franciscans seem prejudiced against the Spanish secular officials, their bias stemmed from the frustration and realization among the fathers that two generations after the reconquest, the conversion of the Pueblos remained incomplete and superficial. In searching for the reasons for their failure, the friars concluded that oppression by the civil government bore the responsibility. In a broadside against the secular government of New Mexico, Fray Carlos Delgado listed the evils perpetrated by the governors and alcalde mayores: forced sales of goods to the Indians, arbitrary requisitions, the consorting with and violation of Indian women, and the whipping or incarceration of Indians for the smallest infractions.[39]

Fray Delgado concluded that the "inequities" of the Spanish officials brought the Indians to the point where: "losing patience and possessed by fear, they turn their backs to our Holy Mother, the church, abandon their pueblos and missions, and flee to the heathen, there to worship the devil, and

most lamentable of all, to confirm in idolatries those who have never been il-
lumined by the light of our holy faith, so that they will never give ear or credit
to the preaching of the gospel. Because of all this, every day new conversions
become more difficult."[40] The Indians did not in fact abandon their pueblos,
and only eight years earlier Fray Delgado himself had led a number of Hopi
and all of the Pueblo Indian refugees, except for the Hano, from the Hopi
mesas to settle at the abandoned pueblo of Sandía, north of Albuquerque.

Fray Delgado's own disappointments help to provide a reason for the
stridency of his accusations. In 1748 he founded the two pueblos of La
Cebolleta and El Encinal, settled by "converted" Apache and Navajo, respectively. The Plains Indians fled their newly constructed pueblos in early 1750,
prompting the report to Fray Jimeno quoted above, which blamed this disaster on the governor and the alcaldes mayores. Fray Juan Sanz de Lezaún,
who worked for five months "catechizing," wrote ten years later that the sight
of the neighboring Acoma and Laguna Indians, forced to build the new
pueblos and their churches, "created such a schism among the Apache that
the latter desisted from their intended conversion and revolted."[41]

In response to the situation described by Delgado, Governor Cachupín
sent his lieutenant governor and Vice-Custo Father Trigo to investigate the
matter, and they arrived at very different conclusions. According to their report, the Indians of La Cebolleta and El Encinal had rebelled against Fray
Manuel Bermejo and Fray Lezaún, not fled as a result of witnessing the labor
of the Pueblo Indians. Fray Juan Miguel Menchero had promised them that
upon settling in a pueblo they would receive "many mares, mules, cows,
sheep, and clothing," much of which they had not seen. The Indians testified
"that they did not want pueblos now nor did they desire to be Christians, nor
had they ever asked for the fathers; and that what they had all said . . . to
Father Menchero was that they were grown up, and could not become like
Christians or stay in one place because they had been raised like deer."[42]

Faced with nomadic Indians who quite consciously rejected Christianity, and by Pueblo Indians who maintained their kivas and traditional ceremonies, the Franciscans directed their bitterness against the secular officials
of the province. Under the circumstances, their accusations reveal less about
the relations of the governor and alcaldes mayores with the Pueblo Indians than about their own sense of failure in attempting to the extend the
spiritual care of the mission to new Indian populations. Stymied within the
Pueblos by the resilience of native institutions—and among the Navajo and
Apache by lack of adequate means of persuasion—the missions in New Mexico lost one of the fundamental reasons for their existence: to teach and expand the faith.

By the end of the eighteenth century, conditions in New Mexico had
changed in ways that compounded the difficulties faced by the Franciscans
and left them increasingly attached to the vecino settlements in the vicinity

of the missions. During the last quarter of the century the number of vecinos living in the province grew significantly (see Figure 9). By the end of the colonial period the vecino population of New Mexico numbered more than 28,000. The Pueblo Indian population, on the other hand, had remained relatively stable, numbering from 9,000 to 10,000 through most of the 1750–1821 period. The cadre of Franciscans available to serve the twenty-two missions and three or so largest vecino towns fluctuated during the same period but generally moved between eighteen and twenty-five missionaries, with the exception of the 1780s. Although the Franciscans established the missions for the conversion and spiritual care of the Pueblo Indians, missionaries in New Mexico also served the spiritual needs of the residents of the neighboring vecino villages. The marked demographic growth among the vecinos, and to some extent within the Pueblos as well toward the end of the century, placed increasing demands on the small group of Franciscans residing in the missions.

In theory, the Franciscan missionaries owed their services primarily to the Indians of the Pueblo missions, not to the vecino communities nearby. In practice, the rapid increase in the vecino population after 1770, the vigorous economy rejuvenated by the vecinos beginning in the 1780s, and the vecino demand for spiritual care not reciprocated to the same degree by the Pueblos drew the Franciscans more closely to the vecinos. After the smallpox epidemic in 1780–1781, the missionaries lost the benefit of the personal servants they had enjoyed. The end of this tradition proceeded from the drastic reduction of the population in many of the missions by smallpox and the steps that Governor Anza then took to reduce the number of resident missionaries from twenty-three to seventeen. Without a missionary living in each mission, the friars could not expect the pueblo to provide the five to ten people weekly to attend the missionary. Only the sacristan continued to aid in the maintenance of the church. The loss of services from the host pueblo caused the missionary to rely more heavily on the obventions of the vecino communities near the pueblos. It also eroded the loyalty that the friar might have felt for his Native American charges. The Franciscan practice of rotating the missionaries throughout the New Mexican missions every few years further exacerbated the forces pulling the friars away from the Pueblo Indians.[43]

In 1789, when Governor Concha wrote to the comandante general to explain why he needed to restore the missions at San Ildefonso, Tesuque, Santo Domingo, San Felipe, and Acoma to residency status, he also initiated a new attack on the privileges of the friars.[44] He explained that when he entered the province, the friars had exaggerated their expenses and had hidden from him "the increases in the obventions and first fruits drawn from the vecindario Español dependent on the missions." Now he had discovered that, except for the friars at Laguna and Zuñi, the *sínodo* and the payments from the vecinos proved more than enough for the missionaries to live decently. These same obligations had become onerous to the vecinos and the Castas. "It is the common opinion in this land," he continued, "that however much the individuals earn and work, the religious absorb it for the baptisms, marriages, and funerals that they perform." Concha explained that the schedule of fees charged for services set in 1730, the *arancel*, still functioned unchanged. Bishop Crespo's arancel pegged fees to values in silver which, by the 1780s, New Mexicans had to pay with increasing amounts of their goods. A more money-conscious society, and the effect of a dose of inflation on New Mexican produce, altered the perception of the vecinos, who found themselves paying for the sacraments in more valuable commodities. The high cost of services caused constant disputes over the just valuation of payment in kind. Concha proposed a thorough investigation of the religious tariff and the revaluation of fees on the basis of goods rather than silver.

The investigation that followed demonstrated that, as a whole, the friars had done quite well. By the early 1790s the vecinos in the vicinity of the missions contributed significantly to the friar's annual stipend of 330 pesos. The vecinos neighboring the mission at Isleta contributed the largest amount, supplementing the income of the missionary by 250 pesos, more than two-thirds of his original stipend.[45] The vecinos at San Juan and Abiquíu each contributed 150 pesos toward the upkeep of their missionaries, in addition to the sínodo. The friar at Santa Clara received 125 pesos from his vecino flock. The missionaries at Cochití, Sandía, and Taos added 75 pesos to their income. The other friars gained less, from the chaplain at the presidio chapel in Santa Fe, a Franciscan due to the lack of secular priests, who supplemented his income of 480 pesos by an additional 70, to the missionary at Zia Pueblo, who received only 25 pesos in obventions. As Concha had mentioned, the missionaries at Zuñi and Acoma received no obventions because of the absence of vecino communities nearby.

While the investigation continued, Governor Concha repeated his call for a change in the tariff for religious services and petitioned Comandante General Pedro de Nava for a new church at Belén to serve the growing population of vecinos and Genízaros. He asked for one-half of a subsidy to supplement the contributions made by the vecinos for the maintenance of the friar, since the forty families of Genízaros at Sabinal could not contribute due to their extreme poverty. If granted, this would bring the number of missions to twenty, supported by twenty-one and a half sínodos. The comandante general supported Concha's request, and in 1792 Viceroy Revillagigedo approved the new mission.[46]

The establishment of the church at Belén with a subsidy from the Crown marked a watershed of sorts. For the first time the civil government approved the commitment of Franciscan missionary resources to a region without an Indian pueblo and dominated by a vecino population, a striking indication of the changing role of the Franciscans in New Mexico.

Meanwhile, the related problem of the schedule of charges for the sacraments still rankled the secular officials. The bishop of Sonora declined to interfere, pointing out that he did not have jurisdiction over New Mexico. The Audiencia of Guadalajara sent the request to the bishop of Durango, who should have received it in the first place, but Bishop Tristán refused to make any changes. After receiving the bishop's decision, Comandante General Nava proposed an alternative method of limiting the contributions collected by the New Mexican friars. After consultation with his fiscal, Nava moved to reduce the remaining obligation paid by each pueblo to its missionary still further, allowing only one-half fanega of maize each year, or other products worth the equivalent of 12 reales. After agreement from the viceroy and the fiscal, the plan won the approval of Bishop Tristán in Durango, who emphasized that even this first fruit was strictly voluntary on the part of the Pueblos.[47] Limiting the contribution to one-half fanega reduced the long tradition of Pueblo Indian service and the provision of food and other supplies to the missionary to no more than a ceremonial offering. The practical effect of this change, and the collapse after 1793 of the high prices brought by New Mexican produce, left the missionaries still more dependent on vecino contributions for their sustenance.

The obventions accepted by the friars from their vecino parishioners reflected a need for spiritual care that only the missionaries could provide in New Mexico and, at the same time, an obligation of pastoral care on the part of the missionary that he could only provide at the expense of the Pueblo Indians. The Franciscan missionaries began to view vecino interests by the mid-1790s within the context of a bond formed by the cultural and economic circumstances that drew them together. In the notes that accompanied the two tables that make up the 1794 census, six friars began a concerted attack on the privileges held by the Pueblo Indians, which they had come to believe hindered the growth of vecino prosperity against the best interests of the province. They depicted the Pueblos as lacking respect for Christianity, shirking work, and not using their land efficiently for production: "But what is most astonishing is that, despite almost 200 years that these Indians have been under the teaching, they do not obey the Church but with very rare exceptions (excepting the Genízaros of Abiquiú). Despite their natural laziness for work, rare is he who does not labor on the most festive days of the year, and they even reprimand those who do not, from which one knows that they work with contempt for the precept of God and the church."[48] The Pueblo Indians held their functions in the kivas "which should be demolished," or outside in the field, "since in those days they are very observant, like Jews on the Sabbath, and on which they guard and they order to keep their inviolate secret." When the missionaries tried to correct these failings through punishment by the fiscales, the Indians ignored and made fun of these Pueblo officials. The friars received little help from secular authorities, and whenever they tried to enforce their authority, the Pueblos petitioned the comandante general or other authorities "without any fear of God," against their actions.

The missionaries suggested two remedies for the situation in the pueblos that illustrate how far they had departed from the protective stance of their counterparts in the 1750s and 1760s. They advocated forcing the Pueblo Indians to speak Castillian instead of their native languages, which they would enforce by placing a royal judge in each pueblo to support the friar. Secondly, they recommended following the process used in Sonora of allowing settlers to claim and enclose the communal lands of the indigenous highland communities.[49] "Where there are surplus lands in the pueblos," wrote the friars, "give them, as they do in Sonora, to the many vecinos, poor men of good reputation and customs, that would live in those same pueblos . . . , and with luck they would go discouraging the vain gentile observances and idolatries that every day are on the rise." The missionaries also used the specter of Pueblo Indian economic domination over landless vecinos to move secular authorities to take action.

The census notes prepared by Fray Diego Turado and Fray Ramón Antonio Gonzalez explained that although the pueblos "enjoy a good deal and fine lands," they did not work as hard as they could at farming maize, wheat, or vegetables. Instead, "part [of their land] they rent to the vecinos for whatever serves them, or for an excessive price," purchasing with pottery whatever provisions they needed from the vecinos. Cochití and Santo Domingo in particular produced enough to sell outside the pueblo. According to the friars, these two pueblos had so much extra, fertile land that they could not work it "without having the assistance of many vecinos, who are obliged from their necessity to serve them, and this service of vecinos to the Indians also occurs in other missions of the province."[50] In a remarkable display of blaming the victims for their predicament, Fray Turado and Fray Gonzalez suggested that taking away the means of Pueblo production, and giving the land to vecinos instead, would provide the solution for Pueblo reluctance to produce for a system that coercively extracted goods for the vecino economy!

The call of the Franciscan hierarchy in 1795 to give Pueblo Indian land to the settlers did not fall on deaf ears, although vecinos proved not to need much encouragement. Another aspect of the assertion of a vecino cultural identity, directly related to the economic boom at the end of the eighteenth century, appears in the aggressive manner in which vecinos began to usurp

Pueblo lands after 1780. In addition to settling new fertile areas that were too dangerous to farm or had previously been vacated due to Comanche and Apache activity, vecinos began wresting choice lands away from Pueblo communal ownership, repeating a pattern well established in other areas of Bourbon New Spain.[51] Unlike in other areas, however, the Franciscan missionaries in New Mexico did not constitute a voice of opposition to vecino encroachment on Pueblo lands.

In general, during most of the eighteenth century the Pueblo Indians had access to Spanish justice in New Mexico. During the period from 1740 to 1770 suits brought by or on behalf of the Pueblos enjoyed a good chance of success.[52] Indian plaintiffs or petitioners won verdicts in their favor in every case brought to the attention of the governor between 1740 and 1770 in which a decision survives.[53] However, beginning in the late 1780s until after 1810, the Indians relied much less heavily on the legal system, either because they found such channels blocked or because they had become of little use in redressing their grievances.

Law suits involving land survive in sufficient number to illustrate the decline in Pueblo Indian participation in the vecino administration of justice. During the 1760s and 1770s, pressure from the growing vecino population also prompted petitions from settlers for new land grants, often nearby and potentially prejudicial to Pueblo territory. A number of cases show a careful consideration of Indian claims by the governor before any making any new land grants. In 1763, for example, Cristóbal and Nerio Montoya sued Antonio Baca over the sale of a piece of land that Santa Ana Pueblo claimed to have purchased from Baca. The proceeding ended with the Indians in possession of the land and Baca in debt to the plaintiffs for the sum of 400 pesos. Governor Mendinueta, who served his second term between 1767 and 1778, took pains to respect the rights of Jémez Pueblo when authorizing a grant to Paulín Montoya. In response to protest that the proposed boundary would endanger the pueblo title to an orchard, Mendinueta ordered the line moved 2,800 varas farther from the pueblo.[54]

As vecino society grew and became more commercial during the last quarter of the eighteenth century, the Pueblo Indians suffered a marked erosion of property rights and protection of their titles, which they had enjoyed under Spanish law and New Mexican practice. Between 1740 and 1820, more than thirty cases for which documents survive involving Indian lands came before the governor for judgment. Of these cases, only one received a hearing between 1770 and 1812, indicating the extent to which the Pueblo Indians had lost the access enjoyed both before and after this period.[55]

The next surviving land action brought to the governor on behalf of the Pueblo Indians dates from August 1812, after the outbreak of the Hidalgo revolt in Mexico two years earlier and the Morelos insurgency of the previous March. Between 1813 and 1819 a relative flood of fourteen Indian petitions and cases reached the governor for investigation and judgment. The timing of the apparent shift in Indian access to vecino justice seems to indicate the desire to prevent any similar uprisings on the part of the Pueblo Indians of New Mexico. After 1810, Governor José Manrique supported the Pueblo Indian use of the newly resurrected office of *Protector de Indios,* dormant in New Mexico since the second decade of the eighteenth century.[56] In fact, a large number of the legal proceedings initiated after 1810 stemmed from vecino purchase of, or encroachment on, Indian lands carried out in the period from the 1780s through the first decade of the nineteenth century.

The case of Taos Pueblo serves as an indicative example. From 1760 until the late 1780s the vecino population of Taos lived in the pueblo because of the danger from Comanche raids. By the mid-1790s the settlers had moved into the recently built plazas of Ranchos de Taos and Don Fernando de Taos, and the population of the valley began to increase rapidly. The growth of the vecino population underlay the subsequent encroachment on Taos Pueblo land and litigation.[57]

In 1795 the Taos Pueblo purchased a tract of land from an heir of Sebastián Martín, a vecino who supposedly had received the land in grant early in the century. The Pueblo in 1800 bought a larger tract from the same person. Both these pieces of land lay inside the time-honored grant of 4 square leagues around the pueblo, so that in theory the Indians already owned the land. Apparently they feared imminent or future trouble if they did not make further efforts to secure their title by whatever means available. During the same time, Governor Chacón gave a grant of land in 1796 to a group of vecinos moving out of the pueblo in order to establish Don Fernando de Taos, also clearly within the Pueblo league. In 1796 and 1797, Alcalde Antonio José Ortiz placed three groups of families in possession of the land. In 1799, Governor Chacón reconfirmed these actions.

In 1815 the governor of Taos Pueblo brought suit against the large number of vecino trespassers settled within the standard 4-league area at Don Fernando de Taos, as well as against the new settlement of Arroyo Hondo, 12 miles to the northwest but abutting land that the pueblo farmed. Significantly, the friar serving at the Taos Mission, José Benito Pereyro, as well as Pedro Martínez, the new alcalde of Taos, came to the defense of the Arroyo Hondo settlers. They argued that "the said descendants of the conquering nation [the Spanish] should be entitled to the lands which the Indians do not develop and cultivate."[58] In his judgment of 1815, Governor Alberto Maynez ruled unequivocally against the settlers of Don Fernando de Taos. In acknowledgment of the impropriety of the previous grants, he ordered the vecinos to vacate the land belonging to the pueblo. As uprooting the newly settled village proved impractical, Maynez ordered the alcalde to try to arrange any possible compromise with the Taos Pueblo, in order to prevent the settlers from losing all of their improvements. In the event, the outcome of the suit did not bring about a complete removal of vecinos from Indian lands, but the Pueblo had reestablished its title and recovered crucial legal rights lost during the 1790s and earlier.

Another case, involving Cochití Pueblo, demonstrates the network of vecino power used to defraud the Indians. In 1792, when Luís María Cabeza de Baca (Vaca) occupied the post of teniente under Alcalde Mayor Don García de la Mora, the governors of Cochití, Santo Domingo, and San Felipe, with the help of the missionary from Santo Domingo, accused Baca of forcing the Indians to cultivate his land without pay, "except for lashes, beatings, and abusive language." He ordered Indians to transport vigas to his property, and, "in one word, he treats the Indians like they were slaves, against the Bulls of the Holy Pope Alexander . . . and against so many Royal cédulas." Governor Concha had Alcalde Mora conduct an examination of these charges. After lengthy hearings, Mora concluded that the accusations made by the Pueblos had no basis in fact. Governor Concha decided that Luís Baca had not improperly used his position, and he asked Alcalde Mora to "determine if the Indians have made any representation against him [the teniente], or if he knows if the vecinos Españoles have established them due to hatred of the teniente, or personal interest could have induced the Indians to [say] that which they exposed to the Reverend Father minister those matters that made up the representation here, with the idea of upsetting the good administration of justice and harmony so necessary and recommended for the peace and for the laws." The alcalde did not record his thoughts on these matters. Upon referral to the legal council for the comandante general, however, Baca had to pay the Cochití Indians for the labor he had suborned and for the legal costs of the case.[59]

In 1805 Baca occupied the land around the Santa Cruz springs, land that Cochití had purchased in 1744, and produced a deed showing that he had bought it from the pueblo for 1,200 pesos. In 1815, representatives from Cochití formally petitioned for the invalidation of Baca's deed, claiming that some members of the pueblo had sold land to him and other vecinos illegally. Governor Maynez decided the case in favor of the plaintiffs in 1815, ordering Baca to give up the property and abandon the improvements he had made to the Cochití. Baca did not leave, however, and the protests of the pueblo went unheeded until 1817, when the Cochití once again renewed their suit before the assessor in Durango. From there the proceedings moved to the Audiencia in Mexico City, before landing at the Audiencia of Guadalajara for a final decision. In 1819, after fourteen years of appeals, the audiencia decided in favor of Cochití Pueblo and ordered Baca to vacate the land and pay court costs.

Despite the victory, the copy of the verdict and restoration of ownership sent by the audiencia never reached Cochití. Even with the knowledge of the verdict, without the documents issued by the Audiencia of Guadalajara, the Pueblo could not prove title to the land to the satisfaction of either the Mexican or American authorities after the end of Spanish colonial government. At the time of the audiencia judgment against Baca, his son, Juan Antonio Cabeza de Vaca, occupied the post of alcalde mayor of the Cochití district. Some years previously, while serving as a justice for Peña Blanca, officials had charged the younger Baca with intercepting and suppressing a letter concerning a debt owed by his father to the Santo Domingo Pueblo. Given the wealth and power of the Baca family in that area of the province, it seems likely that similar action ensured that the critical document never arrived in Cochití Pueblo. By accident, William B. Taylor uncovered the original record of the document transmitting the verdict in 1979 in the archives at Guadalajara, and an act of Congress restored the tract to the pueblo.[60]

In stark contrast to the Franciscan actions of the 1750s and 1760s, at the end of the eighteenth century the missionaries made no accusations against vecinos or the officials who aided them in the taking of Pueblo lands; nor did they react to the general tightening of economic control over the Indians. Toward the end of the century, the Franciscans had by and large identified themselves with the social and economic aspirations that defined the new vecino culture. The Franciscan journey, from protector of the temporal well-being of the Pueblo Indians in the hope of achieving their spiritual transformation, to the recognition that their efforts among the vecinos ultimately held more significance, serves as a marker for the effect that economic change had on social relations inside New Mexico.

The development of the vecino santo industry at the end of the colonial period also suggests that a closer working relationship with the Franciscan missionaries had arisen since midcentury. Due to the difficulty of obtaining religious devotional objects for churches and chapels in New Mexico during the eighteenth century, artisans within the province began making santos shortly after the reconquest.[61] The first pieces fashioned in New Mexico until approximately midcentury conform to a formal, linear style, modeled after the religious frescos created elsewhere in New Spain in a provincial neo-Renaissance style. Grouped by E. Boyd into the "Franciscan F" and "Franciscan B" styles, missionaries executed these religious works, possibly with Indian assistance, for the decoration of the Pueblo missions, rather than the settler-dominated churches of Santa Fe, Santa Cruz de la Cañada, and Albuquerque.

Fray Domínguez's 1776 report and other documentary sources identify by name the earliest santeros to have worked in New Mexico as Fray Andrés García and Capitán Bernardo Miera y Pacheco, the mapmaker, explorer, and painter from the Presidio of Santa Fe. Both men immigrated to New Mexico in midcentury, Fray García from Puebla in 1747 and Spanish-born Miera y

Pacheco around 1754. Boyd attributed extant pieces of sculpture to each of these men and extrapolated from their sculptural style to link to each artist a body of oil paintings executed on cloth, animal hides, and pine panels. García resided in the missions of Santa Fe, Santa Cruz de la Cañada, and Albuquerque and in many of the pueblos during his thirty-two years of service, dying after 1779 in Mexico City. Miera y Pacheco died in Santa Fe in 1785.[62] Although the santos currently in museum collections or New Mexican churches cannot all be attributed to a particular santero at this time, they fit into three recognizable styles, each a provincial rendering of the academic styles of religious painting then prevailing in New Spain.

The late-eighteenth-century works show considerably more stylistic and iconographic complexity than do the simpler, more didactic, early Franciscan styles. Unlike the Franciscan "F" and "B" styles, the artists of the Provincial Academic styles use baroque painting conventions and techniques to portray naturalistic movement and emotional expression characteristic of devotional images. In addition to work done for the Pueblo missions, vecino patrons commissioned santos attributed to both Miera y Pacheco and Fray García for use in vecino churches and chapels. The most clearly documented work by Fray García, an almost life-sized figure of Santo Entierro, resides in the vecino church at Santa Cruz for which it was crafted. One of the sculptures and three panels attributed to Miera y Pacheco have inscriptions commemorating their vecino donors.[63]

Beginning in the 1790s, vecinos undertook an extensive redecoration of New Mexican churches and expanded the availability of santos by creating a local craft tradition. During the same period, vecino santeros developed the religious art first improvised by the Franciscan missionaries for the Pueblo missions into a provincial folk style that fulfilled their need for devotional images. The earlier Franciscan-made religious images in the Provincial Academic style, and the few works of art imported into New Mexico from Mexico and Spain, provided the only stylistic and iconographical models available within the province to the developing santo industry. The Franciscans provided the encouragement and perhaps the prototypes for the vecino tradition that followed. In addition, the success of vecino projects to build, rebuild, and refurbish New Mexican churches, chapels, and oratories depended on the support and active cooperation of the Franciscan missionaries. The friars encouraged or fomented no such development on the part of the Pueblo Indians, in contrast to the early Franciscans in Mexico, for example, who trained and facilitated the decoration of the walls of sixteenth-century missions by Náhuatl artists.[64]

At the turn of the nineteenth century the Franciscan missions in New Mexico continued to offer spiritual services and the sacraments to the Pueblo Indians, in much the same way as they had during the previous century. The role of the missionaries, however, had changed dramatically during the preceding quarter-century. Increasingly, the Franciscans who worked in New Mexico toward the end of the century identified with the young, dynamically evolving vecino society, rather than with their less receptive Pueblo charges.

The shifts in the relationship between Franciscan missionaries, their Pueblo spiritual charges, vecino parishioners, and Spanish officials in New Mexico mirrored profound changes in the position of priests in colonial New Spain. William Taylor has shown that Bourbon administrators focused their power and policies on extending a measure of control over and access to the communal property and financial resources of Indian pueblos in the central regions of New Spain.[65] This often involved identifying and limiting the administrative roles that parish priests customarily had played in pueblo affairs. Bourbon reformers also worked to separate secular functions from the religious ones in areas where custom and tradition had blurred the distinctions between them.

In the 1760s the interest of the Spanish Crown in standardizing and centralizing relationships of power began to reach into the church in New Spain. In 1767 Antonio Lorenzana, the archbishop of Mexico, instituted a new arancel. Disputes over the proper fees for baptisms, funerals, masses, and other services occurred throughout the colonial period, but Taylor shows that the gradual campaign by high secular and ecclesiastical officials to replace local custom with a fixed rule increasingly put local priests at odds with Indian officials. The establishment of the intendancy system in New Spain in the 1780s also curbed "excessive" fees in favor of "equitable aranceles."[66] Bourbon officials provided rural pueblos with the incentive and the tools to restrict their obligations to the lower clergy, and the resulting changes served increasingly to portray the relationship between priest and parishioner as a financial transaction. At the same time, Bourbon officials applied other types of fixed rules, such as the royal monopolies that raised the tax burden for Indian pueblos in central Mexico, thereby worsening the general climate within which the priest had to work.

In New Mexico, the fees charged for religious services provoked the same kind of complaints and official concern. Governor Anza used the smallpox epidemic of 1780–1781 to restrict missionary access to Pueblo labor and services when he consolidated the missions into groups under the care of a single missionary. A few years later, when Governor Concha began his investigation into the arancel in New Mexico, the missionaries had few interests within the Indian pueblos to protect. The Pueblos had not responded to the church with enthusiasm since the reconquest in the 1690s, and in practice the actions of Governors Anza and Concha had ended the customary Pueblo support of the missionaries. In contrast to the dynamics at work in the dioceses of Mexico and Guadalajara, where the arancel created disputes between pueblos and their priests and lawsuits between priests and Spanish district officials, the arancel reforms in New Mexico made it clear to Franciscan missionaries that their future was in the hands of vecino parishioners.

Bourbon innovations also reached the religious cofradías in Indian communities throughout New Spain. Cofradías owned lands and livestock in common, and the parish priest generally managed this property or shared the oversight with Indian majordomos. Bourbon administrators had an interest in defining cofradía wealth as communal, rather than as religious property that could not be taxed. Officials also encouraged individual, rather than communal, sponsorship of civic and pious celebrations, as a means of channeling popular culture into forms that reinforced colonial authority.[67] The Real Ordenanza de Intendentes set up in 1786 called for cofradía members to choose their Indian majordomos in elections presided over by Spanish judges. Cofradías had to submit detailed reports of community property to the regional intendant. In central Mexico, Guadalajara, and elsewhere in New Spain, this drive to separate the communal ownership of assets from the participation of the parish priest in the management of these "pious funds" led to a prolonged struggle that the priests ultimately lost.

In New Mexico, the issue of cofradía wealth and proper management also emerged; hence the detailed accounts of their operation written in 1776 by Fray Domínguez and in 1791 at the request of the archbishop of Durango. Franciscans did not have any success introducing cofradías into Pueblo religious life after the reconquest. Domínguez's account demonstrates the precarious state of the cofradías in the vecino towns of Santa Fe, Santa Cruz de la Cañada, and Albuquerque in 1776. They existed due to gifts from past governors and a few other elite donors and to the perseverance of the missionaries who supervised their management. By 1791, however, vecino cofradías had become a potent vehicle of popular religious expression, individual sponsorship of pious activities, and the owners of great flocks of sheep and other property, just as Bourbon officials might have hoped. By that time the missionaries had given up the management of the cofradías, seemingly without protest.

The Franciscans paid a price for their attention to vecino religious and cultural needs. By giving up their original obligation to the Pueblos, the missionaries in New Mexico placed themselves at the political margin in their dealings with provincial Spanish officials.

Governor Concha's warning to his successor about the new relationship of the friars to the vecino population indicates the extent of Franciscan marginalization at the turn of the nineteenth century. Concha contrasted the lack of Pueblo Indian litigation to the vecino propensity to renew every petition and suit upon the arrival of a new governor. He then described the frequent Pueblo petitions for the removal of their missionary as acts of collusion between the neighboring vecinos and the missionary: "They generally have no other object for this pretense than to oblige the missionaries who seek that specific destination, joining together with the vecindario annexed to the administration of the same pueblos, to which end, one or another [pueblo] implies and alleges a number of deeds against the missionaries in possession that generally turn out to be false. For this reason one needs a very steady hand in order to proceed in these matters. It is necessary to make a tedious examination and take individual notice of what motivates the religious and citizenry to this kind of conduct." The Franciscans had increasingly less political weight to use against Spanish officials toward the end of colonial rule, and the cooperation forged between the missionaries and their vecino parishioners accounts for the lack of interest in secularization or expulsion of the missionaries throughout the Mexican period. In fact, the mission period in New Mexico ended in 1848—and then by attrition—when the last Franciscan, Fray Mariano de Jesús López, died at Isleta.[68]

LOCATING PUEBLO CULTURAL RESISTANCE: THE TEWA SEDITION TRIALS OF 1793

Franciscans responded more readily to the emerging vecino culture than to pastoral obligations owed to the Pueblo Indians by the end of the eighteenth century, in part due to the changing nature of relations between vecino and Pueblo societies. A number of cases against Pueblo Indians for sedition emphasize the fears among Spanish officials and vecinos of another Pueblo rebellion of the same magnitude as the great revolt a century earlier. A close examination of the most spectacular of these trials enables one to delve into the Pueblo cultural response to the assertion of vecino dominance at the end of the colonial period. Like the changes that took place in the attitude of the Franciscans toward Pueblo and vecino lifeways, the Pueblo strategies of self-protection show the broader social and cultural mark left on the Pueblo Indians by the period of late colonial vecino florescence.

The investigation of the Indian leaders of the six Tewa Pueblos for sedition, mounted in 1793 by Spanish officials, provides a rare glimpse of the formation of a pattern of Pueblo resistance to outside vecino influence. This case shows the development of a concerted mode of opposition to the extension of Spanish authority at the end of the eighteenth century. In conjunction with well-established obstruction to religious interference within the Pueblos already discussed, this new form of resistance gave rise to the cultural pattern that, more than a century and a half later, anthropologists dubbed "compartmentalization."[69]

Understanding the significance of the 1793 Tewa trials requires a reordering of current views in two important areas. The first, largely the product of historians, emphasizes one of the results of the Pueblo Revolt of 1680, which drove the Spanish and their Indian collaborators out of the Río

Grande Valley. The system that the Spanish reestablished after their reconquest in 1692 represented less of an imposition on Native American society and culture and allowed for increasingly close cooperation and social contact during the eighteenth century.[70] The second theme concerns an anthropological concept, which Edward H. Spicer and Edward P. Dozier began to apply to the Pueblos in their work published in the 1950s and early 1960s.[71] Spicer's term, "compartmentalization," described a practice of walling off critical portions of Pueblo socioreligious life from the view or influence of outside authority, first from Spanish clergy and officials and later from Anglo-Americans.

Both views have valid implications for interpreting the history of the Río Grande Pueblos, but in their current form they manifest serious historical and methodological difficulties. The notion that the Pueblos fared relatively well under Spanish rule in the eighteenth century and that compartmentalization formed the key Pueblo strategy for their protection have combined to obscure the critical late colonial watershed that marked the end of the period of vecino-Pueblo cooperation and created the conditions for compartmentalization. Compartmentalization began to function effectively at the end of the eighteenth century as a direct result of the changing economic and social relationship with the vecino population of New Mexico. During this period, Pueblo adaptation to the new circumstances of vecino dominance gave rise, for the first time, to a sophisticated, full-fledged strategy calculated to stymie any attempt by Spanish authorities to interfere directly in crucial internal Pueblo matters. The Tewa trials of 1793 demonstrate this type of Pueblo resistance in action.

The trials took place precisely during the period of economic and social ferment, and they reveal the tension introduced into vecino-Pueblo relations during the last decades of Spanish colonial rule. On May 30 the alcalde mayor of the district containing the Tewa Indian pueblo of San Juan convened an extraordinary gathering. "I, the Alcalde Mayor Don Manuel García de la Mora of the pueblo of San Juan de los Caballeros," he recorded, "together with the people of the said pueblo, begin to make the investigations . . . with the goal of knowing the motives that the pueblos of the Tewa nation had in making or forming the meeting that they had in the pueblo of San Ildefonso."[72] Following the order of the previous day from Governor Concha to investigate this illegal gathering, the alcalde and his assistants began the interrogation of one Bentura Piche, Indian of San Juan.

The richly documented case against the Tewa pueblos in 1793 provides a unique opportunity to view aspects of the relationship between the vecino population and the Pueblo Indians at a point when radical change in the provincial demography and economy began to manifest itself in the deterioration of relations between the two primary ethnic groups. For the first time since the early years of the reconquest a century earlier, Spanish officials feared that the Pueblo Indians planned to join the nomadic Indian groups in rebellion, as they had in 1680.[73] The text of the court proceedings speaks of the exercise of Spanish power to determine the extent and tenor of illicit gatherings in the Indian pueblos and to bring to justice those responsible for holding them. The subtext of the same proceedings reflects a change in the underlying relationship between the two peoples. In the face of the hardening of Spanish society in contradistinction to that of the Pueblos, the Tewa responded with more organized and sophisticated forms of cultural resistance. Under the Tewa trial lies a striking demonstration of a complete Pueblo strategy developed to deflect the direct application of vecino authority in important native social and cultural institutions.

The Tewa labyrinth presented here follows the same path along which forty-seven Indians and one vecino led Alcalde Mora and his team during this seventeen-day trial. Among those interrogated figured ten Pueblo Indian officials from the six Pueblos. Both the involvement of so many Indian officials and the sheer scope of the proceedings make this trial unusual, if not unique, among surviving colonial New Mexican materials. In the end, Governor Concha found all but two of these Pueblo officials, and the lone vecino, guilty of sedition.

Alcalde Mora began his investigation with the San Juan Indian, Bentura Piche. Mora asked what had transpired during the meeting at San Ildefonso, apparently led by a San Ildefonso Indian named Asencio Peña. Piche answered in Peña's words "that among the Spanish they endured difficulties; that he had thought this in his heart so that for this they had been congregated; that all were brothers, parents, and friends, and compadres; that they should follow and leave with the Comanche, Ute, or Navajo, or Moqui; and that only in this manner would they be given a mountain with corn and wheat and all that they ate among the Spanish, so that their women and children could eat; and . . . Peña said that it was true that the God of the Spanish was great, but that theirs was also equal."

At first only Antonio Beitia, a vecino from the nearby Plaza de San Rafael, and Juan Diego Pinda, from San Juan, consented to this plan. Piche said that Peña later ordered the governor of San Juan, Miguel Cacugé, to advise his people to consider carefully the consenting position of Antonio Beitia and Juan Diego Pinda "and they should not bring them trouble." According to Piche, Governor Cacugé apparently complied after returning to San Juan.

Any hint of an organized meeting piqued the alcalde's interest, given the recent revolt in 1781 of the Yuma in Sonora, and New Mexico's own Pueblo Revolt of 1680. However, when the Alcalde Mora asked the same question to the second witness from San Juan pueblo, Juan Domingo Tuque, he received a similar answer, along with a conflicting interpretation of the same event.

In Tuque's version, Peña had solicited their presence at the meeting in San Ildefonso and had said that he "called them and congregated them to propose to them what he had in his heart was that among the Spanish they endured difficulties and that if it seemed [correct] they should go with the Comanche, Ute, or Navajo, or Moqui, or Apache."

At this point, according to Tuque, of the twelve men from San Juan attending the meeting, four—namely he, Bentura Piche, another San Juan named Miguel Ortiz, and for good measure the governor of San Juan—refused Peña's proposal, asking for payment in advance for their allegiance: "If six leaders were evil (that is, the assenting six), theirs were not, and that if they gave them a mountain of corn and wheat and of that which the Spanish eat so that they could maintain their children and women, that then they would say yes." Tuque had turned the meaning Piche's version of Peña's speech on its head.

To the Spanish officials attending the trial, the confirmation of Pueblo collaboration intensified the serious tone of the interrogation. Returning to Piche, the alcalde asked him to confirm his previous testimony. Piche refused, declaring "that he had been made crazy [se había hecho loco]; that his testimony had been built up for his people in saying that they wanted to go to the Gentile Nations; [and] that it was only true that they had a meeting." In this version Peña had called the gathering to "give them advice that they should look well to their people and to Antonio Beitia, and to Juan Diego Pinda." In his second declaration, Juan Domingo Tuque agreed with that of Piche, adding that he did not say that the people wanted to go to the Gentile Nations [the Comanche, Ute, Navajo, Moqui, and Apache]. "Perhaps," Tuque offered, "the interpreter did not hear it well."[74] Tuque and Piche had begun to use their answers to counter the intent of the investigation, fighting back with a skillful, subtle pattern of deliberate obfuscation.

Mora reported the information that he had collected from the first two witnesses to Governor Concha, who, due to its alarming nature, ordered the alcalde to change the venue to Santa Fe. There Mora begin the task of taking sworn declarations from all the Indians involved. Between the hearing at the end of May and June 8, when the proceedings reconvened, Spanish authorities assembled at least forty-four Indians from the six Tewa pueblos and the vecino, Antonio Beitia, at the jail in Santa Fe.

Alcalde Mora and his team began taking depositions in Santa Fe, having formulated a set of six standard questions that they put to each of the Pueblo prisoners with little variation. They designed four of the questions to probe the events leading up to and within the meetings: Who suggested to you that you go to the meetings, and what causes moved you to go to them? How many did you go to? Who was the leader of the meeting, and who was the first to speak? What words did you hear, how, and of whom? One question challenged the witness to defend his attendance: Did you not know that this pretext was not sufficient and consequently you should not have gone? The last question revealed somewhat more about the suspicions of the interrogators: In the meeting, was there discussion against any justice or religious, or about any revolt?

The officials slowly pieced together the outlines of the case, even though the Pueblo witnesses tried to contradict each other at every point. All told, the Tewa pueblos held three separate meetings without the required approval of either the appropriate alcalde mayor, the missionary in charge, or the provincial governor.[75] Two took place in Santa Clara and one, later, at San Ildefonso.

The invitation to the various pueblos to attend the large meeting held at San Ildefonso represents a rare view of a network of interpueblo communication. In each case, Peña or the governor of San Ildefonso, Antonio el Guille, visited or sent an envoy to the other Pueblos. The officials of the other Pueblos then instructed their members to attend the meeting at San Ildefonso. In keeping with the established pattern of defense, when asked about who had organized the meeting, Governor Guille and Asencio Peña each blamed the other.

The chain of invitations from Peña or Governor Guille to the various participants seemed to represent a familiarity and trust in representatives from other pueblos that Alcalde Mora found disturbing. "What right or power did you have to convene this meeting," he asked Guille. The governor responded "that he had none, [and] that he knew that he had done wrong in having trampled underfoot the higher orders." Governor Chiche of Nambé answered more diplomatically that "he did not know of any authority vested in Asencio Peña, but that he went because of the order from Governor Guille of San Ildefonso, understanding that [the meeting] was to give him an order from the Señor Governor [Concha] or from the alcalde, just as they have called for various matters in the past."

If the team of local Spanish officials had problems understanding the source of power to convoke such a gathering, they had a much more difficult time sorting out what occurred within the meetings, especially the assembly held at San Ildefonso. Judging from the first declarations of Bentura Piche and Juan Domingo Tuque, in that meeting Peña proposed that the Pueblos rise up against the "troubles" they had endured among the Spanish, joining in some manner with their erstwhile Plains Indians enemies. The Indians of San Juan had at least entertained the notion. From this point on, much like the Pueblo obfuscation of Spanish attempts to investigate Indian religion, the shifting, contradictory, and unpredictable responses of the Tewa Indians seemed calculated to prevent any reconcilable theory as to what really occurred from forming in the minds of the interrogators.

Alcalde Mora reconvened the proceedings in Santa Fe starting with the prisoners from San Juan pueblo. Governor Cacugé further complicated matters by saying that the meeting was about the banishment that he had imposed on Juan Diego Pinda and Juan Ramos (whose deposition does not appear in these records). Asencio Peña had told him "that he should not be involved in fighting with his people, nor should they continue introducing troubles, and that the rest of the group said the same." He added "that he knew that he ought not to have gone to heed the call, but he became crazy and went anyway." Still another Tewa respondent, Miguel Ortiz, felt that Peña had called them to the meeting "to advise them that they should not be involved in conducting lawsuits."

Cacugé and Ortiz had opened the initial salvo in a shifting barrage of language to confuse the matters at issue for the investigators. By offering subtle, continual variations of their answers, the Indians attempted to blur the formal legal language used by the Spanish in the proceedings, keeping them off balance, unable to grasp any single, solid theme. Where Cacugé used the phrase "*no anduvieran peleando*" (they should not be involved in fighting), Ortiz said, "*no anduvieran pleitando*" (they should not be involved in lawsuits). The next witness, the fiscal Juan Luís Trujillo, also said, "*no anduvieran pleitando,*" extending the confusion.

The war captain, Martin Ollí, led the topic away from lawsuits and fighting and toward attempts at communal harmony. According to Ollí, Peña called them to the meeting "to advise them that they should live well with Juan Diego [Pinda]." This new phrase, "*vivieran bien,*" proved most popular with the succeeding witnesses, presumably because it conveyed a suitably vague meaning. The endless variations now developed around just who should live well together. Each respondent had a different group of persons to whom Peña's words applied. Meanwhile, Antonio Cruz added "that they should live like brothers" to the warning against fighting. Manuel Burro elaborated this theme: "they should live like brothers and parents." Juan Diego Pinda, the banished Indian from San Juan, who seemed somehow to be one of the people at the bottom of this battle of words, did not help matters any with his testimony. Asked why he obeyed Peña and came to San Ildefonso, he replied "because something had made his head go crazy."

Similarly, the vecino Antonio Beitia, the other central character and one of the targets for Peña's advice to live well, added little to the alcalde's search for a consistent explanation of what had transpired. Beitia amplified and further deflected the previous responses onto still newer paths, and he continued to perform this service effectively throughout the trial. Beitia had attended two meetings, one in Santa Clara and one at San Ildefonso. He answered that at the San Ildefonso meeting they were advised to "live well and keep the Commandments," here adding another phrase that became popular in subsequent declarations. Beitia seemed to choose the new line specifically to allay the suspicions of the Spanish. As for the Santa Clara meeting, Beitia said that they only dealt with some lost leather breastplates.

The investigation turned to the six prisoners from Santa Clara. Governor Antonio Tafoya told his questioners that he led one of the meetings in his pueblo and that it focused on the matter of lost cuirasses and an irrigation ditch they planned to clean. With his response, Tafoya explained the presence of the outsiders, Beitia the vecino, Asencio Peña from San Juan, Governor Guille of San Ildefonso, and someone named Carlitos. All the other witnesses from Santa Clara agreed with their Governor. Peña led the meeting concerned only with cleaning the ditch and the missing breastplates, although perhaps the latter had been stolen.

When questioned about any discussion of revolt, the pattern of diffuse and opaque answers came full circle, touching once more on the original statements that Piche and Tuque had made to the investigating Alcalde Mora. Governor Tafoya, the first witness to respond with anything but a profession of ignorance, testified that the meeting with Peña and Guille in San Ildefonso took place because of a communication in which Antonio Beitia "had a feeling about Juan Diego [Pinda], who had been exiled the previous winter, that they could raise against him some evidence concerning the suits that they had previously pursued against him."

If this admission sounded like a breakthrough of sorts, other witnesses soon extinguished any ray of hope. Juan Antonio Naranjo claimed that Peña "advised them by the Ten Commandments, telling them that they should look at their neighbor as to themselves, that he knew that they had been engaged in a lawsuit with Antonio Beitia, that they were not going to offer any other evidence such as they had done before, but those that brought evidence in those inquiries were only two people: Bentura [Piche] and Juan Domingo Tuque, and that those two should ask Beitia for his pardon." Instead of confirmation of any portion of Governor Tafoya's description of a lawsuit pitting Antonio Beitia against Juan Diego Pinda, Naranjo turned the story upside down. Peña, now fortified by the Ten Commandments, called on Piche and Tuque, the first two witnesses from San Juan, to beg the pardon of Beitia and put an end to it all. Naranjo not only played havoc with the declaration of his own governor but completely turned around the original testimony of Bentura Piche. Piche had located Beitia and Pinda on the same side, both consenting to the proposals of Peña about leaving with the Plains tribes. Naranjo made Piche and Tuque into troublemakers for stirring up the present suspicions and left Peña preaching the fundamental tenets of Christianity!

Given the complexity of this case and the constant variation of overwhelming detail, further investigation might seem pointless. Nonetheless, Alcalde Mora and his team continued to collect a further twenty-seven depositions during this portion of the proceedings. Other variations from the prisoners of San Ildefonso: Governor Guille said that Peña gathered all the pueblos "to advise them to follow the Commandments as God ordered, and to live well." Juan Pedro Chulo thought that the meeting advocated living well, following the orders of the Governor Concha and his justices (an apt impression under the circumstances) and teaching the children to say their prayers. Francisco Sabe went one step farther, having been advised to take good care of their justices and the missionary father, and live well. Juan Chiracyo further embroidered the theme, saying that "they were advised in the company of Peña, that they will learn Castillian, to pray, and to have respect for their superiors and the father minister like Peña did, and that they should live like brothers." Antonio Caché, who did not attend the meeting at San Ildefonso because he had to help collect the tithe, nevertheless claimed that he heard it said that Peña had advised them only that they should learn to speak Spanish. Finally Asencio Peña testified that Governor Guille advised him to hold the meeting "to advise them that they should live according to the law of God; that they should tell the same to their little ones, teaching them to pray and speak Spanish, since there is not more than one God, he that bestows them favor by providing food, clothing, and the goods they possess, and that by the order of his governor he said all these things in Spanish."

Despite the increasingly tangled web woven by his Pueblo witnesses, Alcalde Mora persevered and questioned the fifteen remaining prisoners from Tesuque, Pojoaque, and Nambé. The Pueblo Indians had already shattered the Spanish judicial proceeding's goal of learning what had actually transpired at the meetings. Through their answers, the point of each question asked by the alcalde from Santa Cruz became at first muddied and then lost entirely in the cacophony of innovative, elaborate, and ultimately conflicting answers. The charges of illegal meetings discussing sedition culled from Bentura Piche's original statement turned into harmless interpueblo meetings intended to settle a host of disconnected internal controversies, aided by the calming, civilizing, and Christian advice imparted by Asencio Peña. The Indians simply ignored the disturbing implications of the alcalde's question about talk of revolt or brushed off the question, as did Juan Pedro Chulo of San Ildefonso, saying amid a flurry of feinting responses: "that which you said above does not express the feeling of anyone."

At first the Tewa witnesses seemed to succeed. Upon receiving the mass of declarations from his alcalde mayor, on June 12 Governor Concha determined that he did not have the evidence necessary to decide the case. Instead, he turned it over to Alcalde Mora again, with instructions to question the leaders of each pueblo and the other principals in a more interrogatory fashion and to determine the level of their participation. This time Mora's questions concentrated on establishing the infractions committed by each of the accused and on eliciting a response to direct charges of collusion with the enemy Indians and of sedition. These efforts ultimately produced no more answers than had the first and second rounds of depositions.

Facing the final and far more rigorous course of questions, the defendants took any of three positions in their answers: acknowledge their error and repent; profess complete ignorance of the matter at hand; or blame someone else. For example, when asked why, if he had any involvement with Juan Diego Pinda, he had not approached the alcalde at San Juan and asked for a sympathetic hearing, Governor Tafoya said "that he erred and that he was ready to suffer the penalty imposed upon him by his superiors."

Against more serious charges, the accused simply pled ignorance. Mora asked Asencio Peña "how come he said in his first declaration that [the meeting] was only a matter of advising them of his benefit and goodness, when it is evident from two [depositions] taken earlier and two other individuals that agree with them that his exhortation was directed to [the end] that all the Pueblos should unite and come out among the barbarous nations because of the bad treatment that they supposedly were receiving from the Spanish?" Peña replied "that nothing of this was touched on in the said meetings." Governor Chiche of Nambé elaborated somewhat ingenuously, "in the said meeting none of those things were touched on, and especially when you know that all of the pueblos are living well adjusted with the Spanish."

Along the same lines, the Spanish asked if any conversations with the Ute people had taken place and if they had used one of these meetings to gather with the Ute. When each of the Indians professed ignorance of any dealings with the Ute, Alcalde Mora asked, "How can you say that they did not gather or treat with the Ute when they have stated to the governor that only by being friends [of the New Mexicans] were the Tewa prisoners, as [the Ute] themselves have informed the Tewa?" Peña answered "that he knew nothing, nor had he heard any talk of this particular matter, and that he was ignorant of the Ute motive for saying it." The teniente of Pojoaque, Ysidro Mutí, deflected the question a bit more cleverly, saying "that he did not know the motives that the Ute might have in saying this, but he himself did not know anything." Intimating that the Ute fabricated the story to damage Pueblo-vecino trust made good strategic sense.

Although this round of interrogations also proceeded using set questions, Alcalde Mora tried to seize upon inconsistencies in the defendants' replies in order to force additional admissions, all to no avail. In the case of Antonio Beitia, the alcalde added a new question prompted by the answers of previous witnesses. After establishing the respondent's sense of the length of each meeting and his version of what took place, Mora asked, "Why did it take so long to talk about these four issues in the two meetings, since don't you know that an hour was enough to speak about them?" Beitia answered "that he knew well that they took a long time, but that they did not talk about more items." In questioning Governor Cacugé, Mora used similarly aggressive tactics. When Cacugé admitted that Peña held no authority worthy of commanding such attention, the alcalde followed, "If you did not recognize any, at the same time it is clear proof that beforehand you had formed a plot of harmful designs, since otherwise it was not natural that all of the heads should gather at one assigned point." Cacugé replied, simply, "that he had not discussed anything beforehand."

On June 13, after the previous day of intense questioning, Alcalde Mora concluded his investigation and handed the case back to Governor Concha for his deliberation. Despite the efforts of the Tewa to confuse the wheels of justice beyond all hope of equilibrium, the governor had no problem discerning the Pueblo tactics and their irreverent undertone from the depositions. Concerning the "certain meetings held by the Indians of the Tewa pueblos," he wrote:

> It is not possible to justify the object of these. With respect to the mutual joining together and convening that one is able to see, in order to declare one more or less unanimous cause; and being morally impossible that these meetings could have been because of any of these issues that they express in their declarations, paying attention that their conduct is diametrically opposed to that which they recounted, since far from striving to teach themselves and instruct their children in the obligations of Christianity, and in observing its precepts with exactitude . . . , they would attempt to free themselves so far as gathering precisely for the exhortations; and, at the same time, avoid obeying the just orders that have been passed by the respective justices under cover of different ill-founded pretexts, such as not knowing the language, and other similar examples.

Governor Concha condemned the Pueblo governors and the other leaders who took part in organizing the meetings, "in order by this means to contain and root out any similar proceedings in the future." Governor Guille and Asencio Peña received the stiffest sentences among the Tewa, since the testimony placed them at the center of the meetings. Alcalde Mora carried out their sentence, administering twenty-five lashes to each and placing them in chains for six months. Each had to serve without pay, working on public projects during that period. They most likely labored at building the new barracks then in progress for the soldiers of the Santa Fe Presidio. The governor fined Guille 30 pesos, which, in New Mexico in 1793, was enough to purchase a flock of 60 sheep. In an economy in which silver entered only by way of presidial salaries or the vecino trade to the south, accumulating the money in specie to pay his fine probably forced Guille to serve longer than his sentence. Due to his lack of official responsibility, Peña only owed 12 pesos.

The other Pueblo officials received similar sentences. Governors Cacugé, Tafoya, and Chiche and Teniente Francisco Pata of Tesuque each spent four months in chains working on public projects without pay. Each man had to pay a fine of 10 pesos. Teniente Mutí served a term of one month and owed 6 pesos. In addition, Governor Concha barred the seven Native Americans from ever holding any official position or employment in their respective pueblos.

Antonio Beitia received a somewhat stiffer sentence. The third round of interrogations referred to Beitia as an Indian, originally from Santa Clara. In 1784, the comandante general of the Provincias Internas confirmed a decision of the governor then in office banishing Beitia from the pueblo for sedition and enjoining him not to participate in any of the normal functions or meetings held by the Tewa for their own government or ceremonies.[76] From that time he had counted as a vecino of the nearby Plaza de San Rafael. Because of his previous troubles and his deep implication in the current case, Governor Concha sentenced Beitia to a year of chains and employment in public works and imposed a fine of 20 pesos "as warning for the future." Beitia's position as an Indian, banished from his pueblo and made a vecino, underscores his role in shifting the direction of the Tewa responses during the investigation.

Juan Diego Pinda also existed between two societies. Bentura Piche mentioned in the first deposition that Pinda was a Coyote, the product of a Plains Indian–Pueblo marriage. It appears that the two men most likely to serve as cultural mediators between the Tewa and non-Tewa peoples functioned in some manner as catalysts for the entire episode.

While the governor's decision looks like a failure of sorts for the Tewa defendants, the front line of Pueblo defenses against the Spanish held admirably. Of the forty-seven Indians interrogated, the governor found only seven guilty, and these represented the civil officials appointed by the Tewa pueblos as intermediaries between the two cultures. Any of the other forty men may have held true religious power and authority in their Pueblo, but neither the Spanish nor we will ever know. Pueblo women do not enter into any part of the proceedings; only one reference appears in the case, ensuring that the Spanish handled the matter entirely within their own patriarchal view of society. Despite the perseverance of Alcalde Mora and his aides, the Spanish judicial machinery could not penetrate more deeply into Pueblo affairs. Even after the sentencing, the Spanish officials had learned little more about what had actually occurred inside the "secret councils" than they did before they began their investigations.

Furthermore, the punishment meted out by Governor Concha to the offenders does not appear harsh in context. Although no consolation to Peña, Guille, and the others, a conviction for sedition could carry with it far greater punishment. Compare, for example, the Tewa punishments to that rendered in the case five years later of Lazaro Sola, who stood trial for subversion as the "principal cause of the meetings and seditions" found at Jémez Pueblo. Sola received three years of hard labor in the public obraje at Encinillas.[77]

Whether due to the governor's stated purpose of "containing" such affairs, to the difficulty of figuring out from the Tewa accounts who had really done what, or to his trepidation for harsher measures that might worsen Pueblo-vecino relations, in 1793 Concha pronounced sentence with a relatively light hand. The Spanish judicial proceeding served to diffuse tensions between the vecino and Pueblo communities, even as each group interpreted its success differently.

The trials of the Tewa appear similar to Spanish responses to rebellion elsewhere in New Spain during the same period.[78] In Oaxaca and the Mixteca Alta, the end of colonial rule saw numerous upheavals that were in some ways reminiscent of the Tewa affair on the Río Grande, including relatively lenient sentences by Oaxacan officials to encourage the affected Indian community to return to live "harmoniously," as before. Two circumstances stand out in the case of the Tewa meetings. Only very rarely did rebellion in Oaxaca and the central valley of Mexico show any of the inter-pueblo interest and communication that the Tewa demonstrated. Also, rebellion formed part of a general pattern in New Spain farther south, intensifying and changing character toward the end of the colonial period in relation to well-documented social and economic changes. In New Mexico, Pueblo resistance sprang rather suddenly upon Spanish officials at the end of the 1780s and, according to current historiography, was not supposed to be happening at all.

If one had any doubt that the actions of the Tewa had brought about this state of affairs, the case that Santo Domingo brought the previous year against Alcalde Mora's lieutenant demonstrates the use of more aggressive tactics when the situation warranted. The Pueblo swore out a detailed statement in front of the Franciscan missionary concerning abuses performed by Teniente Baca. Among other charges, Baca forced the Indians to work without pay or adequate provisions, impressed Indian oxen and their drivers to transport the alcalde's building materials, accompanied the Indians to look at their flocks, made them grind and carry flour for his shepherds, and physically abused them. When excessive abuse of the type likely to gain a hearing by the governor reached the boiling point in Santo Domingo, the entire pueblo came forward and presented its charges, clearly, precisely and vocally, using the missionary to set down their complaints. When, for reasons we do not know, the Tewa pueblos reached that point, they chose secret meetings as an alternative to a public complaint. In the face of the Spanish investigation, the Tewa used their secular officials in a calculated, complex manipulation of cultural, social, and linguistic differences to limit the damage done by the Spanish discovery.[79] The Tewa response to the Spanish investigation of their activities documents for the first time a complete strategy of resistance necessitated by the recent shift in Spanish-Pueblo power relations.

After the trial of the Tewa and the sentencing of Antonio Beitia and the

Pueblo officials, the governor ordered the release of the rest of the Indians from the prison in Santa Fe where they had awaited questioning. Governor Concha addressed the Indians as to "the mode in which they ought to live after they returned to their homes." Concha's phrase, *"como debían vivir,"* immediately recalls the *"vivieran bien"* and its multitude of elaborations by the Tewa deponents. Unfortunately, Concha does not include the text of his speech in the record of the case, but one may gain an idea of his feelings through a comment made before pronouncing sentence: "From all of that which one ought to deduce and the probability of believing that those meetings listed have been and must graduate like news and endanger the good and tranquillity that this province which the king placed in my charge actually enjoys, emanating precisely from the abundance, comfort, and advantages that those Indians achieved, much superior in these to the Spanish that one finds in their environs." Suddenly one can see the Spanish view of the affair, as expressed by Governor Concha, in the light of its Pueblo parody, constructed during the trials from countless repetitions of various parts of the Spanish model, with each variation slightly out of sync with the others.

Whatever the details of the counsel taken at Santa Clara and San Ildefonso in May 1793, the Tewa people did not see their situation with quite the same rosy tint described by Concha. A new, prosperous, self-confident vecino society, emerging from the Spanish settlers replanted in New Mexico, fortified with peace, a burgeoning population, and new opportunities for trade with other regions of Mexico, had permanently altered the context of relations between the Spanish and the Pueblo Indians.

Fray Turado mentioned the Tewa trials in his denunciation of Governor Chacón's proposal to collect the tithe from the pueblos a few years later, as an example of the danger of new exactions:[80]

> A few years ago, during the year of [17]93, we saw that the governor imprisoned the principals of all of the Tewa Pueblos, and gathered from them a summary about why they wanted to revolt. If it was true or not, they did not achieve it, but what is true is that they had the feeling [to rise up] due to having suffered a number of vexations caused by the greed of those who ought to have helped and defended them in similar cases. Also, there occurred the [incident] in [17]92, [where] they wanted to promote the same as now [in 1793], but they feared the unfortunate consequences that they would have brought on themselves, and that all receive who go against the royal spirit of His Majesty.

The Tewa meetings represent one view of the Pueblo response to change in vecino society, as well as the vivid articulation of a maturing system of cultural defense. Pueblo officials in 1793 demonstrated the projection of Tewa cultural power into the forum of Spanish secular justice at just the point when vecino social and economic influence became dominant in colonial New Mexico.

Demographic growth and the late-eighteenth-century economic boom underlay the creation of vecino culture in New Mexico. The genesis of a vibrant, innovative translation of material culture from outside the province paralleled and derived its commercial existence from the growth of vecino production and markets. In each case—textiles, santos, domestic furniture, even religious confraternities—the vecino creation reflected its own cultural stamp molded from rapid change during the last quarter of the century. A growing economy financed the patronage of religious art and architecture, just as it sustained the Franciscan establishment after their original charter proved fruitless. The market forces that fueled the repartimiento of the second commercial system and the vecino pressure on Pueblo Indian communal land also reversed a process of assimilation that the period of cooperation against nomadic enemies had seemingly left as an enduring legacy. Instead, against the aggressive vecino society that threatened to upset the economic balance maintained since the reconquest of the province, the Pueblos felt forced to construct an elaborate defense to protect their own cultural integrity.

George Kubler, in introducing an early exhibition of santos, wrote in explanation of the "astonishing transfers" of material culture throughout the Spanish world: "They violate every expectation based upon political and economic facts. The answer becomes apparent only when we realize that political territories exist because of economic interests, while artistic territories exist because of spiritual affinities and elusive harmonies whose presence has been overlooked. Political geography is often an absurd perpetuation of impossible combinations justified only by necessity and violence. Artistic geography, on the other hand, always commands admiration by an intimate spiritual agreement drawing together those widely separated regions which neither political nor economical needs can otherwise unite."[81] The power that transformed vecinos from frontier settlers in northern New Spain to provincial citizens of New Mexico sprang from the convergence of larger political and economic patterns and a particular social and cultural geography. Out of this brief congruence, vecinos forged a harmonic blend that changed the basic foundations of their culture.

Conclusion

ECONOMIC DEVELOPMENT IN BOURBON NEW MEXICO

The story told here of economic change in late colonial New Mexico has ramifications for a number of areas of Mexican history and for the history of the American Southwest. Significant and measurable economic development took place in New Mexico during the last half-century of Spanish colonial rule. The distance of the province from markets in Nueva Vizcaya made the economic changes of the 1780s and 1790s a particularly interesting example of the power of Bourbon government and the larger economic forces at work in northern New Spain. Officials turned their attention to the military defense of the north in the 1770s, and they offered the leadership and succor that turned the tide against the Comanche, leading to the 1786 alliance. In committing time and resources to the northern provinces the Spanish government saw an opportunity for investment in the defense of the silver-mining areas of Nueva Vizcaya and farther south.

In both interest and action however, Bourbon officials went considerably beyond the measures necessary to retain a defensive perimeter around northern mining areas. Fiscal changes calculated to keep specie in the Provincias Internas, the continual attempt to reform the New Mexican presidio supply system, expenditures for the exploration of roads connecting New Mexico with Texas, Sonora, and California, and the exemption of New Mexicans from taxes and other regulations all exemplified an active policy to encourage and aid the growth of a local economy and to integrate it within the larger regional commercial system that emerged during the latter half of the eighteenth century. Officials made attempts to improve presidio supply in Texas and Florida, for example, but on no other northern frontier province did the Bourbon government lavish such attention.[1] New Mexico received

223

special treatment due to its proximity to markets in Nueva Vizcaya and Sonora relative to Texas, Alta California, and Florida, its comparatively large and rapidly increasing population, and its long history as a Spanish outpost.

Despite the best of Bourbon intentions, one cannot attribute the spurt of New Mexican productivity at the end of the eighteenth century to the planning and largesse of the government of New Spain. Direct actions probably did no more than help foster a positive environment for economic changes that were spurred principally by other factors, such as population growth in northern New Spain and within New Mexico, peace, and the pull of demand for export materials. Some of the concerns of officials did yield economic benefits—the goods purchased from provincial suppliers for gifts to allied Indians, the direct investment in building barracks for the Santa Fe Presidio, the employment of the Bazán brothers to improve local weaving techniques, and similar projects—but even these benefits are not easily quantified. Indeed, the official interest in the Provincias Internas may in itself have strengthened economic ties with other Mexican markets, even if the actual projects fell short of their mark.

The trade boom that began in New Mexico shortly after the defeat of the Comanche groups under Cuerno Verde, and the reordering of the internal markets and social structure of the province that resulted, fits with the general impression of developments in other areas of New Spain, especially aspects of late colonial change in the Bajío and Oaxaca.[2] The location of Spanish settlements created limited points of entry tying New Mexican trade to the economic cycles of Nueva Vizcaya, particularly to that of Chihuahua. Within the province, economic change affected the patterns of production and commerce, as well as vecino pressure on land, labor, and other resources held by the Pueblo Indians, realigning the New Mexican vecino society in the likeness of regional centers of Spanish culture and the metropolis.

In addition to similarities to other regions, a suggestive analogy exists between the developments within the textile industry in the Bajío and the New Mexican economy as a whole.[3] Output from the looms of obrajes and *trapiches* in Querétaro increased substantially after 1780, reflecting the effect of comercio libre, periods of warfare limiting the Atlantic trade and woolen imports from Britain, and the general prosperity of Guadalajara and its region of influence. Like the New Mexican expansion of trade outside the province, demand for woolens from the Bajío increased locally and for export to the central valley of Mexico and other regions from at least the 1770s until the outbreak of the 1810 rebellion.

Among the larger obrajes, the increased labor necessary to raise production came from a combination of higher wages, advances of credit, and outright coercion employed in recruiting and retaining workers. The number of smaller establishments decreased at the same time, because they lacked the economic clout to make similar adjustments. These changes in textile production in the Bajío paralleled the alterations in craft production in New Mexican communities brought about by similar economic incentives and unequal power relations between vecinos and Pueblo Indians.

The late colonial textile industry in the Bajío flourished during this period because it met the demand for particular grades of woolen cloth that fell below those of the highest quality imported from Europe and because it could deliver less expensive finished woolens to the Mexico City market than could obrajes in the metropolis that imported wool from other regions. Obrajes in Querétaro also prospered during times of war, when hostilities reduced the supply of imported cloth from Britain. Consumers substituted smuggled cotton cloth and less desirable Mexican woolen textiles available from the Bajío and other regions when legal imports failed during portions of the 1780s and 1790s.

Beginning in 1810, textile production in Querétaro received blows from which it never recovered. Insurrection against the Spanish state disrupted the supply of wool, labor, and other material needed for weaving textiles and closed the markets in the northern mining areas and Mexico City that had sustained the regional industry. The relaxation of trade regulations by the Bourbons in the 1790s subjected Mexican weavers to competition from Spanish cottons and British cotton and woolen exports, made especially dangerous due to lower production prices caused by mechanization. Reduced demand during the years of rebellion, coupled with greater British textile imports faced by the industry after the violence ended, permanently altered the economic niche occupied by the obrajes.

In some respects, the late colonial New Mexican economy functioned like a giant obraje. Vecinos gathered local products and processed them for the internal market and for export to other regions. Like the obrajes of the Bajío, the New Mexican economy as a unit grew at the end of the colonial period due to the sudden creation of an economic niche for its produce. Population growth in Nueva Vizcaya, damage to agriculture and livestock from hostile Indian raids, and demand from new mines and presidios drew New Mexico into an emerging system of regional trade and commerce. New Mexican goods represented an alternate source and a temporary solution that supplemented an imperfect supply of livestock, wool, and textiles available to markets in the north, just as the obraje production of the Bajío occupied a precarious position between first-quality imports and cheaper goods made available by British industrial techniques. Increased connections between Nueva Vizcaya and markets supplying Mexican or imported manufactures (any change that would lower transportation costs), or the growth of a regional supply of wool and livestock that met demand, would have spelled the end of demand for the principal product of the New Mexican export economy.

New Mexican trade survived the disruptions of the war for independence and the opening of Spanish markets to foreign trade, in contrast to the textile industry of the Bajío. Chihuahua did not sustain the level of destruction from the struggle against the insurgents felt by the Bajío, nor did the insurrections sever trade between New Mexico and Nueva Vizcaya, although they did bring about a similar tendency to encourage regional economic involution. The key difference lay in the ability of the New Mexican economy to adapt to the opening of trade with the United States over the Santa Fe Trail in 1821.

RECONCEPTUALIZING THE SANTA FE TRADE

For many scholars, the opening of the Santa Fe Trail between New Mexico and Missouri "began the process of incorporating the region into the United States."[4] Much like Fray Morfí's interpretation of the economic meaning of the system of "imaginary moneys" operating in New Mexico in the 1770s, discussed in chapter 4, this view assumes that trade with Americans brought *true* capitalist, commercial enterprise to New Mexico for the first time. In contrast to the dominant view, the economic argument presented here for economic growth in late colonial New Mexico provides support for the position that Santa Fe trade reoriented the New Mexican economy, rather than overwhelming it through direct competition and lower prices. The primary New Mexican agricultural and livestock products and manufactured materials that formed the backbone of the colonial trade still found buyers among the American merchants or in Chihuahua during the Mexican period. Even in the realm of textiles, where New Mexican materials faced competition from imports coming from both directions, the better-quality New Mexican sarapes and other weavings retained or increased their markets and value.[5]

Understanding the effect that trade with the United States had on the economic system that New Mexico inherited from New Spain requires a complete reappraisal of the commerce that developed over the Santa Fe Trail. The picture provided of New Mexico's economy in this study emphasizes the importance of reconceptualizing the changes that took place during the Mexican period in terms of continuity rather than wholesale change; as a process of mutual economic adaptation rather than the inevitable replacement of a colonial economic void by the commercial innovation of American merchant entrepreneurs.[6] Ironically, the late colonial economic development of the province may well have provided a compelling reason for the attraction of New Mexico to American merchants as the major point of overland trade connecting Mexico and the United States after 1821.

The history of pottery production by vecinos in New Mexico provides an important illustration of the adaptation of the late colonial economic system to the Santa Fe trade. Charles Carrillo argues that the period of intensive Pueblo production for the vecino export market to the south, discussed in

chapter 4, may have also spurred some of the poorest vecinos to begin producing utilitarian wares for their own use or to trade to within the Spanish villages.[7] Unpainted wares previously available through trade with the Pueblos,
he argues, became dearer or in short supply due to the increased demand for
pottery to export and to sell to New Mexicans who could still afford it. Vecinos without adequate landholdings or who had become otherwise disenfranchised resorted to producing ceramic wares, a craft previously left to Pueblo
potters.

By placing the beginning of vecino specialization of pottery in the 1790–
1810 period, Carrillo's argument raises two problems. For most vecinos, using their labor and other resources to weave woolen textiles would have been
easier to accomplish and more lucrative than taking up pottery making. Unless vecinos needed pottery as a substitute for an inadequate supply of Pueblo
wares for provincial use, they had no overriding reason to turn to a new area
of craft production in lieu of expanding an existing one. Archaeological investigations of vecino sites occupied during the late colonial period have
yielded types of unpainted wares that could be of Spanish manufacture, but
they also confirm that much of the household pottery came from the hands
of Pueblo potters.

The lack of written or oral evidence that can document vecino pottery
making in the late colonial era presents another interpretive difficulty. Carrillo has presented oral, documentary, and archaeological sources to establish vecino pottery production by the 1830s, but no evidence has yet come to
light that can extend the date back in a convincing fashion. The beginning
of vecino pottery production fits more easily with economic trends after
1810, when a series of insurgent armies fighting for Mexican independence
began to unravel the interregional economy that the Bourbons had worked
so hard to forge. The collapse of the demand for New Mexican goods in the
overland trade after 1810 reduced the pressure on the Pueblos to produce
pottery for export. Then the opening of the Santa Fe trade to Missouri and
access to United States markets, after Mexican independence from Spain in
1821, brought a plentiful supply of cheap metal pots, plates, cups, and other
wares, supplanting those previously provided by the Pueblos. Without a market for exports from New Mexico and with the supplanting of the internal
market for pottery, Pueblo producers had no pressure, and very little incentive, to function within the non-Pueblo economy.

At this point, beginning in the 1820s, Carrillo's hypothesis that poorer vecinos adopted the potter's craft to supply a shortage of cheap utilitarian wares
agrees with the general New Mexican economic trends and the available
evidence concerning Hispanic pottery production. Vecinos did not begin to
fashion pottery in the 1790s in response to scarce Pueblo wares because of
the boom in exports from New Mexico to Chihuahua and other southern
markets. Rather, vecinos who had become economically disenfranchised

because of the changes that the Santa Fe trade with the United States brought to New Mexico took advantage of the voluntary Pueblo withdrawal from the market in the 1820s to fill the resulting need for inexpensive ceramic vessels. The economic history of the late colonial period furnishes the perspective necessary to understand how vecinos adapted to the altered currents of trade and capital brought by Mexican independence and the Santa Fe Trail.

CREATING SAINT JOB: VECINO IDENTITY AND CULTURAL MEMORY

One of the central arguments made in this work holds that the period of late colonial economic growth enabled the vecino population of New Mexico to establish a coherent society that took root as a vigorous cultural variant of Spanish colonial life elsewhere in New Spain. The cultural differentiation took place with relative suddenness and depended in part on reversing a pattern of assimilation between vecino and the Pueblo Indians of the Río Grande Valley that had arisen by the third quarter of the eighteenth century. During the process of self-definition, economic pressure—the need to increase production using economic coercion or outright force—went hand in hand with lowering the social status of the Pueblo Indians in the Spanish world. The expression of this process in cultural terms created the basis for the forms of vecino society that have persisted into the twenty-first century.

Works of art often tell stories about their creators and, more broadly, about the culture and historical experience of the people who held and valued them. Among the small proportion of New Mexican santos that have survived to the present, two similar figures exist of a bearded male saint sitting, his legs in front of him, with his knees drawn up toward his chest. In each of these bultos, the man folds his left hand across his lap and balances his right elbow on his knee. He places his cheek on his palm, supporting the weight of his head as if contemplating his unhappy situation with intense concentration (see Plate 18). Bleeding welts or sores cover his body.

The santero used an oil-based pigment to finish these carvings, which indicates that the figures were made around 1880, when commercial oil paints first became available in New Mexico. Anglo collectors purchased these two bultos from the northern New Mexican village communities in which they were held and venerated, one in the 1930s and the other in the 1960s. In each case, their owners or caretakers identified them as "Santo Jo'" (Saint Job) at the time of their sale.[8]

That prior owners should identify these figures as Saint Job seems remarkable since, as an Old Testament figure, Job was never a Christian saint. However, as an example of a man of faith, humility, and patience before God, Job does prefigure the fate that Christ suffered while on earth. The long-standing parallel between Christ and Job in Catholic doctrine suggests that

Plate 18a. *Santo Jo'*. Height 10″. Collected in 1964 from the J. P. Flores family of Placitas, New Mexico. (Photograph by William Acheff; private collection, with permission)

Plate 18b. *Santo Jo'*. Collected in 1936 for the Taylor Museum of the Colorado Springs Fine Arts Center by H. H. Garnett and George Travis. (Courtesy of the Taylor Museum of the Colorado Springs Fine Arts Center, Colorado Springs, Colorado, TM 1580)

the identifications of the santos in Plate 18 as Santo Jo' represent something more than a coincidence. The oral tradition that named these bultos Santo Jo', still current in the 1960s, holds a clue to understanding how New Mexican vecinos have constructed their own identity out of their historical experience, transformed into cultural memory.

The story of Job comes from the Old Testament. Job, who had lived a blameless and upright life, was tested by Satan with God's permission to determine the strength of his faith. Job began his trial a wealthy man, but his calamities mounted rapidly. The Sabeans carried off his plowing oxen and asses in a raid, then lightning struck his sheep and their shepherds. Finally, a great wind killed all of his sons and daughters. As Job did not renounce his faith or the justness of his fate even after suffering these catastrophes, Satan covered Job's body from head to toe with boils. The two santos in Plate 18 show Job suffering from this affliction.

On the face of the matter, Job represents an unusual subject to attract the attention of a New Mexican santero since he is not a Christian saint. Job rarely appeared in the art of New Spain during the eighteenth or early nineteenth centuries. In the early sixth century Pope Gregory the Great published an explanation of the Book of Job that established the Old Testament figure as an exemplar of Christian patience. It took the Catholic Church's search for new and powerful devotional images during the Counter-Reformation to bring Job into the fold of Christianity. During the sixteenth century, Job became known as the patron of syphilitics.[9]

Under the circumstances, the santero in all likelihood did not intend to depict Job when he carved the two figures illustrated in Plate 18. If the figures did not originally represent Santo Jo', they raise further questions. What religious image did the santero have in mind when he fashioned the pieces? How did these pieces become identified as images of Saint Job?

Fortunately, the two retablos pictured in Plate 19 help to clarify which religious subject the santero originally intended to represent when he carved the two bultos in Plate 18. Both of the retablos have a style of workmanship that links them to the New Mexican artist known as the Quill Pen Santero, so named because of characteristically thin lines, which appear to have been painted using a sharp instrument. Given their connection to the work of the Quill Pen Santero, these examples probably date from the 1830s to 1850s.[10] The two retablos portray a similar figure seated on a throne and share a general sense of composition and bearing.

Although the pose of each figure bears a strong resemblance to the bultos of Santo Jo', the full halo clearly indicates that the retablos illustrate Christ rather than a saint. These images depict Christ as the Man of Sorrows, or *Imago Pietatis,* a popular devotional image known throughout Catholic Europe.[11] Devotional images of Christ, in contrast to scenes illustrating historical events taken from his life, illustrate a religious moment out of time. The Man of Sorrows displays the physical pain and mortification of the flesh that Christ suffered during his life. The image functions as an abstraction of the mood and condition of Christ, an emotive symbol used by the devout to intensify their religious contemplation and prayer.

Devotional images of Christ often appear as the subject of the New Mexican santero's art, seeking to draw the viewer closer to the religious significance of his life and death through empathy with his experience and suffering.[12] In the retablo shown in Plate 19a, Christ sits on his throne contemplating the wounds he suffered during the Passion. As he does so, Christ looks in the direction of the viewer as if accepting the burden of the suffering and sin of all mankind. He gives each onlooker the opportunity to make a moral choice to follow him and thereby choose his or her own salvation.

Plate 19a. Man of Sorrows. 9″ × 6.5″.
(Photograph by the author; private
collection)

Plate 19b. El Señor Ecce Homo. 14.5″ ×
9.5″. (Courtesy of Nancy Hunter Warren;
Spanish Colonial Arts Society, on loan to
the Museum of International Folk Art,
Santa Fe, New Mexico, L.5.52–49)

The other related retablo (Plate 19b) bears the title *El Señor Ecce Homo,* referring to a moment from an actual event in the Passion of Christ. After the
flagellation and mocking of Christ by the Romans, Pontius Pilate presented
him to the Jews with the words "Behold the man" and asked them to pass sentence on Jesus for calling himself the Son of God. European and Mexican
versions of the Ecce Homo show either Pilate exhibiting Jesus to a crowd or
Jesus standing alone with his hands bound, showing the wounds of the flagellation. On the other hand, the Man of Sorrows (Plate 19a) represents a devotional image of Christ after the Crucifixion and hence shows his death
wounds.[13]

In the example shown in Plate 19b, the santero actually portrayed Christ
as the Man of Sorrows and labeled it an Ecce Homo. The Quill Pen Santero
or his follower apparently merged these two traditional representations of
Christ in his conception of this devotional image. The santero also painted
the *Arma Christi,* the instruments of the Passion and Crucifixion, distributed

throughout the scene and around the border of the retablo. Christ wears the crown of thorns, and the cords of his imprisonment lie around his neck. The ladder, spear, and ax used during the Crucifixion appear on the left. The Cross, the nails of the Cross (protruding from the upper right-hand corner of the inner frame), and the cane used to flagellate Christ appear on the right. These instruments of the Crucifixion serve as timeless symbols of Christ's Passion, not part of an actual event from the cycle of the Passion; thus, the Arma Christi iconography belongs to the Man of Sorrows, not the Ecce Homo.

The two retablos in Plate 19 and the two bultos in Plate 18 originally represented the same religious scene. Something in the cultural language of the period placed Job into the religious vocabulary of New Mexicans and led the villagers who commissioned and owned the figures to transform Christ into Job. In Catholic doctrine Christ and Job both function as exemplars of patience under adversity, which exposed them to great physical and emotional suffering. Christ, however, came to earth as the Son of God, consciously bearing the destiny imposed on him and accepting the sacrifice of his life among men but, at the same time, sharing the divinity of the Father. Job, on the other hand, could claim only to have lived as an upright, prosperous farmer and rancher, a status with which New Mexicans could easily identify.

New Mexican vecinos seized upon the central idea embodied in the parallel between the life of Christ and their own recent historical experience. In making this connection, they transformed the Man of Sorrows into Santo Jo' to fit their own view of their recent historical experiences. The last decades of the eighteenth century had prepared the ground for an identification with Job. Epidemics, years of warfare with hostile Indians, famine, and the resulting death and impoverishment, recounted in chapter 1, added to the difficulties already associated with life in a remote frontier province. The figure of Job in Plate 18a came from a Penitente house of worship in Placitas, New Mexico, a vecino settlement a few miles north of Taos, in a region that experienced the Comanche and Apache raids of the 1770s (see Map 1 and Map 4b). War against the nomadic Indians and smallpox had challenged the growth and prosperity of the province and had placed its population in almost continual jeopardy. This experience helped to forge the cultural pattern that led to the appearance of the image of Santo Jo' in New Mexico as a symbol of patience and adversity.

At the same time, a marked improvement in material conditions within the province at the end of the eighteenth century and the beginning of the nineteenth served to complete the self-identification of New Mexican vecinos with Job. By the 1790s, population growth and economic expansion in northern New Spain had brought the increasing interconnection of regional markets. These changes outside the province created a new demand for goods, which the New Mexicans filled by developing long-distance trade over the Chihuahua Trail. By the turn of the nineteenth century, the end of fighting with the Comanche and new commercial links with the south began to change the economic options and social choices of those within the province.

When the vecino villagers renamed the Man of Sorrows as Job they created an iconographical link between Christ's torments and their own. In doing so they reached into their past and identified with what their relatives had experienced a century earlier. God restored to Job his family and twice as much property as he had owned before he faced his trials. During a time of relative prosperity in the nineteenth century New Mexicans came to see the period between 1750 and 1790 as the test of their collective faith. Both Christ and Job represented the time of severe travails that the settlers had to endure before they achieved lives of comparative ease. Handed down by vecinos in the form of an oral tradition, the marks of the lash suffered by Christ during his Passion became the boils that scourged unhappy Job.

The transformation of the representations of Christ, the Man of Sorrows, into Santo Jo' by New Mexican villagers displays a collective reaction to their experience of hardship and deprivation followed by relative abundance and prosperity at the end of the colonial period. The image of Santo Jo' represents the personification of torment by warfare and disease (Plate 18). The boils covering Job's body look like the sores from bursting smallpox pustules. Job sits alone on his perch, looking miserable, resigned, and completely self-absorbed. He draws the viewer into his predicament, evoking a mixture of compassion and self-identification.

Bearing his afflictions on earth with human suffering, striving to emulate the patience and faith embodied by Christ, in Saint Job New Mexicans found comfort in a mortal example that resonated with their own experience.[14] The figures of Job express a newly focused aspect that came out of the lived experience of late colonial New Mexicans. When the vecino population created its own new language of cultural expression during the last decades of Spanish rule, its syntax did not arise from the general nature of life in a frontier province of New Spain. Instead, the definition of what it meant to be vecino grew from a specific set of dramatic events, moved by powerful and fleeting demographic and economic forces and rooted to a particular moment in New Mexican history.

NOTES

NOTE TO THE PREFACE

1. See Charles Briggs, "The Politics of Discursive Authority in Research on the 'Invention of Tradition,'" *Cultural Anthropology* 11:4 (1996), 435–79.

NOTES TO THE INTRODUCTION

1. L. Carroll Riley, *Rio del Norte: People of the Upper Rio Grande from Earliest Times to the Pueblo Revolt* (Salt Lake City: University of Utah Press, 1995), 93–100.

2. Joe S. Sando, *Pueblo Nations: Eight Centuries of Pueblo Indian History* (Santa Fe, N.Mex.: Clear Light Publishers, 1992), 30.

3. Fred Eggan, *Social Organization of the Western Pueblos* (Chicago: University of Chicago Press, 1950), 284–87, 291–321; and Edward P. Dozier, *The Pueblo Indians of North America* (New York: Holt, Rinehart and Winston, 1970), 133–76.

4. See Dozier, *Pueblo Indians,* 155–57; E. Charles Adams, "The Katsina Cult: A Western Pueblo Perspective," in *Kachinas in the Pueblo World,* ed. Polly Schaafsma (Albuquerque: University of New Mexico Press, 1994), 35–46; Polly Schaafsma, "The Prehistoric Kachina Cult and Its Origins as Suggested by Southwestern Rock Art," in *Kachinas in the Pueblo World,* ed. Polly Schaafsma (Albuquerque: University of New Mexico Press, 1994), 63–80.

5. The Taos and Picurís have not had masked kachina ceremonies in the recent past, but it can still be said that the northern Tiwa pueblos participated in the cult historically. The southern Tiwa villages, Isleta and Sandía, do have kachina rituals, but in both cases their ceremonies may have come from refugees returning from the western or Hopi pueblos.

6. Albert H. Schroeder, "Shifting for Survival in the Spanish Southwest," *New Mexico Historical Review* 1968, 40:3, 291–310, reprinted in *New Spain's Far Northern Frontier: Essays on Spain in the American West, 1540–1821,* ed. David J. Weber, 237–55 (Albuquerque: University of New Mexico Press, 1979).

7. Ramón A. Gutiérrez, *When Jesus Came, the Corn Mothers Went Away: Marriage, Sexuality, and Power in New Mexico, 1500–1846* (Stanford, Calif.: Stanford University Press, 1991), 155–56.

8. Marc Simmons, "History of Pueblo-Spanish Relations to 1821," in *Southwest*, ed. Alfonso Ortiz, *Handbook of North American Indians* (Washington, D.C.: Smithsonian Institution, 1979), 9:187.

9. Dr. Pedro Tamarón y Romerál, *Bishop Tamarón's Visitation of New Mexico, 1760*, ed. Eleanor B. Adams (Publications in History, 15; Albuquerque: Historical Society of New Mexico, 1954), 78–79. Also published as "Bishop Tamarón's Visitation of New Mexico, 1760," *New Mexico Historical Review* 28:2–4 (1953), 81–114, 192–221, 291–315, and 29:1 (1954), 41–47; and as *Demostración del Vatismo Obispado de la Nueva Vizcaya—1765*, ed. Vito Alessio Robles (Biblioteca Historical Mexicana de Obras Inéditas; Mexico City: Antigua Librería Robredo, de José Porrúa e Hijos, 1937).

10. Tamarón, *Visitation*, 79.

11. Fray Francisco Atanasio Domínguez, *The Missions of New Mexico, 1776*, ed. Eleanor B. Adams and Fray Angélico Chávez (Albuquerque: University of New Mexico Press, 1956), 255.

12. Tamarón, *Visitation*, 80.

13. Domínguez, *Missions*, 257–58.

14. Edward H. Spicer, "Spanish-Indian Acculturation in the Southwest," *American Anthropologist* 56:3 (1954), 663–78. Edward P. Dozier introduced the term "compartmentalization" in "Spanish-Catholic Influences on Rio Grande Pueblo Religion," *American Anthropologist* 60:3 (1958), 441–48.

15. Florence H. Hawley, "Pueblo Indian Social Organization as a Lead to Pueblo History," *American Anthropologist* 39:3 (1937), 508.

16. Ibid., 509, 513, and 515. The eastern Keres pueblos refer to Cochití, Santa Ana, San Felipe, Zia, and Santo Domingo; the western Keres pueblos, Acoma and Laguna.

17. William N. Fenton, *Factionalism at Taos Pueblo, New Mexico* (Bureau of American Ethnology Bulletin 164; Washington, D.C.: Bureau of American Ethnology, 1957), 313–17. See also Gutiérrez, *Corn Mothers*, 156–58.

18. The following discussion draws from Schroeder, "Shifting for Survival," 291–310; and Charles L. Kenner, *A History of New Mexican–Plains Indian Relations* (Norman: University of Oklahoma Press, 1969).

19. Kenner, *History*, 33–34.

20. Albert H. Schroeder, "Rio Grande Ethnohistory," in *New Perspectives on the Pueblos*, ed. Alfonso Ortiz (Albuquerque: University of New Mexico Press, 1972), 61.

NOTES TO CHAPTER 1

1. Oakah L. Jones Jr., *Pueblo Warriors and Spanish Conquest* (Norman: University of Oklahoma Press, 1966), 131–47. Plains Indian–New Mexican relations: Alfred Barnaby Thomas translated and edited three volumes of Spanish documents, each with a useful introductory essay: *Forgotten Frontiers: A Study of the Spanish-Indian Policy of Juan Bautista de Anza, Governor of New Mexico, 1777–1787* (Norman: University of Oklahoma Press, 1932); *The Plains Indians and New Mexico, 1751–1778* (Coronado

Cuarto Centennial Publication No. 11; Albuquerque: University of New Mexico Press, 1940); and *Teodoro de Croix and the Northern Frontier of New Spain, 1776–1783* (Norman: University of Oklahoma Press, 1941). Also see Dorothy L. Keur, "A Chapter in Navaho-Pueblo Relations," *American Antiquity* 10:1 (1944), 75–76; Ernest Wallace and Edward Adamson Hoebel, *The Comanches: Lords of the South Plains* (Norman: University of Oklahoma Press, 1952); Daniel S. Matson and Albert H. Schroeder, trans. and eds., "Cordero's Description of the Apache, 1796," *New Mexico Historical Review* 32:4 (1957), 335–56; Max L. Moorhead, *The Apache Frontier: Jacobo Ugarte and Spanish-Indian Relations in Northern New Spain, 1769–1791* (Norman: University of Oklahoma Press, 1968); and Morris E. Opler and Catherine H. Opler, "Mescalero Apache History in the Southwest," *New Mexico Historical Review* 25:1 (1950), 1–36. Don J. Usner, *Sabino's Map: Life in Chimayo's Old Plaza* (Santa Fe: Museum of New Mexico Press), 1995, 53–68, sets the history of Chimayo within the period.

2. Informe del estado de la Nuevo México a su Majestad según su cédula de 1748, written by ex-custodio Fray Andrés Varo at the behest of Custos Fray Bernardo de Arratia, Hospicio de Santa Barbara, Mexico, January 29, 1749, AFBN 28:553.1, #1773, 5R. See also the report of Fray Varo rebutting the charges of Don Juan Antonio de Ornedal y Maza, Convent of San Francisco, March, no day, 1750, AFBN 29:564.1, #1795, 12R, also translated in Charles W. Hackett, trans. and ed., *Historical Documents Relating to New Mexico and Nueva Vizcaya, and Approaches Thereto, to 1773* (Publication 330; Washington, D.C.: Carnegie Institute, 1937), 3:449, from a copy in AGN:HI 25.

3. Governor Pedro Fermín de Mendinueta to Viceroy Marqués de Cruillas, Teodoro de Croix, Santa Fe, January 28, 1769, AGN:PI 103:1, 60V.

4. Cachupín: Don Vélez de Cachupín to Viceroy Conde de Revillagigedo, October 17, 1757, translated in Thomas, *Plains Indians*, 130. Thomas lists the document from AGN:PI 102; Governor Tomás Vélez de Cachupín to Marqués de Cruillas, Santa Fe, January 3, 1766, AGN:PI 102:10, 427R–430V. Quotation: Report of the Reverend Father Provincial, Fray Pedro Serrano, to Viceroy Croix, no place, day, or month, 1761. Translated from the copy in AGN:HI 25 in Hackett, *Historical Documents*, 3:486–87. Governor Mendinueta mentions giving in exchange to the Comanche "de frenos, alesnas, cuchillos de puro fierro que se fabriquen aqui para ese fin, ropa colorada, y maiz en grano y modo." Mendinueta to Viceroy Antonio Bucareli y Ursúa, Santa Fe, November 14, 1772, AGN:PI 103:1, 194V–195R. See also Domínguez, *Missions*, 252–53. Plains goods exported: See Mendinueta to Croix, Santa Fe, May 11, 1771, AGN:PI 103:1, 153R. Genízaro description: Descripción de la Custodia de Nuevo México, con datos sobre número de familias y situación geográfica de las misiones, ranchos, y pueblos, Fray Juan Miguel Menchero, Santa Fe, May 10, 1748, AFBN 28:537.1, #1737, 5V–6R. Translation in Hackett, *Historical Documents*, 3:401–2.

5. Estimated yield from land planted by the Pueblos for the missionaries: Ross H. Frank, "From Settler to Citizen: Economic Development and Cultural Change in Late Colonial New Mexico, 1750–1820" (Ph.D. diss., University of California, Berkeley, 1992), 458, table 10. Pueblo crop:seed ratio (ratio of amount harvested to seed sown): Domínguez, *Missions*, 49, 55, 63, 69, 87–88, 94, 108, 142, 157, 163, 170–71,

174, 178, 185, 194, 201, 205, 213, and 216. Average ratios (fanegas): wheat 20:1; maize 109.1. In *Hacienda and Market in Eighteenth Century Mexico: The Rural Economy of the Guadalajara Region, 1675–1820* (Berkeley: University of California Press, 1981), 221, Eric Van Young reports an average of 100:1 fanegas for maize in Guadalajara. Wheat had a significantly better crop:seed ratio than it did in Guadalajara (20:1 to 8–10:1). Nueva Vizcaya ratios: wheat 15–20:1; maize 70–80:1, according to Bernardo Bonavía, Lista o noticia de las jurisdicciones . . . de la provincia de Nueva Vizcaya, año de 1803, AGN:HI 917:2, in *Descripciones económicas regionales de Nueva España. Provincias del Norte, 1790–1814,* comp. Enrique Florescano and Isabel Gil Sánchez (Mexico City: Instituto Nacional de Antropología e Historia, 1976), 1:95.

6. Pueblo productivity: Fray Juan Augustín de Morfi, "Account of Disorders, 1778," in *Coronado's Land: Essays on Daily Life in Colonial New Mexico,* ed. and trans. Marc Simmons (Albuquerque: University of New Mexico Press, 1991), 130–32, also mentions the Pueblo communal advantage in defending their nearby fields. Also published as Fray Juan Augustín de Morfi, *Account of Disorders in New Mexico, 1778,* ed. and trans. Marc Simmons (Isleta Pueblo: Historical Society of New Mexico, 1977). Citations will refer to the newer edition. Quotation: AGN:PI 151:2, 229R,V. Translation from Pedro Fermín de Mendinueta, "Indian and Mission Affairs in 1773," in *Coronado's Land: Essays on Daily Life in Colonial New Mexico,* ed. and trans. Marc Simmons (Albuquerque: University of New Mexico Press, 1991), 121–22, originally published as *Indian and Mission Affairs in New Mexico, 1773,* ed. and trans. Marc Simmons (Santa Fe, N.Mex.: Stagecoach Press, 1965).

7. Certificaciones de las missiones . . . Provincia de Nueba Mexico, . . . estado actual & Año de 1794, n.s., n.l., n.d (attributed to Fray Cayetano José Ignacio Bernal, Misión de Belem, September 1, 1794), AASF:MI 1794, #13, 53:108–14.

8. Discussion of Pueblo and vecino weaving: Mark Winter, American Renaissance Inc., Santa Fe, personal communication, December 26, 1996, and September 25, 1998; and Kate Peck Kent, "Spanish, Navajo, or Pueblo? A Guide to the Identification of Nineteenth-Century Southwestern Textiles," in *Hispanic Arts and Ethnohistory in the Southwest,* ed. Marta Weigle, Claudia Larcombe, and Samuel Larcombe (Santa Fe, N.Mex.: Ancient City Press, 1983), 137–43.

9. The Navajo acquired sheep in the 1640s, and probably the knowledge of weaving at the same time; see Joe Ben Wheat, "Yarns to the Navajo: The Materials of Weaving," in *A Burst of Brilliance: Germantown Pennsylvania and Navajo Weaving,* ed. Stanley Chodorow (Philadelphia: Arthur Ross Gallery of the University of Pennsylvania, 1994), 12. Anthony Berlant and Mary Hunt Kahlenburg, *The Navajo Blanket* (Los Angeles: Praeger Publishers, in association with the Los Angeles County Museum, 1972), 9, and Kathleen Whitaker, "Navajo Weaving Design: 1750–1900" (Ph.D. diss., University of California at Los Angeles, 1986), 44–63, reflect the standard view that the Navajo learned to weave closer to 1700, after the Pueblo Revolt.

10. E. Boyd, *Popular Arts of Colonial New Mexico* (Albuquerque: University of New Mexico Press, 1974), 172–73; and Teresa Archuleta-Sagel, "Textiles," in *Spanish New Mexico: The Spanish Colonial Arts Society Collection,* ed. Donna Pierce and Marta Weigle (Santa Fe: Museum of New Mexico Press, 1996), 1:148.

11. Nora Fisher, "The Treadle Loom," in *Spanish Textile Tradition of New Mexico and Colorado,* ed. Nora Fisher (Santa Fe: Museum of New Mexico Press, 1979), 192–

95; and Roland F. Dickey, *New Mexico Village Arts* (Albuquerque: University of New Mexico Press, 1949), 109–12. Vecino preference for wool: see the appendix in Kent, "Spanish, Navajo, or Pueblo?" 164–65.

12. Figure 11 on page 155 of Kent, "Spanish, Navajo, or Pueblo?" is the blanket shown in Plate 2.

13. La Fora quotation: Nicolás de la Fora, *The Frontiers of New Spain*, ed. and trans. Lawrence Kinnaird (Berkeley: Quivira Society, 1958), 94; and Nicolás de la Fora, *Relación del viaje que hizo a los Presidios Internos situados en la frontera de la América Septentrional*, ed. Vito Alessio Robles (Mexico City: Editorial Pedro Robredo, 1939), 104–5. La Fora visited New Mexico between 1766 and 1768. Translation based on Kinnaird. Pecos calamity: Mendinueta to Bucareli, Santa Fe, June 20, 1774, AGN:PI 103:246V–247R. Pueblo Indians transporting goods: Report made by Fray Delgado to Fray Jimeno concerning the abominable hostilities and tyrannies of the governor and alcaldes mayores toward the Indians, Hospicio de Santa Barbara, México, March 27, 1750. In Hackett, *Historical Documents*, 3:427.

14. Reaño's will: Proceedings regarding debt owed to the estate of Juan Reaño, Santa Fe, November 23, 1762, SANM II 9:410–44, TW #559. Sayal: Ward Alan Minge, "*Efectos del país:* A History of Weaving along the Rio Grande," in *Spanish Textile Tradition of New Mexico and Colorado*, ed. Nora Fisher (Santa Fe: Museum of New Mexico Press, 1979), 14.

15. Archaeological survey: Rex E. Gerald, "Spanish Presidios of the Late Eighteenth Century in Northern New Spain," *Museum of New Mexico Research Records* 7 (1968), 41–55. Early Anasazi ceramics: see the discussion of the pre-Pueblo period from about 400 A.D. in Fred Plog, "Western Anasazi," in *Southwest*, ed. Alfonso Ortiz, *Handbook of North American Indians* (Washington, D.C.: Smithsonian Institution, 1979), 9:108–30; and Linda S. Cordell, "Eastern Anasazi," in *Southwest*, ed. Alfonso Ortiz, *Handbook of North American Indians* (Washington, D.C.: Smithsonian Institution, 1979), 9:131–51. Pottery specialization in central Mexico: Murdo MacLeod, "Aspects of the Internal Economy of Colonial Spanish America: Labour; Taxation; Distribution and Exchange," in *The Cambridge History of Latin America*, ed. Leslie Bethell (Cambridge, England: Cambridge University Press, 1984), 2:256. New Mexico pottery making: Charles M. Carrillo, *Hispanic New Mexican Pottery: Evidence of Craft Specialization, 1790–1890* (Albuquerque, N.Mex.: LDP Press, 1997); see also David H. Snow, "Spanish American Pottery Manufacture," *Ethnohistory* 31:2 (1984), 93–113.

16. Don Pedro Alonso O'Crouley, *A Description of the Kingdom of New Spain, 1774,* trans. and ed. Seán Galvin (San Francisco: John Howell Books, 1972), 56.

17. Franciscan supplies: Dr. Pedro Tamarón y Romerál, *Bishop Tamarón's Visitation of New Mexico, 1760,* ed. Eleanor B. Adams (Publications in History, 15; Albuquerque: Historical Society of New Mexico, 1954), 77–78; and Varo (1750), AFBN 29:564.1, #1795, 10V–11R; and Hackett, *Historical Documents*, 3:447–48. Quotation: Letter of Br. don Santiago Roibal to Bishop Tamarón, in Tamarón, *Visitation*, 78. A fanega de sembradura comprised the area of land sown with one fanega of maize, about nine acres (3.57 hectares); an almud equaled one-twelfth of a fanega; a *cuartillo* was one-quarter of an almud. All of these measures also represent a corresponding dry measure.

18. Ornedal sent his report to Viceroy Revillagigedo I (Juan Francisco de Güemes y Horcasitas), Real Presidio del Norte, July 26, 1749, AFBN 29:557.1, #1778, 1V–13V. For a description of the dispute, see Henry W. Kelly, "Franciscan Missions of New Mexico, 1740–1760," *New Mexico Historical Review* 15:4 (1940), 345–68, 16:1 (1941), 41–69, and 16:2 (1941), 148–71, also published in Henry W. Kelly, *Franciscan Missions of New Mexico, 1740–1760* (Albuquerque: Historical Society of New Mexico, 1941); and Tamarón, *Visitation,* 13–18. Also see Hubert Howe Bancroft, *History of the Pacific States of North America: Arizona and New Mexico, 1530–1888* (San Francisco: History Company, 1888), 12:250–51.

19. Informe que manda Fray Manuel de San Juan Nepomuceno y Trigo al procurador general Fray José Miguel de los Ríos, Convento de San Matías de Istacalco, July 23, 1754, AFBN 30:587.1, #1832; translated in Hackett, *Historical Documents,* 3:459–68. See also the earlier rebuttal, Informe de fray Juan Sanz de Lezaún y fray Manuel Bermejo al comisario general fray Juan Antonio Abasolo en que refutan los cargos que hizo a las misiones de Nuevo México, Juan Antonio de Ornedal y Maza, Sía [Zia] y Santa Ana, October 29, 1750, AFBN 29:573.1, #1807, 1R–13R. For a tabulation of the services provided by the Pueblos to the missionaries, see Frank, "Settler to Citizen," 458, table 10. The description and survey of the goods and services provided by each pueblo to which Fray Trigo (1754) refers in this report was in part based on a series of *diligencias* taken at the pueblos in 1750. See Diligencias hechas por fray Manuel de San Juan Nepomuceno y Trigo, comisario vistador, para averiguar lo relativo a la recepción de sínodos por parte de los misioneros de Nuevo México, n.p., July 15–August 22, 1750, AFBN 29:556.1, #1798, 1R–36R.

20. Domínguez, *Missions,* 49. Repuesta y satisfacción dada por parte de la Sagrada Religión de Nuestra Padre San Francisco al informe que hizo Juan Antonio de Ornedal sobre las misiones de Nuevo México [Fray Varo to Viceroy Revillagigedo], Convento de San Francisco [de México?], March 1750, AFBN 29:564.1, #1795, 10R, translated in Hackett, *Historical Documents,* 3:447.

21. Census figures: Antonio de Bonilla, "Apuntes históricos sobre el Nuevo México," copy of September 3, 1903, AGN:HI 25:7, Bancroft Library, University of California, Berkeley (MM–167); and Frank, "Settler to Citizen," appendix 1. Taos and Galisteo: Informe of Fray Trigo (1754), AFBN 30:587.1, #1832, 11V–12R and 9V–10R, translated in Hackett, *Historical Documents,* 3:467–68 and 3:466.

22. G. Emlen Hall, "The Pueblo Grant Labyrinth," in *Land, Water, and Culture: New Perspectives on Hispanic Land Grants,* ed. Charles L. Briggs and John R. Van Ness (Albuquerque: University of New Mexico Press, 1987), 67–138.

23. See Ramón A. Gutiérrez, *When Jesus Came, the Corn Mothers Went Away: Marriage, Sexuality, and Power in New Mexico, 1500–1846* (Stanford, Calif.: Stanford University Press, 1991), 160. Santa Ana example: Leslie A. White, *The Pueblo of Santa Ana* (Memoirs of the American Anthropological Association, 60; Menasha, Wis.: Collegiate Press, 1942), 63.

24. On repartimiento systems in Guadalajara and Mexico (Diocese), the Bajío, and Oaxaca, respectively, see William B. Taylor, *Magistrates of the Sacred: Priests and Parishioners in Eighteenth-Century Mexico* (Stanford, Calif.: Stanford University Press, 1996), 403–4; David A. Brading, *Miners and Merchants in Bourbon Mexico, 1763–1810* (Cambridge, England: Cambridge University Press, 1971), 44–51; Brian R. Hamnett, *Politics and Trade in Southern Mexico, 1750–1821* (Cambridge, England: Cambridge

University Press, 1971), 12–23; Rudolfo Pastor, "El repartimiento de mercancías y los alcaldes mayores novohispanos: Un sistema de explotación, de sus orígenes a la crisis de 1810," in *El gobierno provincial en la Nueva España, 1570–1787*, ed. Woodrow Borah (Mexico City: Universidad Nacional Autónoma de México), 1985, 201–36; and John Lynch, *The Spanish American Revolutions, 1808–1826* (New York: Norton, 1973), 7–9.

25. Stanley J. Stein, "Bureaucracy and Business in the Spanish Empire, 1759–1804: Failure of a Bourbon Reform in Mexico and Peru," *Hispanic American Historical Review* 61 : 1 (1981), 9; and Pastor, "El repartimiento de mercancías," 230–36. For discussion of Bourbon policy and the political debate over repartimiento within the Spanish government, see Stein, "Bureaucracy and Business," 2–28; and the critique of Stein's article by Jacques A. Barbier and Mark A. Burkholder, "Critique of Stanley J. Stein's 'Bureaucracy and Business in the Spanish Empire, 1759–1804: Failure of a Bourbon Reform in Mexico and Peru,'" *Hispanic American Historical Review* 62 : 3 (1982), 460–77, with Stein's reply.

26. Suspiros tristes, sollozos amargos, ayes compasivos y clamorosos validos [*sic*] que . . . expone . . . al virrey Agustín de Ahumada, marqués [de las Amarillas], contra el goberador Francisco Antonio Marín del Valle, no place, New Mexico, no date, 1756, AFBN 30:590.1, #1837, 5V. Lezaún quotations: Noticias lamentables acaecidas en la Nueva México y atrasos cada día se experimentan, así en lo spiritual como lo temporal, por la mala conducta de los gobernadores . . . ; por fray Juan de Lezaún, no location, November 4, 1760, AFBN 30:595.1, #1851, 1R–6V; and translated as "An Account of Lamentable Happenings in New Mexico . . . ," in Hackett, *Historical Documents*, 3 : 475 and 3 : 471. Governor Joaquín Cadallos y Rabal held the tithe for the first time in 1744. The records in Durango for 1735–1743 are missing. See Frank, "Settler to Citizen," 447–48, table 6, for list of colonial tithe holders.

27. Fray Delgado quotation: Report of Fray Delgado, México, March 27, 1750, in Hackett, *Historical Documents*, 3 : 426. Fray Oronzoro quotation: Informe de fray Juan José de Oronzoro al custodio fray Andrés Varo en que consigna algunas de las iniquidades de los gobernadores y alcaldes mayores que fueron disimuladas y aprobadas por el juez visitador Juan [Antonio] de Ornedal, Misión de San Augustín de Isleta, November 7, 1750, AFBN 29:571.1, 1V. This document contains an inventory of activities in almost every pueblo. See also Informe de Andrés García sobre el servicio personal que, como semanaros, prestan los governadores, y alcaldes mayores, Misión de San Estéban de Acoma, August 2, 1750, AFBN 29:569.1, #1801, 1R,V; and Memorial de fray Juan Nepomuceno y Trigo [vice-custos of New Mexico] al virrey Francisco de Güemes y Horcasitas [Revillagigedo I] en que impune un informe de Juan [Antonio] de Ordenal, Santa Fe, September 20, 1750, AFBN 29:570.1, #1804, 1R–8R.

28. Report against Governor Valle (1756), AFBN 30:590.1, #1837, 5V. Fray Lezaún and Fray Bermejo (1750) explained that sheep raising and weaving took place in the southernmost Pueblos, not in the "nine missions of Río Arriba." AFBN 29:573.1, #1807, 4R. Fray Lezaún quotations: Fray Lezaún and Fray Bermejo (1750), AFBN 29:573.1, #1807, 9V; Fray Lezaún (1760), AFBN 30:595.1, #1851; Hackett, *Historical Documents*, 3 : 471. Fray Delgado quotation: Report of Fray Delgado (1750); Hackett, *Historical Documents*, 3 : 427.

29. See Hamnett, *Politics and Trade*, 21.

30. Informe de Andrés García (1750), AFBN 29:569.1, #1801, 1R.

31. Fray Lezaún (1760), AFBN 30:595.1, #1851; Hackett, *Historical Documents,* 3:471.

32. Report of Fray Delgado (1750), Hackett, *Historical Documents,* 3:426.

33. Annual maize consumption: Estéván Lorenzo, Bishop of Durango, to Viceroy Revillagigedo (II), Durango, October 6, 1792, AGN:PI 161:515R. The measure used to make up a fanega varied in New Mexico from 1.5 to 2.5 bushels: Domínguez, *Missions,* 355.

34. Using the number of families provided in the 1752 census for Río Abajo: 1,325 families ÷ 400 blankets = 3.31 blankets per family, or roughly one per year for every 10–17 Indian inhabitants of the Río Abajo Pueblos (using the 1746, 1748, 1750, and 1752 censuses). Using the estimate of Pueblo families compiled from Tamarón (1760): 1,435 families ÷ 400 blankets = 3.59 blankets per family, or roughly one per year for every 15 Pueblo Indians. Fray Varo and Fray Bermejo (1750) commented on the sheep raising and weaving primarily from the Río Abajo Pueblos in AFBN 29:573.1, #1807, 4R.

35. Labor service: Fray Lezaún (1760), AFBN 30:595.1, #1851; Hackett, *Historical Documents,* 3:471. Fray Delgado (1750) maintained that together the alcaldes used "squads of thirty or forty Pueblo Indians and work[ed] them the greater part of the year planting maize and wheat" (Hackett, *Historical Documents,* 3:427), so that the estimate of eighty Pueblo semenaros may be generous. See Frank, "Settler to Citizen," 458, table 10. Census figures: Bonilla, "Apuntes."

36. For a discussion of the reversal of gender roles accompanying the Spanish conquest of the sixteenth century, see Gutiérrez, *Corn Mothers,* 13–36. See also Jones, *Pueblo Warriors,* 135–69 and 175, for Pueblo military organization in the late eighteenth century. The argument here for the increasing ability of male Pueblo leaders to control influences from outside the pueblo pertains specifically to the 1750–1785 period of the "Defensive Crisis."

37. Anglo-Americans referred to the Shoshone who migrated to the Great Basin with the pejorative name "Digger Indians," due to their seemingly characteristic reliance on roots and tubers for subsistence. For western Shoshone migration and culture change, see Dan Flores, "Bison Ecology and Bison Diplomacy: The Southern Plains from 1800 to 1850," *Journal of American History* 78:2 (1991), 465–85; Morris Foster, *Being Comanche: A Social History of an American Indian Community* (Tucson: University of Arizona Press, 1991), 32–35; Stanley Noyes, *Los Comanches: The Horse People, 1751–1845* (Albuquerque: University of New Mexico Press, 1993), xix–xx and 189; and T. R. Fehrenbach, *Comanches: The Destruction of a People* (New York: Alfred A. Knopf, 1974), 32–33 and 117–49.

38. Katherine A. Spielmann, "Interaction among Nonhierarchical Societies," in *Farmers, Hunters, and Colonists: Interaction between the Southwest and the Southern Plains,* ed. Katherine A. Spielmann (Tucson: University of Arizona Press, 1991), 7–13.

39. Furthermore, nutritionists argue that a limit exists to the amount of protein a person can safely consume. When protein consumption exceeds about half of a person's total caloric intake for any length of time, the body cannot metabolize it quickly enough, leading to liver and kidney damage and other serious health problems. During the lean months, game contained more protein relative to other nutrients. This aspect of life on the Plains may have contributed to trade with the Pueb-

los in order to obtain carbohydrates, particularly during the winter and early spring. See the fuller discussion in John D. Speth, "Some Unexplored Aspects of Mutualistic Plains-Pueblo Food Exchange," in *Farmers, Hunters, and Colonists: Interaction between the Southwest and the Southern Plains,* ed. Katherine A. Spielmann (Tucson: University of Arizona Press, 1991), 18–35.

40. See Katherine A. Spielmann, "Coercion or Cooperation? Plains-Pueblo Interaction in the Protohistoric Period," in *Farmers, Hunters, and Colonists: Interaction between the Southwest and the Southern Plains,* ed. Katherine A. Spielmann (Tucson: University of Arizona Press, 1991), 36–50.

41. For seventeenth-century trade, see the complaint of Fray Estevan de Perea against Juan Lopez, October 30, 1633, and the declaration of Captain Andrés Hurtado, Santa Fe, September, 1661, in Hackett, *Historical Documents,* 3:129–31 and 186–93; and Frank Gilbert Roe, *The Indian and the Horse* (Norman: University of Oklahoma Press, 1955), 74–76.

42. Spielmann, "Interaction," 1–7, discusses the term "nonhierarchical." For a discussion of internal Comanche concepts of community and groups, see Foster, *Being Comanche,* 65–74. Quotation: Domínguez, *Missions,* 112.

43. Charles L. Kenner, *A History of New Mexican–Plains Indian Relations* (Norman: University of Oklahoma Press, 1969), 42, cites Cachupín relación to Revillagigedo of September 29, 1752, in Thomas, *Plains Indians,* 124.

44. The original Cachupín price list of December 7, 1754, has not survived, although he describes his edict regulating the Plains Indian trade fairs in his instructions to his successor, Don Martín del Valle, August 12, 1754, AGN: PI 102:10, 444R–452V; translated in Thomas, *Plains Indians,* 129–43. Cachupín also promulgated a bando on May 10, 1753, prohibiting the trade of offensive arms, oxen, horses, mules, and some other items, which he discussed upon taking over the province in 1761 from Governor del Valle; "Instruciones que deverá observar Don Tomas Vélez Cachupín en su Govierno del Nuebo Mexico . . . ," n.d., AGN: PI 102:10, 322R–327V. Fray Atanasio Domínguez mentioned a number of the 1754 prices in *Missions,* 245–46 and 252. Governor Concha mentioned the original bando and his alterations in a report signed in Chihuahua by Pedro Garrido y Durán, December 21, 1786, copy, Janos, May 13, 1788, AGN: PI 65:1, 79R–116V.

45. Governor Francisco Antonio Martín del Valle to Marqués de Amarillas, July 31, 1758, May 12, 1759, May 31, 1760, AGN: PI 102:8, 281R–294V.

46. Report of Governor Mendinueta to Viceroy Bucareli of March 30, 1772, AGN: PI 103:1, 185V; Mendinueta to Bucareli of May 14, 1773, AGN: PI 103:1, 220V; Report of Mendinueta to Bucareli of June 20, 1774, AGN: PI 103:1, 249V–250R, and September 14, 1774, AGN: PI 103:1, 245R,V.

47. Quotation: Bonilla, "Apuntes." The burial records did not always note the reason for death from an unnatural cause, and not all the dead received burial in circumstances that allowed for recording in a book of baptisms. Additionally, not all the church records of colonial New Mexico have survived, but no more comprehensive material exists on which to base a better estimate.
Description from a report from Governor Mendinueta to Viceroy Bucareli, Santa Fe, September 30, 1774, AGN: PI 65:3, 394R–399V.

48. Description from a report from Governor Mendinueta to Viceroy Bucareli, Santa Fe, September 30, 1774, AGN: PI 65:3, 394R–399V.

49. Governor Mendinueta to Viceroy Bucareli, Santa Fe, July 23, 1773, AGN: PI 103:1, 229R–231V; Mendinueta to Bucareli, Santa Fe, August 18, 1775, AGN: PI

244 NOTES TO PAGES 38–43

65:3, 411V–412V; quotation from Mendinueta to Bucareli, Santa Fe, August 19, 1775, AGN:PI 65:3, 414R.

50. Order to proceed with appropriation for the 1,500 horses signed by Hugo O'Connor, Comandante Inspector, Rios, November 1, 1775. Rafael Martinez Pacheco at San Antonio de Bucareli in Coahuila describes problems of organization and transport of the horses due to drought, AGN:PI 65:3, 460R–485V. Quotation, Governor Mendinueta to Viceroy Bucareli, Santa Fe, December 12, 1776, AGN:PI 103:1, 302V; Teodoro de Croix, Comandante General de los Provincias Internas, General Report of January 23, 1780 to Minister of the Indies José de Gálvez, Arispe, No. 458, AGI:GUAD 253, as translated in Thomas, *Croix,* 111.

51. Governor Valle to Marqués de Amarillas, July 31, 1758, May 12, 1759, May 31, 1760, AGN:PI 102:8, 281R–294V. Governor del Valle describes the difficult conditions of 1758 and 1759, and the renewed hostilities of the Indians, but does not explicitly draw any connection. For the 1770s, see the report of Governor Mendinueta to Viceroy Bucareli of March 30, 1772, AGN:PI 103:1, 185V; Mendinueta to Bucareli of May 14, 1772, AGN:PI 103:1, 220V; Report of Mendinueta to Bucareli of June 20, 1774, AGN:PI 103:1, 249V–250R, and September 14, 1774, AGN:PI 103:1, 245R,V.

52. See Francis Haines, "The Northward Spread of Horses among the Plains Indians," *American Anthropologist* n.s., 40:3 (1938), 429–37; Francis Haines, *The Plains Indians* (New York: Thomas Y. Crowell, 1976), 91–104; Frank Raymond Secoy, *Changing Military Patterns on the Great Plains (Seventeenth Century through Early Nineteenth Century)* (Locust Valley, N.Y.: J. J. Augustin, 1953), 34–38. Secoy overemphasizes the role of the Apache in the early spread of horses into the Plains. He identified the "Padouca" found in Spanish and French accounts as an Apachean group, but it generally signified one of the Comanche bands.

53. See Frank, "Settler to Citizen," appendix 1, for the censuses of New Mexico for the colonial period and an explanation of the problems relating to their interpretation.

54. Domínguez, *Missions,* 213–14. See also Fray Juan Augustín de Morfí, "Geographical Description of New Mexico," in *Forgotten Frontiers: A Study of the Spanish-Indian Policy of Juan Bautista de Anza, Governor of New Mexico, 1777–1787,* ed. Alfred Barnaby Thomas (Norman: University of Oklahoma Press, 1932), 93, who says that Pecos "suffered such a considerable decline being the frontier for enemies who, with the pretext of peace, frequented it and took the opportunity to wreak havoc." The translation by Thomas is based on the manuscript in the British Library, Mexico Tratados Varios, Add. Mss 17, 563, 71–94, and a copy in AGN:HI 25:6, 92–116.

55. Quotations from: Domínguez, *Missions,* p. 217; and Morfí, "Description," 87–114. Governor Mendinueta mentioned that flight from Ojo Caliente, Abiquíu, Chama, and Río Arriba had begun in 1770 due to the threat of attack, even when there were no enemy Indians around; Mendinueta to Croix, Santa Fe, November 3, 1770, AGN:PI 103:1, 128R; Santa Fe census of 1821: ACD:PA box 3, folio 7, 12V–13R, 16V, and note on 17V. The Santa Fe census includes 23 families with 123 inhabitants.

56. Identification of Vallecitos, in Thomas M. Pearce, ed. *New Mexico Place Names, A Geographical Dictionary* (Albuquerque: University of New Mexico Press, 1965), 112; Grant, in Ralph E. Twitchell, *The Spanish Archives of New Mexico* (Cedar Rapids, Iowa:

Torch Press, 1914), TW #28, 655, and 656, vol. I (SANM I), 25–27, and 179; San Juan burial book: Lista de los Muertes hechas por los Indios Gentiles en las Parroquias de San Juan y Santa Clara, entre los años de 1726 y de 1842, transcript, HTOZ VIII, #37. This extract of the burial records was made under the direction of Adolph A. Bandelier for the Hemenway Southwestern Expedition. The original San Juan burial records, and the Santa Clara book covering 1806–1840, are not at the Archdioceses of Santa Fe and are not known elsewhere. See Brugge, *Navajos*, 1–15, table 1; Fray Angélico Chávez, *Archives of the Archdiocese of Santa Fe, 1678–1900* (Washington, D.C.: Academy of American Franciscan History, 1957); and Domínguez, *Missions*, 78.

57. At least two versions of the 1779 Miera y Pacheco map exist, one in the British Museum, Add. Mss. 17.651U, published in Thomas, *Frontiers* (insert) and Twitchell SANM, vol. II, facing 264; the other in AGN:MAP, *Catalogo de Ilustraciones* (Mexico City: Centro de Información Gráfica del Archivo General de la Nación, 1979), vol. 1, no. 220, from AGN:HI 25:2, folio 283. See an explanation of the related 1777 and 1778 maps by Miera y Pacheco in Thomas W. Kavanagh, *Comanche Political History: An Ethnological Perspective, 1700–1875* (Lincoln: University of Nebraska Press, 1996), 87–90. The 1779 versions focus on the Province of New Mexico rather than exploration to the north and west.

58. The 1765 census: Donald C. Cutter, trans., "Statistical Report on New Mexico, 1765," *New Mexico Historical Review* 50:4 (1975), 347–52. Raids: Domínguez, *Missions*, 254.

59. There are many differences and discrepancies between the two copies. The AGN map has an incomplete key, but has a scale of leguas and other details that the British Museum map lacks. The British map is missing both Pecos and Galisteo Pueblos entirely. Taken together, the two maps give a good idea of the extent of damage done by the hostile Indian groups. Domínguez, *Missions*, 83, 90–91, and 187.

60. Abiquíu: Domínguez, *Missions*, 124. Taos settlers resettled in 1770 inside the pueblo: Domínguez, *Missions*, 111–13. The first six baptisms performed for vecinos outside the Taos Pueblo took place in "Ranchos" (the new plaza of Ranchos de Taos) in 1787. AASF:BA B–46 (book of baptisms) (Box 69), Taos, 1777–1798. A Taos census of 1796 shows 191 people living in the "Plaza de San Francisco." SANM II 21:545, no TW # (D'Armand Papers, University of New Mexico, Zimmerman Library). Vecinos in Picurís: Governor Mendinueta to Viceroy Bucareli, Santa Fe, July 23, 1773, AGN:PI 103:1, 232V.

61. See Frank, "Settler to Citizen", appendix 1, for the complete census summaries for each point shown. Reading eighteenth-century census material becomes problematic since neither the church nor the governor developed a standard format for counting or reporting population. In 1790 Viceroy Revilligigedo II ordered a general census for all of New Spain and sent census templates to all of the provincial governors for the local officials to follow in recording the population count. New Mexican officials and missionaries began to use template as the basis for future enumeration. No single census from this period can withstand close statistical scrutiny. The Cachupín census figures of 1752, for example, probably undercount the Pueblo Indian population by about one-third, and the vecino population by somewhat less, based on a comparison with the census returns before and after that

year. This creates the dramatic and anomalous dip in the population of the province plotted in Figure 2; no documented event in the early 1750s can account for a demographic collapse of this magnitude.

62. See Marc Simmons, "Settlement Patterns in Colonial New Mexico," *Journal of the West* 8:1 (1969), 7–21 (also in *New Spain's Far Northern Frontier: Essays on Spain in the American West, 1540–1821,* ed. David J. Weber [Albuquerque: University of New Mexico Press, 1979], 97–115). Quotation from Morfí, "Disorders," 131.

63. Quotation: Mendinueta to Croix, Santa Fe, November 3, 1770, AGN: PI 103: 1, 128R,V; Orden dado al Alcalde Mayor de Abiquíu, Marcos Sanchez, para evitar la depoblacion de quel pueblo. Fermín de Mendinueta, Santa Fe, February 7, 1771, PBAN 53:7.

64. For an excellent study of a Genízaro settlement, see Steven M. Horvath Jr., "The Social and Political Organization of the Genízaros of Plaza de Nuestra Señora de los Dolores de Belén, New Mexico, 1740–1812" (Ph.D. diss., Brown University, 1979), 68–108. Quotations: Petitions and diligencias of the settlers of Carnué, Governor Mendinueta, and Alcalde Mayor, Don Francisco Trebol Navarro, April 12, 1771, April 16, 1771, April 24, 1771, May 20, 1771, May 27, 1771, transcript, HTOZ VIII, #35. Documents not listed in Twitchell SANM vol. 1. Grant information: Report to Mendinueta from Navarro, Albuquerque, March 24, 1774, SANM I 1:357–66, TW #46.

65. Abiquíu: Order of Governor Mendinueta, Santa Fe, November 2, 1770, transcript, HTOZ VIII, #34. The original manuscript is in SANM I 1:289–92, TW #36; Governor Mendinueta to Alcalde Mayor Marcos Sánchez, Santa Fe, February 7, 1771, PBAN 53:7, 2R.

66. Quotation: Alfred Barnaby Thomas, trans. and ed., "Governor Mendinueta's Proposals for the Defense of New Mexico, 1772–1779," *New Mexico Historical Review* 6:1 (1931), 29–30; Miera y Pacheco: AGN: MAP, *Catalogo de Ilustraciones,* vol. 1, no. 220, from AGN: HI 25:2, folio 283. See Simmons, "*Settlement Patterns,*" 18; Thomas, *Frontiers,* 92; and Thomas, *Croix,* 107–8.

67. Don Vélez de Cachupín to Viceroy Conde de Revillagigedo, October 17, 1757, translated from AGN: PI 102 in Thomas, *Plains Indians,* 130.

68. Gileño attack: Governor Cachupín to Marquis de Cruillas, Santa Fe, January 2, 1766, AGN: PI 102:10, 420R,V; Quotations: Governor Mendinueta to Inspector General Teodoro de Croix, Santa Fe, November 4, 1769, AGN: PI 103:1, 100R–101R; and Mendinueta to Croix, Santa Fe, January 28, 1769, AGN: PI 103:1, 60V–62V.

69. Mendinueta to Croix, Santa Fe, May 6, 1771, AGN: PI 103:1, 144R–148V. Also see William B. Griffen, *Apaches at War and Peace: The Janos Presidio, 1750–1858* (Albuquerque: University of New Mexico Press, 1988), 30.

70. Appointment of Don Antonio Maria Daroca Teniente del Paso, Mexico, March 30, 1773, AGN: PI 103:1, 201R–202R; Governor Mendinueta to Viceroy Bucareli, Santa Fe, May 14, 1773, AGN: PI 103:1, 218R,V; Bonilla, "Apuntes," 122R,V, paragraph 32. See also Domínguez, *Missions,* 272.

71. Quotation: Governor Mendinueta to Viceroy Bucareli y Ursua, Santa Fe, July 23, 1773, AGN: PI 103:1, 233R,V; bando of Governor Mendinueta, Santa Fe, April 14, 1777, SANM II 10:902–4, TW #697.

72. Comisarios de Ayuntamiento de Chihuahua to Viceroy Teodoro Marquis de

Croix, Chihuahua, December 22, 1767, AGN:PI 95:1, 108R–110V; and letter from Los disputados de mineria y commercio de esta Villa de San Felipe el Real de Chihuahua to Don Pedro Antonio Quiepo de Llano, "corregidor, justicia mayor, y teniente capitan de guerra," Chihuahua, October 24, 1771, transmitted to Julian de Arriaga by Viceroy Antonio Bucareli y Ursua, Mexico, January 22, 1772, AGI: GUAD 512, letter #141, Charles E. Chapman, *Catalogue of the Materials in the Archivo General de Indias for the History of the Pacific Coast and the Southwest* (University of California Publications in History, 8; Berkeley, 1919), #1846.

73. In theory, the bishop of Durango held secular jurisdiction over the Province of New Mexico from the time of the bishopric's foundation in 1621. When Bishop Antonio Crespo y Monroy attempted to carry out a visitation of the province in 1730, the Franciscan custos, Fray Andrés Varo, objected on the grounds that the bishop had no authority over areas ministered to by the regular orders. Legal proceedings followed in which the viceroy upheld the bishop of Durango's right to nominal jurisdiction over the province. The bishop's power extended to the occasional visitation and appointment of ecclesiastical judges and the right to the tithe, which the church collected in 1732 for the first time since the reconquest (ACD:DZ 2:7, 46R, September 9, 1734). See Tamarón, *Visitation,* 1–19; and Bancroft, *Arizona and New Mexico,* 240–41.

74. Letter from the ecclesiastical judge of Santa Fe, B. Santiago Roibal, to the Jueces Hacedores de Diezmos, Santa Fe, June 30, 1762, ACD:DZ 2 (miscellaneous documents), 1R,V of 8 pages beginning at 24R.

75. Morfí, "Disorders," 141–46. Don Clemente Gutiérrez served as the *fiador* for Don Diego Baca, who officially won the bid. ACD:DZ 23:139R bis, 166R.

76. Mexican epidemic: Michael M. Smith, "The 'Real Expedición Marítima de la Vacuna' in New Spain and Guatemala," *Transactions of the American Philosophical Society* n.s., 64:1 (1974), 8; and Donald B. Cooper, *Epidemic Disease in Mexico City, 1761–1813* (Austin: University of Texas Press, 1965). Eastern vector: Marc Simmons, "New Mexico's Smallpox Epidemic of 1780–81," *New Mexico Historical Review* 41.4 (1966), 319–26.

77. Jacobo Ugarte y Loyola to Governor de Anza, September 19, 1786, unique original, HTOZ III, #46. For variolation and Dr. Gil's treatise, see also Smith, "Real Expedición," 8–11. Later program of inoculation: AASF:MI 1805 #10, and SANM II 15:633, 639–40, TW #1823, 1822.

78. Bancroft, *Arizona and New Mexico,* 266. The Picurís registers are: AASF: BU Bur-20 (book of burials), (Box 11) Picurís, 1777–1840, and AASF:BA B–22, (Box 24) Picurís, 1776–1830. Population figures from Frank, "Settler to Citizen," 413–32, table 1. The net population change found in the baptism and burial books between the last representative census and the epidemic was added to the census. The total, plus the baptisms during 1780–1781, yields the divisor of the number who died during the epidemic.

79. The Santa Clara registers are: AASF:BU Bur-30 (Box 20), Santa Clara, 1726–1843, and AASF:BA B–31 (Box 44), Santa Clara, 1728–1805; AASF:BU Bur-33 and Bur-34 (Boxes 23 and 24), Santa Cruz de la Cañada, 1769–1789, 1795–1833, and AASF:BA B–35 and B–26 (Boxes 48 and 49), Santa Cruz de la Cañada, 1769–1794. Santa Fe Presidio Company diary, Santa Fe, February 28, 1781, SANM II 11:215, TW #817a.

80. See Governor Concha to Comandante General Ugarte y Loyola, Santa Fe, November 1, 1790, AGN:PI 161:5, 89R–93V; and Informe of Governor Anza to the Comandante General, Santa Fe, July 20, 1784, copy certified in 1792, AGN:PI 161:5, 83R–88R, list of "reuniones" on 86V.

81. See the Domínguez and Anza censuses for Acoma and Laguna in Frank, "Settler to Citizen," 413–32, table 1.

82. AASF:BU Bur-31, Santa Clara, and Bur-22, Pojoaque. *Párvulo* normally signifies a small child, but in some of the New Mexican censuses it is used to designate older children.

83. Thomas L. Pearcy, "The Smallpox Outbreak of 1779–1782: A Brief Comparative Look at Twelve Borderlands Communities," *Journal of the West* 34 (1997), 26–37; Miguel E. Bustamante, "Aspectos históricos y epidemiológicos del hambre en México," in *Ensayos sobre la historia de las epidemias en México,* ed. Enrique Florescano and Elsa Malvido (Mexico City: Instituto Mexicano del Seguro Social, 1982), 1:56; Germán Somolimos d'Ardois, "La viruela en la Nueva España," in *Ensayos sobre la historia de las epidemias en México,* 1:240.

84. For the role of cofradías in Chihuahua, see Cheryl English Martin, *Governance and Society in Colonial Mexico: Chihuahua in the Eighteenth Century* (Stanford, Calif.: Stanford University Press, 1996), 110–20; Cheryl English Martin, "Public Celebrations, Popular Culture, and Labor Discipline in Eighteenth-Century Chihuahua," in *Rituals of Rule, Rituals of Resistance: Public Celebrations and Popular Culture in Mexico,* ed. William H. Beezley, Cheryl English Martin, and William E. French (Wilmington, Del.: SR Books, 1994), 95–114.

85. Domínguez, *Missions,* 19, 241–249. Also see the note on p. 247.

86. ACD:VA 44:116, 10R, 12R, 14R, 16R.

87. Calculations are based on the percentage increase given by Domínguez, compounded for fifteen years. The same percentage increase was applied to the 1791 rental value to obtain the estimated total number owned by the cofradías in 1791.

88. See Sherburne F. Cook, *The Population of the California Indians, 1769–1970* (Berkeley: University of California Press, 1976); Sherburne F. Cook and Woodrow Borah, *Essays in Population History* (3 vols.; Berkeley: University of California Press, 1979); Henry F. Dobyns, *Their Number Become Thinned: Native American Population Dynamics in Eastern North America* (Knoxville: University of Tennessee Press in cooperation with the Newberry Library Center for the History of the American Indian, 1983), 378; Paul Farnsworth and Robert H. Jackson, "Cultural, Economic, and Demographic Change in the Missions of Alta California: The Case of Nuestra Señora de la Soledad," in *The New Latin American Mission History,* ed. Erick Langer and Robert H. Jackson (Lincoln, University of Nebraska Press, 1995), 109–29; Robert Jackson, *Indian Population Decline: The Missions of Northwestern New Spain, 1687–1840* (Albuquerque: University of New Mexico Press, 1994); Robert H. Jackson, "Grain Supply, Congregation, and Demographic Patterns in the Missions of Northwestern New Spain," *Journal of the West* 36:1 (1997), 19–25; Robert H. Jackson and Edward Castillo, *Indians, Franciscans, and Spanish Colonization* (Albuquerque: University of New Mexico Press, 1995); and Daniel T. Reff, *Disease, Depopulation, and Culture Change in Northwestern New Spain, 1518–1764* (Salt Lake City: University of Utah Press, 1991).

89. See Harry A. Miskimin, *The Economy of Early Renaissance Europe, 1300–1460* (Cambridge, England: Cambridge University Press, 1975), 25–32; A. Elizabeth Levett, *The Black Death on the Estates of the See of Winchester*, vol. 5, no. 9 of *Oxford Studies in Social and Legal History*, edited by Paul Vinogradoff (Oxford: Clarendon Press, 1916), esp. 141; and M. H. Keen, *England in the Later Middle Ages* (London: Methuen, 1973), 169–74. Effects on the peasantry: J. M. W. Bean, "The Black Death: The Crisis and Its Social and Economic Consequences," in *The Black Death: The Impact of the Fourteenth-Century Plague*, ed. Daniel Williman (Binghamton, N.Y.: Center for Medieval and Early Renaissance Studies, 1982), 23, 33, and esp. 30–31. Also see the article by Léopold Genicot, "Crisis: From the Middle Ages to Modern Times," in *The Cambridge Economic History of Europe*, ed. M. M. Postan (2d ed.; Cambridge, England: Cambridge University Press, 1966), 660–94.

90. Miskimin, *Economy*, 34–35. See Philip Ziegler, *The Black Death* (London: Collins, 1969), 239–41, for his comment on the statement to this effect by Sir Frederick Pollock and Frederic William Maitland, *History of English Law before the Time of Edward I* (2 vols.; 2d ed.; Cambridge, England: Cambridge University Press, 1923), 1:106; John Hatcher, *Plague, Population, and the English Economy, 1348–1530* (Studies in Economic and Social History, 13; London: Macmillan, 1977), 32–35.

91. Lorin W. Brown, with Charles L. Briggs and Marta Weigle, *Hispano Folklife of New Mexico: The Lorin W. Brown Federal Writers' Project Manuscripts* (Albuquerque: University of New Mexico Press, 1978), 40.

92. The oldest and most complete version of *Los Comanches* was copied in 1864 from an earlier version: Aurelio M. Espinosa, *The Folklore of Spain in the American Southwest: Traditional Spanish Folk Literature in Northern New Mexico and Southern Colorado*, ed. J. Manuel Espinosa (Norman: University of Oklahoma Press, 1985), 217. The 1864 version: Arthur Leon Campa, *Los Comanches: A New Mexican Folk Drama* (University of New Mexico Bulletin, Language Series, 7:1; Albuquerque: University of New Mexico Press, 1942). Aurelio M. Espinosa published another manuscript owned by Don Amado Chavez of Santa Fe, *Los Comanches: A Spanish Heroic Play of the Year 1780* (University of New Mexico Bulletin, Language Series, 1:1, Albuquerque: University of New Mexico Press, 1907), translated as Gilberto Espinosa, "Los Comanches," *New Mexico Quarterly* 1:2 (1931), 133–46. Lorin Brown describes a performance held at El Rancho New Mexico on December 28, 1938, in Brown, *Hispano Folklife*, 40–43. The author last attended *Los Comanches* at Alcalde, New Mexico, near Española, in late December 1986.

93. Kenner, *History*, 47.

94. Translated from Campa, *Los Comanches*, 42. The original text translated here provides a very different interpretation of the meaning of the play from that of Gilberto Espinosa in "Los Comanches," 145.

NOTES TO CHAPTER 2

1. David A. Brading, *The First America* (Cambridge, England: Cambridge University Press, 1991), 473–77.

2. David A. Brading, *Miners and Merchants in Bourbon Mexico, 1763–1810* (Cambridge, England: Cambridge University Press, 1971), 28–29.

3. Ibid., 129–58; and P. J. Bakewell, *Silver Mining and Society in Colonial Mexico:*

Zacatecas, 1546–1700 (Cambridge, England: Cambridge University Press, 1971), 114–220.

4. Eric Van Young, *Hacienda and Market in Eighteenth-Century Mexico: The Rural Economy of the Guadalajara Region, 1675–1820* (Berkeley: University of California Press, 1981).

5. David A. Brading, *Haciendas and Ranchos in the Mexican Bajío: León, 1700–1860* (Cambridge, England: Cambridge University Press, 1978).

6. John C. Super, *La vida en Querétaro durante la Colonia, 1531–1810* (Mexico City: Fondo de Cultura Económica, 1983); John C. Super, "Querétaro Obrajes: Industry and Society in Provincial Mexico, 1600–1810," *Hispanic American Historical Review* 56:2 (1976), 197–216; and Brian R. Hamnett, *Politics and Trade in Southern Mexico, 1750–1821* (Cambridge, England: Cambridge University Press, 1971), esp. 9–23.

7. Richard L. Garner, with Spiro E. Stefanou, *Economic Growth and Change in Bourbon Mexico* (Gainesville: University Press of Florida, 1993), 25.

8. Ibid., 255. See also Richard Salvucci, "Economic Growth and Change in Bourbon Mexico: A Review Essay," *Americas* 51:2 (1994), 219–30; Paul Gootenberg, "On Salamanders, Pyramids, and Mexico's 'Growth-without-Change': Anachronistic Reflections on a Case of Bourbon New Spain," *Colonial Latin American Review* 5:1 (1996), 117–27; and Richard Garner, "An Exchange on the Eighteenth-Century Mexican Economy," *Americas* 54:1 (1997), 109–23.

9. See Michael M. Swann, *Tierra Adentro* (Boulder, Colo.: Westview Press, 1982), 87–272; and Oakah L. Jones Jr., *Nueva Vizcaya: Heartland of the Spanish Frontier* (Albuquerque: University of New Mexico Press, 1988), 117–226.

10. David J. Weber, *The Spanish Frontier in North America* (New Haven, Conn.: Yale University Press, 1992), 204–35; Jones, *Nueva Vizcaya*, 189–98; and Ignacio del Río, *La aplicación regional de las reformas borbónicas en Nueva España: Sonora y Sinaloa, 1768–1787* (Serie de historia novohispana, 55; Mexico City: Universidad Nacional Autónoma de México, Instituto de Investigaciones Históricas, 1995), 152–65.

11. Edgardo López de Mañón and Ignacio del Río, "La reforma institucional Borbónica," in *Tres siglos de historia sonorense (1530–1830),* ed. Sergio Ortega Noriega and Ignacio del Río (Mexico City: Universidad Nacional Autónoma de México, 1993), 298–300.

12. Gerald E. Poyo, "The Canary Islands Immigrants of San Antonio: From Ethnic Exclusivity to Community," in *Tejano Origins in Eighteenth-Century San Antonio,* ed. Gerald E. Poyo and Gilberto M. Hinojosa (Austin: University of Texas Press, 1991), 41–58; and Jesús F. de la Teja, *San Antonio de Béxar: A Community on New Spain's Northern Frontier* (Albuquerque: University of New Mexico Press, 1995), 18.

13. Sergio Ortega Noriega, *Un ensayo de historia regional: El noroeste de México* (Mexico City: Universidad Nacional Autónoma de México, 1993), 118–26; and Weber, *Spanish Frontier,* 239–61.

14. José Cuello, *El norte, el noreste y Saltillo en la historia colonial de México* (Saltillo, Mexico: Archivo Municipal de Saltillo, 1990), 145–52; and del Río, *La aplicación regional,* 198–203.

15. Cuello, *El norte,* 166–78.

16. See Marc Simmons, *New Mexico: An Interpretive History* (rev. ed.; Albuquerque: University of New Mexico Press, 1988), 91–100, 105–6; and Thomas D. Hall, *Social*

Change in the Southwest, 1350–1880 (Lawrence: University Press of Kansas, 1989), 138–47.

17. Recent works have made a loose connection between the Bourbon reforms and changes in New Mexico: see Ramón A. Gutiérrez, *When Jesus Came, the Corn Mothers Went Away: Marriage, Sexuality, and Power in New Mexico, 1500–1846* (Stanford, Calif.: Stanford University Press, 1991), 299–328; and Weber, *Spanish Frontier,* 230–58.

18. General Report 1781 by Teodoro de Croix, Arispe, April 23, 1781, No. 735, AGI:GUAD 253, published in translation in Alfred Barnaby Thomas, trans. and ed., *Teodoro de Croix and the Northern Frontier of New Spain, 1776–1783* (Norman: University of Oklahoma Press, 1941), 105–6.

19. Thomas, *Croix,* 36–38. See also Mario Hernández Sánchez Barba, *Juan Bautista de Anza: Un hombre de Fronteras* (Madrid: Publicaciones Españolas, 1962); Alfred Barnaby Thomas, trans. and ed., *Forgotten Frontiers: A Study of the Spanish-Indian Policy of Juan Bautista de Anza, Governor of New Mexico, 1777–1787* (Norman: University of Oklahoma Press, 1932), 19–83; and Weber, *Spanish Frontier,* 230–31 and 249–53.

20. Estado que manifesta el numero de Presidios, oficialidad, tropa y Indios exploradores . . . , Mexico, March 1777, AGN:PI 87:3, 39–40 (chart).

21. Oakah L. Jones Jr., *Los Paisanos: Spanish Settlers on the Northern Frontier of New Spain* (Norman: University of Oklahoma Press, 1979), 47. For estimates of the Sonoran population, see Peter Gerhard, *The North Frontier of New Spain* (Princeton, N.J.: Princeton University Press 1982), 250.

22. See Thomas, *Croix,* 35–47.

23. Anza diary of the 1779 Comanche expedition, Santa Fe, September 10, 1779, reprinted in translation by Thomas, *Frontiers,* 121–39.

24. See Max L. Moorhead, *The Apache Frontier: Jacobo Ugarte and Spanish-Indian Relations in Northern New Spain, 1769–1791* (Norman: University of Oklahoma Press, 1968), 144–62.

25. Morris Foster, *Being Comanche: A Social History of an American Indian Community* (Tucson: University of Arizona Press, 1991), 42–44; Elizabeth A. H. John, *Storms Brewed in Other Men's Worlds: The Confrontation of Indians, Spanish, and French in the Southwest, 1540–1795* (College Station: Texas A&M University Press, 1975), 590–91. Quotation from Elizabeth A. H. John, "Inside the Comanchería, 1785: The Diary of Pedro Vial and Francisco Xavier Chaves," trans. Adán Benavides, Jr., *Southwestern Historical Quarterly* 98:1 (1994), 51. Alternative translation in Thomas W. Kavanagh, *Comanche Political History: An Ethnological Perspective, 1700–1875* (Lincoln: University of Nebraska Press, 1996), 103.

26. John, "Inside the Comanchería," 49.

27. Thomas, *Frontiers,* 71–83; documents on the Spanish-Comanche treaty, 294–332. Description of the negotiations in Texas and New Mexico: Kavanagh, *Comanche Political History,* 92–121.

28. See Joseph F. Park, "Spanish-Indian Policy in Northern Mexico, 1765–1810," *Arizona and the West* 4:Winter (1962), 340–44; and Bernardo de Gálvez, *Instructions for Governing the Interior Provinces of New Spain, 1786,* ed. and trans. Donald E. Worcester (Quivira Society Publications, 12; Berkeley, Calif.: Quivira Society, 1951), 79–80.

29. Thomas, *Frontiers*, 305–7. Also see Jack August, "Balance-of-Power Diplomacy in New Mexico: Governor Fernando de la Concha and the Indian Policy of Conciliation," *New Mexico Historical Review* 56:2 (1981), 142–43; and Moorhead, *Apache Frontier*, 151–52.

30. See Governor Anza's summary of events covering the Navajo negotiations, and Jacobo Ugarte y Loyola's response to Anza of October 5, 1786, Thomas, *Frontiers*, 345–57; Frank D. Reeve, "Navaho-Spanish Diplomacy: 1770–1790," *New Mexico Historical Review* 35:3 (1960), 223–25; and Frank D. Reeve, "The Navaho-Spanish Peace: 1720–1770s," *New Mexico Historical Review* 34:1 (1959), 9–40.

31. Lipan and Mescalero Apache: Park, "Spanish-Indian Policy," 341–42; Jicarilla Apache: August, "Balance-of-Power," 149 and 153–56.

32. Jones, *Nueva Vizcaya*, 196. 1787 report: Estado que manifiesta las muertes y robos egecuados por los Indios Enemigos . . . desde Abril 19, 1786 . . . . Jacobo Ugarte de Loyola, Arispe, December 31, 1787, AGN:PI 128:3, 318R. For the 1788 statistics, see Teodoro de Croix, Comandante General de los Provincias Internas, General Report of January 23, 1780, to Minister of the Indies José de Gálvez No. 458, AGI:GUAD 253, in Thomas, *Croix*, 111.

NOTES TO CHAPTER 3

1. Viceroy Antonio Bucareli y Ursua to Governor Pedro Fermín de Mendinueta, Mexico, March 22, 1775, SANM II 10:825, TW #684. A photograph of the document appears in Marc Simmons, "Problems of Research in Spanish Colonial Documents," *El Palacio* (1967), 31–34. A copy of the bando sent by the king on October, 25, 1774, to request pelicans for the Escorial zoo is in AGN:RC 105:113, 1R.

2. Some documents relating to the shipments of elk from New Mexico: 1765, Governor Tomás Vélez Cachupín to Joaquín de Monserrat, Marqués de Cruillas, Santa Fe, November 19, 1765, AGN:PI 102:10, 413R–414R; 1774–1776, Juan Bautista Ugarte to Factor de la Renta Real del Tabaco de Durango, Chihuahua, 1774–1776, AGI:GUAD 402, 104–6–8, Chapman #2498; 1778–1780, Comandante General Teodoro de Croix to Gálvez, Arispe, May 1, 1778, No. 203, AGI:GUAD 267/276, 103–4–9, Chapman #3803; Croix to Gálvez, Arispe, January 23, 1779, No. 357, AGI:GUAD 267, 103–4–9, Chapman #3938; Croix to Gálvez, Arispe, March 29, 1779, No. 385, AGI:GUAD 267, Chapman #3969; Croix to Don Martín de Mayorga, Arispe, December 13, 1779, AGN:PI 161:12, 334R–346R; accounts of Don Joaquín Lain Herrero, Alferez de Presidio de Santa Fe, AGN:PI 161:13, 390R,V, 392R–399R, 404R,V, and 407R–418V; 1782, Croix to Gálvez, Arispe, January 26, 1782, No. 717, AGN:PI 79:1, 3R,V, and AGI:GUAD 267, 103–4–9, Chapman #4481; reply to Croix, Mexico, March 20, 1782, AGN:PI 79:1, 4R; Croix to Don Martín de Mayorga, Arispe, May 15, 1782, AGN:PI 79:1, 16R,V; and Gálvez to Croix, Mexico, October 13, 1782, AGI:GUAD 267, 103–4–9, Chapman #4704. See the description in Marc Simmons, *Taos to Tomé: True Tales of Hispanic New Mexico* (Albuquerque: University of New Mexico Press, 1978), 19–22; and Don Pedro Alonso O'Crouley, *A Description of the Kingdom of New Spain, 1774*, trans. and ed. Seán Galvin (San Francisco: John Howell Books, 1972), 56.

3. "Avisa no hallarse Pelícanos en el expresado Reino." Entry 22 in index of docu-

ments sent from Governor Pedro Fermín de Mendinueta to Viceroy Marqués de Croix, [Santa Fe,] August 22, 1775, AGN:PI 103:1, 264R.

4. John Lynch, *Bourbon Spain, 1700–1808* (Oxford: Blackwell, 1989), 250 and 336–51. See also David A. Brading, *The First America* (Cambridge, England: Cambridge University Press, 1991), 467–91; and David A. Brading, *Miners and Merchants in Bourbon Mexico, 1763–1810* (Cambridge, England: Cambridge University Press, 1971), 33–92.

For a critique of the economic effect of the reforms, see Arij Ouweneel and Catrien C. J. H. Bijleveld, "The Economic Cycle in Bourbon Central Mexico: A Critique of the Recaudación del diezmo líquido en pesos," *Hispanic American Historical Review* 69:3 (1989), 479–530. Rejoinders are: David A. Brading, "Comments on 'The Economic Cycle in Bourbon Central Mexico: A Critique of the Recaudación del diezmo líquido en pesos,'" *Hispanic American Historical Review* 69:3 (1989), 531–37; John H. Coatsworth, "Comments on 'The Economic Cycle in Bourbon Central Mexico: A Critique of the Recaudación del diezmo líquido en pesos,'" *Hispanic American Historical Review* 69:3 (1989), 538–44; Héctor Lindo-Fuentes, "Comments on 'The Economic Cycle in Bourbon Central Mexico: A Critique of the Recaudación del diezmo líquido en pesos,'" *Hispanic American Historical Review* 69:3 (1989), 545–48; and Arij Ouweneel and Catrien C. J. H. Bijleveld, "Comments on 'The Economic Cycle in Bourbon Central Mexico: A Critique of the Recaudación del diezmo líquido en pesos,'" *Hispanic American Historical Review* 69:3 (1989), 549–58. See also Richard L. Garner, with Spiro E. Stefanou, *Economic Growth and Change in Bourbon Mexico* (Gainesville: University Press of Florida, 1993),1–37.

For information on Gálvez, see Herbert I. Priestly, *José de Gálvez, Visitor-General of New Spain, 1765–1771* (University of California, Berkeley, Publications in History, 5; Berkeley: University of California Press, 1916); and Linda K. Salvucci, "Costumbres viejas, 'Hombres Nuevos': José de Gálvez y la burocracia fiscal novo-hispana'" *Historia Mexicana* 33:2 (1983), 224–64.

5. Brading, *Miners and Merchants,* 53. See also an outstanding study: Susan Deans-Smith, *Bureaucrats, Planters, and Workers: The Making of the Tobacco Monopoly in Bourbon Mexico* (Austin: University of Texas Press, 1992), esp. 3–66.

6. Governor Tomás Vélez de Cachupín to Marqués de Cruillas, Santa Fe, January 3, 1766, AGN:PI 102:10, 427R–430V.

7. Equal to 3 or 3.25 pesos (8 reales to 1 peso). See the essay on the gamuza in Marc Simmons, "When New Mexicans Dressed in Skins," in *Coronado's Land: Essays on Daily Life in Colonial New Mexico,* ed. and trans. Marc Simmons (Albuquerque: University of New Mexico Press, 1991), 3–7.

8. Cruillas to Cachupín, Santa Fe, January 3, 1766, AGN:PI 102:10, 428V.

9. Leslie A. White, "Punche Tobacco in New Mexican History," *New Mexico Historical Review* 18:4 (1943), 386–93. Cruillas to Cachupín, Santa Fe, January 3, 1766, AGN:PI 102:10, 430V,R. Request of the viceroy to the Franciscan missionaries for information on tobacco, AFBN 2:9.1, 1R–4R; Ignacio del Río, *Guía del Archivo Franciscano* (Mexico City: Instituto de Investigaciones Bibliográficas, 1975), 1:203.

10. A translation of the bando, signed by Mendinueta on March 4, 1766, appears in Lawrence Kinnaird, "The Spanish Tobacco Monopoly in New Mexico, 1766–1767," *New Mexico Historical Review* 21:4 (1946), 332–34.

254 NOTES TO PAGES 81–85

11. Governor Pedro Fermín de Mendinueta to Viceroy Marqués de Croix, May 19, 1767. Based on the translation by Kinnaird, "Tobacco Monopoly," 334–39. Punche use: Fray Juan Augustín de Morfí, "Account of Disorders, 1778," in *Coronado's Land: Essays on Daily Life in Colonial New Mexico*, ed. and trans. Marc Simmons (Albuquerque: University of New Mexico Press, 1991), 142–44. The tithes remitted for New Mexico included 632 manojos de punche biennially for 1796 and 1797; 956 for 1798 and 1799; 901 for 1800 and 1801; and 799 for the single year 1806. For 1796 and 1797, see ACD:VA 55, 145:26R; for 1798 and 1799, ACD:VA 1801 #2, 2, 3, 4R and 1807, 1R; for 1800 and 1801, ACD:VA 1801 #1, 1R; and for 1806, ACD:VA 1807, 1R.

12. Report of Governor Fernando de Chacón to Comandante General Nemesio Salcido, Santa Fe, August 28, 1803, SANM II 15:85–86, TW #1670a. English translation in Marc Simmons, "The Chacón Economic Report of 1803," *New Mexico Historical Review* 60:1 (1985), 65–88, reprinted in Fernando de Chacón, "Report of Governor Chacón, 1803," in *Coronado's Land: Essays on Daily Life in Colonial New Mexico,* ed. and trans. Marc Simmons (Albuquerque: University of New Mexico Press, 1991), 162–72.

13. Comandante General Pedro de Neve to Governor Juan Bautista de Anza, Arispe, March 15, 1784, SANM II 11:675–76, TW #884a; Neve to Anza, Arispe, April 27, 1784, SANM II 11:721–22, TW #893.

14. Brian R. Hamnett, *Politics and Trade in Southern Mexico, 1750–1821* (Cambridge, England: Cambridge University Press, 1971), 41–55 and 60–71.

15. Morfí, "Disorders," 133.

16. The provisions of the Reglamento, including changes in payroll, are described in Max L. Moorhead, *The Presidio: Bastion of the Spanish Borderlands* (Norman: University of Oklahoma Press, 1975), 64–74.

17. One example: "In the country [New Mexico] money does not circulate except that of the [Presidial] troops, and they always must be self-sufficient on their own account." Letter of Governor Fernando de la Concha to the Señores Jueces Hacedores, Don Manuel del Toro y Casanova and Don Vicente Simon Gonzales de Cosio, Chihuahua, May 29, 1794, ACD:VA 55:145, 6R–9V. Letter draft in SANM II 13:510–13, TW #1286a.

18. Fiscal José Antonio Areche to Viceroy José Antonio de Bucareli, May 29, 1773, AGN:PI 45:2, 151V–153R.

19. An agreement of June 5, 1773, between the Junta de Guerra in Mexico and the Real Hacienda specified that the Real Caja of Guanajuato send funds in specie to Durango, and from there to Chihuahua, to be used for payment of the expenses of the presidios internos. Explanation of the agreement and table of money transfers from the Real Caja de Guadalajara: Ministros Principales de Real Hacienda y Cajas del Distrito de esta Intendencia de Durango, Durango, October 9, 1787, AGN:PI 46:1, 166R,V.

20. John J. TePaske and Herbert S. Klein, *Ingresos y egresos de la Real Hacienda de Nueva España* (Colección Científica Fuentes 41:1; Mexico City: Instituto Nacional de Antropología e Historia, 1986), 16.

21. Apuntes sobre Pagamentos de Situados, Mexico, April 3, 1776, AGN:PI 45:2, 255R.

22. Minutes of the Junta de Guerra meeting of July 10, 1778, AGN:PI 45:2, 327R–334V.

23. References to recoinage: Fabián de Fonseca and Carlos de Urrutia, *Historia general de Real Hacienda escrita por órden del virrey, conde de Revillagigedo* (Mexico City: Imprima por V. G. Torres, 1853), 1:189. See also Brading, *Miners and Merchants,* 143–44; and Garner, *Economic Growth,* 243. Silver content: Pedro Pérez Herrero, *Plata y libranzas: La articulación comercial del México borbónico* (Mexico City: El Colegio de México, 1988), 148. Exemption: Minutes of the Junta de Guerra meeting of July 10, 1778, AGN:PI 45:2, 327R–334V.

24. Brading, *Miners and Merchants,* 101–2; also see Pérez Herrero, *Plata y libranzas,* 195–253.

25. Minutes of the Junta de Guerra meeting of July 10, 1778, AGN:PI 45:2, 327V.

26. See discussion of this point in Garner, *Economic Growth,* 208 and 244.

27. Miguel Francisco de Arroynde to Juan Baptista de Ugarte and Vicente de Muro, Cuencamé, March 29, 1785, AGN:PI 46:1, 129R,V.

28. Juan Baptista de Ugarte and Vicente de Muro to Señores Directores Generales de la Real Renta de Tabaco, Durango, April 7, 1785, AGN:PI 46:1, 131R–132V; John E. Kicza, *Colonial Entrepreneurs: Families and Business in Bourbon Mexico City* (Albuquerque: University of New Mexico Press, 1983), 84–85; and John E. Kicza, *Empresarios Coloniales: Familias y negocios en la ciudad de México durante los Borbones* (Mexico City: Fondo de Cultura Económica, 1986), 101–2.

29. Emphasis in original. Opinion of Parada, Fiscal de Real Hacienda, to Real Caja de Mexico, Mexico, May 31, 1785, AGN:PI 46:1, 141R–143R (missing the beginning portion). Ignacio del Río, *La aplicación regional de las reformas borbónicas en Nueva España: Sonora y Sinaloa, 1768–1787* (Serie de historia novohispana, 55; Mexico City: Universidad Nacional Autónoma de México, Instituto de Investigaciones Históricas, 1995), 218–23, shows the importance of libranzas for the Real Hacienda in Sonora.

30. Vicente de Muro to Señores Directores de la Real Renta del Tabaco, Durango, June 16, 1785, AGN:PI 46:1, 152R,V; Directores de la Real Renta del Tabaco to Viceroy Conde Bernardo de Gálvez, Mexico, July 7, 1785, AGN:PI 46:1, 152R,V; Comandante General José Antonio Rengel to Viceroy Bernardo de Gálvez, Chihuahua, October 1, 1785, AGN:PI 46:1, 175R–176R.

31. Establishment of Real Caja de Chihuahua: TePaske and Klein, *Ingresos y egresos,* 15. Rengel agreement: Ministros Principales de Real Hacienda y Cajas del Distrito de esta Intendencia de Durango, Durango, October 9, 1787, AGN:PI 46:1, 166V. Transfer of funds: Comandante General Jacobo Ugarte de Loyola to Real Audiencia Gobernadora, Chihuahua, January 18, 1787, AGN:PI 46:1, 182R–183R.

32. Comandante General Jacobo Ugarte de Loyola to Viceroy Manuel Antonio Flores, Chihuahua, April 24, 1788, AGN:PI 46:1, 201R–202R.

33. Don Pablo de Ochoa, Alcalde ordinario de segundo voto, Don Francisco de Arrequi, Don Pedro Ignacio Irigoyen, y Don Diego Ventura Marquez, Capitán de Dragones . . . to Señor Comandante General Pedro de Nava, Chihuahua, February 9, 1792, AGN:PI 46:1, 410R–411R. Details of the presidio supply contract for 1791 are given in Moorhead, *Presidio,* 218–19, esp. note 43.

34. Comandante General Pedro de Nava to Viceroy Conde de Revillagigedo II, Chihuahua, February 17, 1792, AGN:PI 46:1, 410R–413R.

35. Estimate based on the following calculation: 1770–1776, 35,000 pesos annually; 1777–1787, 45,000 pesos annually; 1788–1810, 55,000 pesos annually; 1811,

45,000 pesos. Sources: Real Tribunal Audiencia de Cuentas, Antonio de Mier y Teranzas, Fernando de Herrera, [Mexico,] April 26, 1773, AGN:PI 45:2, 141R; Notacion de lo que importa las Situados de los Presidios . . . , Chihuahua, June 30, 1778, AGN:PI 45:3, 337 chart; Estado que manifiesta los caudales . . . , Arispe, September 16, 1784, AGN:PI 46:1 37R; Estado que manifiesta los gastos annuales del Real Herario en las Provincia . . . , Josef Antonio Rengel, Chihuahua, October 1, 1785, AGN:PI 46:1, 171 chart, 247 chart; Razon de las caudales que se invierten annualmente en este Real Caja . . . , Domingo de Beregaña, Chihuahua, May 8, 1788, AGN:PI 46:1, 200R,V; Resumen de fuerzas y gastos en cada Provincia con expresion de las Tesorias donde se pagan . . . , Domingo de Beregaña, Chihuahua, November 6, 1789, November 21, 1789, AGN:PI 46:1, 310R, 314 chart; and Chacón, "Report," 171-72.

36. Thomas Madrid and Francisco Esquibel to Croix, Santa Fe, September 14, 1768, AGN:PI 103:1, 69R,V.

37. Moorhead, *Presidio,* 219.

38. The work of Max L. Moorhead remains basic to any discussion of this topic: "The Presidio Supply Problem of New Mexico in the Eighteenth Century," *New Mexico Historical Review* 36:3 (1961), 210-29; "The Private Contract System of Presidio Supply in Northern New Spain," *Hispanic American Historical Review* 41:1 (1961), 31-54; and *Presidio,* 201-21. Moorhead used AGN:PI 13:1-10, 21-45, 48-324, 401-6, and 407-14. Further information on the Guizarnótegui episode: AGN:PI 46:1, 415R,V (incomplete); AGN:PI 203:8, 170R-187R; and 203:11, 216R-244R.

39. Moorhead, "Presidio Supply," 212.

40. A fanega in this context represents a dry measure equivalent roughly to 1.5-2.5 bushels. Fray Juan Sanz de Lezaún, "An account of lamentable happenings in New Mexico . . . ," in Charles W. Hackett, trans. and ed., *Historical Documents Relating to New Mexico and Nueva Vizcaya, and Approaches Thereto, to 1773* (Publication 330; Washington, D.C.: Carnegie Institution, 1937), 3:474-75.

41. Mendinueta to Croix, Santa Fe, September 15, 1768, AGN:PI 103:1, 64R-65R. Quotation: Mendinueta to Croix, Santa Fe, January 14, 1769, AGN:PI 103:1, 35R-38R; also Mendinueta to Croix, Santa Fe, January 28, 1769, AGN:PI 103: 1, 35R-38R. Supporting letters: Thomas Madrid and Francisco Esquibel to Croix, Santa Fe, September 14, 1768, AGN:PI 103:1, 69R-70R. Mendinueta to Croix, Santa Fe, March 25, 1769, AGN:PI 103:1, 63R. Exemption: Moorhead, "Presidio Supply," 214, citing Croix to Mendinueta, Mexico City, January 28, 1769, SANM II 10:590, TW #644.

42. Moorhead, *Presidio,* 208-9.

43. Ibid., 211.

44. Moorhead, "Contract System," 34; and Moorhead, "Presidio Supply," 215.

45. Bernardo de Gálvez, *Instructions for Governing the Interior Provinces of New Spain, 1786,* ed. and trans. Donald E. Worcester (Quivira Society Publications, 12; Berkeley, Calif.: Quivira Society, 1951), 113. Worcester's translation appears on pp. 53-54.

46. Meeting of September 5, 1786, in Chihuahua: Moorhead, "Contract System," 36-37; and Moorhead *Presidio,* 216-17.

47. Moorhead, "Presidio Supply," 217-18; and Moorhead, "Contract System," 37-41.

48. Moorhead, "Contract System," 38-40.

49. Ibid., 31–49; and Moorhead, "Presidio Supply," 219–29.

50. Moorhead, "Presidio Supply," 220–25. Charges: Francisco Martínez to Joseph Antonio Rengel, Comandante Inspector de las Provincias Internas, Carrizal, March 29, 1788, AGN:PI 203:11, 222R,V.

51. Informe, Governor Concha to Viceroy Manual Antonio de Flores, Santa Fe, September, no day, 1787, AGN:PI 254:2, 13V–14R. The date is supplied by the report of the Fiscal, Ramón Posada, Mexico, March 22, 1789, AGN:PI 161:9, 267R,V.

52. Viceroy Revillagigedo II mentioned that the contract with Guizarnótegui was rescinded in a letter to the intendente of Durango, Mexico, September 8, 1790, AGN:PI 46:1, 415R,V. Consulado contract: Moorhead, "Contract System," 52.

53. Descripción de la Provincia del Nuevo México. [Durango?], no date, probably written in 1797 by Juan Ysidro Campor to the Señores Jueces Hacedores, Dr. Don José Martín Flores and Don Julian Valero de Vicente, ACD:VA 55:145, 16V; see also 19R,V.

54. Marc Simmons, "Spanish Attempts to Open a New Mexico–Sonora Road," *Arizona and the West* 17:1 (1975), 9–10.

55. Informe del Gobernador Don Pedro Fermín de Mendinueta sobre comunicación con Sonora, Santa Fe, November 9, 1775, AGN:HI 52:13, quoted in ibid., 12.

56. Fray Atanasio Domínguez, *The Missions of New Mexico, 1776*, ed. Eleanor B. Adams and Fray Angélico Chávez (Albuquerque: University of New Mexico Press, 1956), 283.

57. Domínguez-Escalante Expedition: Walter Briggs, *Without Noise of Arms: The 1776 Domínguez-Escalante Search for a Route from Santa Fe to Monterey* (Flagstaff, Ariz.: Northland Press, 1976). Quotation: Fray Silvestre Vélez de Escalante to Governor Mendinueta, Guadalupe de Zuñi, October 28, 1775, AFBN 4:79.1, 1R–5V, #320. A copy of the Domínguez-Escalante report appears in AFBN 4:79.3, 1R–4V, #322. Exploration goals are mentioned in a letter from Bernardo de Miera y Pacheco to the King, Chihuahua, October 26, 1777, AFBN 2:22.2, 2R–4R, #233.

58. Memorial de Bernardo de Miera y Pacheco dirigido al rey, Chihuahua, October 26, 1777, AFBN 2:22.2, 2R, #233.

59. Letter from Anza to Croix, Presidio de Altar, January 18, 1774, AGN:PI 237:1, 126R. Also, correspondence of Anza in AGN:PI 237:1, 127R–128R and 134R–141V. Dictamen del Ingeniero D. Miguel Costanzó sobre las distancias del Nuevo Mexico a Sonora y Monterrey, Mexico, March 18, 1776, AGN:PI 169:2, 53R–60V.

60. Bucareli instructions: Papel Instructivo de Exmo. Señor Don Antonio Bucareli y Ursua, Virrey de Nueva España, relativo a las Provincias Internas, para el Señor Don Teodoro de Croix, Comandante General de ellas, Mexico, March 20, 1777, AGN:PI 73:1, 85V–86V, paragraph 21. Anza's appointment: Alfred Barnaby Thomas, trans. and ed., *Forgotten Frontiers: A Study of the Spanish–Indian Policy of Juan Bautista de Anza, Governor of New Mexico, 1777–1787* (Norman: University of Oklahoma Press, 1932), 19, note 56.

61. Anza plans: Two letters of Anza to Croix, Santa Fe, November 1, 1779, Da cuenta con documentos del estado de los Indios del Moqui . . . , Arispe, February 3, 1780, No. 476, AGI:GUAD 512, 104–6–19, published in Thomas, *Frontiers*, 145–50. Anza Hopi expedition: Da cuenta del Descubrimiento del camino desde la Provincia de Nueva Mexico a la de Sonora . . . , Arispe, March 26, 1781, No. 628,

AGI:GUAD 272, 103–4–14, published in Thomas, *Frontiers*, 171–94; and General Report of 1781, in Alfred Barnaby Thomas, ed., *Teodoro de Croix and the Northern Frontier of New Spain, 1776–1783* (Norman: University of Oklahoma Press, 1941), 109.

62. Gold discovery in Sonora: Don Fernando de la Concha, "Diary of Colonel Don Fernando de la Concha," ed. Adlai Feather, *New Mexico Historical Review* 34:4 (1959), 286; and see Bernard E. Bobb, *The Viceregency of Antonio María Bucareli in New Spain, 1771–1779* (Austin: University of Texas Press, 1962), 182–85.

Anza plans for Sonoran expedition: Da cuenta del Descubrimiento del camino desde la Provincia de Nueva Mexico a la de Sonora . . . , Arispe, March 26, 1781, No. 628, AGI:GUAD 272, 103–4–14; Anza's request, Santa Fe, November 1, 1779; Croix's response, Arispe, December 30, 1779; Anza's response, Anza to Croix, Santa Fe, May 26, 1780, published in Thomas, *Frontiers*, 171–94. Thomas, *Frontiers*, 379–80, note 59, mistakenly identifies the "malicious and needless flight of the settlers" (177) of which Anza complains with the reorganization and resettlement program undertaken in 1779 to make the settlements more defensible, as discussed in chapter 1. Anza also mentioned that the settlers who fled "were plotting to instigate a similar project among those who remained by disturbing and inciting them by their bad example." This "project" consisted of plans for a precipitous departure for the new gold finds in Sonora, rather than flight from the reorganized settlements. Of course, Anza's resettlement program could have contributed to the desire of settlers to leave more quickly for Sonora.

63. Simmons, "New Mexico–Sonora Road," 14.

64. Plans: ibid., 14–15. Sonoran expedition: Thomas, *Frontiers*, 37–38, 172, and Anza's journal, 195–205.

65. George P. Hammond, "The Zúñiga Journal, Tucson to Santa Fe: The Opening of a Spanish Trade Route, 1788–1795," *New Mexico Historical Review* 3:1 (1931), 40–51; Simmons, "New Mexico–Sonora Road," 17–19; and Thomas, *Frontiers*, 40–41.

66. Simmons notes a number of expeditions mentioned in SANM, "New Mexico–Sonora Road," 19–20.

67. Noel M. Loomis and Abraham P. Nasatir, *Pedro Vial and the Roads to Santa Fe* (Norman: University of Oklahoma Press, 1967); see the biographical sketch of Vial on pp. xv–xxiii.

68. Fourth Vial and Amangual expeditions: ibid., 370 and 459–534.

69. Galindo Navarro to Croix, Arispe, July 28, 1790, in Thomas, *Frontiers*, 180, 86.

70. Governor Cachupín to Viceroy Joaquín de Monserrat, Marqués de Cruillas, Santa Fe, August 27, 1762, AGN:PI 102:10, 370R–371V.

71. Governor Cachupín to Viceroy Monserrat, Santa Fe, August 27, 1762, AGN: PI 102:10, 374R–376V.

72. Governor Concha to Comandante General Jacobo Ugarte y Loyola, Santa Fe, November 10, 1787, AGN:PI 161:4, 26R–28V. Informe, Concha to Viceroy Flores, Santa Fe, September, no day, 1787, AGN:PI 254:2, 12V–13R.

73. Anza proposal: Croix to Anza, Arispe, July 14, 1780, SANM II 11:79–81, TW #800. See also Moorhead, *Presidio*, 173–76. Concha proposal: Ugarte to Flores, Arispe, December 13, 1787, AGN:PI 161:4, 29R,V.

74. Concha to Ugarte, Santa Fe, June 20, 1788, AGN:PI 161:4, 33R–35V. Tlaxcalans from central Mexico originally settled the Santa Fe barrio of Analco, and

some returned after the Pueblo Revolt of 1680. See Marc Simmons, "Tlaxcalans in the Spanish Borderlands," *New Mexico Historical Review* 39:2 (1964), 108–10. The governor's house is now called the Palace of the Governors.

75. Construction supplies: Ugarte to Concha, Chihuahua, July 22, 1788, AGN: PI 161:4, 36R,V; Ugarte to Concha, San Bartolomé, January 21, 1789, SANM II 12: 112, TW #1029; also Moorhead, *Presidio,* 173–77. Cuartel finance: Ugarte to Flores, Valle de San Bartolomé, October 27, 1788, AGN:PI 161:4, 37R–39V. Skilled labor: Concha to Ugarte, Santa Fe, December 12, 1788, AGN:PI 161:4, 40R,V.

76. Request for more funds: Concha to Ugarte, Santa Fe, July 4, 1789, AGN:PI 161:4, 49R–50V. List of imported goods: Noticia de los Efectos que se han habilitado . . . , Mexico, December 14, 1789, AGN:PI 161:4, 63R,V. Payment for cuartel land: In 1789 Don Diego Antonio Baca and "the soldier" José Pacheco each received 150 pesos for the demolition of their houses, and "corporal" Juan Luís Herrera received 50 pesos. Another 50 "pesos del país" went to Geronimo Esquibel for a piece of land the following year. Construction expenses for the Santa Fe Cuartel, 1789–1791: SANM II 12:705–17, TW #1163. A translated excerpt appears in Richard E. Ahlborn, "Frontier Possessions: The Evidence from Colonial Documents," in *Colonial Frontiers: Art and Life in Spanish New Mexico,* ed. Christine Mather (Santa Fe, N.Mex.: Ancient City Press, 1983), 48.

77. Ugarte to Flores, Chihuahua, September 18, 1789, AGN:PI 161:4, 52R,V; Flores to Beregaña, AGN:PI 161:4, 54R–56R.

78. Rain delay: Concha to Ugarte, Santa Fe, November 15, 1790, SANM II 12: 417, TW #1098. Cuartel expenses: Nava to Concha, Chihuahua, December 11, 1791, SANM II 12:766–67, TW #1174; and Relación jurada . . . de los gastos causados en la Fabrica del Nuevo Quartel . . . , 1789–1791, SANM II 12:717, TW #1163.

79. Zebulon Montgomery Pike, *The Journals of Zebulon Montgomery Pike,* ed. Donald Jackson (Norman: University of Oklahoma Press, 1966), 1:50.

80. AGN:PI 216:8, 249; 245(1):4, 34. Plans shown in AGN, *Catálogo,* 1:188 and 193.

81. Construction employment: bando by Governor Concha, Santa Fe, May 27, 1789, SANM II 12:162–64, TW #1042.

82. Obraje proposal: Informe, Concha to Viceroy Flores, Santa Fe, September, no day, 1787, AGN:PI 254:2, 10R,V. Excepts of the report appear in AGN:PI 161:9, 263R,V. Transcriptions from AGN:PI 161:9 appear in María del Carmen Velázquez, *Notas sobre sirvientes de las Californias y proyecto de obraje en Nuevo México* (Jornadas, 105; Mexico City: El Colegio de México, 1984), 77–83. Chihuahua obraje: Urquidi also won the contract for presidio supply at San Elizario in 1782. Municipal Obraje of Chihuahua records in CPM. Municipal purchase of and investment in the obraje: CPM:HA 54:3, 16R–17V. Obraje accounts, inventories, and reports: 1799, 1801, CPM:HA 51:19, 5R–30R; 1800, CPM:HA 52:6, 1R–3V; 1805, CPM:HA 52:26, 10R–17R; 1806, 1807, CPM:HA 53:6, 1R–5V; 1808, CPM:HA 54:3, 12V–14R; and 1808, 1809, CPM:HA 54:5, 1R–4R.

83. Viceroy Flores request: Flores to Comandante General Ugarte y Loyola, Mexico, September 17, 1788, AGN:PI 161:9, 264R,V. Ugarte response: Ugarte to Flores, Valle de San Bartolomé, October 27, 1788, AGN:PI 161:9, 265R–266V. Durango obraje: Bachiller Miguel Hernández Hidalgo began to set up the obraje in Durango in 1784. Early history of Durango obraje: Franklins Alberto Cañizales Méndez, "El

sector ganadero en la región de Durango en el período colonial (1750–1820): Una aproximación histórica regional" (Maestría thesis, Universidad Nacional Autónoma de México, 1986), 112–35. See also Oakah L. Jones Jr., *Nueva Vizcaya: Heartland of the Spanish Frontier* (Albuquerque: University of New Mexico Press, 1988), 187. Notification of decision: Ramón Posada, Fiscal de Real Hacienda, to Viceroy Flores, Mexico, March 22, 1789, AGN: PI 161:9, 267R,V. Flores to Ugarte, Mexico, April 6, 1789; Ugarte to Flores, Chihuahua, May 1, 1789, AGN: PI 161:9, 268R–269V.

84. Report of Governor Fernando de Chacón to Comandante General Nemesio Salcido, Santa Fe, August 28, 1803, SANM II 15:91, 87, TW #1670a; and Chacón, "Report," 171. Spinners: Chacón to Señor Don Miguel Cañulas, Santa Fe, November 18, 1798, SANM II 14:327, TW #1430a.

85. Contract engaging Don Ignacio Ricardo and Don Juan Bazán, Mexico, September 3, 1805, SANM II 15:845–48, TW #1885. See also the report on the efforts of the Bazán brothers and their accounts submitted to the Real Hacienda. SANM II 16:938–47 and 948–51, TW #2249 and 2250. Correspondence from the Bazán brothers during Ignacio Ricardo's illness: DUR: PG 20:3, 1R–15V. Also see Henry P. Mera, *Spanish-American Blanketry* (Santa Fe, N.Mex.: School of American Research Press, 1987), 18–23.

86. Don Pedro Bautista Pino, Licenciado Don Antonio Barreiro, and Agustín de Escudero, *Three New Mexican Chronicles,* trans. and ed. H. Bailey Carroll and J. Villasana Haggard (Quivira Society Publications, 11; Albuquerque: Quivira Society, 1942), 35–36. Also see E. Boyd, *Popular Arts of Colonial New Mexico* (Albuquerque: University of New Mexico Press, 1974), 200–201; and Ward Alan Minge, "*Efectos del país:* A History of Weaving along the Rio Grande," in *Spanish Textile Tradition of New Mexico and Colorado,* ed. Nora Fisher (Santa Fe: Museum of New Mexico Press, 1979), 21–22. Minge says that Governor Chacón requested that the Bazán brothers be sent to New Mexico, an interpretation not supported by Chacón's report.

NOTES TO CHAPTER 4

1. Concha to Ugarte, Santa Fe, July 4, 1789, AGN: PI 161:4, 49R–50V. Land grants: Victor Westphall, *Mercedes Reales: Hispanic Land Grants of the Upper Rio Grande Region* (Albuquerque: University of New Mexico Press, 1983); a complete listing of the grants filed with the surveyor general of New Mexico arranged chronologically by settlement area appears in appendix 1, pp. 275–80. Forty of the 194 grants filed were approved by the Spanish government between 1785 and 1820. Unlike the grants made from the late 1820s to 1846, the late colonial land grants more closely reflected direct vecino desire for land on which to found new settlements. Vecino expansion: Oakah L. Jones Jr., *Los Paisanos: Spanish Settlers on the Northern Frontier of New Spain* (Norman: University of Oklahoma Press, 1979), 116–17; D. W. Meinig, *Southwest: Three Peoples in Geographical Change, 1600–1970* (New York: Oxford University Press, 1971), 27–32; Taos region: Myra Ellen Jenkins, "Taos Pueblo and Its Neighbors," *New Mexico Historical Review* 41:2 (1966), 98–99; John O. Baxter, *Spanish Irrigation in Taos Valley* (Santa Fe: New Mexico State Engineer Office, 1990), 16–18, 23–29, 102–3, and 124; and Richard L. Nostrand, "The Century of Hispano Expansion," *New Mexico Historical Review* 64:4 (1987), 372–76, also in Richard L. Nostrand,

The Hispano Homeland (Norman: University of Oklahoma Press, 1992), 70–97. Evidence for early occupation of the Mora region: Noticias de las misiones que ocupan los Religiosos de la regular observencia de N. S. P. S. Francisco . . . en los años 1793, 1794 . . . , SANM II 21:540–41, B. M. Read Collection, NMSRCA. See also John L. Kessell, *Kiva, Cross, and Crown: The Pecos Indians and New Mexico, 1540–1840* (Washington, D.C.: National Park Service, U.S. Department of the Interior, 1979), 415–19; Westphall, *Mercedes Reales*, 22–23 and 275; Nostrand, "Hispano Expansion," 367–69; and Fray Angélico Chávez, "Early Settlements in the Mora Valley" *El Palacio* 62:11 (1955), 318–24. Abiquíu area: Frances Leon Swadesh, *Los primeros pobladores: Hispanic Americans of the Ute Frontier* (Notre Dame, Ind.: University of Notre Dame Press, 1974), 48–51; and Nostrand, "Hispano Expansion," 374–77. Expansion west and south of Albuquerque: Concha to Comandante General Jacobo Ugarte de Loyola (Oficio N. 228), Santa Fe, November 1, 1790, AGN:PI 161:5, 93R; and Nostrand, "Hispano Expansion," 382–85.

2. David A. Brading, *Miners and Merchants in Bourbon Mexico, 1763–1810* (Cambridge, England: Cambridge University Press, 1971), 231–32; Miguel Francisco de Arroynde to Juan Baptista de Ugarte and Vicente de Muro, Cuencamé, March 29, 1785, AGN:PI 46:1, 129R,V; CPM:HA, 47:19, Libro borador de salidas diarias del maiz y harina . . . Real Alhondiga de Chihuahua. Prices for October 1784 and November 1785, from Francisco del Valle to Jueces Hacedores de Durango, November 1, 1785, DCA:VA 32:86, 1R,V.

3. Chacón (1803), SANM II 15:90, TW #1670a. See Fernando de Chacón, "Report of Governor Chacón, 1803," in *Coronado's Land: Essays on Daily Life in Colonial New Mexico,* ed. and trans. Marc Simmons (Albuquerque: University of New Mexico Press, 1991), 170, for a translation with significant differences in meaning.

4. Chacón to Comandante General Pedro de Nava, Santa Fe, July 16, 1797, SANM II 14:68–69, TW #1451.

5. Annotated "Informe General de su Provincia," Governor Concha to Viceroy Señor Don Manuel Antonio de Flores, Santa Fe, September, no day, 1788, AGN:PI 254:2, 11R. Royal engineer José Cortés also describes the lack of money in circulation in New Mexico and the fixed value placed on goods of differing quality. He mentions the peso de la tierra at the same time and suggests that he read these same reports in the archives of the Comandancia General in Chihuahua. See José Cortés, *Views from the Apache Frontier: Report on the Northern Provinces of New Spain,* ed. Elizabeth A. H. John, trans. John Wheat (Norman: University of Oklahoma Press, 1989), 61, and "Editor's Introduction," 8.

6. See Ramón A. Gutiérrez, *When Jesus Came, the Corn Mothers Went Away: Marriage, Sexuality, and Power in New Mexico, 1500–1846* (Stanford, Calif.: Stanford University Press, 1991), 323–27; and John O. Baxter, *Las Carneradas: Sheep Trade in New Mexico, 1700–1860* (Albuquerque: University of New Mexico Press, 1987), 28–30 and 47–49. The classic description of the partido system appears in Don Pedro Bautista Pino, Licenciado Don Antonio Barreiro, and Agustín de Escudero, *Three New Mexican Chronicles,* trans. and ed. H. Bailey Carroll and J. Villasana Haggard (Quivira Society Publications, 11; Albuquerque, N.Mex.: Quivira Society, 1942), 40–42, quoting a document from approximately 1817.

7. Prealliance trade: the reports of Mendinueta to Viceroys Croix and Bucareli

emphasize alternating trade and war: Mendinueta to Croix, Santa Fe, May 11, 1771, AGN:PI 103:1, 150R–153V; Mendinueta to Croix, Santa Fe, January 14, 1772, AGN:PI 103:1, 172R–182V; Mendinueta to Bucareli, Santa Fe, July 7, 1772, AGN:PI 103:1, 184R–192R; Mendinueta to Bucareli, Santa Fe, November 14, 1772, AGN:PI 103:1, 193R–196V. Postalliance trade: see Governor Anza to Ugarte y Loyola, #503, Santa Fe, October 15, 1786, AGN:PI 65:1, 207R. "The Comanche are in a querulous mood and every year introduce themselves in greater numbers against the will of many of our people, having been with more excess in the present year . . . . This is harming and destroying the old commerce in skins that they had established with this province."

8. Dr. Pedro Tamarón y Romerál, *Bishop Tamarón's Visitation of New Mexico, 1760,* ed. Eleanor B. Adams (Publications in History, 15; Albuquerque: Historical Society of New Mexico, 1954), 92. The general argument for increasing sheep production and trade is made by Baxter, *Carneradas,* 55–78. Biannual proposal: Comandante General Jacobo Ugarte to Governor Anza, Chihuahua, January 8, 1787, SANM II 11: 1083, TW #947. Suspension mentioned in Zebulon Montgomery Pike, *The Journals of Zebulon Montgomery Pike,* ed. Donald Jackson (Norman: University of Oklahoma Press, 1966), 1:407.

9. Export estimates: Informe, Governor Concha to Viceroy Mañual Antonio de Flores, Santa Fe, September, no day, 1787, AGN:PI 254:2, 13V–14R (date given in report of the fiscal, Ramón Posada, Mexico, March 22, 1789, AGN:PI 161:9, 267R,V). Comandante General Ugarte to Viceroy Flores mentions the goods exported, Valle de San Bartolomé, October 25, 1788, SANM II 12:91, TW #1019; Certificaciones de las missiones . . . Provincia de Nueba Mexico, . . . estado actual & Año de 1794, n.s., n.l., n.d. (attributed to Fray Cayetano José Ignacio Bernal, Misión de Belem, September 1, 1794). AASF:MI 1794 #13, 53:108; Report on tithe collection in Chihuahua, El Paso del Río del Norte, Nuevo México, and the frontier presidios: Juan Ysidro Campor to the Señores Jueces Hacedores, Dr. Don José Martín Flores and Don Julian Valero de Vicente. [Durango?], September 6, 1797, ACD:VA 55:145, 13R.

10. Chacón (1803), SANM II 15:86, TW #1670a; Chacón, "Report," 166. Merchant's strategy: Francisco Antonio Trespalacios to Jueces Hacedores del Durango, Chihuahua, July 3, 1804, ACD:DZ 1805, 1R of 3 folios. Churro sheep: Baxter, *Carneradas,* 55.

11. Unscheduled caravan: Governor Chacón to Comandante General Pedro de Nava, #415, Santa Fe, August 30, 1805, SANM II 14:605, TW #1503, 2R. New trade fair: Comandante General Nemesio Salcedo to Governor Joaquín del Real Alencaster, Chihuahua, February 24, 1806, and May 14, 1806, SANM II 16:84–86, TW #1971, 1972. Another copy of the bando is in AASF:MI 1805 #12, 53:579. See Baxter, *Carneradas,* 62 and 67. Pike's estimate: Pike, *Journals,* 2:50.

12. Chacón (1803), SANM II 15:89, TW #1670a; Chacón, "Report," 169. Report of junta, incomplete, Santa Fe, June 17, 1805, SANM II 15:656–57, TW #1844.

13. Chacón *ibid.,* 169. Joachím del Real Alencaster to Señor Comandante General, Santa Fe, April 1, 1788, AGN:PI 201:2, 307V–308R.

14. Fray Juan Augustín de Morfí, "Account of Disorders, 1778," in *Coronado's Land: Essays on Daily Life in Colonial New Mexico,* ed. and trans. Marc Simmons (Albuquerque: University of New Mexico Press, 1991), 133 and 139. "Manta" is often used

loosely to mean blanket; it did not denote that the blanket came from a Pueblo loom. Chacón (1803), SANM II 15:87–88, TW #1670a; and Chacón, "Report," 168.

15. Payment: Pagos a soldados asi como los raciones y generos . . . , Chihuahua, 1778–1779, CPM:HA 45:6, 4R–95R; New Mexico goods: 1780 receipts, Ignacio Montes de Oca to Don Joseph Yribarren, por mandado de Pascual Melendes, no place, October 4, 1780, and June 5, 1780, CPM:CI 8:8, 1R–2V; 1781 receipts, Ignacio Montes de Oca to Don Joseph Yribarren, por mandado de Pascual Melendes, no place, June 17, 1781, and March 27, 1781, CPM:CI 8:18, 1R–2V; 1785, Pedro Antonio Velarde, Real Carcel de Chihuahua, April 11, 1785, and July 23, 1785, CPM:HA, 46:17, 8R–10R; Zambrano: Nota de lo que he comprado a don Antonio Ondarza . . . , Juan José Zambrano, Durango, March 6, 1804, and October 10, 1804, DUR:PG 29:3, 52V and 65R. Zambrano's wealth and philanthropic activities in Durango: Oakah L. Jones Jr., *Nueva Vizcaya: Heartland of the Spanish Frontier* (Albuquerque: University of New Mexico Press, 1988), 202–3; list of goods of Señor Teniente Colonel Antonio Cordero, Chihuahua, May 26, 1790, CPM:HA, 48:12, 33R–34V. See also Baxter, *Carneradas*, 58–59; copper vessels: Pike, *Journals*, 2:50. Governor Chacón discusses copper deposits in New Mexico in his 1803 report, SANM II 15: 86–87, 88, TW #1670a; Chacón, "Report," 166, 168. For early-nineteenth-century mining of these deposits, see Billy D. Walker, "Copper Genesis: The Early Years of Santa Rita del Cobre," *New Mexico Historical Review* 54:1 (1979), 5–20.

16. Chihuahua obraje: Haviendo tratado la Junta Municipal . . . con don Miguel Ortiz, vecino de la Villa de Santa Fe de Nuevo México, Chihuahua, May 8, 1792, CPM:NO 54:7, 1R; Por el presente pagará el Ylustre Ayuntamiento de esta Villa a Don Diego de Montoya . . . , Chihuahua, January 31, 1793, CPM:CI 9:25, 11R,V. Receipts for wool delivered to the obraje are dated Chihuahua, January 20, 1794, and January 21, 1794, CPM:HA 49:21, 2R, 3R. A contract for 781 arrobas and 14 libras of wool for the obraje made with Don Savino Diego de la Pedrueza in 1790 probably also represented New Mexican wool, Chihuahua, May 21, 1790, CPM:HA 48:16, 1R. Receipt of January 21, 1794, made out to Pedrueza, who received payment for wool from New Mexico delivered by Montoya on the 1794 contract; Reciví de Don Joseph Casados Vecino de Nueva Mexico la cantidad de treinta y ocho arrobas, dies y siete libras de lana sin labrar . . . , Chihuahua, 4 de enero de 1797, Antonio Mendes Son 38 arrobas, 17 libras Importan 64 pesos 5 1/2 reales, CPM: CI 9:30 2R; Cuenta que manifiesta el estado de enseres, efectos, reales, y demas pertenecientes al obraje de esta Villa . . . , Chihuahua, December 18, 1801, CPM:HA 51:19, 6V. Alum as a mineral awaiting development in Chacón (1803), SANM II 15: 87, TW #1670a; Chacón, "Report," 166. Alum appears in the alcabala receipts from New Mexico in 1781, AGN:AC 61:19V.

17. Power of attorney and contract between Don Francisco Manuel de Elguea, Don Felipe Gonzales de Cosío, and Señor Colonel Don Francisco de la Concha, Governor of New Mexico, Chihuahua, January 10, 1795, CHI:RG 34, 1–3–10, vol. 34: 11R–15R. Encinillas obraje: Jones, *Nueva Vizcaya*, note 101.

18. CHI:RG 34:13R,V.

19. In 1792 Governor Concha tried to exchange the ewes he had collected in New Mexico for wethers, in keeping with a policy recommended by Comandante General Ugarte in 1788 to prevent the export of ewes for the protection of New Mexican breeding stock. He offered to trade ewes for wethers at a premium of one-third,

four ewes for three wethers. This offer did not succeed completely, since Campor mentioned that Concha exported a large number of pregnant ewes. Bando: Santa Fe, July 8, 1792, SANM II 13:105–6, TW #1199a; and Baxter, *Carneradas,* 53–55.

20. The year 1784 was used as a dividing point in this comparison because it formed the midpoint in Governor Concha's ten-year administration of the tithe rental, during which time the value remained at 1,600 pesos.

Tithe records for New Mexico and Nueva Vizcaya reside in ACD:DZ, in 4 boxes and 13 packets of documents. Documents relevant to tithe assignment and collection also appear in the 55 boxes marked "Varios" (ACD:VA).

General summary of tithe collection in Mexico: Arij Ouweneel and Catrien C. J. H. Bijleveld, "The Economic Cycle in Bourbon Central Mexico: A Critique of the Recaudación del diezmo líquido en pesos," *Hispanic American Historical Review* 69:3 (1989), 481–82. See one example of historical development of tithe collection: Woodrow Borah, "Tithe Collection in the Bishopric of Oaxaca, 1601–1867," *Hispanic American Historical Review* 19:4 (1949), 498–517. New Mexico follows the eighteenth-century Oaxaca pattern except that the *jueces hacedores* never switched to direct administration of tithe collection. See also Marc Simmons, *Spanish Government in New Mexico* (Albuquerque: University of New Mexico Press, 1968), 107–10, with reference to documents available in SANM.

21. See Richard L. Garner, with Spiro E. Stefanou, *Economic Growth and Change in Bourbon Mexico* (Gainesville: University Press of Florida, 1993), 32–33; Enrique Florescano, *Precios del maíz y crisis agrícolas en México (1708–1810)* (Mexico City: El Colegio de México, 1969; rev. ed. Mexico City: Ediciones Era, 1986). Also see Ouweneel and Bijleveld, "Economic Cycle," 479–81, for a brief review of the literature on price inflation in late colonial Mexico.

22. See Lyman L. Johnson and Enrique Tandeter, eds., *Essays on the Price History of Eighteenth-Century Latin America* (Albuquerque: University of New Mexico Press, 1990). This procedure and the other complications surrounding the use of the tithe rentals to interpret economic development in late colonial New Mexico are discussed in Ross Frank, "'And One Can Only See the Marks': Tithe Rentals and Economic Development in Late Colonial New Mexico" (forthcoming).

23. See the following documents concerning this period of Antonio El Pinto's career: Governor Concha to Comandante General Ugarte y Loyola, #55, Santa Fe, June 26, 1788, AGN:PI 65:1, 221V–225V; Report of Vicente Troncoso to Concha, Santa Fe, April 12, 1788, AGN:PI 65:1, 227R–244R; Ugarte y Loyola to Viceroy Flores, #13, Chihuahua, July 31, 1788, AGN:PI 65:1, 246R–250V. See also J. Lee Correll, *Through White Man's Eyes: A Contribution to Navajo History* (Window Rock, Ariz.: Navajo Heritage Center, 1979), 1:84–86.

24. Report of Vicente Troncoso to Concha, Santa Fe, April 12, 1788, AGN:PI 65:1, 240V–241R; alternative translations of portions in Correll, *White Man's Eyes,* 86; and Joe Ben Wheat, "Early Trade and Commerce in Southwestern Textiles before the Curio Shop," in *Reflections: Papers on Southwestern Culture History in Honor of Charles H. Lange,* ed. Anne V. Poore (Papers of the Archaeological Society of New Mexico, 14; Santa Fe: Ancient City Press for the Archaeological Society of New Mexico, 1988), 62.

25. Cortés, *Apache Frontier,* 60–61.

26. Establishment of fund: Ugarte to Anza, Chihuahua, October 5, 1786, SANM II 11:1056–78, TW #943, published in Alfred Barnaby Thomas, trans. and ed., *For-*

gotten Frontiers: A Study of the Spanish–Indian Policy of Juan Bautista de Anza, Governor of New Mexico, 1777–1787 (Norman: University of Oklahoma Press, 1932), 342. Request, approval, and transmission of funds for the "Indian Allies" for 1787 and 1788: AGN:PI 65:1, 6R–59R.

27. The accounts of the "gastos extraordinarios" are divided into general accounts, which were sent to higher officials to be audited, and collections of supporting receipts. The general accounts cover the years 1786 through 1793, as follows: 1786, AGN:PI 67:1, 32R–34V; 1787, AGN:PI 67:1, 112R–120V; 1788, AGN:PI 67: 1, 203R–214V; 1789, AGN:PI 67:1, 216R–223V; 1790, AGN:PI 67:1, 488R–497V; 1791, AGN:PI 204:15, 337R–341R; 1792, AGN:HI 427:8, 5R–8V; 1793, AGN:HI 427:8, 9R–12R. The individual receipts cover the years 1786 through 1791, as follows: 1786, AGN:PI 65:1, 259R–261V and 67:1, 36R–76R; 1787, AGN:PI 65:1, 268R–278V and 67:1, 84R–109V and 122R–198R,V; 1788, AGN:PI 67:1, 228R–390V and SANM II 12:440–55, TW #1100; 1789, AGN:PI 67:1, 224R and 391R–473R; 1790, AGN:PI 67:1, 500R–595V; 1791, AGN:PI 204:15, 342R–419V and AGN:HI 427:8, 1R–4R.

28. On medias, see Marc Simmons, "On the Trail of the Footless Stockings," in *Coronado's Land: Essays on Daily Life in Colonial New Mexico,* ed. and trans. Marc Simmons (Albuquerque: University of New Mexico Press, 1991), 8–11; and Marc Simmons, "Footwear on New Mexico's Hispanic Frontier," in *Southwestern Culture History: Collected Papers in Honor of Albert H. Schroeder,* ed. Charles H. Lange (Papers of the Archaeological Society of New Mexico, 10; Santa Fe: Ancient City Press for the Archaeological Society of New Mexico, 1985), 223–31.

29. Pueblo mentioned by Thomas, *Frontiers,* 386, note 133, as San Carlos de los Jupes. See also Alfred Barnaby Thomas, "San Carlos: A Comanche Pueblo on the Arkansas River, 1787," *Colorado Magazine,* May 1929, 79–91.

30. Individual receipts: AGN:PI 67:1, 244R, 307V, 406R, 424R, 429R, 432R, 443R, 455R,V, 521R,V, 532R, 538R, 540R, 541R, 549R, 552R, 555R, 568R; AGN: PI 204:15, 368V, 380R.

31. Estimated total: Ross H. Frank, "From Settler to Citizen: Economic Development and Cultural Change in Late Colonial New Mexico, 1750–1820" (Ph.D. diss., University of California, Berkeley, 1992), 435–36, table 3; and Thomas W. Kavanagh, *Comanche Political History: An Ethnological Perspective, 1700–1875* (Lincoln: University of Nebraska Press, 1996), 183, table 4.3. Percentage spent in New Mexico: The estimate is based on the general accounts and receipts listed above. Only goods and services which, due to the type, description, price, or specific context, were virtually certain to have come from New Mexico were counted as "spent in New Mexico." Many other transactions covered items that could have come from New Mexico but were excluded here in order to preserve the conservative nature of this estimate.

32. Expenditures within New Mexico from the *Fondo extraordinario* total of 9,175 pesos. The *sínodos* paid to the missionaries on New Mexico for the year 1787 totaled 9,800 pesos (including the six El Paso missions). See Estado que manifiesta los Gastos que se erogan annualmente en esta Real Caja . . . , Domingo de Bereganãs, Chihuahua, October 10, 1788, AGN:PI 46:1, 247 (table).

33. Alicia V. Tjarks, "Demographic, Ethnic, and Occupational Structure of New Mexico, 1790," *Americas* 35:1 (1978), 82–88, esp. table 15.

34. See Juan Carlos Garavaglia and Juan Carlos Grosso, *Las alcabalas novohispañas*

Alcabala Documents for New Mexico in
the Archivo General de la Nación, Mexico City, Ramo de Alcabalas

Year	Partido	Type	Location
1781	New Mexico	Export	AGN:AC 61:19R,V
1783	New Mexico	Export	AGN:AC 61:20R,V
1783	El Paso	Export	AGN:AC 61:31R–32V
178?	El Paso	Export	AGN:AC 63:3V–31R
1796	New Mexico	Import	AGN:AC 63:2R, 60R,V
1796	El Paso	Import	AGN:AC 63:8R–35R
1811	El Paso	Export	AGN:AC 63:2V–3R
1811	New Mexico	Export	AGN:AC 63:3R
1811	El Paso	Export	AGN:AC 63:7R–11V
1811	New Mexico	Export	AGN:AC 63:12V
1811	El Paso	Export	AGN:AC 63:15R,V
1817	New Mexico	Export	AGN:AC 63:3R
1817	El Paso	Export	AGN:AC 63:16V, 32V

(1776–1821) (Mexico City: Archivo General de la Nación, 1987). The *receptoría de alcabalas* of Chihuahua began to collect the tax in the north in 1777, the first year of operation of the new system. See also Murdo MacLeod, "Aspects of the Internal Economy of Colonial Spanish America: Labour; Taxation; Distribution and Exchange," in *The Cambridge History of Latin America,* ed. Leslie Bethell (Cambridge, England: Cambridge University Press, 1984), 2:245–46.

35. Alcabala origins: Hubert Howe Bancroft, *History of the Pacific States of North America: Arizona and New Mexico, 1530–1888* (San Francisco: History Company, 1888), 12:116–17; and Simmons, *Spanish Government,* 90–91. Application in 1775: Pedro Galindo Navarro, Durango, September 27, 1777, SANM II 10:931–33, TW #706; Croix to Mendinueta, Durango, September 30, 1777, SANM II 10:934, TW #706a.

36. The table above comprises all of the documents pertaining to the alcabala found for late colonial New Mexico and El Paso in AGN:AC. Alcabala extension (1796): The royal order of October 12, 1795 mentioned in Simmons, *Spanish Government,* 91–92, and in Ralph E. Twitchell, *The Spanish Archives of New Mexico* (Cedar Rapids, Iowa: Torch Press, 1914), 373 (TW #1344a), did not reach New Mexico until after October 12, 1796, when Comandante General Pedro de Nava promulgated a bando in Chihuahua embodying the royal order of the previous year: SANM II 13:1012, TW #1372b. Chacón mentions the exemption in his 1803 report to the Consulado de Veracruz. Report of Governor Chacón to Comandante General Nemesio Salcido, Santa Fe, August 28, 1803, SANM II 15:91, TW #1670a; also Marc Simmons, "The Chacón Economic Report of 1803," *New Mexico Historical Review* 60:1 (1985), 87; and Chacón, "Report," 171.

37. Governor Cachupín to Marqués de Cruillas, Santa Fe, January 3, 1766, AGN:PI 102:10, 427V–428R.

38. AGN:PI 151:2, 229R,V. Translation from Pedro Fermín de Mendinueta, "Indian and Mission Affairs in 1773," in *Coronado's Land: Essays on Daily Life in Colonial*

New Mexico, ed. and trans. Marc Simmons (Albuquerque: University of New Mexico Press, 1991), 121.

39. Fray Juan Agustín de Morfí, "Geographical Description of New Mexico," in *Forgotten Frontiers: A Study of the Spanish–Indian Policy of Juan Bautista de Anza, Governor of New Mexico, 1777–1787,* ed. Alfred Barnaby Thomas (Norman: University of Oklahoma Press, 1932), 87–120, translated from British Library, Mexico, Tratados Varios Add. Mss 17,563, 71–94, and a copy in AGN : HI 25 : 6, 92–116. The geographical description dates from 1782, although Morfí collected the material for it in 1778 or 1779. See Thomas, *Frontiers,* 371, note 1; and Morfí, "Account of Disorders," 127–61, translated from AGN : HI 6 : 97R–121R. See Bancroft, *Arizona and New Mexico,* 276–78; and Max L. Moorhead, *New Mexico's Royal Road* (Norman: University of Oklahoma Press, 1958), 50–51.

40. Morfí, "Account of Disorders," 133–38. The translation is by Simmons, as are his comments in square brackets. I have inserted further explanatory comments in curly brackets.

41. "Very rare here is that known to the king as his money because {hence} they make up imaginary pesos" (Morfí, "Geographical Description," 113).

42. Bancroft, *Arizona and New Mexico,* 278.

43. See John E. Kicza, *Colonial Entrepreneurs: Families and Business in Bourbon Mexico City* (Albuquerque: University of New Mexico Press, 1983), for the vast networks of indebtedness extending throughout Mexico that created the major families of business enterprise in Mexico City. Use of *repartimiento de efectos* as income for officials: Brading, *Miners and Merchants,* 44–51.

44. Moorhead, *Royal Road,* 50.

45. See, for example, Marc Simmons, "Colonial New Mexico and Mexico: The Historical Relationship," in *Colonial Frontiers: Art and Life in Spanish New Mexico,* ed. Christine Mather (Santa Fe, N.Mex.: Ancient City Press, 1983), 84; Jones, *Nueva Vizcaya,* 187–88; and Gutiérrez, *Corn Mothers,* 301–2.

46. Fray Atanasio Domínguez, *The Missions of New Mexico, 1776,* ed. Eleanor B. Adams and Fray Angélico Chávez (Albuquerque: University of New Mexico Press, 1956), 19.

47. Ibid., 245.

48. Fray Juan Sanz de Lezaún, "An Account of Lamentable Happenings in New Mexico," translated in Charles W. Hackett, trans. and ed., *Historical Documents Relating to New Mexico and Nueva Vizcaya, and Approaches Thereto, to 1773* (Publication 330; Washington, D.C.: Carnegie Institution, 1937), 3 : 468–79; and Domínguez, *Mission,* 245–46.

49. Don Jacobo Ugarte y Loyola to Exmo. Don Manuel Antonio Flores, Numero 352, Valle de San Bartolomé, October 25, 1788, SANM II 12 : 91–92, TW #1019.

50. Peso Antiguo: Fray Lezaún, no location, November 4, 1760, AFBN 30 : 595.1, #1851, 1R–6V; and Hackett, *Historical Documents,* 3 : 475. Peso de Proyecto: anonymous description of El Paso, September 1, 1773, AGN : HI 25. This translation is Hackett's from a copy in Bancroft Library, Berkeley, CA (M–A 4 : 3, vol. 2). Hackett, *Historical Documents,* 3 : 508.

51. Domínguez, *Missions,* 30 and 245; the tariff for services performed in the Dioceses of Durango appears on pp. 244–45. Certificaciones de los misioneros de Nuevo Mexico en las que se especifica el número de bautizmos, matrimonios, y defunciones

habidos en sus misiones . . . , enero 1749 a agosto de 1750, August 29, 1750, AFBN 29:567.1, #1799, 19 folios.

52. See discussions of mission finances in Domínguez, *Missions*, 30–31, 75–77, and 100–101. Quotation: Relaciones juradas del subsidio pertenecen a la misiones del Paso y Nuevo Mexico, various dates, various authors, ACD:VA 44:116, 24 folios. The description of pesos de la tierra is found on 19R. This report calculated the New Mexican portion of a 6 percent ecclesiastical contribution levied by the Crown. The bishop of Durango sent a cédula to Governor Concha from Durango on December 20, 1790, enclosing the order to the custodio of New Mexico for the assessment: SANM II 12:436–39, TW #1109. Further correspondence: SANM II 12:538–39, TW #1123. See also Viceroy Conde de Revillagigedo to the bishop of Durango, Mexico, December 1, 1790, ACD:VA 44:116, 3 folios.

53. List of prices: 1776, Domínguez, *Missions*, 245; 1791, Relaciones juradas del subsidio pertenecen a la misiones del Paso y Nuevo Mexico, various dates, various authors, ACD:VA 44:116, 19R of 24 folios. Column six presents the ratio of the 1791 peso de la tierra price to the price in silver reales for the same year. Column seven shows the ratios between the value of the goods in silver reales in 1776 and 1791.

54. Construction expense for the Santa Fe Cuartel, 1789–1791: SANM II 12: 705–18, TW #1163.

55. Annotated "Informe General de su Provincia," Governor Concha to Viceroy Señor Don Manuel Antonio de Flores, Santa Fe, September, no day, 1787, AGN:PI 254:2, 11R. Quotation: Don Jacobo Ugarte y Loyola to Exmo. Don Manuel Antonio Flores, Numero 352, Valle de San Bartolomé, October 25, 1788, SANM II 12:93 and 12:96, TW #1019.

56. Ignacio del Río, *La aplicación regional de las reformas borbónicas en Nueva España: Sonora y Sinaloa, 1768–1787* (Serie de historia novohispana, 55; Mexico City: Universidad Nacional Autónoma de México, Instituto de Investigaciones Históricas, 1995), 167–69; and Brading, *Miners and Merchants*, 130.

57. Razon de caudal que se remite a Chihuahua perteneciente al Donativo gratuito que se ha colectado en la Provincia del Nuevo Mexico, assi en Dinero como efectos, Santa Fe, September 18, 1799, SANM II 14:466–68, TW #1471a. Final accounting and congratulations concerning the donativo of 1799, Pedro de Nava to Governor Chacón, Chihuahua, January 24, 1800, SANM II 14:494–96, TW #1481. Report of Governor Chacón to Comandante General Nemesio Salcedo, Santa Fe, August 28, 1803, SANM II 15:90, TW #1670a; Chacón, "Report," 170. Gutiérrez, *Corn Mother*, 321, mentions that in 1774 the confraternity of Our Lady of Mount Carmel in Santa Cruz de la Cañada changed its annual dues from 1 peso de la tierra to "2 reales in silver, and if that was too much, then to 1 real" (AASF:MI 1794 #11, 53:103). This also suggests that the peso de la tierra originally served to value local produce for payment of the 2 reales annual fee. With the introduction of specie into the province, the confraternity wished to change back to silver but realized that the full amount in reales might be too much for its members to bear. Also note the difference between this and Gutiérrez's translation of Chacón's 1803 report. Gutiérrez notes the increase in circulation of specie after 1800 but confuses instances of money used in colonial transactions during the 1750–1770s with more fundamental changes in the monetary system that took place later.

58. Cortés, *Apache Frontier*, 61.

59. Cuenta de cargo y data del común de companía del año de 1805 . . . , SANM II 15:494–552, TW #1818a.

60. Quotations: Chacón (1803), SANM II 15:85, TW #1670a. See also translation in Chacón, "Report," 165; and Pike, *Journals*, 1:51.

61. Instruccion formada por el colonel Don Francisco de la Concha, Governador que ha sido de la Provincia de Nuevo México para el subcesor el teniente coronel Don Fernando Chacón . . . , Chihuahua, June 28, 1794, AGN:HI 41:11, paragraph 30, 349R,V.

62. Ward Alan Minge, "*Efectos del país:* A History of Weaving along the Rio Grande," in *Spanish Textile Tradition of New Mexico and Colorado,* ed. Nora Fisher (Santa Fe: Museum of New Mexico Press, 1979), 21; Dorothy Boyd Bowen, "A Brief History of Spanish Textile Production in the Southwest," in *Spanish Textile Tradition of New Mexico and Colorado,* ed. Nora Fisher (Santa Fe: Museum of New Mexico Press, 1979), 6; and E. Boyd, *Popular Arts of Colonial New Mexico* (Albuquerque: University of New Mexico Press, 1974), 171–90.

63. Labor: Boyd, *Popular Arts,* 18; David M. Brugge, *Navajos in the Catholic Church Records of New Mexico, 1694–1875* (rev. ed.; Tsaile, Ariz.: Navajo Community College Press, 1985), 22–23, table 2; extant baptism records listed on pp. 2–9. Slaves: Gutiérrez, *Corn Mothers,* 171–72 and 180–90.

Gutiérrez, *Corn Mothers,* 171, overestimates the number of Genízaros in New Mexico, suggesting that in 1793 they numbered about one-third of the population, or "as many as 9,690." According to Brugge, *Navajos* (1985), 22–23, table 2, at least 3,500 non-Pueblo Indians entered New Mexican baptismal records from 1693 to 1846. Of these, about 1,700 entered the province through slave raids after 1800.

The remaining 1,800 did not all become enslaved in New Mexican households: Franciscan expeditions around midcentury led non-Pueblo and Pueblo Indians to occupy new or revived mission sites as autonomous villages (Brugge, *Navajos* [1985], 24–29); Jicarilla Apache settled in the Taos region in 1733 (Hackett, *Historical Documents,* 3:403); Fray García brought about 440 Tano refugees and other Hopi refugees in 1742 to resettle the site of the abandoned Sandía pueblo (Hackett, *Historical Documents,* 3:411); perhaps 500 Indians resettled at Isleta and Jémez (Hackett, *Historical Documents,* 3:472); Fray Menchero and Fray Delgado resettled Apaches and Navajo at Cebolleta and El Encinal in the 1740s (Hackett, *Historical Documents,* 3: 421–22, 432–37, and 471–72); and 150 or so Hopi returned to the Río Grande Valley as refugees from drought in 1780 (Joseph F. Park, "Spanish-Indian Policy in Northern Mexico, 1765–1810," *Arizona and the West* 4: Winter [1962], 227).

Thus, an estimated 1,100 of the 1,800 autonomous non-Pueblo peoples baptized before 1800, according to Brugge, *Navajos* (1985), 22–23, table 2, were not incorporated into "Spanish" households (Jicarilla, near Taos, 100; Sandía, 1742, 200; Isleta and Jémez, 1745, 250; Cebolleta and Encinal, 1740s, 350; 1780s drought refugees, 200; total, 1,100). This leaves about 700 people who entered New Mexican households as Genízaros before 1800, plus those absorbed by vecino society from Pueblo intermarriage or the incorporation of outcasts (Gutiérrez, *Corn Mothers,* 154–56).

Note the minimum number of clearly non-Genízaro baptisms included in Brugge, *Navajos* (1985), 22–23, table 2: Jicarilla, 100 (est.); Sandía, 165; Isleta and Jémez, 80; Cebolleta and Encinal, 350; Hopi in 1780, 74; total, 770.

64. Boyd, *Popular Arts,* 205.

65. Dorothy Boyd Bowen, "Introductory Remarks," in *Spanish Textile Tradition of New Mexico and Colorado,* ed. Nora Fisher (Santa Fe: Museum of New Mexico Press, 1979), 55; Roland F. Dickey, *New Mexico Village Arts* (Albuquerque: University of New Mexico Press, 1949), 112–13. Imported dyes: Chacón (1803), SANM II 15:87–88, TW #1670a; Chacón, "Report," 168; Dorothy Boyd Bowen and Trish Spillman, "Appendix D: Natural and Synthetic Dyes," in *Spanish Textile Tradition of New Mexico and Colorado,* ed. Nora Fisher (Santa Fe: Museum of New Mexico Press, 1979), 208–9; and Henry P. Mera, *Spanish-American Blanketry* (Santa Fe, N.Mex.: School of American Research Press, 1987), 2. Eye-dazzlers: Mera, *Blanketry,* 22; Joe Ben Wheat, "Río Grande, Pueblo, and Navajo Weavers: Cross-Cultural Influence," in *Spanish Textile Tradition of New Mexico and Colorado,* ed. Nora Fisher (Santa Fe: Museum of New Mexico Press, 1979), 31–32; and also see James Jeter and Paula Marie Juelke, *The Saltillo Sarape: An Exhibition Organized by the Santa Barbara Museum of Art* (Santa Barbara, Calif.: New World Arts, 1978), 24–25.

66. Fray Bernal (1794), AASF:MI 1794 #13, 53:109. Notes for the 1794 census returns from Río Arriba (paragraph 5) describe vecino weaving as: "the second principal branch of commerce in this province, and that which also assists the first [sheep raising]." Noticias de las missiones que ocupan los religiosos . . . , Fray Diego Turado, Fray Ramón Gómez, Abiquíu, November 3, 1795, AASF:MI 1795 #13, 53:156.

67. See Wheat, "Weavers," 31–32.

68. Quotations: Fray Bernal (1794), AASF:MI 1794 #13, 53:110–14. Notes for the 1794 census returns from Río Abajo (paragraph 5) also include this information. Noticias de las missiones que ocupan los religiosos . . . , Abiquíu, October 30, 1795, SANM II 21:537, no TW #, B.M. Read Collection, NMSRCA. Noticias de las missiones que ocupan los religiosos . . . , Santa Clara, November 3, 1795, AASF: MI 1795 #13, 53:156.

69. Alcabala payments: 1781, AGN:AC 61:19R,V; 1783, AGN:AC 61:20R,V; 1811, AGN:AC 63:3R, 12V; 1817, AGN:AC 63:16V, 32V.

70. Governor Anza to Viceroy Gálvez, Santa Fe, November 12, 1785, AGN:CA 29:3, 159R.

71. See Gutiérrez, *Corn Mothers,* 154–56; and Teresa Archuleta-Sagel, "Textiles," in *Spanish New Mexico: The Spanish Colonial Arts Society Collection,* ed. Donna Pierce and Marta Weigle (Santa Fe: Museum of New Mexico Press, 1996), 1:148.

72. Brugge, *Navajos* (1985), 56–84.

73. Fray Pedro Serrano, Report of Fray Serrano (1761), in Hackett, *Historical Documents,* 3:486; Chacón (1803), SANM II 15:88, TW #1670a; and Chacón, "Report," 169. Pueblo potters did use glazes before the Pueblo Revolt of 1680.

74. Morfí, "Account of Disorders," 133 and 137. The "defective and corrupt trade" refers to the system of barter using the different values for pesos discussed above; Pike, *Journals,* 2:50.

75. Rex E. Gerald, "Spanish Presidios of the Late Eighteenth Century in Northern New Spain," *Museum of New Mexico Research Records* 7 (1968), 41–55, esp. 9–10 and 41–55.

76. See Henry P. Mera, *Style Trends in Pueblo Pottery in the Rio Grande and Little Colorado Cultural Areas from the Sixteenth to the Nineteenth Century* (Laboratory of Anthropology Memoir No. 3; Santa Fe, N.Mex.: Laboratory of Anthropology, 1939), 13–14

and 62; Kenneth M. Chapman and Francis H. Harlow, *The Pottery of San Ildefonso Pueblo* (Monograph Series No. 28; Santa Fe, N.Mex.: School of American Research, 1970); Francis H. Harlow, *Matte-Paint Pottery of the Tewa, Keres, and Zuni Pueblos* (Albuquerque: Museum of New Mexico Press, 1973); Larry Frank and Francis H. Harlow, *Historic Pottery of the Pueblo Indians, 1600–1880* (Boston: New York Graphic Society, 1974); Larry Frank and Francis H. Harlow, *Historic Pottery of the Pueblo Indians, 1600–1880* (2d ed.; West Chester, Pa.: Schiffer Publishing, 1990); Ken Hedges and Alfred Edward Dittert Jr., *Heritage in Clay: The 1912 Pueblo Pottery Collections of Wesley Bradfield and Thomas S. Dozier* (San Diego Museum of Man Papers, 17; San Diego, Calif.: San Diego Museum of Man, 1984); Jonathan Batkin, *Pottery of the Pueblos of New Mexico, 1700–1940* (Colorado Springs, Colo.: Taylor Museum, 1987); and Rick Dillingham, with Melinda Elliot, *Acoma and Laguna Pottery* (Santa Fe, N.Mex.: School of American Research Press, 1992).

77. Discussion of the Franciscan "F" and "B" styles: Boyd, *Popular Arts,* 118–43. Mission church decoration: Domínguez, *Missions;* and inventories ordered taken by Governor Fernando de la Concha in 1789, RHUN, box 2: Laguna, RHUN 1849; Taos, RHUN 51; Picurís, RHUN 335; San Juan, RHUN 337; Pojoaque, RHUN 1837; Abiquíu, RHUN 1835; San Ildefonso, RHUN 1836; Nambé, RHUN 1838; Santa Clara, RHUN 1839; Cochití, RHUN 1849; San Felipe, RHUN 1841; Santo Domingo, RHUN 1842. Church refurbishment: Marsha Bol, "The Anonymous Artist of Laguna and the New Mexican Altar Screen" (M.A. thesis, University of New Mexico, 1980), 28–49 and 130. Destruction of paintings on animal skin began with the visitation of the bishop of Durango's *visitador,* don Juan Bautista Ladrón de Guevara, in 1817–1820 (Boyd, *Popular Arts,* 125–28).

78. See Bol, "Anonymous Artist," 114–27; William Wroth, *Christian Images in Hispanic New Mexico* (Colorado Springs, Colo.: Taylor Museum, 1982), 69–72; and Boyd, *Popular Arts,* 163–66.

79. See for example, Frank and Harlow, *Historic Pottery* (1974), 8–9.

80. The following discussion is informed by Batkin, *Pottery,* 37–43; Frank and Harlow, *Historic Pottery* (1974), 29–73; Harlow, *Matte-Paint,* 28–36; and Chapman and Harlow, *Pottery of San Ildefonso,* esp. 37–51. Ogapoge Polychrome: Mera, *Style Trends,* 13–14 and 62; and Batkin, *Pottery,* 38.

81. For a discussion of Kiua Polychrome and its northeastern Keres successors, see Batkin, *Pottery,* 93–98; Frank and Harlow, *Historic Pottery* (1974), 74–115; and Harlow, *Matte-Paint,* 44–50.

82. Alan Ferg, *Historic Archeology on the San Antonio de las Huertas Grant, Sandoval County, New Mexico* (CASA Papers, 3; Cortez, Colo.: Complete Archeological Service Association, 1984), esp. 68–72; Frank and Harlow, *Historic Pottery* (1974), 34 and 74–75; Batkin, *Pottery,* 94; and Harlow, *Matte-Paint,* 32. See also Curtis F. Schaafsma, "Review of *Archaeological Notes Concerning Two Colonial Period Settlements in the Tijeras Canyon Area, New Mexico,*" by Michael P. Marshall, in *Report of New Mexico State Archaeologist* (Santa Fe, N.Mex.: Laboratory of Anthropology, 1984), 4–6. Change from stone to rag-polished slips: Frank and Harlow, *Historic Pottery* (1974), 39, 75–76, 157; and Batkin, *Pottery,* 94.

83. Nambé production: see Frank and Harlow, *Historic Pottery* (1974), 39, 72–73. Fray Bernal (1794), AASF:MI 1794 #13, 53:110; Fray Turado and Fray Gomez, Abiquíu, November 3, 1795, AASF:MI 1795 #13, 53:156. Christine A. Rudecoff and

Charles Carillo, "Test Excavations at San Antonio de Los Poblanos: A Spanish Colonial Community on the Middle Rio Grande," in *Secrets of a City: Papers on Albuquerque Area Archaeology in Honor of Richard A. Bice,* ed. Anne V. Poore and John Montgomery (Papers of the Archaeological Society of New Mexico, 13; Santa Fe: Ancient City Press for the Archaeological Society of New Mexico, 1987), 51.

84. Dillingham, *Acoma and Laguna Pottery,* 135–37, notes that the argument presented in Ross Frank, "Changing Pueblo Indian Pottery Tradition: The Underside of Economic Development in Late Colonial New Mexico, 1750–1820," *Journal of the Southwest* 33:3 (1991), 282–321, and refined here helps to explain the abruptness of the change from the Ako style to the Acomita style.

85. Even the Hopi pueblos underwent a significant and related change in style and technique. Polacca Polychrome formed a striking departure from earlier Hopi pottery styles and took on aspects of pottery-producing pueblos nearby, such as Zuñi's Kiapkwa transition style. See Edwin L. Wade and Lea S. McChesney, *Historic Hopi Ceramics: The Thomas V. Keam Collection of the Peabody Museum of Archaeology and Ethnology* (Cambridge, Mass.: Peabody Museum Press, Harvard University, 1981), 102–3 and plates on pp. 104–42. The catalog (p. 120) notes the brief Spanish influence but dates it a little too late (1800–1830). The appearance of the Polacca B style and the brief Spanish influence are a part of the same phenomenon occurring elsewhere in the New Mexican pottery-making region.

NOTES TO CHAPTER 5

1. Ramón A. Gutiérrez, *When Jesus Came, the Corn Mothers Went Away: Marriage, Sexuality, and Power in New Mexico, 1500–1846* (Stanford, Calif.: Stanford University Press, 1991), 281; and Ross H. Frank, "From Settler to Citizen: Economic Development and Cultural Change in Late Colonial New Mexico, 1750–1820" (Ph.D. diss., University of California, Berkeley, 1992), 413–32, table 1, census returns of 1789, 1794, 1804, 1810, 1811, and 1821. Durango: Michael M. Swann, *Tierra Adentro* (Boulder, Colo.: Westview Press, 1982), 207–14. *Diligencias:* Gutiérrez, *Corn Mothers,* 278–81.

2. Ethnic labels: Gutiérrez, *Corn Mothers,* 284–85 and 289. Closer cooperation between vecinos and Indios during the 1760–1780 period: Oakah L. Jones Jr., "Pueblo Indian Auxiliaries in New Mexico, 1763–1821," *New Mexico Historical Review* 37:2 (1962), 81–109; and Oakah L. Jones Jr., *Pueblo Warriors and Spanish Conquest* (Norman: University of Oklahoma Press, 1966), 131–86.

3. Gutiérrez, *Corn Mothers,* 287–92.

4. Ibid., 288; Leslie Scott Offut, *Una sociedad urbana y rural en el norte de México* (Saltillo, Mexico: Archivo Municipal de Saltillo, 1993), 260–63; and Leslie Scott Offut, "Urban and Rural Society in the Mexican North: Saltillo in the Late Colonial Period" (Ph.D. diss., University of California, Los Angeles, 1982), 278–81. See the discussion of changing racial designations in colonial censuses in Sherburne F. Cook and Woodrow Borah, *Essays in Population History* (Berkeley: University of California Press, 1971), 2:182–91. Examples of the process of changing racial status by declaration to officials appear in Patricia Seed, *To Love, Honor, and Obey in Colonial Mexico: Conflicts over Marriage Choice, 1574–1821* (Stanford, Calif.: Stanford University Press, 1988), 147–57.

5. James F. Brooks, "'This Evil Extends Especially . . . to the Feminine Sex': Negotiating Captivity in the New Mexico Borderlands," *Feminist Studies* 22:2 (1996), 294–95; Adrian Bustamante, "'The Matter Was Never Resolved': The Casta System in Colonial New Mexico, 1693–1823," *New Mexico Historical Review* 66:2 (1991), 150–57.

6. See Alicia V. Tjarks, "Demographic, Ethnic, and Occupational Structure of New Mexico, 1790," *Americas* 35:1 (1978), 45–88; Adrian José Ríos-Bustamante, "A Contribution to the Historiography of the Greater Mexican North in the Eighteenth Century," *Aztlán* 7:3 (1976), 347–90; Adrian José Ríos-Bustamante, "New Mexico in the Eighteenth Century: Life, Labor and Trade in the Villa de San Felipe de Albuquerque, 1706–1790," *Aztlán* 7:3 (1976), 391–426; Bustamante, "Casta System," 150–57; Janie Louise Aragón, "The People of Santa Fe in the 1790s," *Aztlán* 7:3 (1976), 391–418; and Oakah L. Jones Jr., *Los Paisanos: Spanish Settlers on the Northern Frontier of New Spain* (Norman: University of Oklahoma Press, 1979), 132–35.

7. See letter and census returns from Governor Concha to Viceroy Revillagigedo, Santa Fe, November 20, 1790, AGN:HI 522:38, 244R–256R. Concha explained that the lack of assistants who could write made it difficult to follow the forms that the viceroy had sent. Even after clear explanations and examples, they had spoiled the printed forms, so the returns used handwritten copies of the originals (244R–245R). Steven M. Horvath Jr., "The Social and Political Organization of the Genízaros of Plaza de Nuestra Señora de los Dolores de Belén, New Mexico, 1740–1812" (Ph.D. diss., Brown University, 1979), 96–102, observes that the 1790 census takers were far more rigorous in their identification of people as Castas or Genízaros than were most of the contemporary missionaries.

8. Horvath, "Genízaros," 100, also notes that the term "Genízaro" disappeared from civil and religious records between 1812 and 1821.

9. Cynthia Radding, *Wandering Peoples: Colonialism, Ethnic Spaces, and Ecological Frontiers in Northwestern Mexico, 1700–1850* (Durham, N.C.: Duke University Press, 1997), 153–68. See also Ignacio del Río, *La aplicación regional de las reformas borbónicas en Nueva España: Sonora y Sinaloa, 1768–1787* (Serie de historia novohispana, 55; Mexico City: Universidad Nacional Autónoma de México, Instituto de Investigaciones Históricas, 1995), 79–80, and 126–27.

10. José Manuel Espinosa, *Spanish Folk Tales from New Mexico* (Memoirs of the American Folklore Society, 30; New York: G. E. Stechart, 1937; reprint: Millwood, N.Y.: Kraus Reprint, 1976), 157–60.

11. Racial designations "Spanish" and "Coyote" given by the informant. "Coyote" was used at times to describe both products of Plains-Pueblo and Spanish-Pueblo marriages. See Ríos-Bustamante, "New Mexico," 365; and Gutiérrez, *Corn Mothers,* 197.

12. Libro extraordinario de gobierno. Illmo. Señor D. José Antonio de Zubiría, Obispo de Durango, Visita, February 19, 1833, ACD:CB 54:15R–18V.

13. See Frank, "Settler to Citizen," 459–60, table 11 and sources. Description of refurbishment in the early 1790s described in notes to two parts of the 1794 census: custos, Fray José de la Prada and others, Noticias de las missiones que ocupan los religiosos . . . , Abiquíu, October 10, 1795, SANM II 21:535–36, no TW #, B. M. Read Collection, NMSRCA; and Noticias de las missiones que ocupan los religiosos . . . , Fray Diego Turado, Fray Ramón Gomez, Abiquíu, November 3, 1795, AASF:MI 1795 #13, 53:153–54.

14. Fray Angélico Chávez, *Origins of New Mexico Families* (Santa Fe: Historical Society of New Mexico, 1954, 247–50, 150); Marsha Bol, "The Anonymous Artist of Laguna and the New Mexican Altar Screen" (M.A. thesis, University of New Mexico, 1980), 38; and Fray Juan Augustín de Morfí, "Account of Disorders, 1778," in *Coronado's Land: Essays on Daily Life in Colonial New Mexico,* ed. and trans. Marc Simmons (Albuquerque: University of New Mexico Press, 1991), 144–45.

15. Alcabala: AGN:AC 61:20V. Positions: Pregones for the 1785 tithe contract. ACD:VA 32:86, 7 folios; Instruccion formada por el colonel Don Francisco de la Concha, Governador que ha sido de la Provincia de Nuevo México para el subcesor el teniente coronel Don Fernando Chacón . . . , Chihuahua, June 28, 1794, AGN: HI 41:11, paragraph 24, 344V–345R.

16. See Bol, "Anonymous Artist," 38–43; and George Kubler, *Religious Architecture of New Mexico* (Colorado Springs, Colo.: Taylor Museum, 1940; reprinted, Chicago: Rio Grande Press, 1962), 79 and 100–101.

17. Bol, "Anonymous Artist," 41; translation from Col. José D. Sena, "The Chapel of Don Antonio José Ortiz," *New Mexico Historical Review* 13:4 (1938), 350.

18. Bol, "Anonymous Artist," 42–43 and 50–95; E. Boyd, *Popular Arts of Colonial New Mexico* (Albuquerque: University of New Mexico Press, 1974), 155–62; and Marie Romero Cash, *Santos: Enduring Images of Northern New Mexican Village Churches* (Niwot: University of Colorado Press, 1999), 49–54. Cash argues that the Laguna Santero created two of the altar screens at the Santa Cruz de la Cañada church in 1786. The early date depends on her identification of the Laguna Santero as Fray Ramón Antonio Gonzalez, who served in New Mexico from 1769 until his death in 1815. The relationship between Don Antonio and Doña Maria follows: Maria Manuela Ortiz was the second child of José Reaño II and Ana Maria Ortiz (Chávez, *Origins,* 265; and see discussion of Reaño's will in chapter 1 [Proceedings regarding debt owed to the estate of Juan Reaño, Santa Fe, November 23, 1762, SANM II 9:410–44, TW #559]). Ana María Ortiz was the second child of Francisco Ortiz and Francisca Montoya (the first died in infancy) (Chávez, *Origins,* 249). Since Francisco Ortiz was the brother of Nicholas Ortiz III, Antonio José Ortiz's father, Don Antonio José Ortiz, and Doña Maria Manuela Ortiz were second cousins.

19. Boyd, *Popular Arts,* 155–69; William Wroth, *Christian Images in Hispanic New Mexico* (Colorado Springs, Colo.: Taylor Museum, 1982), 69–71; Bol, "Anonymous Artist," 97; and Cash, *Santos,* 49–60. All cite an unpublished dendrochronological study of New Mexican retablos of William S. Stallings Jr., located in the archives of the Taylor Museum of the Colorado Springs Fine Arts Center, Colorado Springs, circa 1951. See also Wroth, *Christian Images,* 98–200, appendix 2.

Cash (pp. 55–57) makes the argument that Fray Ramón Antonio Gonzalez was the Laguna Santero based a comparison of handwriting from documents written by Gonzalez and the inscriptions painted on attributed altar screens at the churches of San Miguel in Santa Fe, Santa Cruz de la Cañada, and Acoma Pueblo. Cash also shows that Gonzalez served at Pojoaque (near Santa Fe) in 1789–1792, Santa Cruz in 1782–1784, and Acoma in 1769 and 1787–1789.

Cash also suggests—without foundation—that the date inscribed on the Laguna altar screen may be 1780, instead of 1808, and that the nave altar screen at Santa Cruz de la Cañada might read 1793, instead of 1796. Absent Cash's interpretation of these inscriptions, no documentary evidence confirms that before 1795 the Laguna Santero made any work attributed to the artist on stylistic grounds, and the dates of Fray Gonzalez's service at or near the sites of these three altar screens do not match the dates inscribed on them: Santa Cruz, 1795; San Miguel, 1798; and Acoma, 1808. Fray Gonzalez may have painted the inscriptions precisely because of the "neatness and clarity" of his hand noted by Cash.

The assumption that the person who painted the inscriptions also painted the altarpieces must be weighed against the testimony of numerous ecclesiastical inventories that carefully note who commissioned and financed these works, not who carved and painted them. In 1795, for example, the same year in which the Laguna Santero finished the nave altar screen at Santa Cruz de la Cañada, Fray Gonzalez himself wrote the inventory, along with Fray José de la Prada, Fray Esteven Aumatell, Fray Jaime Canals, and Fray Diego Muñoz Turado: "The church of the mission Santa Cruz de la Cañada one finds roofed a few years since, at the expense of the R. P. Fr. Sebastian Fernandez referred to above. The side altars, sacristy, and a chapel were done at his expense, and with the help of other benefactors, while R. P. Fr. Jose Carral was the minister, and at this chapel and another there, Fray Francisco Martin Bueno and Fray Ramon Antonio Gonzalez made the respective side altar at their expense and, and being minister of said Villa, the latter [Gonzalez] made another of the side altars of the church, painted the three pulpits, the two doors of the chapel, gave three colored friezes for the dais of the altars, and made the living quarters that the convent has today, all at his expense" (Notes to NM Census of 1793–1794, November 3, 1795, AASF 1795 #13:154). In contrast, Fray Domínguez directly mentioned "the altar screen, the image of Nuestra Señora del Rosario, the large Jesús Nazareno, the [Santo Entierro], casket and balustrade were made and designed by Fray Andrés García who worked day and night with his own hands" (Domínguez, *Missions*, 75).

Santa Cruz church restoration: Gustavo Victor Goler, "Technical Report for the Restoration of the Altar Screen on the North Nave at La Iglesia de Santa Cruz de la Cañada, Santa Cruz, New Mexico" (unpublished report, 1997). See also Santa Cruz Parish, *La Iglesia de Santa Cruz de la Cañada, 1733–1983* (Santa Cruz, N.Mex.: Parish of Santa Cruz de la Cañada, 1983).

20. The following discussion of the style of the Laguna Santero is based on Bol, "Anonymous Artist," 51–113; Boyd, *Popular Arts*, 155–69; Wroth, *Christian Images*, 69–71; Thomas J. Steele, *Santos and Saints: Essays and Handbook* (Albuquerque, N.Mex.: Calvin Horn, 1974); and Thomas J. Steele, *Santos and Saints: The Religious Folk Art of Hispanic New Mexico* (rev. ed.; Santa Fe, N.Mex.: Ancient City Press, 1982), 1–43.

21. See Joseph A. Baird Jr., *Los retablos del siglo XVIII en el sur de España, Portugal, y México* (Mexico City: Universidad Nacional Autónoma de México, 1987). On Laguna Santero bulto style, see: Wroth, *Christian Images*, 69; on 92 Wroth identifies a niche with a crucifixion scene inside with two sculptured witnesses, which he compares with the niche in Boyd, *Popular Arts*, 119, fig. 98. See also Larry Frank, *The New Kingdom of the Saints* (Santa Fe, N.Mex.: Red Crane Books, 1992), chap. 4, plates 38 and 39, for possible examples.

22. Clara Bargellini, *La Catedral de Chihuahua* (Mexico City: Universidad Nacional Autónoma de México, 1984), plates 14–32 and 98–99; and Baird, *Retablos del siglo XVIII*, plates 42–43.

23. Boyd, *Popular Arts*, 327–40; Frank, *New Kingdom*, 35–66; Wroth, *Christian*

Images, 171–84; and Cash, *Santos,* 71–83. Effect of prints on New Mexican santeros: Yvonne Lange, "In Search of San Acacio: The Impact of Industrialization on Santos Worldwide," *El Palacio* 94:1 (1987), 18–24; and Yvonne Lange, "Lithography, an Agent of Technological Change in Religious Folk Art: A Thesis," *Western Folklore* 23:1 (1974), 53–57. Molleno: Boyd, *Popular Arts,* 349–65; Wroth, *Christian Images,* 93–95; Frank, *New Kingdom,* 84–108; and Cash, *Santos,* 60–71. See also Steele, *Santos and Saints* (1982), 13–14. Molleno may have worked on the original altar screen on the north nave of the church at Santa Cruz de la Cañada. See Goler, "Technical Report," 16–19.

24. George Kubler, "Indianism, *Mestizaje,* and *Indigenismo* as Classical, Medieval, and Modern Traditions in Latin America," in *Studies in Ancient American and European Art: The Collected Essays of George Kubler,* ed. Thomas F. Reese (New Haven, Conn.: Yale University Press, 1985), 77–78; Christine Mather, "Works of Art in Frontier New Mexico," in *Colonial Frontiers: Art and Life in Spanish New Mexico,* ed. Christine Mather (Santa Fe, N.Mex.: Ancient City Press, 1983), 21–25; Bol, "Anonymous Artist," 101–2; Wroth, *Christian Images,* 36; and Steele, *Santos and Saints* (1982), 1–27.

25. Itinerant folk tradition: Roland F. Dickey, *New Mexico Village Arts* (Albuquerque: University of New Mexico Press, 1949), 135–86; and José Edmundo Espinosa, *Saints in the Valley: Christian Sacred Images in the History, Life, and Folk Art of Spanish New Mexico* (Albuquerque: University of New Mexico Press, 1960); José Edmundo Espinosa, *Saints in the Valley: Christian Sacred Images in the History, Life, and Folk Art of Spanish New Mexico* (rev. ed., Albuquerque: University of New Mexico Press, 1967); and a charming rendition by Paul Horgan, *The Saintmaker's Christmas Eve* (New York: Farrar, Straus and Cudahy, 1955). Fresquis: Boyd, *Popular Arts,* 330; and Fray Angélico Chávez, *La conquistadora* (Paterson, N.J.: St. Anthony Guild Press, 1954). Molleno: Bol, "Anonymous Artist," 116–17; Wroth, *Christian Images,* 93–94; and Frank, *New Kingdom,* 37.

26. José Aragón emigrated from Spain, but his technique and style are purely vecino: Boyd, *Popular Arts,* 395–407; and William Wroth, *The Chapel of Our Lady of Talpa* (Colorado Springs, Colo.: Taylor Museum, 1979), 54–58. See also the work done by José Aragón (no relation to José Rafael Aragón, called Rafael Aragón to avoid confusion) for the church at Arroyo Hondo (circa 1828), discussed in Robert L. Shalkop, *Arroyo Hondo* (Colorado Springs, Colo.: Taylor Museum, 1976), 5–10.

27. Penitentes: Marta Weigle, *Brothers of Light, Brothers of Blood* (Albuquerque: University of New Mexico Press, 1976); and Thomas J. Steele S.J. and Rowena A. Rivera, *Penitente Self-Government: Brotherhoods and Councils, 1797–1947* (Santa Fe, N.Mex.: Ancient City Press, 1985), 1–11; Fray Angélico Chávez, "The Penitentes of New Mexico," *New Mexico Historical Review* 29:2 (1954), 110–12; and see the 1791 census of cofradía in New Mexico (ACD:VA 44:116, 10R–22R). As mentioned in chapter 1, these documents show a tremendous increase in wealth and membership, as well as new confraternities, compared with the Domínguez report of 1776. See also the membership roll of the Cofradía de Benditas Animas in Albuquerque, which in 1802 contained most of the population of the town (AASF:MI 1802 #30).

28. See Alan C. Vedder, *Furniture of Spanish New Mexico* (Santa Fe, N.Mex.: Sunstone Press, 1977), 9. Vedder argued that early-eighteenth-century furniture made in New Mexico has not survived, "no doubt due to constant reusing and reworking of every piece of furniture until it was literally worn out, as was the case with tools."

Although all scraps of metal were scarce and constantly reused, it is difficult to imagine that vecino craftsman could reuse old boards in new furniture, after traditional methods of patching had failed, in a manner that could not be detected in surviving late-eighteenth-century examples. It is more likely that the general lack of furniture in use in the province earlier in the eighteenth century, coupled with the new quality of vecino carpentry encouraged by growing internal demand for furniture, accounts for the survival of late-eighteenth-century specimens rather than of earlier material.

29. See A. D. Williams, *Spanish Colonial Furniture* (Milwaukee, Wis.: Bruce Publishing, 1941), 2–3; Lonn Taylor and Dessa Bokides, *New Mexican Furniture, 1600–1940* (Santa Fe: Museum of New Mexico Press, 1987), ix; and Josiah Gregg, *Commerce of the Prairies,* ed. Max L. Moorhead (Norman: University of Oklahoma Press, 1954), 146.

30. List of furniture mentioned in wills from 1704 to 1843 found in SANM I compiled by Taylor and Bokides, *New Mexican Furniture,* 3–7 (copy of data in the possession of the author, courtesy of Lonn Taylor); and Frank, "Settler to Citizen," 461, table 12. See Taylor and Bokides, *New Mexican Furniture,* xvi and 19–21. Inventory of Clemente Gutiérrez, San Ysidro del Pajarito, 1785, SANM I 8:994–1136, TW #371; and Taylor and Bokides, *New Mexican Furniture,* 19–20; see also John O. Baxter, *Las Carneradas: Sheep Trade in New Mexico, 1700–1860* (Albuquerque: University of New Mexico Press, 1987), 51–52. Settlement of the estate of Tomasa Benavides, Santa Fe, 1762: SANM I 1:776–88, TW #104.

31. Inventory of Manuel Delgado, Santa Fe, 1815: SANM I 2:365–87, TW #252; Taylor and Bokides, *New Mexican Furniture,* 20–22; and Boyd, *Popular Arts,* 251. Three estates: Juan Montes Vigil, alcalde mayor of the northeastern Keres Pueblos (Santo Domingo, Cochití, and San Felipe), 1762; will of the estate of Miguel Lucero, alcalde mayor of Albuquerque, Santa Fe, 1768 (copy of 1827), SANM I 3:489–90, TW #48; settlement of the estate of Gertrudes Armijo, wife of Martín Vigil, alcalde mayor of San Geronimo de Taos, Taos, 1776, SANM I 1:372–87, TW #48.

32. Taylor and Bokides, *New Mexican Furniture,* 23; and Donna L. Pierce, "New Mexican Furniture and Its Spanish and Mexican Prototypes," in *The American Craftsman and the European Tradition, 1620–1820,* ed. Francis J. Puig and Michael Conforti (Minneapolis, Minn.: Minneapolis Institute of Arts, 1989), 183. The chest shown here as Plate 15 appears in Taylor and Bokides, *New Mexican Furniture,* plate 27.

33. See the late-seventeenth-century Spanish example in Pierce, "New Mexican Furniture," catalog no. 75.

34. Ibid., 183 and 195–96; and Taylor and Bokides, *New Mexican Furniture,* 24.

35. See Taylor and Bokides, *New Mexican Furniture,* plates 1–10, 24, and 33. The chest shown here as Plate 16 appears in Taylor and Bokides, *New Mexican Furniture,* plate 5, and Pierce, "New Mexican Furniture," catalog no. 76. The chest shown here as Plate 17 appears in Taylor and Bokides, *New Mexican Furniture,* plate 10. For an example of the system of apprenticeship for blacksmiths that probably functioned among santeros and furniture makers, see the contract of Juan de Jesus Peña in Marc Simmons and Frank Turley, *Southwestern Colonial Ironwork: The Spanish Blacksmithing Tradition from Texas to California* (Santa Fe: Museum of New Mexico Press, 1980), 32.

36. Three large harineros appear in the will of Manuel Mares, Santa Fe, 1804, SANM I 3:1399–1402, TW #604; see Taylor and Bokides, *New Mexican Furniture,* 21

and 24–25. Inventory of Manuel Delgado, Santa Fe, 1815, SANM I 2:365–87, TW #252. One harinero is described as "small." Inventory of Clemente Gutiérrez, San Ysidro del Pajarito, 1785, SANM I 8:994–1136, TW #371. The Gutiérrez estate was valued at 58,668 pesos, as opposed to 23,887 pesos assessed for the estate of Delgado. See also: Inventory of José Durán y Chavez, San Francisco de Bernalillo, 1783, SANM I 2:316–53, TW #250; settlement of the estate of Juan Antonio Fernández, Santa Fe, 1784, SANM I 8:811–77, TW #280; the will of Juliana Fernández, Santa Fe, 1785, SANM I 2:485–91, TW #279; and the will of José Antonio Griego, Santa Fe, 1789, SANM I 2:1051–67, TW #372.

37. Boyd, *Popular Arts*, 251–54, discusses the relationship between the possession of furniture and vecino social status.

38. The evidence from the inventories suffers due to small samples, 27 over a period of 70 years. Arguing on the basis of what does not exist in the material record is clearly even weaker. However, earlier eighteenth-century examples of Santos and Pueblo pottery do survive. Pottery was valued and prized in a manner similar to furniture and was far more breakable. Of other vecino manufactures, only textile styles such as the Río Grande blanket have left no early- or mid-eighteenth-century samples. In the case of these textiles, they were not made before the end of the century, precisely the argument for the new furniture styles. For a list of the inventories, see Frank, "Settler to Citizen," 461, table 12.

39. Report of Fray Delgado to Fray Jimeno concerning the abominable hostilities and tyrannies of the governor and alcaldes mayores toward the Indians, [Hospicio de Santa Barbara, México], March 27, 1750, in Charles W. Hackett, trans. and ed., *Historical Documents Relating to New Mexico and Nueva Vizcaya, and Approaches Thereto, to 1773* (Publication 330; Washington, D.C.: Carnegie Institution, 1937), 3:425–30.

40. Ibid., 3:429.

41. Fray Lezaún, n.p., November 4, 1760, AFBN 30:595.1, #1851, 1R–6V; Hackett, *Historical Documents*, 3:471–72; and letter of Governor Tomás Vélez de Cachupín to Vice-Custos Fray Manuel Trigo, Santa Fe, March 24, 1750, in Hackett, *Historical Documents*, 3:424–25.

42. Auto of Don Bernardo de Bustamente y Tagle, Acoma, April 18, 1750 (signed Fray Trigo), in Hackett, *Historical Documents*, 3:435. Also see letter of Fray Trigo, 3: 432–433, and other depositions, 3:433–38.

43. Services: Gutiérrez, *Corn Mothers*, 312. Visita rotations: John L. Kessell, *Kiva, Cross, and Crown: The Pecos Indians and New Mexico, 1540–1840* (Washington, D.C.: National Park Service, U.S. Department of the Interior, 1979), 352.

44. Governor Concha to Comandante General Ugarte y Loyola, Santa Fe, November 1, 1790, AGN:PI 161:5, 91V–93V.

45. The figures are for 1791 and 1793. Expediente formado en virtud de oficios del Exmo. Virrey de México para la guía publica . . . , Santa Fe, no date, 1794, ACD: VA 51:132, 14R,V.

46. Concha to Comandante General Pedro de Nava, #228, Santa Fe, July 12, 1790, AGN:PI 161:5, 94R–95R; and summary by Galindo Navarro, Chihuahua, January 9, 1792, AGN:PI 161:5, 95R–98V. See also Horvath, "Genízaros," 64–65. Nava to Viceroy Revillagigedo, Chihuahua, January 20, 1792, AGN:PI 161:5, 99R–102R; approval of mission and sínodo at Belén by Revillagigedo, Posada, Fiscal de Real Hacienda, México, February 31, 1792, AGN:PI 161:5, 103R,V.

47. Teniente Colonel Don Diego Borica, Chihuahua, July 15, 1792, AGN:PI 161:5, 116V–119V and 123R–131V; Nava to Revillagigedo, Chihuahua, July 12, 1792, AGN:PI 161:5, 132R–136V; Fiscal Posada to Revillagigedo, México, August 16, 1792, AGN:PI 161:5, 138R,V; and acceptance of plan by the bishop of Durango, Estevan Lorenzo de Tristán, AGN:PI 161:5, 140R,V; opinion of the Señor Fiscal de lo Civil to Nava, Chihuahua, September 1, 1792, AGN:PI 161:5, 83V–84V; Nava to Concha, Chihuahua, October 19, 1793, SANM II 13:422–24, TW #1263; Concha to Nava, Chihuahua, January 17, 1794, SANM II 13:477–78, TW #1274; and Nava to Concha, Chihuahua, February 3, 1794, SANM II 13:483–84, TW #1278. See also Marc Simmons, *Spanish Government in New Mexico* (Albuquerque: University of New Mexico Press, 1968), 110. Bishop Estevan Lorenzo de Tristán to Revillagigedo, Durango, October 6, 1792, AGN:PI 161:5, 149R.

48. Noticias de las missiones que ocupan los religiosos . . . , Abiquíu, October 30, 1795, signed Custos Fray José de la Prada, Fray Ramón Antonio Gonzalez, Fray Esteban Aumantell, Fray Jaime Canal, and Fray Diego Martinez Turado, SANM II 21:539–40, no TW #, B. M. Read Collection, NMSRCA.

49. See Radding, *Wandering Peoples,* 171–207.

50. Noticias de las missiones que ocupan los religiosos . . . , Santa Clara, November 3, 1795, AASF:MI 1795 #13, 53:156. Noticias de las missiones que ocupan los religiosos . . . , Abiquíu, October 30, 1795, SANM II 21:537, no TW #, B. M. Read Collection, NMSRCA.

51. For an example of the process of land aggrandizement elsewhere in Bourbon New Spain, see Eric Van Young, *Hacienda and Market in Eighteenth-Century Mexico: The Rural Economy of the Guadalajara Region, 1675–1820* (Berkeley: University of California Press, 1981), 297–324.

52. See the description of legal procedure in New Mexico during the later eighteenth century in Charles R. Cutter, *The Legal Culture of Northern New Spain* (Albuquerque: University of New Mexico Press, 1995), esp. 82–94; and Charles R. Cutter, *The Protector de Indios in Colonial New Mexico, 1659–1821* (Albuquerque: University of New Mexico Press, 1986), 61–80. Cutter, *Protector,* 69–75, provides a number of examples of Pueblo access and general success before the governor. See also Woodrow Borah, *Justice by Insurance: The General Indian Court of Colonial Mexico and the Legal Aides of the Half-Real* (Berkeley: University of California Press, 1983), esp. 376–78.

53. The records perused contain only the cases that reached the governor during their proceedings. Cutter, *Protector,* 69, argues that most Pueblo petitions for justice went directly to the governor in order to circumvent the political, economic, and social power held by the local alcalde and his assistants. However, the extant documents probably represent only a fragment of the original material, and obvious gaps occur in the records between about 1770 and 1777, the period of most intensive Plains Indian incursions into the province. The documents include land-related and criminal cases involving Pueblo Indians from the 1740–1820 period. Cases consulted: SANM I, TW #208, 529, 531, 532, 610, 643, 668, 699, 703, 786, 792, 965, 971, 972, 1234, 1243, 1279, 1280, 1348, 1349, 1351–59, and 1361–64; SANM II, TW #431, 432, 440, 447, 448, 466, 485, 507a, 510, 512, 517, 521, 523, 541, 541b, 553, 555, 558, 562, 570, 574, 595a, 596, 631, 636, 662, 673, 687, 690, 850a, 850b, 876, 1004, 1188, 1237a, 1249, 1273, 1394, 1427, 1462, 1531, 1627, 1821, 1869, and 1870; and PBAN 50:3, 52:5, 52:8, 52:15, 52:27, 53:1, and 53:5.

54. Cristóbal and Nerio Montoya versus Antonio Baca over sale of land belonging to Santa Ana Pueblo, Santa Fe, August 9–25, 1761, SANM II 9:509–21, TW #570. See Elizabeth Nelson Patrick, "Land Grants during the Administration of Spanish Colonial Governor Pedro Fermín de Mendinueta," *New Mexico Historical Review* 51:1 (1976), 9–10.

55. The single case heard during this period involved the pueblos of Santa Clara and San Ildefonso against Mateo Trujillo. This case involved land in almost continual litigation from around 1700 until 1786, when Governor Anza threw out the original grant in favor of the pueblo claims, and hence does not reflect upon the Indian's ability to bring fresh grievances before the authorities. See Myra Ellen Jenkins, "Spanish Land Grants in the Tewa Area," *New Mexico Historical Review* 47:2 (1972), 113–34, esp. 127–29.

56. Juan José Quintana, from Cochití Pueblo, asked Comandante General Nemesio Salcedo to appoint a protector in early 1810. Felipe Sandoval (vecino) was appointed in August 1810, before the Hidalgo revolt. All the Pueblo cases that he represented, however, occurred in the context of the rebellion to the south. See Cutter, *Protector,* 82–84.

57. Discussion of this case is from Jenkins, "Taos Pueblo and Its Neighbors," *New Mexico Historical Review* 41:2 (1966), 95–104.

58. Translation from SANM II 16:1639–54, TW #1357, in ibid., 103.

59. Case against Luís Baca for mistreatment of Pueblo Indians, Santa Fe, February 2–20, 1792, SANM II 13:25–51, TW #1188. Fiscal Galindo Navarro to Concha, opinion on the cases of Luís María Baca and Marcos Sanchez, Chihuahua, September 13, 1793, SANM II 13:413–15, TW #1259.

60. Expert witness testimony for H.R. 3259, presented to the U.S. House of Representatives by William B. Taylor, "Cochití Lands and the Disputed Sale to Luis María Cabeza de Vaca" (expert witness testimony for H.R. 3259, presented to the U.S. House of Representatives, July 26, 1983), 36–37. Case against Juan Antonio Baca, Santa Fe, September 3–13, 1808, SANM II 16:611–29, TW #2154. See "Cochiti Indians to Regain Land Lost in 1805," *Washington Post,* June 23, 1984; and "Indians Will Get Back Stolen Land," *Oakland Tribune,* June 23, 1984.

61. See discussion of the Provincial Academic Style I and II, and the attribution of specific styles and works to Fray García, Miera y Pacheco, and the eighteenth-century Novice, in Boyd, *Popular Arts,* 96–139; and Wroth, *Christian Images,* 47–68.

62. Fray Atanasio Domínguez, *The Missions of New Mexico, 1776,* ed. Eleanor B. Adams and Fray Angélico Chávez (Albuquerque: University of New Mexico Press, 1956), 333 and 345.

63. Boyd, *Popular Arts,* 102–109.

64. Donald Robertson, "The Treatment of Architecture in the Florentine Codex of Sahagún," in *Sixteenth-Century Mexico: The Work of Sahagún,* ed. Munro S. Edmonson (Albuquerque: University of New Mexico Press, 1974), 151–64, esp. 156.

65. Willam B. Taylor, *Magistrates of the Sacred: Priests and Parishioners in Eighteenth-Century Mexico* (Stanford, Calif.: Stanford University Press, 1996), esp. 301–23, 345–46, 406–8, and 422–47.

66. Ibid., 435.

67. See Cheryl English Martin, *Governance and Society in Colonial Mexico: Chihuahua in the Eighteenth Century* (Stanford, Calif.: Stanford University Press, 1996), 97–124.

68. Instruccion formada por el colonel Don Francisco de la Concha, Governador que ha sido de la Provincia de Nuevo México para el subcesor el teniente coronel Don Fernando Chacón . . . , Chihuahua, June 28, 1794, AGN:HI 41:11, paragraph 23, 343V–344R. See David J. Weber, *The Mexican Frontier, 1821–1846: The American Southwest under Mexico* (Albuquerque: University of New Mexico Press, 1982), 60.

69. Edward H. Spicer, "Spanish-Indian Acculturation in the Southwest," *American Anthropologist* 56:3 (1954), 663–84; Edward P. Dozier, "Spanish-Catholic Influences on Rio Grande Pueblo Religion," *American Anthropologist* 60:3 (1958), 445–47; Edward P. Dozier, "The Pueblo Indians of the Southwest," *Current Anthropology* 5:2 (1964), 90; and Edward P. Dozier, "The Rio Grande Pueblo," in *Perspectives in American Indian Culture Change*, ed. Edward H. Spicer (Chicago: University of Chicago Press, 1961), 147.

70. This idea begins as early as Hubert Howe Bancroft, *History of the Pacific States of North America: Arizona and New Mexico, 1530–1888* (San Francisco: History Company, 1888), 270–71. See also Marc Simmons, "History of Pueblo-Spanish Relations to 1821," in *Southwest*, ed. Alfonso Ortiz, *Handbook of North American Indians* (Washington, D.C.: Smithsonian Institution, 1979), 9:187–91.

71. Spicer, "Spanish-Indian Acculturation," 663–84; and Dozier, "Spanish-Catholic Influences," 445–47.

72. The case appears in SANM II 13:237–40 and 13:241–326, TW #1237 and 1237a.

73. Bancroft, *Arizona and New Mexico*, 225. Substantial concern had surfaced in 1715, and a rumor circulated in 1759 that the Indians would revolt on the day of Corpus Christi, according to Tamarón, but the trials of 1793 appeared far more serious to provincial officials. See Bancroft, *Arizona and New Mexico*, 224–33; and Dr. Pedro Tamarón y Romerál, *Bishop Tamarón's Visitation of New Mexico, 1760,* ed. Eleanor B. Adams (Publications in History, 15; Albuquerque: Historical Society of New Mexico, 1954), 73–74.

74. The document is cut short at the end of Tuque's declaration. That of Juan Ramos may have followed.

75. The most recent bando before the trial concerning the regulation of interior travel had been sent by Comandante General Jacobo Ugarte y Loyola and promulgated by Governor de la Concha in Santa Fe on September 17, 1790, SANM II 12:303–14, TW #1091.

76. Comandante General Felipe de Nava to Governor Juan Bautista de Anza, Chihuahua, January 24, 1784, SANM II 10:623–24, TW #876.

77. Governor Fernando de Chacón, Santa Fe, June 18, 1798, SANM II 14:300, TW #1427. See similar sentences meted out in the case against "an Indian from San Juan," n.p., May 4–August 15, 1805, SANM II 15:555–62, TW #1869; and the case against Patricio Cerda, Santa Fe, August 5–October 3, 1805, SANM II 15:752–63, TW #1870.

78. William B. Taylor, *Drinking, Homicide, and Rebellion in Colonial Mexican Villages* (Stanford, Calif.: Stanford University Press, 1979), 113–70.

79. Case against Luís Baca for mistreatment of Pueblo Indians, Santa Fe, February 2–20, 1792, SANM II 13:25–51, TW #1188.

80. Patente of Fray Diego Muñoz Turado, Santa Clara, April 9, 1796, AASF: MI 1796 #7, 53:179–80.

81. George Kubler, *Santos: An Exhibition of the Religious Folk Art of New Mexico* (Fort Worth, Tex.: Amon Carter Museum of Western Art, 1964), 1–2; reprinted as "Santos: An Exhibition of the Religious Folk Art of New Mexico," in *Studies in Ancient American and European Art: The Collected Essays of George Kubler,* ed. Thomas F. Reese (New Haven, Conn.: Yale University Press, 1985), 61.

NOTES TO THE CONCLUSION

1. For Texas, see Jesús F. de la Teja, *San Antonio de Béxar: A Community on New Spain's Northern Frontier* (Albuquerque: University of New Mexico Press, 1995), 301–3 and 314–22; for Florida, see John Jay TePaske, "Economic Problems of the Governor," in *America's Ancient City: Spanish Saint Augustine, 1565–1763,* ed. Kathleen A. Deagan (Spanish Borderlands Sourcebooks, 25; New York: Garland Publishing, 1991), 577–608.

2. See the comparison between New Mexican markets and those in other regions of New Spain in chapter 5.

3. See Richard J. Salvucci, *Textiles and Capitalism in Mexico: An Economic History of the Obrajes, 1539–1840* (Princeton, N.J.: Princeton University Press, 1987), esp. 135–69.

4. Thomas D. Hall, *Social Change in the Southwest, 1350–1880* (Lawrence: University Press of Kansas, 1989), 147–48.

5. Josiah Gregg, *Commerce of the Prairies,* ed. Max L. Moorhead (Norman: University of Oklahoma Press, 1954), 147–48; Ward Alan Minge, "*Efectos del país:* A History of Weaving along the Rio Grande," in *Rio Grande Textiles: A New Edition of Spanish Textile Tradition of New Mexico and Colorado,* comp. and ed. Nora Fisher (Santa Fe: Museum of New Mexico Press, 1994), 18–21; and Joe Ben Wheat, "Saltillo *Sarapes* of Mexico," in *Rio Grande Textiles: A New Edition of Spanish Textile Tradition of New Mexico and Colorado,* comp. and ed. Nora Fisher (Santa Fe: Museum of New Mexico Press, 1994), 60–63.

6. Some aspects of continuity with colonial commerce are noted in Angel Moyano Pahissa, *El comercio de Santa Fe y la guerra del '47* (Mexico City: Sep Setentas, 1976).

7. Charles M. Carrillo, *Hispanic New Mexican Pottery: Evidence of Craft Specialization, 1790–1890* (Albuquerque, N.Mex.: LDP Press, 1997), esp. 45–56.

8. The bulto in Plate 18a came from J. P. Flores of Placitas, New Mexico, in 1964. The Flores family owned the figure from the time it was fashioned, and J. P.'s father had passed on the name of the santo to his son. Information from the owner, personal communication, July 24, 1989. For the attribution of Plate 18b as *Santo Jo'*, see Mitchell A. Wilder and Edgar Breitenbach, *Santos: The Religious Folk-Art of New Mexico* (Colorado Springs, Colo.: Taylor Museum, 1943), plate 12; and Robert L. Shalkop, *Wooden Saints: The Santos of New Mexico* (Feldafing, Germany: Buchheim Verlag, 1967), 44–45. The bulto was collected for the Taylor Museum of the Colorado Fine Arts Center, Colorado Springs, Colorado by H. H. Garnett and George Travis in 1936. Both of these bultos are painted in oil and indicate a date in the 1880s. However, both appear related in style to the retablos made by the "followers" or "school" of the Quill Pen Santero. The Taylor Museum has another "Job," TM 1392, collected by Frank Applegate and acquired by the museum in 1928.

9. In a related usage, see the mention of Job by Fray Toribio Motolinía to describe

the patience and faith that the Nahuatl and other Indians of the Central Valley of Mexico exhibited when sick or receiving medical treatment. Fray Toribio Motolinía, *Historia de los indios de la Nueva España* (Mexico City: Editorial Porrúa, 1984), 58–59.

10. The work of the Quill Pen Santero is generally dated 1835–1850, and that of his "school" or "followers" extended into the 1870s. See William Wroth, *Christian Images in Hispanic New Mexico* (Colorado Springs, Colo.: Taylor Museum, 1982), 99–100; and William Wroth, *Images of Penance, Images of Mercy: Southwestern Santos in the Late Nineteenth Century* (Norman: University of Oklahoma Press, 1991), 65. Both retablos in Plate 19 are shown in Frank, *New Kingdom,* plates 146 and 144.

11. The *Man of Sorrows,* or *Imago Pietatis,* represents a devotional image of Christ after the crucifixion and hence depicts his death wounds. *Ecce Homo* refers to a scene from the Passion made into a devotional image of Christ. It shows Christ after he had been whipped and mocked by the Romans, as he was presented to the Jews by Pontius Pilate. The Quill Pen Santero has apparently confused the two representations of Christ. See Gertrud Schiller, *Iconography of Christian Art,* trans. Janet Seligman (Greenwich, Conn.: New York Graphic Society, 1968), 2:76 and 197–99.

12. See Ross H. Frank, "The Life of Christ and the New Mexican Santo Tradition," *Catholic Southwest: A Journal of History and Culture* 7 (1996), 32–80.

13. The *Christ as the Man of Sorrows* at the Minneapolis Institute of Arts by Luis Morales (El Divino) provides an excellent example (Minneapolis Institute of Art, *Slide Catalog,* no. 221). The comparison with religious images found elsewhere in Mexico is based on the analysis of Gloria Fraser Giffords, *The Art of Private Devotion: Retablo Painting of Mexico* (Dallas/Fort Worth: Meadows Museum, Southern Methodist University / InterCultura, 1991), 44–46. An example of an *Ecce Homo* showing Christ standing and with his hands bound together survives in the collection of the Taylor Museum of the Colorado Fine Arts Center in Colorado Springs (TM 592). The eighteenth-century Novice santero created this example, which has much more in common with contemporary Mexican retablos than do the later examples in Plates 18 and 19.

14. For a further analysis of images of Christ in New Mexican santos and the religious response that they were created to evoke, see Frank, "Life of Christ," 32–80.

GLOSSARY OF COLONIAL SPANISH TERMS

abrigo	An overcoat made from woolen cloth woven in New Mexico.
aguardiente	Brandy or hard liquor, often of local manufacture. El Paso produced a good deal of aguardiente until it was surpassed by Parras and, to a lesser extent, Nombre de Dios, sometime around 1800 or shortly thereafter.*
alcabala	An excise tax levied on specified commodities that moved between jurisdictions, normally 2–6 percent of the value of the products.
alcalde mayor	In New Mexico, an official appointed by the governor with civil jurisdiction over the judicial and executive functions of one of the eight districts of the province; district magistrate.
alférez	A second lieutenant in the Spanish military; a standard bearer.
alhóndiga	A public granary for maize and wheat flour.
almud	A dry measure normally used for grain. There are 12 *almudes* in a fanega and 4 *cuartillos* in an almud. Also a measure of planted land (see *fanega de sembradura*).

---

* "Until now [wines] have only been produced in the Jurisdiction of El Paso del Norte. However, in the Interior of the Province they are propagating the planting of vineyards and the production of wine and brandy." Report of Governor Fernando de Chacón to Comandante General Nemesio Salcido, Santa Fe, August 28, 1803, SANM II 15:89, TW #1670a; also Fernando de Chacón, "Report of Governor Chacón, 1803," in *Coronado's Land: Essays on Daily Life in Colonial New Mexico,* ed. and trans. Marc Simmons (Albuquerque: University of New Mexico Press, 1991), 169. Tithe records show El Paso's loss of preeminence beginning around 1800. See Ross H. Frank, "From Settler to Citizen: Economic Development and Cultural Change in Late Colonial New Mexico, 1750–1820" (Ph.D. diss., University of California, Berkeley, 1992), 439–46, Table 5.

arancel   A published schedule of fees; for example, Governor Cachupín's 1754 list of prices governing Comanche trade fairs, and the tariff for religious services set in 1730 by Bishop Crespo and under review in the 1780s.

armario   An eighteenth-century term for a closed cabinet in which to store clothing.

arras   The part of a marriage ceremony in which the bridegroom gave a pledge of 13 coins to the bride. The arras was not used in New Mexico through the 1770s, in part because of the unavailability of specie.

arroba   A dry measure equivalent to 25.35 pounds; a liquid measure equivalent to 3.32 gallons.

audiencia   Royal high court of justice and appeals, organized by region in Spanish America. During the late colonial period, New Mexico fell under the jurisdiction of the Real Audiencia of Guadalajara.

ayuntamiento   The municipal council of a town or city.

bando   An official document promulgating a rule, law, event, or other official act.

bayeta   Baize; in eighteenth- and early-nineteenth-century New Mexico, a kind of simple yardage woven on the treadle loom. Later in the nineteenth century the term referred to cloth woven out of unraveled commercial baize.

belduque   A broad "peasant" knife used in the Spanish colonial period; one of the primary trade items between New Mexicans and the Comanche, Ute, Navajo, and Apache.

bretaña   Fine, bleached linen, named for its place of origin, Brittany.

bulto   A *santo* sculpted in the round, normally out of cottonwood root.

cabildo   A cathedral chapter; a municipal council; a council or chapter meeting hall.

cacique   Chief, or head spiritual or political leader. The Spanish imported the term from the Arawak in the Caribbean by way of Mexico.

Camino Real   The royal road connecting Mexico City with the north, ultimately ending in Chihuahua. From there branches carried goods and travelers to the various provincial towns and *presidios* on the northern frontier. The branch of the Camino Real that ended in Santa Fe was named the Chihuahua Trail.

Casta   The offspring of a mixed Spanish-Indian marriage. In late colonial New Mexico, this term came to mean any racial mixture. Synonymous with *mestizo*.

churro   A variety of sheep that adapted well to the semiarid conditions of New Spain. Diego de Vargas introduced churros into New Mexico in 1697. They are smaller than the

	better-known merino sheep and yield coarse, long-staple wool.
coa	A sticklike implement used for tilling in place of a hoe.
cofradía	A Catholic lay ecclesiastical brotherhood dedicated to a particular devotion and responsible for paying for specific religious services and for the maintenance of an attached church or endowed chapel.
colcha	From the word "embroidery," this term in New Mexico came to mean a thick, embroidered woolen weaving made using a distinctive couching, or "colcha" stitch.
Color Quebrado	A person of "broken color"; in other words, not white (Spanish) or dark (Indian); a half-breed.
comandante general	The commander of a political and military district, a *comandancia general.*
comercio libre	A decree of 1778 that allowed trade to the Spanish colonies in America to enter and leave Spain from all peninsular ports, not just Cádiz.
compañía volante	A special, lightly armed cavalry unit, literally a "flying company." Compañías volantes were created in 1782 by Teodoro de Croix, first *comandante general* of the *Provincias Internas,* to respond quickly to Indian raids over a greater territory than could regular presidial troops.
consulado	A merchant guild involved in fomenting trade, gathering economic information, and influencing economic policies that affected their interests.
cordón	A military cordon formed by a series of forts or troops; a caravan, normally with military escort.
costal	A dry measure equivalent to 0.5 *fanega* or 6 *almudes.*
cotone	A Pueblo Indian textile blanket made of cotton. Defined by Fray José Cayetano as "a type of wide scapular," woven by the northeastern Keres and Puname Pueblos.*
Coyote	A racial category describing the product of Spanish or *Casta (mestizo)* and Indian parents. Often referred to off-spring of Plains Indians born in Spanish households as captives or servants.
criado	Literally, a servant. In New Mexico, Plains Indian captives or slaves and Pueblo or *Casta* servants were referred to as criados.
cuartel	A military barracks.
cuartillo	One-quarter of an *almud* (see *fanega de sembradura*).
custos	The provincial head of a Franciscan *custodia* (Franciscan ecclesiastical subdivision).

*Certificaciones de las missiones . . . Provincia de Nueba Mexico, . . . estado actual & Año de 1794, n.s., n.l., n.d (attributed to Fray Cayetano José Ignacio Bernal, Misión de Belem, November 1, 1794), AASF:MI 1794 #13, 53:112.

diezmo
The ecclesiastical tax (tithe) of one-tenth collected annually on agricultural produce and the increase in livestock. Also, a tax of one-tenth levied by the royal treasury on silver produced by licensed miners.

diligencia matrimonial
An investigation of a couple seeking marriage in order
to determine whether any impediment existed, such
as consanguinity, affinity, or marriage or religious vows
made previously.

donativo
A type of voluntary contribution called for by the king
to raise emergency revenue, such as for war. These donations normally functioned as forced loans.

encomienda
A grant of tribute from Indians living on a specified tract
of land. In return for tribute (in goods or labor), the
grantee (*encomendero*) was responsible for the welfare
of the Indians and for their religious instruction as
Christians.

Españoles
Spaniards; people born in Spain. In New Mexico and
elsewhere on the northern frontier of late colonial New
Spain, Españoles came to mean people who were cultur-
ally Spanish.

estanco de tabaco
The state monopoly for tobacco set up in 1765 by José
de Gálvez as part of his program of fiscal reform in
New Spain.

fanega
A dry measure roughly equivalent to 1.5 to 2.5 bushels,
12 *almudes,* or 48 *cuartillos.* A *fanega de sembradura* was
an area sown with one fanega of maize, about 9 acres
(3.57 hectares).

feria
Trade fair held between Plains and Pueblo Indians. Taos
and Pecos were primary trade-fair locations.

fiscal
A royal attorney appointed as a watchdog over bureaucratic departments. During the second half of the eighteenth century a fiscal presided over civil and criminal
matters, and in 1780 the Crown appointed a *fiscal de
Real Hacienda.* Also an attorney for a city, municipality,
or other organization; in New Mexican *vecino* villages
and Indian *pueblos,* an official with responsibility for the
maintenance of community lands and irrigation ditches;
a *pueblo* official appointed by the missionary to assist Indians in performing their religious duties.

fondo de gratificación
A common fund provided with 10 pesos per year from
the salary of each soldier of a *presidio* company. The fund
covered the expenses of feeding and clothing captive
Indians, purchasing small gifts for visiting Indian delega-
tions, and retiring debts of soldiers who died or deserted.
Money spent from this fund on rations and hospitality
for Indians was generally repaid by the Crown.

fondo de retención   The fund of a *presidio* company created to assure that soldiers and their families had money for private expenses. The fund paid 2 reales per day and could also be used to replace worn-out or lost horses, saddlery, uniforms, or weapons.

fresada   A heavy cotton or woolen blanket. Also spelled *frasada* or *frazada* in modern Spanish.

gamuza   A heavy, good-quality buckskin used for clothing in New Mexico.

Genízaro   A captured or ransomed Indian from the nomadic tribes near New Mexico, or his or her offspring, who was baptized and acculturated into *vecino* society. A contemporary source described Genízaros as "Indians of all nations of gentiles that surround us, but all who had been, or were [at the time] servants of the *vecinos*. They had been purchased from the gentiles [and] speak no language other than Spanish." The term derived from the Moorish word "Janissary" (devoted Turkish infantrymen). Captured or ransomed Indians served within *vecino* households and generally adopted many elements of Hispanic culture. After a period of service, some Genízaros were freed from any obligation. Beginning in the 1740s, groups of landless Genízaros petitioned for and received permission from the governor to settle on lands in frontier areas, such as Abiquíu or Belén, as bulwarks against incursions by Plains Indians. Genízaros also settled San Miguel de Carnué.*

gente de razón   Literally, "people of reason": Christians, as opposed to *gentiles*, as the Plains Indians were often called. In New Mexico the term normally included the Pueblo Indians.

gentile   Literally, "Gentile": unconverted or pagan, in contrast to *gente de razón*.

grano   A monetary unit and coin valued at one-twelfth of a *real*.

habilitado   The supply master and, by virtue of the of the task, the paymaster of each *presidio* company. After the *Reglamento* of 1772, the habilitado was elected by the company.

harinero   A flour bin; in New Mexico, a wooden chest made for the storage of flour (*harina*).

índigo   A plant that produces various medium and deep blue dyes. The *Indigofera suffruticosa* variety is a native of Mexico and the West Indies and may have been used in New Mexico as well.

---

*Noticias de las misiones que ocupan los Religiosos de la regular observancia de N. S. P. S. Francisco . . . en los años 1793, 1794 . . . , SANM II, 21:538, B. M. Read Collection, NMSRCA.

intendente
: Appointee to govern an *intendencia,* a regional administrative unit introduced into New Spain between 1764 and 1790 as a part of the Bourbon reform. Intendentes replaced regional *gobernadores, corregidores,* and *alcaldes.*

jerga
: Twill-woven fabric used primarily as a floor covering and also for packing material, under mattresses, and for clothing. Also spelled *gerga, herga,* and *xerga* in colonial documents.

jícara
: A small cup or gourd. In this case, "*xicaras*" was used by Vicente Troncoso to describe Navajo pottery, clay vessels dipped in pitch to enable them to hold water.

juez hacedor
: An ecclesiastical official appointed by the bishop or the archbishop to make decisions relating to the administration of the church tithe.

junta de diezmos
: A committee made up church officials in charge of renting and collecting the *diezmo,* the ecclesiastical tax of one-tenth collected annually on agricultural produce and the increase in livestock.

kiva
: A Pueblo Indian ceremonial chamber, often constructed underground.

koshari
: A sacred clown used by the Río Grande Pueblos in both religious and social ceremonies.

legua (league)
: The Spanish league in the eighteenth century was a measure of distance covering about 2.6 miles.

libramiento
: A bill to be paid in money to the holder; essentially a *libranza* converted into specie.

libranza
: A bill of exchange employed by merchants in New Spain. Libranzas often functioned as currency among merchants and financial officials.

Lobo
: A racial category describing the product of Pueblo and Plains Indian parents, or used synonymously with *Coyote.*

maíz (maize)
: Corn, a grain native to the New World.

manojo
: A dry measure similar to a bale.

manta
: A blanket or shawl worn by men woven on a Pueblo (indigenous) loom. Measured by the wefts, the manta is longer than it is wide, in contrast to *sarapes* made on Spanish-style looms.

marco (mark)
: A monetary unit, originally composed of 8 ounces of silver.

mata
: A wild herb that grew in the mountains near Taos and Pecos. Pueblo Indians and *vecinos* used mata as a tobacco substitute when they could not obtain *punche.* Also referred to sometimes as *oja.*

medias
: Stockings woven out of wool or cotton in New Mexico and elsewhere New Spain, named for their length up to the knee.

Moqui
: The Spanish colonial designation for Hopi *pueblos,* today often spelled "Moki"; the striped or banded pattern

characteristic of early colonial Pueblo textiles. Early Anglo traders in blankets attributed the origin of this design style to the Hopi.

Mulato A racial category used generally in New Mexico to mean the offspring of a Spanish-Indian marriage. Replaced by *Casta* during the eighteenth century.

Naturale A Native, one who originally inhabited or was born in the area (indigenous).

obraje A workshop, often for the production of textiles.

obrajero An owner of or worker in an *obraje.*

oratorio A private chapel licensed by the church to use for Mass.

paño Coarse woolen cloth.

partido A district or other type of administrative division; the jurisdiction of a *teniente alcalde;* a contract governing future distribution of sheep in a herd let out to rent.

párvulo(a) A child, usually under the age of 12–15.

peso The basic monetary unit and silver coin used in finance and commercial transactions. Pesos held the value of 8 *reales* or 96 *granos.*

peso antiguo The designation for silver peso coins of the old mintage after the 1772 devaluation of the peso; also used in financial transactions after 1772 to identify the value of local goods by the customary price that originally appeared in Governor Cachupín's 1754 schedule of trade prices. Pesos de antiguos were worth 4 *reales.*

peso de plata Standard circulating silver coin in Spain and its colonial possessions, worth 8 *reales.*

peso de proyecto One of the "imaginary moneys" mentioned by Fray Morfí in his "Account of Disorders," this unit appears to represent the value of a *peso antiguo* lent at interest, literally, for a commercial project. A peso de proyecto was worth 6 *reales.*

peso de la tierra Another unit of "imaginary money" that grew out of the need to set the value of the produce that *vecinos* gave to the mission fathers in obventions, first fruits, and payments for other services. These pesos often, but not always, were worth 2 *reales* and were also called *pesos de común.*

piloncillo A cone-shaped loaf of raw sugar.

Plan de Intendencias The system of intendants extended to New Spain in 1785 by Viceroy Bernardo de Gálvez.

presidio A frontier garrison.

presidios internos Garrisons within the *Provincias Internas,* which included the Californias, New Mexico, Texas, Coahuila, Nueva Vizcaya, and Sonora.

Protector de Indios The office for the legal representation of Indians, which functioned in New Mexico from the early seventeenth

	century until around 1717 and was reestablished in 1810.
Provincias Internas	The designation for the administrative unit set up in 1776 in order to provide centralized military authority separate from the viceroy. In 1777 the Provincias Internas included the Californias, New Mexico, Texas, Coahuila, Nueva Vizcaya, and Sonora.
pueblo	A Native American town or village; a small, incorporated town.
punche	A variety of tobacco produced in New Mexico.
ranchería	A ranch (agricultural compound) inhabited by Spanish settlers; a nomadic Native American (Ute, Navajo, Apache, or Comanche) encampment.
real	A monetary unit and coin valued at one-eighth of a *peso.*
Real Audiencia	The Real Audiencia de México functioned as the royal judicial and legislative council administering affairs throughout New Spain and acting in consultation with the viceroy.
real caja	A local branch or office of the *Real Hacienda.*
real estanco	A royal monopoly, as in the *Real Estanco de Tabaco.*
Real Hacienda	The royal treasury or exchequer of Spain or New Spain.
Real Ordenanza de Intendentes	The major reorganization of the royal government of New Spain, which was signed by King Carlos III on December 4, 1786, but which took effect in 1789. Twelve intendancies were created: Yucatán, Oaxaca, Puebla, Mexico, Veracruz, Valladolid, Guanajuato, Guadalajara, Zacatecas, San Luis Potosí, Durango, and Sonora. Each indendant had a legal advisor and a lieutenant, and all were under the *superintendente subdelgado de Real Hacienda,* who also held the Intendancy of Mexico.
reducción	The forcible relocation by Spanish missionaries or civil authorities of Indian villages into larger communities. Authorities used the reducción at various times in New Mexico, the Sonoran Pimería Alta, the Californias, and elsewhere in New Spain, in order to force religious conversion and cultural change toward Spanish norms.
Reglamento	The document promulgated in 1772 reorganizing the northern frontier based on a perimeter defended by *presidios* and resident troops at royal expense.
remate	The painted crest of an altar screen or *retablo.*
repartimiento	A distribution; a system of distribution of Indian labor used in sixteenth-century New Spain; a forced distribution of trade goods to Indians on credit in exchange for Indian products. Found in many areas of colonial New Spain. The last definition was also referred to as *repartimiento de efectos.*

reredo	A painted altar screen, often made up of individual *retablos* or a series of painted *santos*.
rescate	Trade; normally used to refer to commercial activity involving barter.
retablo	Retable; a *santo* painted on a flat pine board.
Río Abajo	The southern half of the province of New Mexico, proceeding south from the Alcaldía de los Queres (south of Cochití, Jémez, and Santo Domingo Pueblos).
Río Arriba	The northern half of the province of New Mexico, proceeding north from the Alcaldía of Santa Fe (north of Pecos and Galisteo).
sabanilla	Literally "little sheet"; handspun woolen yardage woven on a treadle loom by *vecinos*.
sacristán	A Pueblo Indian official in charge of maintaining the cleanliness and order in the sacristy and the church. Pueblo Indian boys who attended the missionary were also referred to as *sacristanes*.
santero	A saint maker; in New Mexico, an itinerant craftsman who fashioned holy images for churches, chapels, and family devotional altars.
santo	A saint; an image of a saint painted on hide, canvas, linen, or wood; a carved wooden statue. See *bulto, retablo,* and *reredo*.
sarape	A blanket or shawl, worn by men, woven on a Spanish-style loom. Measured by the wefts, the sarape is shorter than it is wide, in contrast to Pueblo-made *mantas*.
sarga	Serge; a durable twill-weave fabric.
sayal	Originally a sackcloth type of fabric made for Franciscan friars, sayal came to mean a harsh, unfinished cloth woven on the treadle loom. Also spelled *sallal* in colonial documents.
semanero	A Pueblo Indian labor obligation; Pueblo workers drafted weekly to serve in the house of the governor and *alcaldes mayores* or to perform public works.
sínodo	The annual allowance paid by the Spanish government to missionaries in the provinces.
situado	The salary drawn by soldiers stationed in *presidios* or other garrisons.
teniente	A lieutenant, as in lieutenant governor or lieutenant colonel. Also *teniente alcalde,* a lieutenant mayor.
tilma	A woven blanket worn over the shoulders as a shawl, made normally of cotton.
trapiche	A household or small weaving operation; a small *obraje* of less than about twenty workers.
vara	A unit of length measuring 32.99 inches (0.838 meters).
vecindario	A neighborhood; citizenry.

vecino	A householder or resident of a community; citizen; neighbor.
venado	New Mexican elk. Also referred to in documents as *alazán venado,* or sorrel deer.
viga	A wooden ceiling beam made from a pine trunk laid across the width of an adobe building to support the roof. For practical purposes the length of the vigas determined the maximum width of the building.
villa	An incorporated settlement of the second rank; smaller than a city (*ciudad*) but larger than a *pueblo.*
visita	A mission without a resident priest, administered to by a priest residing in another nearby parish; a formal inspection by a religious or civil official of his jurisdiction.
visitador	A religious or secular official responsible for carrying out a formal inspection (*visita*).

BIBLIOGRAPHY

ARCHIVAL SOURCES

Archives of the Archdiocese of Santa Fe, New Mexico

Book of Baptisms
Book of Burials
Diligencias Matrimoniales
Loose Documents, Mission

Archivo de Catedral de Durango, Mexico

Archivo del Cabildo
Archivo Histórico, Ramo de Diezmos
Archivo Histórico, Ramo de Padrones
Archivo Histórico, Ramo de Varios

*Archivo Franciscano, Biblioteca San Augustín
(old Biblioteca Nacional), Mexico City*

Archivo General de Indias, Seville

Ramo de Guadalajara

Archivo General de la Nación, Mexico City

Mapoteca
Ramo de Alcabalas
Ramo de Californias
Ramo de Historias
Ramo de Provincias Internas
Ramo de Reales Cédulas

Archivo Histórico, Palacio Gobierno, Durango, Mexico

Archivo Histórico, Palacio Municipal, Chihuahua, Mexico

Sección Civil
Sección Hacienda
Sección Notaria

Bonilla, Antonio de. "Apuntes históricos sobre el Nuevo México."
Copy of September 3, 1903. AGN:HI 25:7, Bancroft Library,
University of California, Berkeley (MM–167)

Hemenway Collection, Tozzer Library,
Harvard University, Cambridge, Massachusetts

Pinart Collection, Bancroft Library, University of California, Berkeley, California

Registro de Propiedades, Archivos Históricos, Chihuahua, Chihuahua

Ritch Collection, Huntington Library, San Marino, California

Spanish Archives of New Mexico,
New Mexico State Records Center and Archives, Santa Fe, New Mexico

Series I, land grant records
Series II, provincial records

PRINTED PRIMARY SOURCES

Bonavía, Bernardo. "Lista o noticia de las jurisdicciones . . . de la provincia de Nueva Vizcaya, año de 1803." In *Descripciones económicas regionales de Nueva España. Provincias del Norte, 1790–1814,* compiled by Enrique Florescano and Isabel Gil Sánchez, 85–96. Mexico City: Instituto Nacional de Antropología e Historia, 1976.

Bonilla, Antonio de. "Notes Concerning New Mexico." Translated by George P. Hammond. In *Antonio de Bonilla and Spanish Plans for the Defense of New Mexico, 1772–1778,* edited by Alfred Barnaby Thomas, 1:191–201. New York: Kraus Reprint, 1969.

Briggs, Walter. *Without Noise of Arms: The 1776 Domínguez-Escalante Search for a Route from Santa Fe to Monterey.* Flagstaff, Ariz.: Northland Press, 1976.

Brown, Lorin W., with Charles L. Briggs and Marta Weigle. *Hispano Folklife of New Mexico: The Lorin W. Brown Federal Writers' Project Manuscripts.* Albuquerque: University of New Mexico Press, 1978.

Campa, Arthur Leon. *Los Comanches: A New Mexican Folk Drama.* University of New Mexico Bulletin, Language Series, 7:1. Albuquerque: University of New Mexico Press, 1942.

Chacón, Fernando de. "The Chacón Economic Report of 1803." *New Mexico Historical Review* 60:1 (1985), 65–88.

———. "Report of Governor Chacón, 1803." In *Coronado's Land: Essays on Daily Life in Colonial New Mexico,* edited and translated by Marc Simmons, 162–72. Albuquerque: University of New Mexico Press, 1991.

Concha, Don Fernando de la. "Diary of Colonel Don Fernando de la Concha." Edited by Adlai Feather. *New Mexico Historical Review* 34:4 (1959), 285–303.

Correll, J. Lee. *Through White Man's Eyes: A Contribution to Navajo History.* 6 vols. Window Rock, Ariz.: Navajo Heritage Center, 1979.

Cortés, José. *Views from the Apache Frontier: Report on the Northern Provinces of New Spain.* Edited by Elizabeth A. H. John. Translated by John Wheat. Norman: University of Oklahoma Press, 1989.

Cutter, Donald C., trans. "Statistical Report on New Mexico, 1765." *New Mexico Historical Review* 50:4 (1975), 347–52.

Domínguez, Fray Francisco Atanasio. *The Missions of New Mexico, 1776.* Translated and edited by Eleanor B. Adams and Fray Angélico Chávez. Albuquerque: University of New Mexico Press, 1956.

Espinosa, Aurelio M. *Los Comanches: A Spanish Heroic Play of the Year 1780.* University of New Mexico Bulletin, Language Series, 1:1. Albuquerque: University of New Mexico Press, 1907.

Espinosa, Gilberto. "Los Comanches." *New Mexico Quarterly* 1:2 (1931), 133–46.

Espinosa, José Manuel. *Spanish Folk Tales from New Mexico.* Memoirs of the American Folklore Society, 30. New York: G. E. Stechart, 1937. Reprinted, Millwood, N.Y.: Kraus Reprint, 1976.

Fonseca, Fabián de, and Carlos de Urrutia. *Historia general de Real Hacienda escrita por orden del virrey, conde de Revillagigedo.* 6 vols. Mexico City: Imprima por V. G. Torres, 1853.

Fora, Nicolás de la. *The Frontiers of New Spain.* Edited and translated by Lawrence Kinnaird. Quivira Society Publications, 13. Berkeley: Quivira Society, 1958.

———. *Relación del viaje que hizo a los Presidios Internos situados en la frontera de la América Septentrional.* Edited by Vito Alessio Robles. Mexico City: Editorial Pedro Robredo, 1939.

Gálvez, Bernardo de. *Instructions for Governing the Interior Provinces of New Spain, 1786.* Edited and translated by Donald E. Worcester. Quivira Society Publications, 12. Berkeley, Calif.: Quivira Society, 1951. Reprinted, New York: Arno Press, 1967.

Gregg, Josiah. *Commerce of the Prairies.* Edited by Max L. Moorhead. Norman: University of Oklahoma Press, 1954.

Hackett, Charles W., trans. and ed. *Historical Documents Relating to New Mexico and Nueva Vizcaya, and Approaches Thereto, to 1773.* Vol. 3. Carnegie Institute Publication 330. Washington, D.C.: Carnegie Institute, 1937.

Hammond, George P. "The Zúñiga Journal, Tucson to Santa Fe: The Opening of a Spanish Trade Route, 1788–1795." *New Mexico Historical Review* 3:1 (1931), 40–51.

John, Elizabeth A. H., ed. "Inside the Comanchería, 1785: The Diary of Pedro Vial and Francisco Xavier Chaves." Translated by Adán Benavides, Jr. *Southwestern Historical Quarterly* 98:1 (1994), 26–56.

Matson, Daniel S., and Albert H. Schroeder, trans. and eds. "Cordero's Description of the Apache, 1796." *New Mexico Historical Review* 32:4 (1957), 335–56.

Mendinueta, Pedro Fermín de. *Indian and Mission Affairs in New Mexico, 1773.* Edited and translated by Marc Simmons. Santa Fe, N.Mex.: Stagecoach Press, 1965.

————. "Indian and Mission Affairs in 1773." In *Coronado's Land: Essays on Daily Life in Colonial New Mexico,* edited and translated by Marc Simmons, 118–26. Albuquerque: University of New Mexico Press, 1991.

Morfí, Fray Juan Augustín de. *Account of Disorders in New Mexico, 1778.* Edited and translated by Marc Simmons. Isleta Pueblo: Historical Society of New Mexico, 1977.

————. "Account of Disorders, 1778." In *Coronado's Land: Essays on Daily Life in Colonial New Mexico,* edited and translated by Marc Simmons, 127–61. Albuquerque: University of New Mexico Press, 1991.

————. "Geographical Description of New Mexico." In *Forgotten Frontiers: A Study of the Spanish-Indian Policy of Juan Bautista de Anza, Governor of New Mexico, 1777– 1787,* translated and edited by Alfred Barnaby Thomas, 85–114. Norman: University of Oklahoma Press, 1932.

Motolinía, Fray Toribio. *Historia de los indios de la Nueva España.* Mexico City: Editorial Porrúa, 1984.

O'Crouley, Don Pedro Alonso. *A Description of the Kingdom of New Spain, 1774.* Translated and edited by Séan Galvin. San Francisco: John Howell Books, 1972.

Pike, Zebulon Montgomery. *The Journals of Zebulon Montgomery Pike.* 2 vols. Edited by Donald Jackson. Norman: University of Oklahoma Press, 1966.

Pino, Don Pedro Bautista, Licenciado Don Antonio Barreiro, and Agustín de Escudero. *Three New Mexican Chronicles.* Translated and edited by H. Bailey Carroll and J. Villasana Haggard. Quivira Society Publications, 11. Albuquerque, N.Mex.: Quivira Society, 1942. Reprinted, New York: Arno Press, 1967.

Simmons, Marc. "The Chacón Economic Report of 1803." *New Mexico Historical Review* 60:1 (1985), 65–88.

Tamarón y Romerál, Dr. Pedro. "Bishop Tamarón's Visitation of New Mexico, 1760." *New Mexico Historical Review* 28:2 (1953), 81–114.

————. "Bishop Tamarón's Visitation of New Mexico, 1760." *New Mexico Historical Review* 28:3 (1953), 192–221.

————. "Bishop Tamarón's Visitation of New Mexico, 1760." *New Mexico Historical Review* 28:4 (1953), 291–315.

————. "Bishop Tamarón's Visitation of New Mexico, 1760." *New Mexico Historical Review* 29:1 (1954), 41–47.

————. *Bishop Tamarón's Visitation of New Mexico, 1760.* Edited by Eleanor B. Adams. Publications in History, 15. Albuquerque: Historical Society of New Mexico, 1954.

————. *Demostración del Vatismo Obispado de la Nueva Vizcaya—1765.* Edited by Vito Alessio Robles. Biblioteca Historical Mexicana de Obras Inéditas. Mexico City: Antigua Librería Robredo, de José Porrúa e Hijos, 1937.

TePaske, John J., and José and Mari Luz Hernández Palomo. *La Real Hacienda de Nueva España: La Caja de México (1576–1816).* Colección Científica Fuentes, 1. Mexico City: Instituto Nacional de Antropología e Historia, 1976.

TePaske, John J., and Herbert S. Klein. *Ingresos y egresos de la Real Hacienda de Nueva*

España. Colección Científicas Fuentes, 41 : 1. Mexico City: Instituto Nacional de Antropología e Historia, 1986.

Thomas, Alfred Barnaby, trans. and ed. *Forgotten Frontiers: A Study of the Spanish-Indian Policy of Juan Bautista de Anza, Governor of New Mexico, 1777–1787*. Norman: University of Oklahoma Press, 1932.

———. "Governor Mendinueta's Proposals for the Defense of New Mexico, 1772–1779." *New Mexico Historical Review* 6 : 1 (1931), 21–39.

———. *The Plains Indians and New Mexico, 1751–1778*. Coronado Cuarto Centennial Publication No. 11. Albuquerque: University of New Mexico Press, 1940.

———. *Teodoro de Croix and the Northern Frontier of New Spain, 1776–1783*. Norman: University of Oklahoma Press, 1941.

Velázquez, María del Carmen. *Notas sobre sirvientes de las Californias y proyecto de obraje en Nuevo México*. Jornadas, 105. Mexico City: El Colegio de México, 1984.

SECONDARY SOURCES

Adams, E. Charles. "The Katsina Cult: A Western Pueblo Perspective." In *Kachinas in the Pueblo World*, edited by Polly Schaafsma, 35–46. Albuquerque: University of New Mexico Press, 1994.

Ahlborn, Richard E. "Frontier Possessions: The Evidence from Colonial Documents." In *Colonial Frontiers: Art and Life in Spanish New Mexico*, edited by Christine Mather, 35–58. Santa Fe, N.Mex.: Ancient City Press, 1983.

———. "Glossary of Material Culture Terms in Documentary Sources." In *Colonial Frontiers: Art and Life in Spanish New Mexico*, edited by Christine Mather, 59–70. Santa Fe, N.Mex.: Ancient City Press, 1983.

Ahlborn, Richard E., Pauline Núñez, and Marvette Perez. "Material Culture Terms from the Report of Fray Atanasio Domínguez on the Missions of New Mexico." *Southwestern Mission Research Center Newsletter* 1990 (insert and corrected version, 1992).

Aragón, Janie Louise. "The People of Santa Fe in the 1790s." *Aztlán* 7 : 3 (1976), 391–418.

Archuleta-Sagel, Teresa. "Textiles." In *Spanish New Mexico: The Spanish Colonial Arts Society Collection*, edited by Donna Pierce and Marta Weigle, 1 : 144–63. Santa Fe: Museum of New Mexico Press, 1996.

August, Jack. "Balance-of-Power Diplomacy in New Mexico: Governor Fernando de la Concha and the Indian Policy of Conciliation." *New Mexico Historical Review* 56 : 2 (1981), 141–60.

Baird, Joseph A., Jr. *Los retablos del siglo XVIII en el sur de España, Portugal, y México*. Mexico City: Universidad Nacional Autónoma de México, 1987.

Bakewell, P. J. *Silver Mining and Society in Colonial Mexico: Zacatecas, 1546–1700*. Cambridge, England: Cambridge University Press, 1971.

Bancroft, Hubert Howe. *History of the Pacific States of North America: Arizona and New Mexico, 1530–1888*. Vol. 12. San Francisco: History Company, 1888.

Barbier, Jacques A., and Mark A. Burkholder. "Critique of Stanley J. Stein's 'Bureaucracy and Business in the Spanish Empire, 1759–1804: Failure of a Bourbon Reform in Mexico and Peru.'" *Hispanic American Historical Review* 62 : 3 (1982), 1–28. (Includes Stanley Stein's reply.)

Bargellini, Clara. *La Catedral de Chihuahua.* Mexico City: Universidad Nacional Autónoma de México, 1984.

Batkin, Jonathan. *Pottery of the Pueblos of New Mexico, 1700–1940.* Colorado Springs, Colo.: Taylor Museum, 1987.

Baxter, John O. *Las Carneradas: Sheep Trade in New Mexico, 1700–1860.* Albuquerque: University of New Mexico Press, 1987.

————. *Spanish Irrigation in Taos Valley.* Santa Fe: New Mexico State Engineer Office, 1990.

Bean, J. M. W. "The Black Death: The Crisis and Its Social and Economic Consequences." In *The Black Death: The Impact of the Fourteenth-Century Plague,* edited by Daniel Williman, 23–38. Binghamton, N.Y.: Center for Medieval and Early Renaissance Studies, 1982.

Beck, Warren A., and Ynez D. Haase. *Historical Atlas of the American West.* Norman: University of Oklahoma Press, 1989.

Berlant, Anthony, and Mary Hunt Kahlenburg. *The Navajo Blanket.* Los Angeles: Praeger Publishers, in association with the Los Angeles County Museum, 1972.

Bobb, Bernard E. *The Viceregency of Antonio María Bucareli in New Spain, 1771–1779.* Austin: University of Texas Press, 1962.

Bol, Marsha. "The Anonymous Artist of Laguna and the New Mexican Altar Screen." M.A. thesis, University of New Mexico, 1980.

Borah, Woodrow. *Justice by Insurance: The General Indian Court of Colonial Mexico and the Legal Aides of the Half-Real.* Berkeley: University of California Press, 1983.

————. "Tithe Collection in the Bishopric of Oaxaca, 1601–1867." *Hispanic American Historical Review* 19:4 (1949), 498–517.

Bowen, Dorothy Boyd. "A Brief History of Spanish Textile Production in the Southwest." In *Spanish Textile Tradition of New Mexico and Colorado,* edited by Nora Fisher, 5–7. Santa Fe: Museum of New Mexico Press, 1979.

————. "Introductory Remarks." In *Spanish Textile Tradition of New Mexico and Colorado,* edited by Nora Fisher, 54–56. Santa Fe: Museum of New Mexico Press, 1979.

Bowen, Dorothy Boyd, and Trish Spillman. "Appendix D: Natural and Synthetic Dyes." In *Spanish Textile Tradition of New Mexico and Colorado,* edited by Nora Fisher, 207–11. Santa Fe: Museum of New Mexico Press, 1979.

Boyd, E. *Popular Arts of Colonial New Mexico.* Albuquerque: University of New Mexico Press, 1974.

Brading, David A. "Comments on 'The Economic Cycle in Bourbon Central Mexico: A Critique of the Recaudación del diezmo líquido en pesos.'" *Hispanic American Historical Review* 69:3 (1989), 531–37.

————. *The First America.* Cambridge, England: Cambridge University Press, 1991.

————. *Haciendas and Ranchos in the Mexican Bajío: León, 1700–1860.* Cambridge, England: Cambridge University Press, 1978.

————. *Miners and Merchants in Bourbon Mexico, 1763–1810.* Cambridge, England: Cambridge University Press, 1971.

Briggs, Charles. "The Politics of Discursive Authority in Research on the 'Invention of Tradition.'" *Cultural Anthropology* 11:4 (1994), 435–79.

Brooks, James F. "'This Evil Extends Especially . . . to the Feminine Sex': Negotiating Captivity in the New Mexico Borderlands." *Feminist Studies* 22:2 (1996), 279–309.

Brugge, David M. *Navajos in the Catholic Church Records of New Mexico, 1694–1875.*

Research Reports, 1. Window Rock, Ariz.: Research Section, Parks and Recreation Department, Navajo Tribe, 1968.

———. *Navajos in the Catholic Church Records of New Mexico, 1694–1875*. Rev. ed. Tsaile, Ariz.: Navajo Community College Press, 1985.

Bustamante, Adrian. "'The Matter Was Never Resolved': The Casta System in Colonial New Mexico, 1693–1823." *New Mexico Historical Review* 66:2 (1991), 143–64.

Bustamante, Miguel E. "Aspectos históricos y epidemiológicos del hambre en México." In *Ensayos sobre la historia de las epidemias en México*, edited by Enrique Florescano and Elsa Malvido, 1:37–66. Mexico City: Instituto Mexicano del Seguro Social, 1982.

Cañizales Méndez, Franklins Alberto. "El sector ganadero en la región de Durango en el período colonial (1750–1820): Una aproximación histórica regional." Maestría thesis, Universidad Nacional Autónoma de México, 1986.

Carrillo, Charles M. *Hispanic New Mexican Pottery: Evidence of Craft Specialization, 1790–1890*. Albuquerque, N.Mex.: LDP Press, 1997.

Cash, Marie Romero. *Santos: Enduring Images of Northern New Mexican Village Churches*. Niwot: University of Colorado Press, 1999.

Chapman, Kenneth M., and Francis H. Harlow. *The Pottery of San Ildefonso Pueblo*. Monograph Series No. 28. Santa Fe, N.Mex.: School of American Research, 1970.

Chávez, Fray Angélico. *La conquistadora*. Paterson, N.J.: St. Anthony Guild Press, 1954.

———. "Early Settlements in the Mora Valley." *El Palacio* 62:11 (1955), 318–24.

———. "The Penitentes of New Mexico." *New Mexico Historical Review* 29:2 (1954), 97–123.

Coatsworth, John H. "Comments on 'The Economic Cycle in Bourbon Central Mexico: A Critique of the Recaudación del diezmo líquido en pesos.'" *Hispanic American Historical Review* 69:3 (1989), 538–44.

"Cochiti Indians to Regain Land Lost in 1805." *Washington Post*, June 23, 1984.

Cook, Sherburne F. *The Population of the California Indians, 1769–1970*. Berkeley: University of California Press, 1976.

Cook, Sherburne F., and Woodrow Borah. *Essays in Population History*. 3 vols. Berkeley: University of California Press, 1979.

Cooper, Donald B. *Epidemic Disease in Mexico City, 1761–1813*. Austin: University of Texas Press, 1965.

Cordell, Linda S. "Eastern Anasazi." In *Southwest*, edited by Alfonso Ortiz, 131–51. Vol. 9 of *Handbook of North American Indians*. Washington, D.C.: Smithsonian Institution, 1979.

Cuello, José. *El norte, el noreste y Saltillo en la historia colonial de México*. Saltillo, Mexico: Archivo Municipal de Saltillo, 1990.

Cutter, Charles R. *The Legal Culture of Northern New Spain*. Albuquerque: University of New Mexico Press, 1995.

———. *The Protector de Indios in Colonial New Mexico, 1659–1821*. Albuquerque: University of New Mexico Press, 1986.

Deans-Smith, Susan. *Bureaucrats, Planters, and Workers: The Making of the Tobacco Monopoly in Bourbon Mexico*. Austin: University of Texas Press, 1992.

De la Teja, Jesús F. *San Antonio de Béxar: A Community on New Spain's Northern Frontier*. Albuquerque: University of New Mexico Press, 1995.

Del Río, Ignacio. *La aplicación regional de las reformas borbónicas en Nueva España: Sonora y Sinaloa, 1768–1787*. Serie de historia novohispana, 55. Mexico City: Universidad Nacional Autónoma de México, Instituto de Investigaciones Históricas, 1995.

Dickey, Roland F. *New Mexico Village Arts*. Albuquerque: University of New Mexico Press, 1949.

Dillingham, Rick, with Melinda Elliot. *Acoma and Laguna Pottery*. Santa Fe, N.Mex.: School of American Research Press, 1992.

Dobyns, Henry F. *Their Number Become Thinned: Native American Population Dynamics in Eastern North America*. Knoxville: University of Tennessee Press in cooperation with the Newberry Library Center for the History of the American Indian, 1983.

Dozier, Edward P. *The Pueblo Indians of North America*. New York: Holt, Rinehart and Winston, 1970.

———. "The Pueblo Indians of the Southwest." *Current Anthropology* 5:2 (1964), 79–97.

———. "The Rio Grande Pueblo." In *Perspectives in American Indian Culture Change*, edited by Edward H. Spicer, 94–166. Chicago: University of Chicago Press, 1961.

———. "Spanish-Catholic Influences on Rio Grande Pueblo Religion." *American Anthropologist* 60:3 (1958), 441–48.

Eggan, Fred. *Social Organization of the Western Pueblos*. Chicago: University of Chicago Press, 1950.

Espinosa, Aurelio M. *The Folklore of Spain in the American Southwest: Traditional Spanish Folk Literature in Northern New Mexico and Southern Colorado*. Edited by J. Manuel Espinosa. Norman: University of Oklahoma Press, 1985.

Espinosa, José Edmundo. *Saints in the Valley: Christian Sacred Images in the History, Life, and Folk Art of Spanish New Mexico*. Albuquerque: University of New Mexico Press, 1960.

———. *Saints in the Valley: Christian Sacred Images in the History, Life, and Folk Art of Spanish New Mexico*. Rev. ed. Albuquerque: University of New Mexico Press, 1967.

Farnsworth, Paul, and Robert H. Jackson. "Cultural, Economic, and Demographic Change in the Missions of Alta California: The Case of Nuestra Señora de la Soledad." In *The New Latin American Mission History*, edited by Erick Langer and Robert H. Jackson, 109–29. Lincoln: University of Nebraska Press, 1995.

Fehrenbach, T. R. *Comanches: The Destruction of a People*. New York: Alfred A. Knopf, 1974.

Fenton, William Nelson. *Factionalism at Taos Pueblo, New Mexico*. Bureau of American Ethnology Bulletin 164. Washington, D.C.: Bureau of American Ethnology, 1957.

Ferg, Alan. *Historic Archeology on the San Antonio de las Huertas Grant, Sandoval County, New Mexico*. CASA Papers, 3. Cortez, Colo.: Complete Archeological Service Association, 1984.

Fisher, Nora. "The Treadle Loom." In *Spanish Textile Tradition of New Mexico and Colorado*, edited by Nora Fisher, 192–95. Santa Fe: Museum of New Mexico Press, 1979.

Flores, Dan. "Bison Ecology and Bison Diplomacy: The Southern Plains from 1800 to 1850." *Journal of American History* 78:2 (1991), 465–85.

Florescano, Enrique. *Precios del maíz y crisis agrícolas en México (1708–1810)*. Mexico City: El Colegio de México, 1969.

———. *Precios del maíz y crisis agrícolas en México (1708–1810)*. Rev. ed. Mexico City: Ediciones Era, 1986.

Foster, Morris. *Being Comanche: A Social History of an American Indian Community.* Tucson: University of Arizona Press, 1991.

Frank, Larry. *The New Kingdom of the Saints.* Santa Fe, N.Mex.: Red Crane Books, 1992.

Frank, Larry, and Francis H. Harlow. *Historic Pottery of the Pueblo Indians, 1600–1880.* Boston: New York Graphic Society, 1974.

———. *Historic Pottery of the Pueblo Indians, 1600–1880.* 2d ed. West Chester, Pa.: Schiffer Publishing, 1990.

Frank, Ross. "'And One Can Only See the Marks': Tithe Rentals and Economic Development in Late Colonial New Mexico." Forthcoming.

———. "Changing Pueblo Indian Pottery Tradition: The Underside of Economic Development in Late Colonial New Mexico, 1750–1820." *Journal of the Southwest* 33:3 (1991), 282–321.

———. "From Settler to Citizen: Economic Development and Cultural Change in Late Colonial New Mexico, 1750–1820." Ph.D. diss., University of California, Berkeley, 1992.

———. "The Life of Christ and the New Mexican Santo Tradition." *Catholic Southwest: A Journal of History and Culture* 7 (1996), 32–80.

Garavaglia, Juan Carlos, and Juan Carlos Grosso. *Las alcabalas novohispañas (1776–1821).* Mexico City: Archivo General de la Nación, 1987.

Garner, Richard. "An Exchange on the Eighteenth-Century Mexican Economy." *Americas* 54:1 (1997), 109–23.

Garner, Richard L., with Spiro E. Stefanou. *Economic Growth and Change in Bourbon Mexico.* Gainesville: University Press of Florida, 1993.

Genicot, Léopold. "Crisis: From the Middle Ages to Modern Times." In *The Cambridge Economic History of Europe,* edited by M. M. Postan, 660–94. 2d ed. Cambridge, England: Cambridge University Press, 1966.

Gerald, Rex E. "Spanish Presidios of the Late Eighteenth Century in Northern New Spain." *Museum of New Mexico Research Records* 7 (1968), 7–60.

Gerhard, Peter. *The North Frontier of New Spain.* Princeton, N.J.: Princeton University Press, 1982.

Giffords, Gloria Fraser. *The Art of Private Devotion: Retablo Painting of Mexico.* Dallas / Fort Worth: Meadows Museum, Southern Methodist University / InterCultura, 1991.

Goler, Gustavo Victor. "Technical Report for the Restoration of the Altar Screen on the North Nave at La Iglesia de Santa Cruz de la Cañada, Santa Cruz, New Mexico." Unpublished report, 1997.

Gootenberg, Paul. "On Salamanders, Pyramids, and Mexico's 'Growth-without-Change': Anachronistic Reflections on a Case of Bourbon New Spain." *Colonial Latin American Review* 5:1 (1996), 117–27.

Griffen, Willam B. *Apaches at War and Peace: The Janos Presidio, 1750–1858.* Albuquerque: University of New Mexico Press, 1988.

Gutiérrez, Ramón A. *When Jesus Came, the Corn Mothers Went Away: Marriage, Sexuality, and Power in New Mexico, 1500–1846.* Stanford, Calif.: Stanford University Press, 1991.

Haines, Francis. "The Northward Spread of Horses among the Plains Indians." *American Anthropologist* n.s., 40:3 (1938), 429–37.

———. *The Plains Indians.* New York: Thomas Y. Crowell, 1976.

Hall, G. Emlen. "The Pueblo Grant Labyrinth." In *Land, Water, and Culture: New Perspectives on Hispanic Land Grants,* edited by Charles L. Briggs and John R. Van Ness, 67–138. Albuquerque: University of New Mexico Press, 1987.

Hall, Thomas D. *Social Change in the Southwest, 1350–1880.* Lawrence: University Press of Kansas, 1989.

Hamnett, Brian R. *Politics and Trade in Southern Mexico, 1750–1821.* Cambridge, England: Cambridge University Press, 1971.

Harlow, Francis H. "Glaze-Matte Transitions in Pueblo Pottery." Unpublished book manuscript. 1983.

———. *Matte-Paint Pottery of the Tewa, Keres, and Zuni Pueblos.* Albuquerque: Museum of New Mexico Press, 1973.

Hatcher, John. *Plague, Population, and the English Economy, 1348–1530.* Studies in Economic and Social History, 13. London: Macmillan, 1977.

Hawley, Florence H. "Pueblo Indian Social Organization as a Lead to Pueblo History." *American Anthropologist* 39:3 (1937), 504–22.

Hedges, Ken, and Alfred Edward Dittert Jr. *Heritage in Clay: The 1912 Pueblo Pottery Collections of Wesley Bradfield and Thomas S. Dozier,* San Diego Museum of Man Papers, 17. San Diego, Calif.: San Diego Museum, 1984.

Hernández Sánchez Barba, Mario. *Juan Bautista de Anza: Un hombre de Fronteras.* Madrid: Publicaciones Españolas, 1962.

Horgan, Paul. *The Saintmaker's Christmas Eve.* New York: Farrar, Straus and Cudahy, 1955.

Horvath, Steven M., Jr. "The Social and Political Organization of the Genízaros of Plaza de Nuestra Señora de los Dolores de Belén, New Mexico, 1740–1812." Ph.D. diss., Brown University, 1979.

"Indians Will Get Back Stolen Land." *Oakland Tribune,* June 23, 1984.

Jackson, Robert H. "Grain Supply, Congregation, and Demographic Patterns in the Missions of Northwestern New Spain." *Journal of the West* 36:1 (1997), 19–25.

———. *Indian Population Decline: The Missions of Northwestern New Spain, 1687–1840.* Albuquerque: University of New Mexico Press, 1994.

Jackson, Robert H., and Edward Castillo, *Indians, Franciscans, and Spanish Colonization.* Albuquerque: University of New Mexico Press, 1995.

Jenkins, Myra Ellen. "Spanish Land Grants in the Tewa Area." *New Mexico Historical Review* 47:2 (1972), 113–34.

———. "Taos Pueblo and Its Neighbors." *New Mexico Historical Review* 41:2 (1966), 85–114.

Jeter, James, and Paula Marie Juelke. *The Saltillo Sarape: An Exhibition Organized by the Santa Barbara Museum of Art.* Santa Barbara, Calif.: New World Arts, 1978.

John, Elizabeth A. H. *Storms Brewed in Other Men's Worlds: The Confrontation of Indians, Spanish, and French in the Southwest, 1540–1795.* College Station: Texas A&M University Press, 1975.

Johnson, Lyman L., and Enrique Tandeter, eds. *Essays on the Price History of Eighteenth-Century Latin America.* Albuquerque: University of New Mexico Press, 1990.

Jones, Oakah L., Jr. *Nueva Vizcaya: Heartland of the Spanish Frontier.* Albuquerque: University of New Mexico Press, 1988.

———. *Los Paisanos: Spanish Settlers on the Northern Frontier of New Spain.* Norman: University of Oklahoma Press, 1979.

————. "Pueblo Indian Auxiliaries in New Mexico, 1763–1821." *New Mexico Historical Review* 37:2 (1962), 81–109.

————. *Pueblo Warriors and Spanish Conquest.* Norman: University of Oklahoma Press, 1966.

Kavanagh, Thomas W. *Comanche Political History: An Ethnological Perspective, 1700–1875.* Lincoln: University of Nebraska Press, 1996.

Keen, M. H. *England in the Later Middle Ages.* London: Methuen, 1973.

Kelly, Henry W. "Franciscan Missions of New Mexico, 1740–1760." *New Mexico Historical Review* 15:4 (1940), 345–68.

————. "Franciscan Missions of New Mexico, 1740–1760." *New Mexico Historical Review* 16:1 (1941), 41–69.

————. "Franciscan Missions of New Mexico, 1740–1760." *New Mexico Historical Review* 16:2 (1941), 148–83.

————. *Franciscan Missions of New Mexico, 1740–1760.* Historical Society of New Mexico Publications in History, 10. Albuquerque: Historical Society of New Mexico, 1941.

Kenner, Charles L. *A History of New Mexican–Plains Indian Relations.* Norman: University of Oklahoma Press, 1969.

Kent, Kate Peck. "Spanish, Navajo, or Pueblo? A Guide to the Identification of Nineteenth-Century Southwestern Textiles." In *Hispanic Arts and Ethnohistory in the Southwest,* edited by Marta Weigle, Claudia Larcombe, and Samuel Larcombe, 135–67. Santa Fe, N.Mex.: Ancient City Press, 1983.

Kessell, John L. *Kiva, Cross, and Crown: The Pecos Indians and New Mexico, 1540–1840.* Washington, D.C.: National Park Service, U.S. Department of the Interior, 1979.

Keur, Dorothy L. "A Chapter in Navaho-Pueblo Relations." *American Antiquity* 10:1 (1944), 75–76.

Kicza, John E. *Colonial Entrepreneurs: Families and Business in Bourbon Mexico City.* Albuquerque: University of New Mexico Press, 1983.

————. *Empresarios coloniales: Familias y negocios en la ciudad de México durante los Borbones.* Mexico City: Fondo de Cultura Económica, 1986.

Kinnaird, Lawrence. "The Spanish Tobacco Monopoly in New Mexico, 1766–1767." *New Mexico Historical Review* 21:4 (1946), 328–39.

Kubler, George. "Indianism, *Mestizaje,* and *Indigenismo* as Classical, Medieval, and Modern Traditions in Latin America." In *Studies in Ancient American and European Art: The Collected Essays of George Kubler,* edited by Thomas F. Reese, 75–80. New Haven, Conn.: Yale University Press, 1985.

————. *Religious Architecture of New Mexico.* Colorado Springs, Colo.: Taylor Museum, 1940. Reprinted, Chicago: Rio Grande Press, 1962.

————. *Santos: An Exhibition of the Religious Folk Art of New Mexico.* Fort Worth, Tex.: Amon Carter Museum of Western Art, 1964.

————. "Santos: An Exhibition of the Religious Folk Art of New Mexico." In *Studies in Ancient American and European Art: The Collected Essays of George Kubler,* edited by Thomas F. Reese, 61–65. New Haven, Conn.: Yale University Press, 1985.

Lange, Yvonne. "In Search of San Acacio: The Impact of Industrialization on Santos Worldwide." *El Palacio* 94:1 (1987), 18–24.

————. "Lithography, an Agent of Technological Change in Religious Folk Art: A Thesis." *Western Folklore* 23:1 (1974), 51–64.

Levett, A. Elizabeth. *The Black Death on the Estates of the See of Winchester.* Vol. 5, No. 9 of *Oxford Studies in Social and Legal History,* edited by Paul Vinogradoff. Oxford: Clarendon Press, 1916.

Lindo-Fuentes, Héctor. "Comments on 'The Economic Cycle in Bourbon Central Mexico: A Critique of the Recaudación del diezmo líquido en pesos.'" *Hispanic American Historical Review* 69:3 (1989), 545–48.

Loomis, Noel M., and Abraham P. Nasatir. *Pedro Vial and the Roads to Santa Fe.* Norman: University of Oklahoma Press, 1967.

López de Mañon, Edgardo, and Ignacio del Río. "La reforma institucional Borbónica." In *Tres siglos de historia sonorense (1530–1830),* edited by Sergio Ortega Noriega and Ignacio del Río, 287–326. Mexico City: Universidad Nacional Autónoma de México, 1993.

Lynch, John. *Bourbon Spain, 1700–1808.* Oxford: Blackwell, 1989.

———. *The Spanish American Revolutions, 1808–1826.* New York: Norton, 1973.

MacLeod, Murdo. "Aspects of the Internal Economy of Colonial Spanish America: Labour; Taxation; Distribution and Exchange." In *The Cambridge History of Latin America,* edited by Leslie Bethell, 2:219–64. Cambridge, England: Cambridge University Press, 1984.

Martin, Cheryl English. *Governance and Society in Colonial Mexico: Chihuahua in the Eighteenth Century.* Stanford, Calif.: Stanford University Press, 1996.

———. "Public Celebrations, Popular Culture, and Labor Discipline in Eighteenth-Century Chihuahua." In *Rituals of Rule, Rituals of Resistance: Public Celebrations and Popular Culture in Mexico,* edited by William H. Beezley, Cheryl English Martin, and William E. French, 95–114. Wilmington, Del.: SR Books, 1994.

Mather, Christine. "Works of Art in Frontier New Mexico." In *Colonial Frontiers: Art and Life in Spanish New Mexico,* edited by Christine Mather, 7–33. Santa Fe, N.Mex.: Ancient City Press, 1983.

Meinig, D. W. *Southwest: Three Peoples in Geographical Change, 1600–1970.* New York: Oxford University Press, 1971.

Mera, Henry P. *Spanish-American Blanketry.* Santa Fe, N.Mex.: School of American Research Press, 1987.

———. *Style Trends in Pueblo Pottery in the Rio Grande and Little Colorado Cultural Areas from the Sixteenth to the Nineteenth Century.* Laboratory of Anthropology Memoir No. 3. Santa Fe, N.Mex.: Laboratory of Anthropology, 1939.

Minge, Ward Alan. *"Efectos del país:* A History of Weaving along the Rio Grande." In *Spanish Textile Tradition of New Mexico and Colorado,* edited by Nora Fisher, 8–28. Santa Fe: Museum of New Mexico Press, 1979.

———. *"Efectos del país:* A History of Weaving along the Rio Grande." In *Rio Grande Textiles: A New Edition of Spanish Textile Tradition of New Mexico and Colorado,* compiled and edited by Nora Fisher, 5–21. Santa Fe: Museum of New Mexico Press, 1994.

Miskimin, Harry A. *The Economy of Early Renaissance Europe, 1300–1460.* Cambridge, England: Cambridge University Press, 1975.

Moorhead, Max L. *The Apache Frontier: Jacobo Ugarte and Spanish-Indian Relations in Northern New Spain, 1769–1791.* Norman: University of Oklahoma Press, 1968.

———. *New Mexico's Royal Road.* Norman: University of Oklahoma Press, 1958.

————. *The Presidio: Bastion of the Spanish Borderlands.* Norman: University of Oklahoma Press, 1975.

————. "The Presidio Supply Problem of New Mexico in the Eighteenth Century." *New Mexico Historical Review* 36:3 (1961), 210–29.

————. "The Private Contract System of Presidio Supply in Northern New Spain." *Hispanic American Historical Review* 41:1 (1961), 31–54.

Moyano Pahissa, Angela. *El comercio de Santa Fe y la guerra del '47.* Mexico City: Sep Setentas, 1976.

Nostrand, Richard L. "The Century of Hispano Expansion." *New Mexico Historical Review* 64:4 (1987), 361–86.

————. *The Hispano Homeland.* Norman: University of Oklahoma Press, 1992.

————. "The Hispano Homeland in 1900." *Annals of the Association of American Geographers* 70:3 (1980), 382–96.

Noyes, Stanley. *Los Comanches: The Horse People, 1751–1845.* Albuquerque: University of New Mexico Press, 1993.

Offut, Leslie Scott. *Una sociedad urbana y rural en el norte de México.* Saltillo, Mexico: Archivo Municipal de Saltillo, 1993.

————. "Urban and Rural Society in the Mexican North: Saltillo in the Late Colonial Period." Ph.D. diss., University of California, Los Angeles, 1982.

Opler, Morris E., and Catherine H. Opler. "Mescalero Apache History in the Southwest." *New Mexico Historical Review* 25:1 (1950), 1–36.

Ortega Noriega, Sergio. *Un ensayo de historia regional: El noroeste de México.* Mexico City: Universidad Nacional Autónoma de México, 1993.

Ouweneel, Arij, and Catrien C. J. H. Bijleveld. "Comments on 'The Economic Cycle in Bourbon Central Mexico: A Critique of the Recaudación del diezmo líquido en pesos.'" *Hispanic American Historical Review* 69:3 (1989), 549–58.

————. "The Economic Cycle in Bourbon Central Mexico: A Critique of the Recaudación del diezmo líquido en pesos." *Hispanic American Historical Review* 69:3 (1989), 479–530.

Park, Joseph F. "Spanish-Indian Policy in Northern New Mexico, 1765–1810." *Arizona and the West* 4:Winter (1962), 325–44.

Pastor, Rudolfo. "El repartimiento de mercancías y los alcaldes mayores novohispanos: Un sistema de explotación, de sus orígenes a la crisis de 1810." In *El Gobierno Provincial en la Nueva España, 1570–1787,* edited by Woodrow Borah, 201–36. Mexico City: Universidad Nacional Autónoma de México, 1985.

Patrick, Elizabeth Nelson. "Land Grants during the Administration of Spanish Colonial Governor Pedro Fermín de Mendinueta." *New Mexico Historical Review* 51:1 (1976), 5–18.

Pearce, Thomas M., ed. *New Mexico Place Names: A Geographical Dictionary.* Albuquerque: University of New Mexico Press, 1965.

Pearcy, Thomas L. "The Smallpox Outbreak of 1779–1782: A Brief Comparative Look at Twelve Borderland Communities." *Journal of the West* 34:1 (1997), 26–37.

Pérez Herrero, Pedro. *Plata y libranzas: La articulación comercial del México borbónico.* Mexico City: El Colegio de México, 1988.

Pierce, Donna L. "New Mexican Furniture and Its Spanish and Mexican Prototypes." In *The American Craftsman and the European Tradition, 1620–1820,* edited by Francis J. Puig and Michael Conforti, 179–201. Minneapolis, Minn.: Minneapolis Institute of Arts, 1989.

Plog, Fred. "Western Anasazi." In *Southwest,* edited by Alfonso Ortiz, 108–30. Vol. 9 of *Handbook of North American Indians.* Washington, D.C.: Smithsonian Institution, 1979.

Pollock, Sir Frederick, and Frederic William Maitland. *History of English Law before the Time of Edward I.* 2 vols. 2d ed. Cambridge, England: Cambridge University Press, 1923.

Poyo, Gerald E. "The Canary Islands Immigrants of San Antonio: From Ethnic Exclusivity to Community." In *Tejano Origins in Eighteenth-Century San Antonio,* edited by Gerald E. Poyo and Gilberto M. Hinojosa, 41–58. Austin: University of Texas Press, 1991.

Poyo, Gerald E., and Gilberto M. Hinojosa. "Introduction." In *Tejano Origins in Eighteenth-Century San Antonio,* edited by Gerald E. Poyo and Gilberto M. Hinojosa, ix–xxii. Austin: University of Texas Press, 1991.

———. "Spanish Texas and Borderlands Historiography in Transition: Implications for United States History." *Journal of American History* 75:2 (1988), 393–416.

Priestly, Herbert I. *José de Gálvez, Visitor-General of New Spain, 1765–1771.* University of California, Berkeley, Publications in History, 5. Berkeley: University of California Press, 1916.

Radding, Cynthia. *Wandering Peoples: Colonialism, Ethnic Spaces, and Ecological Frontiers in Northwestern Mexico, 1700–1850.* Durham, N.C.: Duke University Press, 1997.

Reeve, Frank D. "Navaho-Spanish Diplomacy: 1770–1790." *New Mexico Historical Review* 35:3 (1960), 223–25.

———. "The Navaho-Spanish Peace: 1720–1770s." *New Mexico Historical Review* 34:1 (1959), 9–40.

Reff, Daniel T. *Disease, Depopulation, and Culture Change in Northwestern New Spain, 1518–1764.* Salt Lake City: University of Utah Press, 1991.

Riley, L. Carroll. *Rio del Norte: People of the Upper Rio Grande from Earliest Times to the Pueblo Revolt.* Salt Lake City: University of Utah Press, 1995.

Ríos-Bustamante, Adrian José. "A Contribution to the Historiography of the Greater Mexican North in the Eighteenth Century." *Aztlán* 7:3 (1976), 347–90.

———. "New Mexico in the Eighteenth Century: Life, Labor and Trade in the Villa de San Felipe de Albuquerque, 1706–1790." *Aztlán* 7:3 (1976), 391–426.

Robertson, Donald. "The Treatment of Architecture in the Florentine Codex of Sahagún." In *Sixteenth-Century Mexico: The Work of Sahagún,* edited by Munro S. Edmonson, 151–64. Albuquerque: University of New Mexico Press, 1974.

Roe, Frank Gilbert. *The Indian and the Horse.* Norman: University of Oklahoma Press, 1955.

Rudecoff, Christine A., and Charles Carillo. "Test Excavations at San Antonio de los Poblanos: A Spanish Colonial Community on the Middle Río Grande." In *Secrets of a City: Papers on Albuquerque Area Archaeology in Honor of Richard A. Bice,* edited by Anne V. Poore and John Montgomery, 48–56. Papers of the Archaeological Society of New Mexico, 13. Santa Fe: Ancient City Press for the Archaeological Society of New Mexico, 1987.

Salvucci, Linda K. "Costumbres viejas, 'Hombres Nuevos': José de Gálvez y la burocracia fiscal novo-hispana." *Historia Mexicana* 33:2 (1983), 224–64.

Salvucci, Richard. "Economic Growth and Change in Bourbon Mexico: A Review Essay." *Americas* 51:2 (1994), 219–30.

————. *Textiles and Capitalism in Mexico: An Economic History of the Obrajes, 1539–1840.* Princeton, N.J.: Princeton University Press, 1987.

Sando, Joe S. *Pueblo Nations: Eight Centuries of Pueblo Indian History.* Santa Fe, N.Mex.: Clear Light Publishers, 1992.

Santa Cruz Parish. *La Iglesia de Santa Cruz de la Cañada, 1733–1983.* Santa Cruz, N.Mex.: Parish of Santa Cruz de la Cañada, 1983.

Schaafsma, Curtis F. "Review of *Archeological Notes Concerning Two Colonial Period Settlements in the Tijeras Canyon Area, New Mexico*, by Michael P. Marshall." In *Report of New Mexico State Archeologist*, 1–9. Santa Fe, N.Mex.: Laboratory of Anthropology, 1984.

Schaafsma, Polly. "The Prehistoric Kachina Cult and Its Origins as Suggested by Southwestern Rock Art." In *Kachinas in the Pueblo World*, edited by Polly Schaafsma, 63–80. Albuquerque: University of New Mexico Press, 1994.

Schiller, Gertrud. *Iconography of Christian Art.* Translated by Janet Seligman. 2 vols. Greenwich, Conn.: New York Graphic Society, 1971.

Schroeder, Albert H. "Rio Grande Ethnohistory." In *New Perspectives on the Pueblos*, edited by Alfonso Ortiz, 41–70. Albuquerque: University of New Mexico Press, 1972.

————. "Shifting for Survival in the Spanish Southwest." *New Mexico Historical Review* 40:3 (1968), 291–310. Reprinted in *New Spain's Far Northern Frontier: Essays on Spain in the American West, 1540–1821*, edited by David J. Weber, 237–55. Albuquerque: University of New Mexico Press, 1979.

Secoy, Frank Raymond. *Changing Military Patterns on the Great Plains (Seventeenth Century through Early Nineteenth Century).* Locust Valley, N.Y.: J. J. Augustin, 1953.

Seed, Patricia. *To Love, Honor, and Obey in Colonial Mexico: Conflicts over Marriage Choice, 1574–1821.* Stanford, Calif.: Stanford University Press, 1988.

Sena, Col. José D. "The Chapel of Don Antonio José Ortiz." *New Mexico Historical Review* 13:4 (1938), 347–59.

Shalkop, Robert L. *Arroyo Hondo.* Colorado Springs, Colo.: Taylor Museum, 1976.

————. *Wooden Saints: The Santos of New Mexico.* Feldafing, Germany: Buchheim Verlag, 1967.

Simmons, Marc. "Colonial New Mexico and Mexico: The Historical Relationship." In *Colonial Frontiers: Art and Life in Spanish New Mexico*, edited by Christine Mather, 71–90. Santa Fe, N.Mex.: Ancient City Press, 1983.

————. *Coronado's Land: Essays on Daily Life in Colonial New Mexico.* Albuquerque: University of New Mexico Press, 1991.

————. "Footwear on New Mexico's Hispanic Frontier." In *Southwestern Culture History: Collected Papers in Honor of Albert H. Schroeder*, edited by Charles H. Lange, 223–31. Papers of the Archaeological Society of New Mexico, 10. Santa Fe: Ancient City Press for the Archaeological Society of New Mexico, 1985.

————. "History of Pueblo-Spanish Relations to 1821." In *Southwest*, edited by Alfonso Ortiz, 178–93. Vol. 9 of *Handbook of North American Indians*. Washington, D.C.: Smithsonian Institution, 1979.

————. *New Mexico: An Interpretive History.* Rev. ed. Albuquerque: University of New Mexico Press, 1988.

————. "New Mexico's Smallpox Epidemic of 1780–81." *New Mexico Historical Review* 41:4 (1966), 319–26.

————. "On the Trail of the Footless Stockings." In *Coronado's Land: Essays on Daily Life in Colonial New Mexico,* edited and translated by Marc Simmons, 8–11. Albuquerque: University of New Mexico Press, 1991.

————. "Problems of Research in Spanish Colonial Documents." *El Palacio* 74:3 (1967), 31–34.

————. "Settlement Patterns in Colonial New Mexico." *Journal of the West* 8:1 (1969), 7–21.

————. "Settlement Patterns in Colonial New Mexico." In *New Spain's Far Northern Frontier: Essays on Spain in the American West, 1540–1821,* edited by David J. Weber, 97–115. Albuquerque: University of New Mexico Press, 1979.

————. "Spanish Attempts to Open a New Mexico–Sonora Road." *Arizona and the West* 17:1 (1975), 5–20.

————. *Spanish Government in New Mexico.* Albuquerque: University of New Mexico Press, 1968.

————. *Taos to Tomé: True Tales of Hispanic New Mexico.* Albuquerque, N.Mex.: Adobe Press, 1978.

————. "Tlaxcalans in the Spanish Borderlands." *New Mexico Historical Review* 39:2 (1964), 101–10.

————. "When New Mexicans Dressed in Skins." In *Coronado's Land: Essays on Daily Life in Colonial New Mexico,* edited and translated by Marc Simmons, 3–7. Albuquerque: University of New Mexico Press, 1991.

Simmons, Marc, and Frank Turley. *Southwestern Colonial Ironwork: The Spanish Blacksmithing Tradition from Texas to California.* Santa Fe: Museum of New Mexico Press, 1980.

Smith, Michael M. *The "Real Expedición Marítima de la Vacuna" in New Spain and Guatemala.* Transactions of the American Philosophical Society n.s., 64:1. Philadelphia: American Philosophical Society, 1974.

Snow, David H. "Spanish American Pottery Manufacture." *Ethnohistory* 31:2 (1984), 93–113.

Somolimos d'Ardois, Germán. "La viruela en la Nueva España." In *Ensayos sobre la historia de las epidemias en México,* edited by Enrique Florescano and Elsa Malvido, 1:237–48. Mexico City: Instituto Mexicano del Seguro Social, 1982.

Speth, John D. "Some Unexplored Aspects of Mutualistic Plains-Pueblo Food Exchange." In *Farmers, Hunters, and Colonists: Interaction between the Southwest and the Southern Plains,* edited by Katherine A. Spielmann, 18–35. Tucson: University of Arizona Press, 1991.

Spicer, Edward H. "Spanish-Indian Acculturation in the Southwest." *American Anthropologist* 56:3 (1954), 663–78.

Spielmann, Katherine A. "Coercion or Cooperation? Plains-Pueblo Interaction in the Protohistoric Period." In *Farmers, Hunters, and Colonists: Interaction between the Southwest and the Southern Plains,* edited by Katherine A. Spielmann, 36–50. Tucson: University of Arizona Press, 1991.

————. "Interaction among Nonhierarchical Societies." In *Farmers, Hunters, and Colonists: Interaction between the Southwest and the Southern Plains,* edited by Katherine A. Spielmann, 1–17. Tucson: University of Arizona Press, 1991.

Steele, Thomas J. *Santos and Saints: Essays and Handbook*. Albuquerque, N.Mex.: Calvin Horn, 1974.

————. *Santos and Saints : The Religious Folk Art of Hispanic New Mexico*. Rev. ed. Santa Fe, N.Mex.: Ancient City Press, 1982.

Steele, Thomas J., S.J., and Rowena A. Rivera. *Penitente Self-Government: Brotherhoods and Councils, 1797–1947*. Santa Fe, N.Mex.: Ancient City Press, 1985.

Stein, Stanley J. "Bureaucracy and Business in the Spanish Empire, 1759–1804: Failure of a Bourbon Reform in Mexico and Peru." *Hispanic American Historical Review* 61:1 (1981), 2–28.

Super, John C. "Querétaro Obrajes: Industry and Society in Provincial Mexico, 1600–1810." *Hispanic American Historical Review* 56:2 (1976), 197–216.

————. *La vida en Querétaro durante la Colonia, 1531–1810*. Mexico City: Fondo de Cultura Económica, 1983.

Swadesh, Frances Leon. *Los primeros pobladores: Hispanic Americans of the Ute Frontier*. Notre Dame, Ind.: University of Notre Dame Press, 1974.

Swann, Michael M. *Tierra Adentro*. Boulder, Colo.: Westview Press, 1982.

Taylor, Lonn, and Dessa Bokides. *New Mexican Furniture, 1600–1940*. Santa Fe: Museum of New Mexico Press, 1987.

Taylor, Willam B. "Cochití Lands and the Disputed Sale to Luis María Cabeza de Vaca." Expert witness testimony for H.R. 3259, presented to the U.S. House of Representatives, July 26, 1983, 1–49.

————. *Drinking, Homicide, and Rebellion in Colonial Mexican Villages*. Stanford, Calif.: Stanford University Press, 1979.

————. *Magistrates of the Sacred: Priests and Parishioners in Eighteenth-Century Mexico*. Stanford, Calif.: Stanford University Press, 1996.

TePaske, John Jay. "Economic Problems of the Governor." In *America's Ancient City: Spanish Saint Augustine, 1565–1763*, edited by Kathleen A. Deagan, 577–608. Spanish Borderlands Sourcebooks, 25. New York: Garland Publishing, 1991.

Thomas, Alfred Barnaby. "San Carlos: A Comanche Pueblo on the Arkansas River, 1787." *Colorado Magazine*, May 1929, 79–91.

Tjarks, Alicia V. "Demographic, Ethnic, and Occupational Structure of New Mexico, 1790." *Americas* 35:1 (1978), 45–88.

Usner, Don J. *Sabino's Map: Life in Chimayo's Old Plaza*. Santa Fe: Museum of New Mexico Press, 1995.

Van Young, Eric. *Hacienda and Market in Eighteenth-Century Mexico: The Rural Economy of the Guadalajara Region, 1675–1820*. Berkeley: University of California Press, 1981.

————. "Mexican Rural History since Chevalier." *Latin American Research Review* 18:3 (1983), 5–61.

Vedder, Alan C. *Furniture of Spanish New Mexico*. Santa Fe, N.Mex.: Sunstone Press, 1977.

Wade, Edwin L., and Lea S. McChesney. *Historic Hopi Ceramics: The Thomas V. Keam Collection of the Peabody Museum of Archaeology and Ethnology*. Cambridge, Mass.: Peabody Museum Press, Harvard University, 1981.

Walker, Billy D. "Copper Genesis: The Early Years of Santa Rita del Cobre." *New Mexico Historical Review* 54:1 (1979), 5–20.

Wallace, Ernest, and Edward Adamson Hoebel. *The Comanches: Lords of the South Plains.* Norman: University of Oklahoma Press, 1952.

Weber, David J. *The Mexican Frontier, 1821–1846: The American Southwest under Mexico.* Albuquerque: University of New Mexico Press, 1982.

———. *The Spanish Frontier in North America.* New Haven, Conn.: Yale University Press, 1992.

Weigle, Marta. *Brothers of Light, Brothers of Blood.* Albuquerque: University of New Mexico Press, 1976.

Westphall, Victor. *Mercedes Reales: Hispanic Land Grants of the Upper Rio Grande Region.* Albuquerque: University of New Mexico Press, 1983.

Wheat, Joe Ben. "Early Trade and Commerce in Southwestern Textiles before the Curio Shop." In *Reflections: Papers on Southwestern Culture History in Honor of Charles H. Lange,* edited by Anne V. Poore, 57–72. Papers of the Archaeological Society of New Mexico, 14. Santa Fe: Ancient City Press for the Archaeological Society of New Mexico, 1988.

———. "Río Grande, Pueblo, and Navajo Weavers: Cross-Cultural Influence." In *Spanish Textile Tradition of New Mexico and Colorado,* edited by Nora Fisher, 29–36. Santa Fe: Museum of New Mexico Press, 1979.

———. "Saltillo *Sarapes* of Mexico." In *Rio Grande Textiles: A New Edition of Spanish Textile Tradition of New Mexico and Colorado,* compiled and edited by Nora Fisher, 60–63. Santa Fe: Museum of New Mexico Press, 1994.

———. "Yarns to the Navajo: The Materials of Weaving." In *A Burst of Brilliance: Germantown Pennsylvania and Navajo Weaving,* edited by Stanley Chodorow, 12–25. Philadelphia: Arthur Ross Gallery of the University of Pennsylvania, 1994.

Whitaker, Kathleen. "Navajo Weaving Design: 1750–1900." Ph.D. diss., University of California, Los Angeles, 1986.

White, Leslie A. *The Pueblo of Santa Ana.* Memoirs of the American Anthropological Association, 60. Menasha, Wis.: Collegiate Press, 1942.

———. "Punche Tobacco in New Mexican History." *New Mexico Historical Review* 18:4 (1943), 386–93.

Wilder, Mitchell A., and Edgar Breitenbach. *Santos: The Religious Folk-Art of New Mexico.* Colorado Springs, Colo.: Taylor Museum, 1943.

Williams, A. D. *Spanish Colonial Furniture.* Milwaukee, Wis.: Bruce Publishing, 1941.

Wroth, William. *The Chapel of Our Lady of Talpa.* Colorado Springs, Colo.: Taylor Museum, 1979.

———. *Christian Images in Hispanic New Mexico.* Colorado Springs, Colo.: Taylor Museum, 1982.

———. *Images of Penance, Images of Mercy: Southwestern Santos in the Late Nineteenth Century.* Norman: University of Oklahoma Press, 1991.

Ziegler, Philip. *The Black Death.* London: Collins, 1969.

GUIDES AND FINDING AIDS

Almada, Francisco R. *Diccionario historia, geografía y biografía chihuahuenses.* Chihuahua, Mexico: Universidad de Chihuahua, Departamento de Investigaciones Sociales, Sección de Historia, 1928 (2d ed., 1987).

Archivo General de la Nación. *Catálogo de ilustraciones.* Vol. 1. Mexico City: Centro de Información Gráfica del Archivo General de la Nación, 1979.

————. *Índice del Ramo Clero Regular y Secular.* Guías y Catálogos, 22. Mexico City: Archivo General de la Nación, 1982.

Bancroft Library. "Key to Alphonse Louis Pinart Collection." *Colección de documentos sobre Nuevo México. 1681–1841.* P-E 37–61 key.

Barnes, Thomas C., Thomas H. Naylor, and Charles W. Polzer. *Northern New Spain: A Research Guide.* Tucson: University of Arizona Press, 1981.

Beers, Henry Putney. *Spanish and Mexican Records of the American Southwest: A Bibliographical Guide to Archive and Manuscript Sources.* Tucson: University of Arizona Press, 1979.

Chapman, Charles E. *Catalogue of the Materials in the Archivo General de Indias for the History of the Pacific Coast and the Southwest.* University of California Publications in History, 8. Berkeley, 1919.

Chávez, Fray Angélico. *Archives of the Archdiocese of Santa Fe, 1678–1900.* Washington, D.C.: Academy of American Franciscan History, 1957.

————. *Origins of New Mexico Families.* Santa Fe: Historical Society of New Mexico, 1954.

Del Río, Ignacio. *Guía del Archivo Franciscano.* Vol. 1. Mexico City: Instituto de Investigaciones Bibliográficas, 1975.

González Ponce, Enrique. *Catálogo del Ramo Misiones.* Guías y Catálogos, 16. Mexico City: Archivo General de la Nación, 1981.

Hammond, George P. *A Guide to the Manuscript Collections of the Bancroft Library.* Berkeley: University of California Press, 1972.

Heredia, Roberto. *Catálogo del Ramo Provincias Internas, I.* Mexico City: Archivo General de la Nación, 1967.

————. *Catálogo del Ramo Provincias Internas, II.* Mexico City: Archivo General de la Nación, 1967.

Herrera Huerta, Juan Manuel, and Victoria San Vicente Tello. *Archivo General de la Nación: Guía general.* Mexico City: Archivo General de la Nación, 1990.

Jenkins, Myra Ellen, comp. and ed. *Calendar to the Microfilm Edition of the Land Records of New Mexico, 1621–1821, Series II.* Santa Fe: New Mexico State Records Center and Archives, 1968.

————. *Guide to the Microfilm Edition of the Spanish Archives of New Mexico, 1621–1821.* Santa Fe: State of New Mexico Records Center and Archives, 1975.

Martínez Peñaloza, Ma. Teresa. *Vocabulario de términos en documentos históricos.* Guías y Catálogos, 1. Mexico City: Archivo General de la Nación, 1977.

Minneapolis Institute of Art. *Slide Catalog.* 3d ed. Minneapolis: Minneapolis Institute of Art, 1987.

Navarro y Noriega, Fernando. *Catálogo de los curatos y misiones que tiene la Nueva España, en cada una de sus diócesis.* . . . Mexico City: Casa de Arizpe, 1813.

Rodríguez de Lebrija, Esperanza. *Catálogo del Ramo Provincias Internas, I: Índice Analítico V. 3.* Guías y Catálogos, 17. Mexico City: Archivo General de la Nación, 1981.

————. *Catálogo del Ramo Provincias Internas, II: Índice Analítico V. 4.* Guías y Catálogos, 17. Mexico City: Archivo General de la Nación, 1981.

Twitchell, Ralph E. *The Spanish Archives of New Mexico.* 2 vols. Cedar Rapids, Iowa: Torch Press, 1914.

Tyler, Daniel. *Sources for New Mexican History, 1821–1848.* Santa Fe: Museum of New Mexico Press, 1984.

Weber, David J. "Mexico's Far Northern Frontier, 1821–1825: A Critical Bibliography." *Arizona and the West* 19:3 (1977), 225–66.

Weigle, Marta. *A Penitente Bibliography.* Albuquerque: University of New Mexico Press, 1976.

Wilson, John P. "Examination of Adolph F. Bandelier's Transcripts of Spanish Documents." Hemenway Southwestern Expedition Collections, Peabody Museum Library, Ottawa, Ont., 1974. Unpublished manuscript.

INDEX

Abiquíu: "Defensive Crisis," 43, 47, 49–50,
    244 n55; Genízaros, 200; missionary
    funds, 199
Acoma Pueblo, 5, 7; altar screen, 184,
    274 n19; labor exploitation, 197; mis-
    sions, 23, 27, 57, 59, 198, 199; popula-
    tion, 59; pottery, 163, 165; repartimiento
    de effectos, 26; smallpox, 57, 59; textiles,
    16, 16 *Plate*, 155, 156
Acomita Polychrome, 165, 166 *Plate*, 167,
    174. *See also* Acoma Pueblo
ages, vecino (1780s), 177
agriculture: Apache, 31, 75; Bourbon Re-
    forms and, 66–67; "Defensive Crisis,"
    34–35, 42, 43, 47–49; hunting and
    gathering vs., 31–32; interregional trade
    and, 108; missionaries' supplies, 23–25,
    29; Pueblo, 3, 7, 8, 15, 21–30, 47–49,
    79–80, 140, 152, 201, 242 n35; punche,
    15, 79–81, 100–101; smallpox epidemic
    and, 60, 62; Sonora, 180; vecino, 8, 15,
    21, 52, 54, 80–81, 108, 119, 152. *See also*
    grain; livestock
Ako Polychrome, 163, 165, 165 *Plate*, 167,
    169, 174. *See also* Acoma Pueblo
Albuquerque: alcades mayores, 54; cofradías,
    208; "Defensive Crisis," 37, 43, 45 *map*,
    49, 50; ethnic geography (c. 1750), 5, 7,
    10; interregional exploration, 105; mis-
    sion, 206; pottery, 174; vecino artisans,
    135–37

alcabala tax, 67, 69, 125, 137–39, 155, 183,
    266 nn35,36, 266 *table*
alcades mayores, 9, 54, 183; "Defensive Crisis,"
    50; furniture owners, 190; repartimiento
    de effectos, 8, 25–30
Alencaster, Joaquín Real, 112, 125
Alta California: missions, 71, 196; San Fran-
    cisco Presidio, 113; Spanish settlers, 69;
    trade, 101, 103, 104, 108
Amangual, Francisco, 107
Anasazi people, 6–7
Anglo-American settlers, 12, 55
Antonio "El Pinto," 131
Anza, Juan Bautista de: Indian Policy, 71–
    72, 73, 74, 124; and interregional trade,
    104–8; and missionaries, 57, 198, 207;
    and Pueblo economic participation,
    155–56; and Pueblo land, 280 n55; set-
    tlement plans, 50, 105, 110, 258 n62;
    and smallpox, 56; and tobacco, 81; and
    trade convoy to Chihuahua, 124; victory
    over Cuerno Verde, 39, 63, 72, 110
Apache Indians, 7, 10–12, 34, 71–74; Bour-
    bon Reforms and, 2, 65, 70–75; gifts to,
    133; Guizarnótegui attacked by, 98; and
    horses, 31, 33, 244 n52; Jicarilla, 10, 12,
    31, 34, 74, 133, 269 n63; and money,
    150; resettled, 10–12, 197, 269 n63;
    Spanish-Comanche alliance and, 71, 72–
    75; trade, 10, 33, 158; warfare, 1, 2, 7,
    10–12, 13, 30–54, 57, 68–75, 123, 232.

Apache Indians (*continued*)
    See also Gila (Gileño) Apache; Navajo Indians; Plains Indians
Aragón, Don José Manuel, 184, 185
Aragón, José Rafael, 188. See also *santos*
Arispe, 68, 70, 105–6
Arizona, Hopi Pueblos, 5, 10, 12; interregional trade and, 103, 104–5; kachina rituals, 235n5; pottery, 272n85; resettlement, 10, 105, 197, 269n63; weaving laborers, 153
Arroynde, Miguel Francisco de, 87
Arroyo Hondo, 203
art: kiva, 6; Spanish/vecino religious, 3, 166–69, 166 *Plate*, 182–95, 205, 228–33. See also craft production; *santos*
Ashiwi Polychrome, 174. *See also* Zuñi Pueblo
Ayuntamiento, Chihuahua, 52, 126

Baca, Don Antonio, 27, 202, 259n76
Baca, Luís María Cabeza de, 204–5, 220
Bajío, 119–20, 167, 224–26
Bancroft, Hubert Howe, 56, 142–43
barter, 13, 78–79, 82, 85, 140–51, 152–53
Bazán brothers, Juan and Ignacio Ricardo, 116, 154, 185
Beitia, Antonio, 211–21
Belén, church, 199–200
Benavides, Alonso de, 188
Benavides, Tomasa, 190
Bermejo, Manuel, 27, 29, 197, 242n34
Bernal, Custos Cayetono José Ignacio, 154–55, 172–73
birthrates, smallpox epidemic, 55, 56, 57, 58 *fig*, 60
blankets, 226; fresadas, 126; mantas, 15–17, 16 *Plate*, 27, 122, 155; Río Abajo Pueblos, 29, 242n34; Río Grande, 17–19, 18 *Plate*, 153–54, 175, 176, 278n38; Santa Fe Presidio supply, 151
Bokides, Dessa, 194–95
Bonilla, Antonio, 35, 51, 84
Bourbons: administrators, 2, 56, 62, 65–175, 180–81, 207, 223–33; Carlos III, 2, 65, 66, 68, 76–77, 98, 99; Reforms, 2, 65–118, 132, 139, 207–8. See also Spanish officials
Boyd, E., 205–6
Brading, David A., 65–66, 67
bretaña, 121
bubonic plague, Europe, 61–62

Bucareli y Ursúa, Antonio, 50, 56, 76, 83, 104
buffalo, 20, 31, 32, 33, 38
Burro, Manuel, 214
Bustamante, Antonio Cadero y, 107
Bustamante, Rosa, 153, 183, 190

Caché, Antonio, 216
Cachupín, Tomás Vélez de: vs. alcabala tax, 139; on Apache threats, 50, 197; census (1752), 245n61; and currency, 140; and gunpowder factory, 109; Ojo Caliente land, 43; on Plains trade, 14; and prices, 34, 140, 141, 144, 145, 146, 243n44; tithe rental, 54; and tobacco monopoly, 78, 79–80
cacique, 9–10
Cacugé, Miguel, 211, 214, 218–19
Cádiz, trade, 66
Calderón, Don Joseph González, 93–94
Californias: fiscal system, 88; trade, 101, 103–4, 108. See also Alta California
"Calligraphic Santero," 187, 188. See also *santos*
Camino Real, 104
Campor (investigator), 127–28, 264n19
Carlana Apache, 10, 34
Carlos III, 2, 65, 66, 68, 76–77, 98, 99
Carnué, San Miguel Laredo de, 43, 49
Caroca, Don Antonio, 51
Carrillo, Charles, 21, 226–27
Carrizal, Presidio, 95–96, 99, 158
Cash, Marie Romero, 274–75nn18,19
Castas, 1, 178, 180, 181, 199, 273n7
Cathedral of Durango, tithes, 53, 54, 83, 127
Cebolleta Pueblo, 197, 269n63
Chaco Canyon, 5
Chacón, Fernando de: alcabala exemption, 139; on export trade, 120–22, 124, 125, 155, 156; and "imaginary moneys," 150, 268n57; land grants, 203; Ortiz commended to, 183; on Pueblo production, 152, 155, 158; on tobacco, 81; and vecino crafts, 116, 154, 185
Chama, 43, 58 *fig*, 60, 244n55
Chaves, Francisco Xavier, 73
Chiche, Governor, 213, 217, 218–19
Chihuahua: Ayuntamiento, 52, 126; Camino Real, 104; consulado, 95, 96, 100; Council of War, 71, 85, 91; crafts production, 115, 126, 137; merchants, 89–90, 94–100, 143, 149; treasury, 83, 86–89, 90,

94, 96, 98, 101, 111, 112. *See also* Chihuahua Trail/Chihuahua trade

Chihuahua Trail/Chihuahua trade, 14–15, 20–21, 62, 68, 224–26, 232–33; annual New Mexican convoy, 78–79, 120, 122–26, 140, 183; "Defensive Crisis," 50–51, 52, 53; Extraordinary Fund goods, 134, 139; furniture owners, 190; "imaginary moneys" and, 149; interregional trade and, 105, 107, 108; missionaries' supplies, 22; Moorhead work on, 143; pottery, 158–59; produce, 140; religious structures financed by, 183; sheep, 124; tobacco, 79, 80; vecinos using Pueblo production for, 28

children: smallpox, 60. *See also* birthrates, smallpox epidemic

Chimayo church, 182, 188

Chiracyo, Juan, 216

Christ, images of, 230–32, 231 *Plate,* 233, 283nn11,13

Christianity, 8–9, 103; fees for services, 147–48, 199–200, 207–8; Indians and, 3, 7–10, 13, 21–25, 29, 196–209; religious art, 3, 166–69, 166 *Plate,* 182–95, 205, 228–33; "Saint" Job and, 230; structures, 182–95. *See also* Franciscan missionaries; *santos;* tithes, church

Chulo, Juan Pedro, 216

churches. *See* Christianity; Franciscan missionaries; tithes, church

clans, Pueblo, 5–6, 7

Claramonte, Andrés, 56

Coahuila, 154; Bourbon Reforms, 68, 69, 88, 117; drought, 244n50

Cochití Pueblo, 5; "Defensive Crisis," 37; land issues, 201, 204–5; mission, 57, 59, 199; pottery, 171; textiles, 155

Cofradía Nuestra Señora del Carmen, Santa Cruz de la Cañada, 61, 188

cofradías, 60–61, 182, 183, 188, 208

Color Quebrado, 180

Comanche Indians, 31; Bourbon policy, 2, 65, 70–75; gifts to, 133; peace treaty/Spanish alliance, 2, 55, 70–75, 90, 124, 132; smallpox, 73; trade, 2, 10, 12, 14, 20, 31–32, 33, 51, 73, 74, 79–80, 123, 158; warfare, 1, 2, 10–12, 13, 20, 30, 33–54, 63–64, 70, 72–73, 110, 123, 232

Los Comanches (play), 63–64

comercio libre decree (1778), 66

compañías volantes, 68–69, 85, 89, 96

"compartmentalization," 9, 209

Concha, Fernando de la: on barter for horses, 152–53; on commercial repartimiento, 121; on convoy to Chihuahua, 124; gifts to Indians, 133; and interregional trade, 106, 107; on land availability, 119; and missionaries, 57, 59, 198–99, 204, 207, 208–9; Navajo chief imprisonment, 131; obraje establishment, 114–16; Ortiz commended by, 183; on peso de la tierra, 149; and prices, 34, 145; retirement enterprise, 126–28, 131; and Santa Fe cuartel, 110–14; sheep, 126–27, 263–64n19; and soldiers' pay, 99–100; and Tewa sedition trials, 210–21; tithe rental, 127–28, 264n20; and vecino weaving, 154, 185

Coronado, Francisco Vásquez de, 3

Cortés, José María, 150, 261n5

Corvalán, Pedro de, 88

Cosío, Don Phelipe Gonzales, de, 126–27

Costanzó, Miguel, 104

cotton, Pueblo, 155

Council of War, 71, 72, 85–87, 91

Coyotes, 181, 273n11

craft production, 2–3, 15–17; Navajo, 17, 19–20, 131–32, 153, 238n9. *See also* art; pottery; Pueblos' crafts; textiles; vecino crafts

Crespo, Don Benito, 147, 199, 247n73

Crespo, Francisco Antonio, 101–3, 107

Cristóbal, 202

Croix, Teodoro de, Marqués de Cruillas, 101; and "Defensive Crisis," 52; fiscal system, 84, 85, 86, 139; and interregional trade, 104, 105, 106, 108; Morfí as consultant to, 141; and presidio funds, 91–95; and Saltillo militia, 69; and Santa Fe resettlement, 110; and Spanish-Comanche alliance, 71–72, 73

Cruz, Antonio, 214

Cuartelejo Apache, 10–12, 34

cuarteles, presidio, 110–14, 113 *fig,* 132, 137, 148–49, 218, 259n76

Cuencamé funds, 87

Cuerno Verde (Green Horn), 39, 47, 63, 72, 110

cultural changes: Plains Indians, 12; Pueblo resistance, 9, 209–22; vecino identity,

cultural changes (*continued*)
176–222, 228–33. *See also* demography;
ethnic identity; religion
cultural patronage, 3, 183–85, 187–88,
189, 206. *See also* art
currency: circulating, 34, 78–79, 82–90,
95, 100, 114, 140–51, 254n17, 261n5,
268n57; "imaginary moneys," 139–51,
226, 267n41; silver, 85–86, 114, 148;
and soldiers' salaries, 28, 93–94, 95–96.
See also peso
custos, 8, 14

dance ceremonies, Pueblo, 6–7, 9
deaths, 243n47; by hostile Indians (1700–
1819), 35, 36 *fig*, 42, 54, 75; by smallpox,
55, 56–57, 58 *fig*, 60
"Defensive Crisis" (1770s), 14, 34–55, 62–
64, 100, 242n36
Delgado, Carlos, 26, 27, 29, 196–97, 269n63
Delgado, Don Manuel, 190, 194
demography: "Defensive Crisis," 42–43, 46–
50, 52–53, 54; marriage data (1780s),
177; New Mexican household occupations (1790), 135–37, 138 *fig*, 153; smallpox epidemic, 55, 56, 57, 58 *fig*, 60. *See
also* deaths; ethnic geography; population; settlement patterns
diligencias matrimoniales, 177, 178–79
diseases: epidemics, 7, 13, 14, 55–62. *See
also* smallpox epidemics
Domínguez, Francisco Atanasio, 182; on cofradías, 60–61, 208; on Comanche ac-
quisitions, 33; "imaginary moneys," 140,
144–45, 147–48; on Indian services for
friars, 23; on Indians' lack of Christian
commitment, 8, 9; interregional expedition, 103; population figures, 56, 57;
santeros identified by, 205–6, 275n19;
on settlement patterns, 42, 43–44, 47
Dozier, Edward P., 210
droughts: Coahuila, 244n50; "Defensive Crisis," 34–35, 37–38, 42, 47, 52; fiscal system and, 88; Hopi and, 105, 269n63;
horses during, 34–35, 37–38, 244n50;
New Mexico's economic boom during,
119; Tompiro pueblos and, 7, 10
Durango: bishop of, 182, 200, 247n73; Cathedral tithes, 53, 54, 83, 127; crafts production, 137; intendant, 98; merchants,
126; obraje, 115, 259n83; tobacco mo-

nopoly, 88; trade, 68, 125; treasury, 82,
83, 84 *fig*, 85, 86–87, 89, 90, 101

Ecce Homo, 231–32, 231 *Plate*, 283nn11,13
Echeagaray, Manuel de, 106
economics, 3; barter, 13, 78–79, 82, 85,
140–51, 152–53; boom (1780s), 2–3,
108, 118–32, 151, 176, 201–2, 221–24;
Bourbon administrators and, 2, 65–175,
180–81, 207–8, 223–33; church service
fees, 147–48, 199–200, 207–8; coercive,
7, 8, 13, 21–30, 156–75, 196–209, 220,
242n35; cofradías, 60–61, 208; cultural
patronage, 3, 183–85, 187–88, 189,
206; "Defensive Crisis" and, 50–55, 62–
63; encomiendas, 7, 8; Extraordinary
Fund, 90, 132–39, 135–36 *figs;* fines for
Tewa sedition defendants, 218; market,
139–51; missionaries', 21–25, 29, 82,
90, 198–200; New Mexico (through
1770s), 13–64; New Mexico development, 119–75, 223–33; New Mexico development obstacles, 76–118; obraje,
115; Pueblo participation, 21–25, 122–
23, 151–56; repartimiento de effectos, 8,
25–30; Santa Fe cuartel, 110, 111, 112,
113–14, 259n76; smallpox epidemic
and, 55–62; trade fair regulations, 34;
vecino culture as product of, 176, 182.
See also fiscal system; labor; markets; mining; prices; products; salaries; taxes;
tithes, church; trade
Ecueracapa, 73
El Encinal Pueblo, 197, 269n63
Elguea, Don Francisco Manuel de, 126
Elizondo, Domingo, 68
El Paso: alcabala tax, 139; exports, 79, 125;
gunpowder factory, 109; interregional
route, 107; Presidio, 51, 101; pueblo,
51, 71
"El Pinto," Antonio, 131
El Príncipe Presidio, 158
Encinillas, Real Hacienda, 126–28
encomiendas, 7, 8
England, 12, 55, 61–62, 69, 109
Escalante, Silvestre Vélez de, 103–4
Esquibel, Francisco, 91–92
Esquibel, Geronimo, 259n76
ethnic geography, 222; New Mexico
(c. 1750), 3–5, 4 *map*, 10–12, 11 *map;*
settlement patterns affected by war, 39–

44, 40–46 *maps*, 47–50. *See also* Plains Indians; Pueblo Indians; *vecinos*
ethnic identity, 180–81; intermarriages, 3, 177, 178, 180; preoccupation with (1760–1800), 177, 178–80; vecino, 3, 177, 180, 182, 201–2, 228–33. *See also* ethnic geography
Europe, 20, 56, 61–62, 225. *See also* England; European settlers; France; Russia, and Alta California; Spain
European settlers, 12, 31, 55. *See also* Spanish settlers
exports, 2–3, 15, 30, 116, 120–26; "imaginary moneys" and, 143, 148; Pueblo pottery, 158, 169, 174–75, 226–27; Pueblos excluded, 122, 155–56; textiles, 152–56, 225, 226. *See also* Chihuahua Trail/Chihuahua trade
Extraordinary Fund, 90, 132–39, 135–36 *figs*

family: Pueblo, 5–6. *See also* marriages
famine, 119–20, 133
Faraone Apache, 10
Fernández, Don Carlos, 63
First Mesa, 10
fiscales, 8, 9, 29, 30, 201
fiscal system, 82–91, 117, 139, 223; libranzas, 85–101; presidio expenses, 82–85, 84 *fig*, 89, 90, 91–101, 91 *fig*, 223. *See also* currency; taxes; treasuries
Flores, Manuel Antonio, 121; Guizarnótegui case, 98, 99; and libranzas, 89; and obraje in New Mexico, 114, 115; and Santa Fe cuartel, 110, 112
food, 2–3, 242–43 n39; drought effects, 34–35; famine, 119–20, 133; furniture used for, 194; gathering, 31–32, 242 n37; gifts to Indians, 133; hunting, 20, 31–32, 33–34; pottery used for, 158–59; prices, 119, 128–30, 140–41, 200; raids, 31, 32–33. *See also* agriculture; grain; livestock
"form-splitting" (*Formenspaltungen*), 187
France, 12, 31, 72–73, 109
Franciscan missionaries, 3, 7–10, 14, 15, 177; art, 166–67, 189, 205–6; diligencias matrimoniales, 177, 178–79; dispute with officials, 21–22, 25–26, 29, 196–209; economics, 21–25, 29, 82, 90, 198–200; population classifications, 47; priest work, 182; and Pueblos, 3, 7–10,

13, 21–25, 29, 196–209, 220; smallpox epidemic, 57, 207; stipend, 22, 199; Texas, 69; tobacco use, 81; and vecino culture, 196–209
fresadas, 126
Fresquis, Don Pedro Antonio ("Calligraphic Santero"), 187, 188. *See also* santos
furniture, vecino, 3, 182, 189–95, 191–93 *Plates*, 276–77 n28. *See also* craft production

Galisteo Pueblo, 3, 24, 34, 42–43, 54–55
Gálvez, Bernardo de, 74, 88, 89, 95
Gálvez, José de, 56, 66–71, 78, 82, 104, 106
gamuzas, 15, 79
Garcés, Francisco, 103, 105
García, Andrés, 27, 205–6, 269 n63, 275 n19
García, Valencia, 25
Garner, Richard L., 68
gender roles, 30, 172–73
Genízaros, 180, 181, 199; Abiquíu, 200; communities, 15; cuartel labor, 113–14; population, 199, 269 n63, 273 n7; San Fernando del Río Puerco, 49; textile work, 153, 155, 156
geography. *See* ethnic geography
Gerald, Rex E., 158
gifts, to Indians, 90, 132–39, 135–36 *figs*
Gil, Francisco, 56
Gila (Gileño) Apache, 10, 74; and interregional trade route, 101–3, 106; Spanish-Comanche alliance against, 71, 72–74; warfare, 34, 37, 38, 50–51
Gobernador Canyon, 169
gold, 105, 258 n62
Goldschmidt, Adolf, 187
Gómez, Ramón, 155
Gonzalez, Ramón Antonio, 201, 274–75 nn18,19
governors, 9; vs. alcabala tax, 139; "Defensive Crisis," 34–38, 42–43, 47, 49–54; repartimiento de effectos, 8, 25–30; smallpox epidemic, 57, 59. *See also* Alencaster, Joaquín Real; Anza, Juan Bautista de; Cachupín, Tomás Vélez de; Chacón, Fernando de; Concha, Fernando de la; Maynez, Alberto; Mendinueta, Pedro Fermín de
grain: famine, 119–20, 133; gifts for Indians, 133; for missionaries, 23–25, 29; pottery to store, 158–59; prices, 129,

grain (*continued*)
140–41; Pueblo production, 15, 152;
repartimiento de effectos, 26–27, 29;
Santa Fe Presidio supply, 26, 123, 151;
stored, 32; trade, 21, 24, 31, 32
Gregg, Josiah, 189–90
Gregory the Great, Pope, 230
Grimarest, Enrique de, 106
Guadalajara, 15, 66, 67, 78
Guadalupe chapel, La Cuesta, 182
Guanajuato, 82, 83, 86, 89, 120, 254n19
guilds: craft, 194; merchant, 89–90, 95–
100
Guille, Antonio el, 213, 215, 216, 218, 219
Guizarnótegui, Francisco de, 95–100, 144
gunpowder monopoly, 88–89, 109
Gutiérrez, Don Clemente, 54, 190, 194
Gutiérrez, Ramón A., 177, 178, 268n57

habilitado, presidio, 94–99
Hano, 10
harineros, 189, 193 *Plate,* 194–95
La Hermanidad Nuestro Padre Jesús Nazareno (*Los Penitentes*), 182, 188, 232
Herrera, Juan Luís, 259n76
Hidalgo, Bachiller Miguel Hernández, 115,
259n83
Hidalgo rebellion (1810), 115, 202, 224
Hopi Pueblos, 5, 10, 12; interregional
trade and, 103, 104–5; kachina rituals,
235n5; pottery, 272n85; resettlement,
10, 105, 197, 269n63; weaving laborers,
153
horses: Apache and, 31, 33, 244n52; Comanche, 12, 31, 33–38, 54, 73; "Defensive Crisis," 34–38, 54; during drought,
34–35, 37–38, 244n50; northward
spread, 38, 39 *map;* repartimiento de
effectos, 152–53; Santa Fe Presidio, 151;
smallpox epidemic and, 62; tithes and,
127
hunting, 20, 31–32, 33–34

"imaginary moneys," 139–51, 226, 267n41
Imago Pietatis, 230
imports, 20, 66, 225, 226
Indians. *See* Plains Indians; Pueblo Indians;
see also under individual groups and tribes
intendants, 98, 207
Iribarren, Don José Antonio, 126
Irigoyen, Don Pedro Ignacio de, 89

Isleta Pueblo, 5, 6, 26, 269 n63; El Pinto, 131;
kachina rituals, 235n5; mission, 199

Janos Presidio, 158
Jémez Pueblo, 3, 6, 7; "Defensive Crisis,"
37; land ownership, 202; mission, 57; re-
settlements, 269n63; Sola trial, 219; tex-
tiles, 155
Jenner, Edward, 56
Jicarilla Apache, 10, 12, 31, 34, 74, 133,
269n63
Jimeno, Fray, 197
Job, Saint, 228–33, 229 *Plate,* 282n8
Jones, Oakah, 14
Junta de Diezmos, jueces hacedores of, 53, 54
justice: Spanish, 13, 202–4, 209–22,
279n53. *See also* law suits

kachina cult, 6–7, 235n5
Kansas Indians, 107
Keres pueblos, 3; missions, 59; Navajo
raids, 37; officials, 9; pottery, 162, 169;
social structure, 5, 6, 7; textiles, 155. *See
also* Acoma Pueblo; Cochití Pueblo; La-
guna Pueblo; San Felipe Pueblo; Santa
Ana Pueblo; Santo Domingo Pueblo;
Zia Pueblo
Kiapkwa Polychrome, 174, 272n85. *See also*
Zuñi Pueblo
Kiua Polychrome, 171–72, 172 *Plate,* 174.
See also Cochití Pueblo; Santo Domingo
Pueblo
kiva societies, 6, 7, 8–9, 197, 200–201
Kubler, George, 187, 222

labor: Bourbon Reforms and, 67, 69–70;
epidemics and, 62; gender roles, 30,
172–73; Pueblo coerced, 7, 8, 13, 21–
30, 156–75, 196–209, 220, 242n35; Río
Napestle pueblo, 137; Santa Fe cuartel,
111, 113–14, 137, 148–49, 218; Tewa
sedition prisoners, 218–19; textile, 115,
153, 156, 224–25. *See also* servants; slaves
La Cuesta, Guadalupe chapel, 182
la Fora, Nicolás de, 20, 125
Laguna Pueblo, 5, 7; "Defensive Crisis,"
37, 38, 46 *map;* mission church art, 167,
168 *Plate,* 169, 184–87, 274–75n19;
mission jurisdiction, 57, 59; population,
59; pottery, 165; Pueblo coerced services, 23, 24, 197; textiles, 155, 156

Laguna Santero, 167, 184–87, 188, 274–75nn18,19

land ownership: cofradías, 208; Pueblo, 201–5, 280n55; vecino, 119, 201–5, 260n1. *See also* settlement patterns

languages: mission, 8, 201; Pueblo, 3–5, 201; Shoshone, 5

Las Nutrias, 43

Las Trampas de Taos, 47

law suits: Pueblo, 202–4, 279n53, 280n55; vecino, 208. *See also* sedition trials, Tewa (1793)

Lezaún, Juan Sanz de, 26–29, 93, 145, 146, 197

libramientos, 87, 89, 90. *See also* currency

libranzas, 85–101. *See also* currency

Lino, Don Ignacio, 83

Lipan Apache, 71, 72–73, 74

livestock: cofradías, 208; Concha company, 126–27; "Defensive Crisis," 34, 37, 42, 43, 52, 54, 124; missionaries', 23, 28; prices, 148; raids, 31, 32–33; repartimiento de effectos, 25; smallpox epidemic and, 55, 62; trade, 20–21, 108, 123. *See also* horses; sheep

López, Mariano de Jesús, 209

Lorenzana, Antonio, 207

Louisiana, 56, 72–73, 101, 107

Madariaga, Justo Pastor de, 98

Madrid, Thomas, 91–92

Maldonado, Don José, 133

Manrique, José, 203

mantas, Pueblo, 15–17, 16 *Plate*, 27, 122, 155

Mares, José, 107

Mares, Manual, 194

Mariñelarena, Don Martín, 115

markets: barter, 13, 78–79, 82, 85, 140–51, 152–53; fiscal system and, 89–90, 92, 139–51; New Mexico, 14–21, 78–79, 108, 114, 121–25, 139–51. *See also* exports; imports; products; trade fairs

Márquez, Don Diego Ventura, 89

marriages: Pueblo, 5; vecino, 177; vecino-Indian, 3, 177, 178, 180

Martín, Sebastián, 203

Martínez, Pedro, 203

matrilineal clans, Pueblo, 5, 6

Maynez, Alberto, 203–4

Maza, Juan Antonio de Ornedal y, 23

medicine societies, 6

men: agricultural roles, 30; vecino ratio (1780s), 177

Menchero, Juan Miguel de, 10, 101, 105, 106, 197, 269n63

Mendinueta, Pedro Fermín de: vs. alcabala tax, 139; Anza replacing, 72; Bourbon Reforms, 77; Council of War, 71; "Defensive Crisis," 33, 34–35, 37, 38, 42, 47, 49–52, 244n55; and interregional trade, 101–3; land grants, 202; and Pecos Indians, 20; and pelicans, 76, 77; and presidio funds, 93–94; on prices, 140–41; on Pueblo agriculture, 15; resettlements, 110, 197; and tobacco growing, 80; on trade fairs, 14, 33

merchants: American, 226; Chihuahua, 89–90, 94–100, 143, 149; guild, 89–90, 95–100; "imaginary moneys," 141–51; New Mexico, 126; Nueva Vizcaya, 126; presidio suppliers, 94–101; repartimiento de effectos, 25, 120

Mescalero Apache, 34, 74

Mexico: art styles, 186–87; Bourbon Reforms and, 66–70, 117–18, 132; famine, 119–20; furniture, 190–91; independence from Spain, 3, 151, 156, 227; treasury, 83, 84 *fig*, 86, 88; weavers, 225. *See also* Guadalajara; Mexico City; Oaxaca; Provincias Internas; Veracruz

Mexico City: art, 187, 188; Camino Real, 104; cigar manufacturing, 78; finance, 88; silver production, 66; smallpox, 55; trade, 67

Michoacán, 96, 98, 195

Miera y Pacheco, Bernardo de, 103–4; maps, 40–46 *maps*, 43–44, 50, 54, 245n57; santos, 205–6. See also *santos*

military. *See* militias; presidios; soldiers; Spanish military; warfare

militias, 69, 105–6, 183

mining: Bourbon Reforms, 2, 66–70; gold, 105; gunpowder and, 109; Mexico, 52, 68; silver, 66–67, 68, 108; Sonora, 66, 69–70, 105, 108, 180

missions. *See* Franciscan missionaries

Missouri, Santa Fe Trail, 156, 226–28

Mixteca Alta, rebellions, 220

Mogollón, Ignacio Flores, 93

moieties, Pueblo social, 6, 7, 9

Molleno, santero, 187, 188

money. *See* currency; treasuries

Monserrat, Joaquín de, Marqués de Cruillas, 109
Monterey, trade, 103, 104
Montoya, Don Diego de, 126
Montoya, Nerio, 202
Montoya, Paulín, 202
Moorhead, Max L., 143, 256n38
Mora, Don Manuel García de la, 204, 210–19
Morelos insurgency (1811), 202
Morfí, Augustín de: and "Defensive Crisis," 43, 49; on money, 82, 140, 141–47, 144–46 *figs*, 150, 226, 267n41; population records, 56; on Pueblo pottery, 158; on textiles, 125, 185; on tithe, 54, 81
Muro, Vicente de, 87–88
Mutí, Ysidro, 217, 219

Nambé Polychrome, 173 *Plate*, 174
Nambé Pueblo, 6; blankets, 155; Comanche attack, 35; missionaries, 22, 57; pottery, 172, 173, 173 *Plate;* and Tewa sedition trials, 213, 216, 217
Naranjo, Juan Antonio, 215
Naturales, 180. *See also* ethnic identity
Nava, Pedro de, 90, 106, 199, 200, 266n36
Navajo Indians: chief returned to, 131; craft production, 17, 19–20, 131–32, 153, 238n9; gifts to, 133; and money, 150; resettled, 197, 269n63; slaving raids against, 156; Spanish-Comanche alliance and, 74, 131; trade, 131, 158; warfare, 2, 12, 35, 37, 38, 43
Navarro, Pedro Galindo, 96–97, 108, 139
Neve, Felipe de, 73
Neve, Pedro de, 81
New Mexico: Bourbon Reforms, 68, 69, 70–82, 108–9, 207–8; "Defensive Crisis," 14, 34–55, 62–63; development obstacles, 76–118; economic boom (1780s), 2–3, 108, 118–32, 151, 176, 201–2, 221–24; economic development, 119–75, 223–33; economy (through 1770s), 13–64; ethnic geography (c. 1750), 3–5, 4 *map*, 10–12, 11 *map;* fiscal system, 85, 86–87, 88, 90, 139; household occupations (1790), 135–37, 138 *fig*, 153; population (1740–1785), 47, 48 *fig*; products and markets, 14–21, 78–79, 108, 114–16, 121–25, 133–51, 136 *fig*, 157–75; tithe rentals, 53–54, 53 *fig*, 83, 127–31, 129–30 *figs*, 151, 183, 190, 264n20. *See*

also demography; Franciscan missionaries; New Spain; Pueblo Indians; Santa Fe; Spanish officials; trade; *vecinos*
New Spain: art, 23, 185–87; Bourbon administrators, 2, 56, 62, 65–175, 180–81, 207, 223–33; churrigueresque churches, 167; competition for control over Indians, 196; "Defensive Crisis," 52, 62; land usurpation, 202; rebellions (1790s), 220; repartimiento de effectos, 25–26, 27; smallpox, 56, 60, 61; Spanish entering Pueblo-Plains relationship, 32, 34; trade, 20, 140. *See also* Louisiana; Mexico; Provincias Internas; Spanish officials
nomadic/nonsedentary Indians. *See* Plains Indians; *see also under individual groups and tribes*
Nombre de Dios, 137
Nuestra Señora de Guadalupe, 182, 184
Nuestra Señora del Rosario, 61, 183–84, 188
Nueva Vizcaya: agriculture, 15; Apache Indians, 10, 68; Bourbon Reforms, 66, 68, 117; "Defensive Crisis," 38, 50, 52; drought and dearth, 120; fiscal system, 85, 86–87, 88; household occupations (1790), 135–37, 138 *fig;* New Mexican textiles, 125–26; presidio expenses, 85, 94, 95, 96, 98; sheep, 124; silver production, 66, 223; trade, 79, 126, 223–26. *See also* Chihuahua; Durango
Nuevo León, 113, 117
Nuevo Santander, 73, 113

Oaxaca, 67, 81, 220, 224
obrajes, 114–16, 126, 224–25, 259n83
Ochoa, Don Pablo de, 89
O'Connor, Hugo, 94
O'Crouley, Don Pedro Alonso, 76
officials. *See* Spanish officials
Ogapoge Polychrome, 169–70, 170 *Plate*, 171, 174. *See also* San Ildefonso Pueblo
Ojo Caliente, "Defensive Crisis," 43, 44 *map*, 49, 54–55, 244n55
Ollí, Martin, 214
Oñate, Juan de, 137, 176
Opata Indians, 180
oratorios, 182, 183
Orizaba, 78
Oronzoro, Juan José de, 26

Ortiz, Doña María Manuela, 184, 185, 274n18
Ortiz, Don Antonio José, 274n18; land grants, 203; patron of religious structures, 183–85, 188; textiles owned by, 153; tithe rental, 54; wife (Rosa Bustamante), 153, 183, 190
Ortiz, Don Miguel, 126, 150, 212, 214
Ostimuri, 69–70

Pacheco, José, 259n76
Pacheco, Rafael Martinez, 244n50
Páez Hurtado, Gertrudis, 183
Pajarito, San Ysidro de, 49
Paloma Apache, 34
Parral, crafts production, 137
Pata, Francisco, 218–19
Pawnee Indians, Louisiana, 73
peace: Extraordinary Fund for, 90, 132–39, 135–36 *figs;* Spanish-Comanche treaty (1785–1786), 55, 70, 73–74, 124, 132
Pecos Pueblo, 3, 20; Apache allies, 10–12; "Defensive Crisis," 34, 37, 42, 244n54; Spanish-Comanche peace treaty and, 74
pelicans, 76, 77, 101
Peña, Asencio, 211–19
Los Penitentes, 182, 188, 232
Pereyro, José Benito, 203
Peru, Joaquín, 125
peso: common, 148; imaginary, 144–50, 267n41; price valuation on, 144; recoinage of, 85, 146–47; silver/real, 148
peso antiguo, 146–47
peso de la tierra, 147–50, 149*table,* 261n5, 268n57
peso de proyecto, 147
Philip V (1700–1746), 65
Piche, Bentura, 210–16, 219
Picurís Pueblo, 3, 24, 35, 47, 56, 235n5
Pike, Zebulon, 112, 124, 126, 152, 156, 158
Pima Indians, 180
Pimería Alta, 106, 196
Pinda, Juan Diego, 211, 212, 214, 215, 217, 219
Pineda, Juan Rafael, 133
Pino, Pedro Bautista, 116
Piro Pueblo, 5, 7, 10
Placitas, 232
Plains Indians, 10–12, 11 *map;* and Christianity, 196–97; drought and dearth (1789–1791), 120; Extraordinary Fund

for, 90, 132–39, 135–36 *figs;* Spanish alliances, 2, 55, 70–75, 90, 124, 132; and Tewa sedition trials, 211–19; trade, 14–15, 20–37, 51, 74, 123, 126, 242–43nn39,44; vecino intermarriages, 177; warfare, 13, 14, 30–55, 62–64. *See also* Apache Indians; Comanche Indians; Navajo Indians; Ute Indians
Plaza de San Rafael, 211, 219
Pojoaque Pueblo, 6, 29; mission, 22, 57, 59, 183–84, 186; pottery, 172; smallpox, 56–57, 59, 60; and Tewa sedition trials, 216, 217; textiles, 155
Polacca Polychrome, 272n85. *See also* Hopi Pueblos
population, 245–46n61; artisan (1790), 135–37; "Defensive Crisis," 42–43, 46–50, 52–53; and food prices, 128–30; Genízaros, 199, 269n63, 273n7; Mexico (Bourbon period), 68; New Mexico (1740–1785), 47, 48 *fig;* presidio soldiers (1700s), 71, 72; Pueblo, 7, 29, 59, 59 *fig,* 151, 198, 245n61; smallpox epidemics and, 7, 55, 56–60, 59 *fig,* 247n78; Texas non-Indian (1777), 71; tithe rentals and, 129–31, 130 *fig;* vecino, 57–60, 129–31, 130 *fig,* 151, 176–77, 182, 198, 221–22, 245n61. *See also* deaths; demography
Posada, Ramón, 115
pottery: Pueblo, 15–16, 21, 31, 122, 156–75, 157 *map,* 160–61 *Plates,* 226–27, 272n85, 278n38; Spanish influence, 21, 227, 272n85; vecino, 226–27
Powhoge Polychrome, 169–71, 171 *Plate,* 174. *See also* San Ildefonso Pueblo; Tesuque Pueblo
presidios: Chihuahua, 125–26; cuarteles, 110–14, 113 *fig,* 132, 137, 148–49, 218, 259n76; El Paso, 51, 101; new, 68–69, 70, 82, 112; pottery shards, 158–59; San Bernadino, 105; San Elizario, 95, 126; supplies, 82–85, 84 *fig,* 89–101, 91 *fig,* 223, 254n19; Tubac, 104; Tucson, 106. *See also* Santa Fe Presidio; soldiers
prices: Cachupín and, 34, 140, 141, 144, 145, 146, 243n44; food, 119, 128–30, 140–41, 200; "imaginary moneys," 140–45, 148; inflation, 119, 128–29
products: bretaña, 121; imported from Europe, 20, 225; missionaries' supplies, 13, 21–25; New Mexico, 14–21, 78–79,

products (*continued*)
108, 121–25, 133–37, 136 *fig*, 157–75;
officials' supplies, 13, 21–22, 25–30;
Pueblo Indians' supplies, 25. *See also*
agriculture; craft production; markets
Protector de Indios, 203
Provincial Academic styles, 206
Provincias Internas, 11 *map*, 56, 81; fiscal
affairs, 82, 88, 90, 119, 137–39, 223; Indian attacks, 70, 74; interregional trade,
106, 108; officials' support for economic
projects, 108–17, 139, 223–24; presidio
supply system, 92, 95, 100, 101, 223. *See
also* Californias; Coahuila; New Mexico;
Nueva Vizcaya; Sonora; Spanish officials;
Texas
Puebla, 78, 162, 164 *Plate*
Pueblo Indians, 1, 2, 3–7; agriculture, 3, 7,
8, 15, 21–30, 47–49, 79–80, 140, 152,
201; coerced services and labor of, 7,
8, 13, 21–30, 156–75, 196–209, 220,
242n35; cultural resistance, 9, 209–22;
"Defensive Crisis," 33–55, 62; economic
participation, 21–25, 122–23, 151–
56; Hispanicized, 13; law suits, 202–4,
279n53, 280n55; missionaries and, 3, 7–
10, 13, 21–25, 29, 196–209, 220; Plains
Indians relationships, 31–34; population, 7, 29, 59, 59 *fig*, 151, 198, 245n61;
religion, 5–7, 8–10, 25, 196–209; Revolt (1680), 7, 8, 10, 13, 176, 209–10,
211; smallpox, 55, 56, 57, 59–60, 62; social structure, 5–7; Spanish-Comanche
peace treaty and, 74; trade, 13, 14–21,
28, 31–33, 114, 122–23, 151–56, 242–
43n39; vecino/Spanish settler relationships, 3, 13, 122–23, 177–81, 209, 221;
warfare vs., 1, 2, 7, 10–12, 13, 20, 33,
34–38, 46–47, 55. *See also* Keres pueblos; Pueblos' crafts; Tanoan pueblos;
Zuñi Pueblo
Pueblos' crafts, 19–20, 21, 152; Plains Indians trade, 31; pottery, 15–16, 21, 31,
122, 156–75, 157 *map*, 160–61 *Plates*,
226–27, 272n85, 278n38; repartimiento de effectos, 25–30, 152, 156–
58; textiles, 15–17, 16 *Plate*, 21, 27, 122,
151, 155–56, 169, 174–75, 242n34
Puname Polychrome, 159–61, 163, 165,
169, 174. *See also* Zia Pueblo
punche, 15, 79–81, 100–101, 133

Querétaro, 20, 67, 78, 224, 225
Quill Pen Santero, 230, 231–32, 282n8,
283nn10,11

Rabal, Joaquín Cadallos y, 27, 43
Radding, Cynthia, 180
Ramos, Juan, 214
rancherías, Comanche, 12
Ranchos de Taos, 182, 185, 188, 203, 245n60
Real Audiencia, 98
Real Hacienda, 83, 87–90, 98–99, 132, 141;
and currency, 150; of Encinillas, 126–
28; and textiles, 115–16; and tobacco,
78–79
Real Ordenanza de Intendentes (1786), 98, 208
Reaño, Joseph, 20–21
rebellions: Apache, 197; Hidalgo (1810),
115, 202, 224; New Spain (1790s), 220;
Pueblo Revolt (1680), 7, 8, 10, 13, 176,
209–10, 211; Sonora, 71–72, 211; Tewa
sedition trials (1793), 209–22, 281n73
Reforms, Bourbon, 2, 65–118, 132, 139,
207–8
Reglamento (1772), 68–69, 82–83, 94
religion: Pueblo, 5–7, 8–10, 25, 196–209;
vecino, 182–95, 205, 228–33. *See also*
Christianity
Rendón, Pedro, 133
Rengel, José Antonio, 88–89, 124
repartimiento de effectos, 8, 25–30, 120, 121,
123, 152–53, 156–58
Revillagigedo II, Conde de, 89, 90, 107,
179, 199, 245n61
Río Abajo, 28; blankets, 29, 242n34; furni-
ture, 195; repartimiento de effectos, 29
Río Arriba, 28, 241n28; "Defensive Crisis,"
244n55; furniture, 193–94, 195; pueb-
los, 155, 188; religious buildings, 188;
repartimiento de effectos, 29
Río Napestle pueblo, 133, 137
Ríos, José Miguel de los, 23
Roibal, Santiago, 22
Roybal, B. Santiago de, 54
Rubí, Marqués de, 20, 68–69, 93
Rubí de Celís, Alonso Victories, 101
Rubio, Don José, 86
Russia, and Alta California, 69

Sabe, Francisco, 216
sacristanes, 9, 23
Saint Job, 228–33, 229 *Plate*, 282n8

St. Louis, Santa Fe Trail, 156, 226–28
salaries: cuartel workers, 111, 114; interregional militia and settlers, 105; missionaries, 22, 199; officials, 143; soldiers, 26, 28, 82–83, 85, 89, 91–100, 125–26, 132
Salcido, Nemesio, 115–16, 124
Saltillo, Bourbon Reforms, 68, 69
Saltillo blanket design, 154
San Antonio de Béxar, 69, 71, 107
San Antonio de Bucareli, 244n50
San Antonio de las Huertas, 172
San Antonio de los Poblanos, 173–74
San Bernadino Presidio, 105
Sánchez, Marcos, 50
Sandía Pueblo, 5, 6, 29; kachina rituals, 235n5; missionary income, 199; resettled Indians at, 10, 197, 269n63
Sandoval, Vitor, 184, 185
San Elizario Presidio, 95, 126
San Felipe Pueblo, 5, 57, 59, 155, 198, 204
San Fernando del Río Puerco, 43, 49
San Fernando de Taos, 182, 184
San Francisco, California, 104, 113
San Ildefonso de Cieneguilla, 105
San Ildefonso Pueblo, 6; land suit, 280n55; mission, 57, 59, 198; pottery, 169; and Tewa sedition trials, 210–16, 221; textiles, 155
San Juan del Río, 87, 119, 137
San Juan Pueblo, 6; mission, 24, 199; and Tewa sedition trials, 210, 211–12, 214, 215; textiles, 155
San Luis Potosí, 83
San Miguel chapel, Santa Fe, 183–84, 186, 274n19
San Pablo Polychrome, 159–61, 162 Plate, 165, 167–69. See also Zia Pueblo
Santa Ana Pueblo, 5; land ownership, 202; mission, 24, 25, 57, 184; pottery, 159–61; textiles, 155
Santa Clara Pueblo, 6; land suit, 280n55; mission, 57, 199; population change (1776–1790), 59 fig; Santa Fe cuartel land, 110; smallpox, 56, 57, 58 fig, 59, 59 fig, 60; Tewa sedition trials and, 213, 214–15, 221; textiles, 155
Santa Cruz de la Cañada: church art, 185, 188, 206, 274–75 nn18,19; cofradías, 61, 188, 208, 268n57; "Defensive Crisis," 43, 44 map, 49–50; interregional exploration, 105; smallpox, 56

Santa Fe: alcades mayores, 54, 183; cofradías, 60–61, 208; crafts production, 137; ecclesiastical judge, 54; ethnic geography (c. 1750), 3, 5; interregional trade exploration, 104–7; militia, 183; missionaries, 22; obraje, 115; religious buildings, 183–84, 186, 188, 206; settlement patterns, 42, 43, 50; social and economic divisions, 120–21; Tewa sedition trials, 212–14; vecinos, 37, 135–36. See also Santa Fe Presidio; Santa Fe Trail
Santa Fe Presidio: chapel, 199; vs. Comanches, 71, 72; cuartel, 110–14, 113 fig, 132, 137, 148–49, 218, 259n76; "Defensive Crisis," 37; expenses, 26, 90, 91–93, 99–100; grain supply, 26, 123, 151; interregional exploration, 106; money economy, 28, 150–51; smallpox, 57; teniente, 91, 183; tobacco revenues for, 81–82, 85; Troncoso of, 111, 131
Santa Fe Trail, 156, 226–28
Santo Domingo Pueblo, 5; Baca family and, 204, 205, 220; "Defensive Crisis," 34; land issues, 204; mission, 57, 59, 198; pottery, 171; production, 201; Santa Fe cuartel land, 110
santos, 3, 166–67, 182–89, 205–6, 222, 274–75 nn18,19; Christ images, 230–32, 231 Plate, 233, 283 nn11,13; Ecce Homo, 231–32, 231 Plate, 283 nn11,13; Laguna Santero, 167, 184–87, 188, 274–75 nn18,19; Quill Pen Santero, 230, 231–32, 282n8, 283 nn10,11; Santo Jo', 228–33, 229 Plate, 282n8
Santuario del Señor de Esquipulas, 182
San Xavier de Bac, Mission of, 103
sarapes, 226; Río Grande blankets, 17–19, 18 Plate, 153–54, 175, 176, 278n38
scalp dances, 9
Secoy, Frank Raymond, 244n52
secularization, of missions, 196
sedition trials, Tewa (1793), 209–22, 281n73
semaneros, 28, 29
Seri Indians, 71–72
Serrano, Pedro, 158
servants, 15, 21–30, 153, 198. See also Genízaros
settlement patterns: "Defensive Crisis," 39–44, 40–46 maps, 47–50. See also demography; ethnic geography

Seven Years' War (French and Indian War), 72–73, 109

sheep, 241n28; *churro,* 124; cofradías, 60, 61; Concha, 126–27, 263–64n19; "Defensive Crisis," 34, 37; missionaries', 23; Navajo, 238n9; Nueva Vizcaya, 124; prices, 129; repartimiento de effectos, 27, 29; Santa Fe Presidio, 151; smallpox epidemic and, 55, 60, 62; Spanish settlers', 16; tithes and, 127–28; trade in, 20, 124–25, 127

Shoshone, 5, 31, 242n37

silver: currency, 85–86, 114, 148; and food prices, 128–29; mining, 66–67, 68, 108, 223

slaves, 14–15, 153, 156, 181, 269n63

smallpox epidemics, 2, 14, 55–62, 232; Comanche, 73; and interregional trade, 106; population effects, 7, 55, 56–60, 59*fig,* 247n78; and Pueblo services for missionaries, 198, 207; Santa Fe resettlement and, 110

social structure: Apache and Comanche, 33; ethnic status, 180–81, 228; Pueblo, 5–7

Sola, Lazaro, 219

soldiers: Bourbon Reforms, 69, 70, 71–72; "Defensive Crisis," 34–35, 37–38, 50–51, 62; populations (1700s), 71, 72; repartimiento de effectos, 26, 27; salaries, 26, 28, 82–83, 85, 89, 91–100, 125–26, 132. *See also* presidios; Spanish military

Sonora: Apache Indians, 10, 68; Bourbon Reforms, 66, 68, 69–70; "Defensive Crisis," 50, 52; fiscal system, 88, 149–50; gold, 105, 258n62; Indian rebellions, 71–72, 211; interregional exploration, 105–6; land ownership process, 201; mining, 66, 69–70, 105, 108, 180; presidios, 104, 105; *reducción* policy, 180; trade, 14, 69, 101–8, 224

Spain: art styles, 186, 187; Cádiz trade, 66; conquistadors from, 3, 7; folktales, 181; furniture, 190–91, 195; Mexican independence from, 3, 151, 156, 227; pottery, 21, 227, 272n85; war against England, 109. *See also* Bourbons; New Spain; Spanish officials; Spanish settlers

Spanish military, 13, 30, 68–73, 90, 117, 223; reconquest (1692), 6–8, 10, 188, 207, 208, 210–11. *See also* presidios; soldiers

Spanish officials, 2, 9–10, 76–77; alliances with Indians, 2, 55, 70–75, 90, 124, 132; Bourbon administrators, 2, 56, 62, 65–175, 180–81, 207, 223–33; "Defensive Crisis," 51, 52, 62, 100; encomiendas, 7, 8; Franciscan dispute with, 21–22, 25–26, 28, 196–209; on New Mexican trade dependency on Chihuahua, 143; peace treaty with Comanches (1785–1786), 55, 70, 73–74, 124, 132; population classifications, 47; Pueblo coercion by, 7, 8, 13, 21–22, 25–30, 196–209, 220; Pueblo Revolt against (1680), 7, 8, 10, 13, 176, 209–10, 211; repartimiento de effectos, 8, 25–30, 120, 121, 123, 152–53, 156–58; sacristánes, 9, 23; salaries, 143; tenientes, 51, 91, 183; Tewa sedition trials, 209–22, 281n73. *See also alcades mayores;* governors; New Spain; Provincias Internas; Spanish military

Spanish settlers, 1, 2, 176; Apache vs., 13; Bourbon Reforms to increase, 69, 71; Comanche and, 12, 31, 43; Pueblo Revolt effects, 13, 176, 209–10; trade, 2, 13, 14–21, 32–33; warfare vs., 1, 2, 13, 33–55. *See also* Franciscan missionaries; soldiers; Spanish officials; *vecinos*

Spicer, Edward H., 210

Spielmann, Katherine A., 32

Squash (or Pumpkin) People, 6

Summer People, 6

Supreme Council of the Indies, 115

Sure Method to Preserve the Pueblos from Smallpox (Gil), 56

Tafoya, Antonio, 215, 217, 218–19

tailors, vecino, 133

Tamarón y Romerál, Pedro, 8–9, 22, 123–24, 182, 242n34, 281n73

Tanoan pueblos, 3–5, 6, 7, 10. *See also* Galisteo Pueblo; Piro Pueblo; Tewa pueblos; Tiwa pueblos; Tompiro pueblos; Towa pueblos

Taos Pueblo, 3, 6, 9–10, 235n5; Comanche raid, 72; land ownership, 203–4; mission, 199; trade fairs, 24, 33, 37; vecinos living in, 47, 203 taxes: alcabala, 67, 69, 125, 137–39, 155, 183, 266nn35,36, 266 *table;* Bourbon Reforms, 65, 67, 69–70, 77–82, 139, 207–8

Taylor, Lonn, 194–95

Taylor, William B., 205, 207

tenientes, 51, 91, 183

Tesuque Pueblo, 6; mission, 23–24, 57, 59, 184, 198; pottery, 172; and Tewa sedition trials, 216, 218–19; textiles, 155

Tewa pueblos, 3, 6, 9, 10; pottery, 162, 169, 172–73; sedition trials, 209–22, 281n73; textiles, 155. *See also* Nambé Pueblo; Pojoaque Pueblo; San Ildefonso Pueblo; San Juan Pueblo; Santa Clara Pueblo; Tesuque Pueblo

Texas: vs. Apaches, 71; Comanche in, 73; fiscal system, 88; missions, 69, 196; trade, 101, 107, 108

textiles, 224–25, 241n28; dyes, 154; master weavers, 116, 154; Navajo, 17, 19–20, 131–32, 153, 238n9; obrajes, 114–16, 126, 224–25, 259n83; Pueblo, 15–17, 16 *Plate,* 21, 27, 122, 151, 155–56, 169, 174–75, 242n34; Querétaro, 20, 67, 224, 225; repartimiento de effectos, 25; trade, 15–20, 108, 123, 125–26, 151–56, 174–75, 226; vecino, 17–21, 18 *Plate,* 114–16, 122–23, 125–26, 137, 151–56, 174–75, 185, 270n66, 278n38. *See also* blankets

Tiguex, 5. *See also* Isleta Pueblo; Sandía Pueblo

tithes, church, 26, 27–28, 81; New Mexico tithe rentals, 53–54, 53 *fig,* 83, 127–31, 129 *fig,* 130 *fig,* 151, 183, 190, 264n20

Tiwa pueblos, 3, 5, 6, 235n5. *See also* Picurís Pueblo; Taos Pueblo

tobacco: gifts to Indians, 133; monopoly (*estanco de tabaco*), 78–82, 85–86, 87–89

Tompiro pueblos, 5, 7, 10

Towa pueblos, 3, 6. *See also* Jémez Pueblo; Pecos Pueblo

trade, 3, 225–26; Apache, 10, 33, 158; barter, 13, 78–79, 82, 85, 140–51, 152–53; Bourbon Reforms and, 2, 66–67, 139; Cádiz, 66; Comanche, 2, 10, 12, 14, 20, 31–32, 33, 51, 73, 74, 79–80, 123, 158; "Defensive Crisis," 37, 50–52; economic boom (1780s), 2–3, 108, 122–32, 176, 224; fiscal system and, 85; grain, 21, 24, 31, 32; interregional, 2–3, 101–8, 102 *map,* 125–26, 140, 176, 225, 227, 232–33; Navajo, 131, 158; Plains Indians (general), 14–15, 20–37, 51, 74, 123, 126, 242–43nn39,44; Pueblo, 13, 14–21, 28, 31–33, 114, 122–23, 151–56, 242–43n39; Santa Fe Trail, 156, 226–28; smallpox epidemic and, 55, 60, 106; Sonora, 14, 69, 101–8, 224; textile, 15–20, 108, 123, 125–26, 151–56, 174–75, 226; Ute, 14, 50, 51; vecino, 2, 13, 14–21, 32–33, 51, 55, 74, 108, 122–26, 140, 151–56, 158–59; war captives, 14–15, 20, 32, 33, 37. *See also* Chihuahua Trail/Chihuahua trade; exports; imports; markets; prices; trade fairs

trade fairs, 13, 14–15, 27–28; Navajo, 131; Plains Indians and New Mexicans, 14–15, 20–21, 24, 31, 33–34, 37, 51, 123, 126, 243n44; regulations, 34; Saltillo, 154; Spanish-Comanche peace treaty and, 74; at Valle de San Bartolomé (December 1806), 124; vecino products, 123

treasuries, 88–90, 92, 97; Chihuahua, 83, 86–89, 90, 94, 96, 98, 101, 111, 112; Durango, 82, 83, 84 *fig,* 86–87, 89, 90, 101; Guanajuato, 82, 86, 89, 254n19; Mexico, 83, 84 *fig,* 86, 89; San Luis Potosí, 83. *See also* currency; taxes

Trigo, Manuel de San Juan Nepomuceno y, 23, 24, 197

Trios Polychrome, 161–62, 163 *Plate,* 165, 169. *See also* Zia Pueblo

Tristán, Bishop, 200

Troncoso, Vicente, 111, 131–32

Tubac, 104, 106

Tucson, 106

Tuque, Juan Domingo, 211–12, 213, 215

Turado, Diego, 155, 201, 275n19

Turquoise People, 6

Ugalde, Juan de, 74, 95

Ugarte, Juan Baptista de, 87–88

Ugarte y Loyola, Jacobo, 57; on hostile Indian activity (1787), 75; and "imaginary moneys," 149; and obrajes, 115; and presidio supply systems, 95–100; and Santa Fe cuartel, 110–12; and smallpox, 56; and soldier salaries,

Ugarte y Loyola, Jacobo (*continued*)
89; and trade convoy to Chihuahua,
124
United States, Santa Fe Trail trade, 156,
226–28
Urquidi, Don Manuel de, 95, 115
Urrisola, Manuel Portillo de, 54
Urtundúa, Juan de Lagaza, 112
Ute Indians: gifts to, 133; and money, 150;
Spanish-Comanche peace treaty and, 73,
74; Tewa sedition trials and, 217; trade,
14, 50, 51; warfare, 10, 12, 33, 35, 38,
43, 72, 123

Vaca, Juan Antonio Cabeza de, 205
vaccination, smallpox, 56
Valdez family, carpenters, 194
Valle, Francisco Antonio Martín del, 26,
243n44, 244n51
Valle de San Bartolomé, 124, 127
Van Young, Eric, 67
Vargas, Diego de, 6–8, 176, 183, 188
variolation, smallpox, 56
Varo, Andrés, 14, 29, 242n34
vecino crafts, 119, 135–37, 176, 225; furniture, 3, 182, 189–95, 191–93 *Plates*,
276–77n28; pottery, 226–27; textiles,
17–21, 18 *Plate*, 114–16, 122–23, 125–
26, 137, 151–56, 174–75, 185, 270n66,
278n38. See also *santos*
vecinos, 1, 121–22; agriculture, 8, 15, 21, 52,
54, 80–81, 108, 119, 152; creation of,
176–222; "Defensive Crisis," 1, 37, 43,
46–50, 51–52, 55, 62–64; defined, 1n,
180; drought and dearth effects, 34–35;
encroachments on Pueblos (1700s), 8;
ethnic identity, 3, 177, 180, 182, 201–
2, 228–33; Franciscans reorienting to,
196–209; Galisteo Pueblo reoccupied
by, 43; gifts to Indians, 133–37; household occupations (1790), 135–37, 153;
interregional exploration, 105–6; population, 57–60, 129–31, 130 *fig*, 151,
176–77, 182, 198, 221–22, 245n61;
products and markets, 14–21, 108,
114–16, 121–25, 133–51, 136 *fig*;
Pueblo pottery of, 158, 173–74; Pueblo
relationships, 3, 13, 122–23, 177–81,
209, 221; repartimiento de effectos, 121;
and Santa Fe cuartel, 110–11, 113–14;

settlements, 43, 44 *map*, 47–50, 119,
201–5, 260n1; smallpox, 55, 56, 57–60,
58 *fig*, 61, 62, 232; Spanish-Comanche
peace treaty and, 74; in Tewa sedition
trials, 214–15; and tithe rental growth,
129–31, 130 *fig*; trade, 2, 13, 14–21,
32–33, 51, 55, 74, 108, 122–26, 140,
151–56, 158–59; usurpation of Pueblo
textile trade, 151–56, 174–75; warfare
vs., 1, 2, 13, 33–55, 62–64. *See also* European settlers; Genízaros; Spanish officials; vecino crafts
Vedder, Alan C., 276–77n28
Velarde, 194
Veracruz, 66, 78, 115–16
Vial, Pedro, 7, 107

war captives, 31, 54–55; Comanche, 72;
trade in, 14–15, 20, 32, 33, 37. *See also*
Genízaros
War Council, 71, 72, 85–87, 91
warfare: Apache, 1, 2, 7, 10–12, 13, 30–54,
57, 68–75, 123, 232; Comanche, 1, 2,
10–12, 13, 20, 30, 33–54, 63–64, 70,
72–73, 110, 123, 232; "Defensive Crisis,"
14, 34–55, 62–64; demographic effects,
35, 36 *fig*, 42–43, 46–50, 52–53, 54; Navajo, 2, 12, 35, 37, 38, 43; vs. Pueblos, 1,
2, 7, 10–12, 13, 20, 33, 34–38, 46–47,
55; settlement pattern effects, 39–44,
40–46 *maps*, 47–50; Seven Years' War
(French and Indian War), 72–73, 109;
slaving raids, 156; Ute, 10, 12, 33, 35,
38, 43, 72, 123; vs. vecinos, 1, 2, 13, 33–
55, 62–64. *See also* peace; rebellions;
Spanish military
weaving. *See* textiles
wills: furniture, 189, 190, 194; smallpox epidemic, 60
Winter People, 6
women: agricultural roles, 30; craft production roles, 30, 172–73; smallpox, 60;
Tewa sedition trials and, 219; vecino ratio (1780s), 177
wool/woven goods. *See* sheep; textiles

Yaqui revolt (1781), Sonora, 211

Zambrano, Don Juan José, 126
Zarte, Francisco, 60–61

Zia Pueblo, 5; mission, 57, 184, 199; pottery, 159–62, 161 *Plate,* 163 *Plate,* 167–69; textiles, 155
Zongolica, 78
Zubiría, Don José Antonio de, 182, 188
Zúñiga, José de, 106–7

Zuñi Polychrome, 174. *See also* Zuñi Pueblo
Zuñi Pueblo, 3, 5, 7; interregional trade route, 106–7; missions, 23, 199; pottery, 17, 162, 174, 272n85; textiles, 155, 156

Text and Display:	Baskerville
Composition:	G&S Typesetters, Inc.
Printing and binding:	Data Reprographics
Maps and illustrations:	Bill Nelson
Index:	Barbara Roos